The Cultural Logic of Politics in Mainland China and Taiwan

Tianjian Shi shows how cultural norms affect political attitudes and behavior through two causal pathways, one at the individual level and one at the community level. Focusing on two key norms – definition of self-interest and orientation to authority – he tests the theory with multiple surveys conducted in mainland China and Taiwan. Shi employs multilevel statistical analysis to show how, in these two very different political systems, similar norms exert similar kinds of influence on political trust, understanding of democracy, forms of political participation, and tolerance for protest. The approach helps explain the resilience of authoritarian politics in China and the dissatisfaction of many Taiwan residents with democratic institutions. Aiming to place the study of political culture on a new theoretical and methodological foundation, Shi argues that a truly comparative social science must understand how culturally embedded norms influence decision making.

The late Tianjian Shi was an associate professor of political science at Duke University. He also taught at Tsinghua University in China. Shi was the author of *Political Participation in Beijing* (1997). He specialized in comparative politics with an emphasis on political culture and political participation in China and Taiwan.

"Over the course of his career, Tianjian Shi came to realize that culture could not be dismissed as irrelevant to the politics of nations. Instead, it kept resurfacing as a critical determinant of political legitimacy, participation, interests, and leadership. This final casebook of a great detective solves once and for all the puzzle of culture. It will serve as a model for anyone on the trail of culture."

– Bruce Gilley, Associate Professor of Political Science,
Portland State University

"This book is Shi's most ambitious. It is at once both a circling back to his personal and scholarly roots and a stretching of his reach and ambition. He develops this account – of individual and social norms and how they shape cultural understandings of rationality and orientations to authority – remarkably well. Nothing is a 'fitting tribute,' but his own words come close."

– John Aldrich, Pfizer-Pratt University Professor of
Political Science, Duke University

"Tianjian Shi has written an important book that investigates culture as norms. Through comparative survey work in mainland China and Taiwan, Shi illuminates the workings of cultural commonalities in distinctly different institutional settings. Not least of all, Shi reveals a common hierarchical orientation to authority, with roots in traditional Chinese culture, that provides legitimacy to a communist party–state in one setting and is the source of democratic tensions in the other. A theoretical and empirical tour de force."

– Melanie Manion, Vilas-Jordan Distinguished Achievement Professor
of Public Affairs and Political Science, University of Wisconsin-Madison

"A pioneer of survey research in China, the late Tianjian Shi left a rich intellectual legacy in this book. Using multiyear survey data from China and Taiwan, one authoritarian and one democratic, to examine the interactions between political culture and political behavior, Shi demonstrated that cultural changes are relatively independent of social structural and political institutional changes. A fascinating study, this book provides many fresh and original insights into the ongoing debate of political modernization."

– Suisheng Zhao, Professor of International Studies, University of Denver,
and Editor of *Journal of Contemporary China*

"This groundbreaking study offers not only a new full-fledged theory of political culture but also the most credible answer to East Asia's political puzzle of democratic underdevelopment. It also challenges the increasingly popular claims among neo-modernization theorists in the West that China and all other East Asian economic powerhouses will join the exclusive club of fully liberal democracies in a couple of decades. Among Asian-born scholars, therefore, the late Tianjian Shi should be remembered as the most brilliant theoretical pioneer."

– Doh Chull Shin, Center for the Study of Democracy,
University of California, Irvine

"This is a remarkable achievement: not just a cultural explanation of Chinese politics, but a new theory of culture that has applications well beyond China. Innovative ideas, sophisticated data analysis, provocative conclusions – it is the culmination of Tianjian Shi's lifetime of scholarship and will stand as his ultimate legacy."

– Bruce Dickson, Director, Sigur Center for Asian Studies, and
Professor of Political Science and International Affairs,
George Washington University

The Cultural Logic of Politics in Mainland China and Taiwan

TIANJIAN SHI
Duke University

CAMBRIDGE
UNIVERSITY PRESS

University Printing House, Cambridge CB2 8BS, United Kingdom

One Liberty Plaza, 20th Floor, New York, NY 10006, USA

477 Williamstown Road, Port Melbourne, VIC 3207, Australia

314-321, 3rd Floor, Plot 3, Splendor Forum, Jasola District Centre, New Delhi - 110025, India

79 Anson Road, #06-04/06, Singapore 079906

Cambridge University Press is part of the University of Cambridge.

It furthers the University's mission by disseminating knowledge in the pursuit of education, learning and research at the highest international levels of excellence.

www.cambridge.org
Information on this title: www.cambridge.org/9781316608463

© The Estate of Tianjian Shi 2015

This publication is in copyright. Subject to statutory exception and to the provisions of relevant collective licensing agreements, no reproduction of any part may take place without the written permission of Cambridge University Press.

First published 2015
First paperback edition 2020

A catalogue record for this publication is available from the British Library

Library of Congress Cataloging in Publication data
Shi, Tianjian.
The cultural logic of politics in mainland China and Taiwan / Tianjian Shi.
  pages cm
Includes bibliographical references and index.
ISBN 978-1-107-01176-2 (hardback)
1. Politics and culture – China.   2. Politics and culture – Taiwan.   3. Political culture – China.   4. Political culture – Taiwan.   5. Political sociology – China.   6. Political sociology – Taiwan.   I. Title.
JQ1516.S55   2014
306.20951–dc23   2014018496

ISBN 978-1-107-01176-2 Hardback
ISBN 978-1-316-60846-3 Paperback

Cambridge University Press has no responsibility for the persistence or accuracy of URLs for external or third-party internet websites referred to in this publication, and does not guarantee that any content on such websites is, or will remain, accurate or appropriate.

This book is dedicated to Christine, Eleanor, and Sarah

Contents

List of Tables and Figures	*page* ix
Editor's Note	xiii
Acknowledgments	xv
Introduction	1

PART I: THEORY OF POLITICAL CULTURE

1. Political Culture Theory and Regime Stability	13
2. Cultural Norms East and West	41
3. Measuring Cultural Norms in Mainland China and Taiwan	60
4. Culture, Social Structure, and Political Institutions	76

PART II: CULTURE'S IMPACT ON POLITICAL
ATTITUDES AND BEHAVIORS

5. Culture's Impact on Political Trust	107
6. Cultural Impacts on Political Participation	147
7. The Impact of Culture on Understandings of Democracy	192
Conclusion and Theoretical Reflections	221

Appendix A. Sample Design for the Surveys	229
Appendix B. Validity of Measurements	239
Appendix C. Comparing Different Measurement Models: IRT versus CMT	246

vii

viii   *Contents*

Appendix D. The Mechanism of Cultural Shifts: The Cases of Yu Luojin and "Running Fan"	250
Appendix E. Analyzing Cross-County Variation in Government Salience and Political Participation: A Prerequisite for HLM	258
References	261
Additional Works Consulted	277
Index	283

Tables and Figures

Tables

2.1	Two Normative Traditions	*page* 50
3.1	Reciprocal Orientation toward Authority and Idiocentric Definition of Self-Interest in Mainland China and Taiwan	67
3.2	Confirmatory IRT Model for 1993 Mainland China Data	70
3.3	Confirmatory IRT Model for Combined Mainland China and Taiwan Data	73
3.4	Confirmatory IRT Model for Combined Mainland China Data	74
4.1	Reciprocal Orientation toward Authority by Age Group and Cohort in Mainland China	90
4.2	Idiocentric Definition of Self-Interest by Age Group and Cohort in Mainland China	92
4.3	Reciprocal Orientation toward Authority by Age Group and Cohort in Taiwan	94
4.4	Idiocentric Definition of Self-Interest by Age Group and Cohort in Taiwan	95
4.5	Changes in Idiocentric Definition of Self-Interest by Level of Education in Mainland China	100
4.6	Changes in Idiocentric Definition of Self-Interest by Level of Education in Taiwan	101
5.1	Correlations of Structural and Institutional Variables with Political Trust	113
5.2	Exploratory Factor Analysis of Political Trust in Mainland China	120
5.3	Effects of Individual-Level Variables on Political Trust in Mainland China	128

5.4	Hierarchical Intercept Model of Cultural Environment's Effects on Incumbent-Based Trust in Mainland China	134
5.5	Full HLM Model of Incumbent-Based Trust with Cross-Level Interaction in Mainland China	137
5.6	Exploratory Factor Analysis of Political Trust in Taiwan	140
5.7	Effects of Individual-Level Variables on Political Trust in Taiwan	142
5.8	Full HLM Model for Trust in Partisan Institutions/Agents in Taiwan	143
6.1	Non-Electoral Participation in Mainland China	153
6.2	Cultural Impacts on Government Salience in Mainland China	160
6.3	Comparing the Effects of Culture and Education on Government Salience in Mainland China	162
6.4	Cultural Impacts on the Likelihood of Political Participation in Mainland China	168
6.5	Comparing the Effects of Cultural and Psychological Variables on Participation in Mainland China	171
6.6	Cultural Impacts on Choice of Confrontational Political Acts in Mainland China	179
6.7	Comparing the Effects of Culture and Political Interest on the Likelihood of Choosing Confrontational Acts of Participation in Mainland China	182
6.8	Protest Potential in Mainland China (Percent of Sample Approving)	185
6.9	Cultural Impacts on Protest Potential in Mainland China	188
7.1	Understanding of Democracy in Mainland China and Taiwan	203
7.2	"Don't Know" Answers in Mainland China	208
7.3	"Don't Know" Answers in Taiwan	209
7.4	Cultural Impacts on People's Understanding of Democracy in Mainland China	214
7.5	Cultural Impacts on People's Understanding of Democracy in Taiwan	217
7.6	Different Understandings of Democracy (2002)	218
7.7	Multinomial Analysis of Cultural Impacts on People's Understanding of Democracy (2002)	219
A.1	Test–Retest for Whether Respondent Voted	236
A.2	Test–Retest for Respondent's Vote (Choice of Party)	236
A.3	Population Division and Sample Breakdown	237
A.4	Checking Representativeness of Taiwan Survey Sample (Data before Raking)	237
A.5	Checking Representativeness of Taiwan Survey Sample (Data after Raking)	238

Tables and Figures xi

B.1 Political Fear in Mainland China and Taiwan: Changes
and Continuity 241
B.2 Correlation between Political Fear and Political Trust 242
B.3 Missing Values in Democratic Supply and Demand
Questions 244
B.4 Impacts of Education, Political Interest, and Fear on Item
Nonresponses 245
E.1 Hierarchical Logit ANOVA Model for Government
Salience 259
E.2 Hierarchical Logit ANOVA Model for Political
Participation 259

Figures

5.1 Institutional trust around the world, 2001–2005 111
7.1 "How suitable is democracy for your country?" 195
7.2 "What is the level of democracy in your country now?" 195

Editor's Note

Tianjian Shi passed away unexpectedly on December 25, 2010, leaving this book's completed manuscript, which had been accepted by Cambridge University Press. I undertook the final editing with the professional assistance of Mary Child and the technical help of Tianjian's former student, Jie Lu. As peer reviewers for the Press, Dorothy J. Solinger and Doh Chull Shin provided valuable suggestions for revisions. I thank John Aldrich for finding the funds to support Mary Child's work. Some minor queries that came up in the course of editing could not be resolved. I regret any errors or confusion that I may have introduced into the text.

Andrew J. Nathan

Acknowledgments

Many organizations sponsored the surveys that were critical for collecting the data used in this book. The surveys in mainland China were sponsored by various grants from the U.S. National Science Foundation (Grants SES-88-12023 and NSF-SBR-94-96313), the Henry Luce Foundation, the Ford Foundation, and the World Bank. The surveys in Taiwan were funded by the Ministry of Education of Taiwan under the MOE-NSC Program for Promoting Academic Excellence of Universities as well as various grants from National Taiwan University (NTU) and the Institute of Political Science of Academia Sinica. I also would like to thank the Carnegie Endowment for International Peace for providing me with an opportunity to work in their Beijing office while writing this book.

Numerous people in China have helped me with the surveys. I have greatly benefited from valuable support from the Survey Research Center of the People's University of China, the Institute of Sociology of the Chinese Social Sciences Academy, and the Research Center for Contemporary China of Peking University. For the 1993 survey, I would like to thank Zheng Hangsheng, Li Qiang, Hao Hongsheng, Hong Dayong, Song Shige, and Xu Ping for their valuable assistance. Professor Shen Rendao also helped me with various political complications.

For the 2002 survey, I would like to thank Li Peilin, Li Wei, Lu Hongxin, and Zuo Xinhua of the Institute of Sociology of the Chinese Academy of Social Science for their assistance. I would like to express my thanks especially to Xu Xinxin for her efforts in obtaining the required permit from the authorities to make the survey possible, as well as her ability to overcome various political and other difficulties.

For the 2008 survey, I would like to thank Shen Mingming, Yang Ming, Yan Jie, and Zuo Cai from the Research Center for Contemporary China of Peking University for helping me accomplish the survey successfully. I am also grateful to Jennifer Li.

I would also like to thank Andrew J. Nathan, Bruce Dickson, Daniel Bell, Doh C. Shin, Daniela Stockmann, and Jie Lu, all of whom provided me with detailed comments on various drafts of this manuscript. I am especially grateful for the extremely proficient research assistance provided by Jie Lu when he was a graduate student at Duke. I am also indebted to my students for the valuable lessons I learned at Duke. The project also benefited from the able assistance of Liu Da, Stuart Wiggin, Colin Feehan, Mariya Kovalenko, Ma Jiansu, Martin Rivlin, and Meredith Wen. Joy Ding provided efficient and valuable editorial assistance at the final stages of this project. I am extremely grateful for their support and help.

I am indebted to my wife, Christine Chiu, and our children, Eleanor and Sarah, who have borne my absences from the family during the valuable summers when I needed to be in China to direct various surveys. I profoundly appreciate the personal sacrifices they have made to enable me to complete this book. This book is dedicated to them.

Tianjian Shi

Introduction

The intellectual journey that led to this book can be traced back to my graduate school years at Columbia University. My interest in culture was generated by a puzzle in the field of political science: Why have scholars of Asian politics failed to make major theoretical contributions to political science in the way that their counterparts studying European, Latin American, and African politics have done over the past half century? Why haven't students of Asian politics developed general theories that can be applied to the study of political behavior and processes in other parts of the world?

Over several decades of studying Chinese politics I gradually realized that the answers to these questions lie in the existence of distinct cultural traditions across regions. Culture moderates and even directly shapes political attitudes, behavior, and the dynamics of political systems. Truly general theories cannot be established without systematically theorizing and appropriately modeling the impacts of culture. Without a general theory of culture, scholars of comparative politics are left with isolated research fields that are compartmentalized by geographic and linguistic barriers with few overarching links to political behavior overall. Since the behavioral revolution, scholars of political science have tended to assume that people in different societies are all instrumentally rational, that is, that their choices are guided by similar norms, which emphasize utility-maximization, usually centered on actors' material interests. When political scientists find that similar social-structural and institutional variables in societies with different cultural environments play different roles, they tend to attribute this to differences in access to information. For example, when they find that people in China trust their government more than

I

people in other societies, they are inclined to attribute the difference primarily to regime media control. In this way, the impacts of culture have mostly been ignored.

But what if rationality – understood here as the process of deciding what goals to aim for and what means to use to achieve them – is culturally embedded, or, as I call it here, normative? That is, what if individuals' interest calculations are based on socially shared ideas about acceptable and expected behavior rather than on a universal, materialist concept of utility? I argue that norms shape people's interpretations of outside stimuli, define goals to pursue in their responses to the outside world, and guide them to choose appropriate means to pursue those goals. Culture, therefore, has an independent effect on people's political attitudes and behavior. Rationality is norm-infused rather than norm-free. One theoretical contribution that scholars of Asian politics can make to the general theory of political science is to theorize how culturally defined normative rationality can – by itself, or in interaction with social structures and institutions – shape people's choices in politics. The range of unique cultural heritages present in Asia, along with the diversity of distinct political institutions, and varying levels of economic development, provide researchers with an excellent variety of cases with which to develop and test theory about the impact of culture on politics.

This study seeks to discover whether and how cultural norms shape people's approaches and responses to politics. In such an investigation, the most difficult challenge is to rule out *endogeneity* – that is, to show that culture is an independent cause of certain behaviors and not the effect of structural or institutional factors that are the real causes of those behaviors. To control for the impacts of social structure and political institutions on behavior, social scientists cannot rely solely on cross-sectional data collected from one country at one time, as this would not provide the necessary variation to sort out the endogeneity issue. To establish the independent impact of culture from those of social structure and institutions, scholars of political culture need data from societies with different social structures and political institutions and also data across time. This study uses three waves of data from two Asian societies with different social structures and political institutions – mainland China and Taiwan – to explore the independent effects of culture on political behavior.

In the early 1990s, Professors Hu Fu and Chu Yun-han from the National Taiwan University visited Columbia University. We shared an interest in political culture, and we sought the help of Professors Hsin-chi Kuan and S. K. Lau of the Chinese University of Hong Kong. In 1993 our

Introduction 3

three research teams conducted our first comparative study of political culture – the 1993 Survey of Political Culture and Political Participation in Mainland China, Taiwan, and Hong Kong – with the support of the Henry Luce Foundation. After the three surveys were done and we began analyzing the data, I painfully realized that the data did not allow me to test thoroughly my ideas about the role of culture. Although data from societies with different social-structural resources and political institutions allowed me to control for structural and institutional variables in order to examine the impacts of culture, my findings were limited to a single point of time in two rapidly changing societies: a Taiwan just undergoing democratic transition and a mainland China in the midst of economic reform. To systematically test the theory that culture did not change in direct response to changes in social structures or political institutions, I needed to wait for more time to elapse and then gather additional data.

After the 1993 survey, our three research teams were joined by teams from Japan, South Korea, Thailand, the Philippines, and Mongolia to constitute the East Asian Barometer (EAB), which conducted its first wave of surveys from 2001 to 2003. Because the EAB's mainland China survey was conducted in 2002, I refer to it as the 2002 China Survey. Fortunately, I was able to persuade my colleagues in the project to include in our core questionnaire the key items necessary to test my cultural theory. The Taiwan survey for this same period is referred to here as the 2002 Taiwan Survey.

By 2005 the EAB had been joined by research teams from another five countries (Vietnam, Cambodia, Indonesia, Malaysia, and Singapore), and the name of the project was changed to the Asian Barometer Survey (ABS).[1] We conducted surveys in all thirteen societies during the period 2005–2008 and called them the "second wave surveys," or Asian Barometer Survey II. The mainland China survey in this set was fielded in 2008, and I refer to it as the 2008 China Survey.

With the involvement of more country teams, negotiations over items to be included in the common questionnaire became tougher. I was able to persuade my colleagues to include only a limited number of questionnaire items on cultural norms, fewer than those included in the 1993 and 2002 surveys. I therefore use the 2008 data here only to examine whether structural and institutional changes in China altered culture over

---

[1] The Asian Barometer Survey (ABS) project Web site can be found at: http://www.asianbarometer.org.

the fifteen years under study. I do not use the 2008 data in my analyses of political trust, participation, and understanding of democracy.

AN OVERVIEW OF THE BOOK

The book is divided into two parts. In the first, I bring the original meaning of culture – the distinctive normative rationality of a given society – back to the center of cultural studies. To understand how normative rationality influences the choices of individuals, researchers must focus on norms. While mainland China and Taiwan are the loci of the puzzles that I use to explore the role of culture and the source of the data that I employ to test my analysis, the scope of the argument is intended to reach beyond any particular region, to address the role and influence of culture in political behavior in general.

Chapter 1 begins with a brief review of the intellectual origins of cultural studies, showing that early studies of culture focused on the meanings that lie behind social actions. When Almond and Verba borrowed the concept of culture for use in political science, they understood it as simply another kind of resource (Almond and Verba 1963). For them, the impacts of cultural variables were similar to the impacts of sociological resources: they can either increase the benefits or reduce the costs associated with various participatory activities. Normative utility, which had occupied a central position in traditional cultural studies, became a secondary consideration.

To return cultural studies to its roots, I define culture as a kind of mental software that sets up standards of appropriate behavior for a group or category of people, thereby distinguishing that group from other groups or categories. Culture constitutes socially shared guidance for accepted and expected patterns of conduct. As such, it shapes the definitions of normative rationality employed by political actors. This definition reasserts and refines the idea of culture as a pattern of social meaning in three ways. First, it makes a clear distinction between values and norms on one hand and attitudes and beliefs on the other. I argue that students of political culture should concentrate on values and norms in order to avoid treating culture as a proxy of structures and institutions. Second, I argue that the nation-state is not always the proper unit of analysis for the study of how culture affects individual action. Because culture exerts influence through both individual psychology and social pressure, the cultural environment at the community level can be expected to have a more important influence on an individual than the larger cultural

Introduction

environment in the country as a whole. (This is not to suggest that countries can never be used as units of analysis in cultural study. The proper unit of analysis depends on the particular dependent variable one wishes to explain.) Third, while recent cultural theory often sees cultural change as a response to social-structural and institutional changes in a society, I argue that struggles within cultures can play a critical role in bringing about cultural change in a society.

Chapter 2 begins to illustrate the argument by a comparison of the roots of traditional Chinese and modern Western liberal cultures. I stylize their differences as alternative solutions to the core problem of collective action: how to foster cooperation among people to achieve collective goals and thus make social life possible. Eastern and Western philosophers offered different visions of how humans escape from a pre-societal state or state of nature; the cultural norms they chose to sustain their solutions are also fundamentally different. Among the various cultural norms developed from those solutions, two of them – which I label orientation toward authority (OTA) and definition of self-interest (DSI) – have perhaps the most important impact on a person's orientation toward political life and therefore on political processes in different societies. The analyses in this book concentrate on these two cultural norms. Chapter 2 goes on to describe the mechanisms by which these cultural norms influence political attitudes and behavior.

Still in Part I, the theoretical discussion is followed by an empirical examination of culture in China and Taiwan. Using data collected from these two societies at different times, I test whether culture is a causal force that operates independently of social structure and political institutions. The first question is whether structural and institutional changes drive cultural changes. If they do, there would be little need to study culture. I show that rapid, modernizing social change in mainland China and far-reaching, democratizing political change in Taiwan did not bring about significant cultural shifts in these societies, confirming that culture changes independently from social structure and institutions.

I then use culture as an independent variable to explain certain puzzles of political life in China and Taiwan. Why does the authoritarian Chinese government enjoy a high level of political trust from people who claim that they have a strong desire for democracy? Why do people in Taiwan perceive their regime to offer a greater degree of democracy than they want? I show that people holding traditional cultural norms are more likely to trust their government, less likely to confront the regime, and more likely to define the meaning of democracy as government by guardianship. An analysis of causal relationships in mainland China and Taiwan shows that the structural and institutional differences between the two societies do not diminish the impact of culture. Culture has an independent effect on political attitudes and political behavior.

Chapter 3 begins by specifying how the cultural norms in this study are measured. I then use confirmatory factor analysis to test whether the observable variables used in the surveys tap into actual clusters of values and norms and whether these norms have the features specified by my theory of culture. Finally, I compare the configurations of cultural norms in China and Taiwan. I find that the common culture they started out with has retained its basic structure in each society, despite their separation for many years and the dramatic changes each has undergone.

Chapter 4 is designed to examine the endogeneity problem discussed above: that is, whether culture is merely a product of social structure and political institutions. I explore whether social and institutional changes in China and Taiwan between 1993 and 2002 led to cultural shifts in these societies. If cultural norms changed in response to social and institutional changes, then culture is merely an intervening variable with no independent effects. I show that structural and institutional changes in these two societies actually reinforced people's commitment to traditional cultural norms rather than converting them to new norms as suggested by other theories. The finding confirms that culture is independent from structure and institutions.

Part II takes culture as an independent variable and tests its impacts on political attitudes and behavior. Chapter 5 examines the effects of culture on political trust. Scholars of political trust have generally held that people's attitudes toward government are shaped primarily by government performance as well as by people's ability to understand the government's impact on their lives. Empirical research on political trust has concentrated on these two factors and on variables related to them, such as education and access to media. The theory advanced in this book challenges the assumption that all people use the same standards to evaluate government performance. I argue that different cultural norms lead people to hold different expectations of government, which creates a diversity of standards for evaluating government performance. The same governmental behavior may lead people with different cultural orientations to respond in different ways. For this reason, normative rationality can have a significant impact on political trust.

Introduction 7

The empirical test of culture's impact on political trust confirms that both individual-level norms and the normative environment in which the individual lives play a role in the way in which cultural norms influence political trust. The impact of the social environment on political trust is complex. It is not linearly associated with the percentage of people holding dominant cultural norms in a community; instead, a smaller group of deviating norm holders may be able to provide the crucial social support that makes it difficult for dominant norm holders to socially isolate deviating norm holders. Unless researchers in comparative politics understand how political actors' preferences are defined by culture, their analyses will suffer from the "omitted variable problem," and they will misunderstand the formation of political attitudes and behaviors of the populations they study.

Chapter 6 explores the impact of culture on people's participatory behavior. I argue that people's decisions to participate in politics can be divided into three stages:

1. Facing outside stimuli, actors need to assign responsibility;
2. If they hold their government responsible for a problem, they need to decide whether to engage in political acts to address the problem; and
3. If the answer is positive, they need to choose a particular political act.

I show that cultural norms have a statistically significant impact on each stage of the decision-making process, and that the impacts of culture are more important than those of social structure and political institutions. The impacts of culture on participation, however, are complicated. While one dimension of traditional culture – what I call an "allocentric" (or community-minded) definition of self-interest – encourages people to be more politically passive, another dimension of traditional culture – a "hierarchical" orientation toward authority – encourages people to be more politically active. Although the hierarchical orientation encourages people to get involved in various political acts, including unconventional political acts like strikes and demonstrations, the goals legitimated by the norm are different from those authorized by what I call a reciprocal orientation toward authority, in which the governed understand authority as operating by grace of their consent. Rather than authorizing people to oppose their government, a hierarchical orientation toward authority encourages people to remonstrate. Thus, similar political acts undertaken by people holding different cultural norms may have dissimilar implications for the citizen and therefore also for the regime.

Chapter 7 tests the way in which cultural norms affect people's understanding of democracy. After the Third Wave of democratization, which started in Southern Europe in the 1970s and extended through Latin America, East Asia, and Eastern and Central Europe and the former Soviet space in the 1990s, democracy seems to have become a universally preferred value (see, for example, Chu, Diamond, Nathan, and Shin 2008). In China and Taiwan, the Asian Barometer Survey confirmed that the majority of people desire democracy. Yet a majority of respondents in authoritarian China reported that they already enjoyed a high level of democracy, and respondents in Taiwan claimed that the system was more democratic than they wanted it to be. Both of these surprising responses suggest that the democracy people in these two societies claimed that they wanted may have been different from the mainstream Western conception of democracy.

Although there is no democratic tradition in China, there is an ancient doctrine of "people as the basis" (*minben*) that remains influential. While minben and democracy are identical in their expectation that the goal of government is to benefit the people, they differ in (1) the means used to achieve this goal; (2) the standards for evaluating governmental legitimacy; and (3) the rights and responsibilities assigned to people vis-à-vis government. Precisely because the goal of good government is understood in the same way in both democratic and minben thinking, people with traditional cultural views may understand the meaning of democracy in terms of the minben tradition.

I test structural, institutional, and cultural explanations for differences in understanding of democracy. I show that more modern cultural norms incline people to define democracy as a set of procedural arrangements to constrain political power, whereas traditional cultural norms make people more likely to understand democracy as government by benevolent guardians. The finding is true in both authoritarian China and democratic Taiwan. A government's legitimacy, according to minben doctrine, may be judged on its policy outcomes; accordingly, citizens in a society where people are deprived of the right to elect public officials or are denied certain civil liberties in the name of collective interest may not necessarily downgrade their assessment of democratic development in their societies. This finding confirms that the authoritarian regime in China is sustained by a different kind of legitimacy than that of democratic regimes.

Introduction

In the Conclusion, I argue that these insights into the role of culture throw light on the evolution of the political regimes in China and Taiwan. In China, the prevalence of traditional cultural norms of hierarchical orientation to authority and allocentric definition of self-interest undergird the legitimacy of a regime that styles itself as a guardian of the people and bases its claim to authority on its ability to provide for the people's welfare. Traditions of deference to authority provide the authoritarian mainland regime with considerable leeway to exercise authority in the absence of procedures to guarantee citizens' rights or influence. In Taiwan, the persistence of traditional norms, despite the modernization of social structures and the democratization of political institutions, creates friction between the regime's open and sometimes turbulently democratic political practices and the normative expectations of its citizens, which are influenced by traditional cultural norms. As a result, despite its authenticity as a democracy, the political system in Taiwan is a disappointment to some of its citizens.

PART I

THEORY OF POLITICAL CULTURE

I

Political Culture Theory and Regime Stability

What explains the resilience of the authoritarian regime in mainland China? Why do people in China express a high level of trust toward the government even though they strongly desire democracy? Conversely, why do many people in Taiwan say they would prefer a government less democratic than the one they actually have? These findings run counter to Western scholars' expectations about democracy and contradict current theories of politics. An understanding of prevailing cultural norms about politics in these political systems can help resolve these puzzles.

In the aftermath of the 1989 Tiananmen Square incident, most observers of Chinese politics believed that the Chinese Communist Party (CCP) had permanently lost its legitimacy and that continuation of its rule would necessitate a reliance on brute force. The collapse of the Soviet Union in 1991 reinforced this belief. Scholars argued that the CCP had only two choices: to join the "third wave" of democratization, which would bring about the party's collapse, or to initiate serious political reforms, which would delay collapse but weaken the party's authority. In effect, the CCP could choose between painless euthanasia or a prolonged and painful dying process.[1]

---

[1] For example, in an interview with ABC television, Liu Binyan, a former *People's Daily* journalist, predicted that the regime would collapse within forty-eight hours. May 22, 1989 Vanderbilt Television News Archive, available at: http://tvnews.vanderbilt.edu/program.pl?ID=646443 (accessed December 17, 2013). A multiauthor symposium on Chinese democracy in the *Journal of Democracy* (January 1998) expressed the mindset of many Western observers. The discussion dealt with how the CCP was able to consolidate its power after the 1989 crisis and whether this consolidation was real. The questions were based on the assumption that the regime should not have been able to remain in power.

Observers also believed that the survival of the CCP and successful economic reform were incompatible. In one group were scholars influenced by modernization theory, who held that successful economic reform would require concomitant political change. Because the CCP refused to introduce meaningful political reform, its economic reforms were unsustainable. The late Gordon White described the CCP's dilemma – the democratic transition it would have to contend with after unleashing economic reform – as "riding the tiger" (a reference to the Chinese saying "If you are riding a tiger it is hard to get off") (White 1993, 2). Bruce Gilley argued that democratization was inevitable, despite the regime's efforts to obstruct it (Gilley 2004).

In a second camp were scholars who doubted the long-term viability of the Chinese economic reform program. In its first stage, reform could create a win-win situation: economic gains for the majority would translate into support for the regime or at least for its reform program. However, support would depend on the regime's continuing ability to provide economic gains. This would become increasingly difficult in a second stage, when the necessary reform of obsolete state-owned enterprises (SOEs) would jeopardize the interests of a large part of the population. The provisional peace between state and society would vanish, and a disgruntled majority would challenge the regime, leading to a crisis. If the CCP tried to avoid this crisis by refusing to move from the first stage to the second stage, the resulting financial burden of the SOEs would drag the banking system into insolvency, leading eventually to regime collapse (Chang 2001).

Such predictions aligned with mainstream theories of comparative politics and democratic transitions. Authoritarian leaders, by definition, hold political power without the periodically renewed consent of their people, but they do allow their people certain freedoms not allowed in totalitarian societies, including the freedom to criticize the government in private settings. According to mainstream theory, the weak legitimacy and overcentralization of power built into Chinese authoritarianism – combined with a decline, brought by economic reform, in the regime's capacity to control the economic life of its citizens and the existence of a space for citizens to criticize the government – would make a transition to democracy highly likely (see, for example, Linz 2000).

Yet, at least as of this writing, the CCP has escaped this fate. China demonstrated a viable path for growing out of a planned economy, showing that sequencing economic and political change is possible in the transition from communism. China's economy expanded beyond expectations,

Political Culture Theory and Regime Stability

achieving an average annual growth rate, starting in 1998, of 8 to 9 percent. The government weathered the risky period of SOE reform beginning in the late 1990s, laying off some 20 million workers in the process. Although the layoffs triggered scattered protests and demonstrations, the policy did not generate the major turmoil and social unrest predicted by outside observers.

Even among workers who lost their jobs and peasants who lost their land, few joined social movements to protest against the regime (Shi and Lou 2010a). To be sure, the frequency of protests increased, but their incidence was low in comparison to the scale of SOE layoffs.[2] Among citizens who chose to engage in such regime-challenging political activities, most wanted to remonstrate with rather than oppose the regime.[3] Why did Chinese workers behave differently from workers in Poland's Solidarity, who also faced regime suppression?

The scale of repression did not increase. On the contrary, surveys showed that most Chinese perceived an increase in civil liberties and political freedoms during the period of reform. Instead, the successful political navigation of SOE reform must be attributed to widespread public normative support for the regime. Survey after survey conducted by Western scholars showed levels of popular satisfaction with the regime at around 80 percent (Chen 2004; Chu et al. 2008; Li 2004; Shi 2001).

Some scholars dismiss the ability of surveys to gain true information in China, due to the regime's suppression. Others argue that information control in China forces people to evaluate their government based on incomplete information. Even if survey responses reflect the true feelings of people at a given time, those feelings are fragile. The removal of information barriers, these scholars believe, would result in a change of attitude toward the government. Some demonize all surveys done in China. He Qinglian, for example, asserts that all joint research projects

[2] In 1995, there were 10,000 "collective mass incidents," a category used by the government to refer to such political acts as protests, riots, and mass petitioning. In 2004, the number of collective mass incidents rose to 74,000 and then to 87,000 in 2005 (Kahn 2006). This increase happened despite the fact that the regime's use of repression remained more or less constant. What changed was the willingness of citizens to confront the regime.

[3] A well-known example was Guo Haifeng's behavior in front of the Great Hall of the People on April 25, 1989. Guo knelt down and begged the government to accept the students' appeal. A stream of research by Kevin O'Brien and Lianjiang Li found that "resistance" in rural China was usually aimed not at challenging the regime but at persuading local bureaucrats to implement central government policies (Li and O'Brien 1996; O'Brien 1994a, 1996; O'Brien and Li 2006). A survey by Wenfang Tang also revealed that many workers who lost their jobs in the reform tried to understand the government's difficulties rather than challenge its decisions (Tang 2005).

16 *Theory of Political Culture*

involving Western and Chinese academics are infiltrated by the State Security Bureau and that all survey data are screened by the bureau. She alleges that scholars involved in survey research in China know the real situation but do not confess because doing so would jeopardize their credibility (He 2004).

Among scholars who recognize regime resilience as genuine, many attribute the phenomenon primarily to the country's economic performance.[4] The problem with this argument is that even though economic performance may partially explain why people who benefited from economic reforms supported the government, it cannot explain why the victims of reform, such as laid-off SOE workers, support it. Yet a survey conducted by Wenfang Tang shows that laid-off workers in China's rust belt supported the regime no less than other respondents did (Tang 2005).

Another theory attributes the resilience of the regime to institutional changes. For example, the institutionalization of succession made it possible for the regime to avoid the turmoil that accompanies succession in most authoritarian regimes (Nathan 2003). Although this argument explains the lack of political breakdown at the top during leadership transitions, it does not explain why ordinary people express high levels of trust in their government, nor the apparent contradiction that a majority of people say they want democracy but refrain from engaging in the regime-challenging political actions that would bring it about.

If neither economic performance nor institutional change explains authoritarian resilience, how did the CCP achieve such a miracle? The question has application beyond the single case of China. The histories of Japan, South Korea, Singapore, and Taiwan reveal the existence of authoritarian regimes that enjoyed genuine support from their people for extended periods of time even though their policies caused significant economic difficulties for large segments of their populations. Before their democratic transitions, people living in these countries were found to tolerate their governments more than people living in authoritarian societies outside of East Asia. This led Chalmers Johnson to argue that rulers in East Asia possessed "a particular kind of legitimacy that allows them to be much more experimental and undoctrinaire than the typical authoritarian regime" (Johnson 1982).[5]

---

[4] See the multiauthor symposiums in the *Journal of Democracy* vol. 9, no. 1 (1998) and vol. 14, no. 1. For instance, see Nathan (1998) and Oksenberg (1998) in the former and Nathan (2003) in the latter.

[5] Many students of East Asian politics in general and political economy in particular reject the cultural explanation. For example, Woo-Cummings says, "Western observers have

Political Culture Theory and Regime Stability

To be sure, authoritarianism eventually yielded peacefully to democracy in three of these cases. But this was not necessarily due to a massive collapse of support for the predemocratic regimes. The United States played a critical role – an undeniable outside factor – in supporting democratic transitions in these countries, all of which faced similar security threats that forced them to rely on U.S. support and respond to U.S. concerns. Moreover, the Asian Barometer Survey I (2001–2003) found that the level of popular commitment to democracy in many newly democratized East Asian societies was lower than that on other continents (Chu et al. 2008). In Southern Europe more than three-quarters of the mass public believed that democracy was preferable to authoritarianism under all circumstances, with overwhelming levels of public support demonstrated by multiple surveys. By contrast, less than half the public in South Korea and Taiwan thought that democracy was the best form of government, and more than half of those countries' citizens supported possible authoritarian alternatives. When respondents were asked to rate both the level of democracy that was suitable for their political system and the level that it had achieved on a scale of 1 to 10, residents of Taiwan rated their system as being more democratic than they wanted it to be: that is, democratic "supply" was higher than democratic "demand." Even in Japan, the region's oldest democracy, citizens showed low enthusiasm for its democratic political system and little desire for more democracy. Yet despite the low levels of popular support for democracy in Asian societies, their democratic regimes remain stable.

The study of political culture offers a way to explain these puzzles found in mainland China, Taiwan, and other Asian countries. To understand people's responses to political regimes, we need to understand the normative rationality of each population. Yet culture has been misunderstood in recent studies of political behavior. Most scholars conceptualize political culture as simply another kind of resource, arguing that culture can either increase the benefits or reduce the costs associated with various political activities.[6] This definition removes the essence of political culture – assigning meanings to political action – from political culture studies. I argue instead that culture defines for political actors what constitutes a cost and what constitutes a benefit and in that way shapes the

---

had a hard time understanding the legitimacy of the developmental regime in East Asia, often confusing it with a cultural (i.e., Confucian) penchant for political acquiescence" (Woo-Cumings 1999, 20).

[6] For example, Almond and Verba (1963) and Verba and Nie (1972).

18   *Theory of Political Culture*

logic underlying an actor's choices. To understand the puzzles identified in mainland China and Taiwan, we need to study the specifics of political culture in these societies.

INTELLECTUAL ORIGINS OF MODERN CULTURE STUDIES

Theories of political culture constitute a response to a fundamental problem of the social sciences, that is, "how a genuinely positive social science would differ from the other positive sciences that had developed before it" (Eckstein 1996, 471). In the words of Max Weber, "The distinctive (not sole) task of social science [is]: trying to 'understand' the meanings, or motivations, that underlie actions."[7] Culturally defined meaning plays a critical role in human behavior. Meaning systems not only relate the self to situations that confront actors and in which they are forced to act but also orient people to situations, similar to the way that maps orient travelers.

Following Weber, Talcott Parsons claimed that social action is influenced by the "normative orientation" of actors. When actors choose the means to pursue their ends, their normative orientation plays two critical roles insofar as the situation allows for alternatives: (1) it shapes the ends that actors decide to pursue; and (2) it constrains the means that actors consider available to them to pursue such ends (Parsons 1968 [1937], 44, 74–75). Parsons and Edward Shils argued further that normative orientations play major roles in three distinct but related components of decision making:

1. Cognitive decoding: since the same situation can be cognitively decoded in a variety of ways, actors must interpret the situation in a certain way before choosing an action. People with different cognitive orientations may interpret the same event in fundamentally different ways;

2. Affective[8] encoding: cognitively decoded situations can have positive or negative emotional meaning for actors, in turn supplying energy for action;

3. Evaluative encoding: alternative actions left open by cognition plus affects must be assigned positive or negative valuations in light of one's normative system. Such normative systems may sanction or

---

[7] Weber as summarized in Eckstein (1996, 483).
[8] This more commonly used term is substituted for Parsons' term "cathexis," as documented in Eckstein (1996, 489).

Political Culture Theory and Regime Stability

prohibit certain actions. Although in some areas, human actions can be straight responses to feelings, in most cases, cognition plus affect plus evaluation together shape people's choices of action (Parsons and Shils 1951, 53).

After decoding the meaning of an event, actors need to decide whether to respond and, if so, in what way. An actor responding to a political event with which he or she disagrees may choose to protest, write to newspaper editors; donate money to a cause supporting his or her view; support a particular political party or candidate in the next election; block the entrances to government buildings; join secret societies or, in an extreme case, become a terrorist. Each actor's evaluative and affective orientations help him/her decide on the proper goals and the proper means for pursuing such goals.

Those subdimensions of orientation work together to produce a single response to a single stimulus (Parsons 1968). People with different cognitive orientations may interpret the same event in fundamentally different ways. Affective orientation can cause an actor to sample information selectively so as to avoid cognitive dissonance.[9] Different evaluative orientations will lead actors to different views about the rightness or wrongness of a given act. How people decode an event is shaped by the yardsticks they use to measure the event.

Evaluative and affective orientations may cause actors not only to use different standards to gauge the meaning of an event but also to weigh the importance of various pieces of information differently. As a result, a single piece of information can trump all other conflicting information for a particular actor. From this perspective, differences in actors' interpretations of situations are often due not to differences in the information they receive, as argued by rational choice theorists, but to differences in the ways in which affective and evaluative orientations lead them to decode the same information. This implies that actors from different cultural backgrounds will differ systematically in the meanings that they derive from the same information. Unfortunately, contemporary students of political culture usually interpret action theory in a different way, one that constitutes a barrier to the advance of studies of political culture.

---

[9] The social psychologist Leon Festinger found that when inconsistency exists between people's predispositions and social reality, people can experience an unpleasant state of arousal called cognitive dissonance. The arousal of dissonance motivates people to act to reduce or eliminate this sensation and strive to achieve consonance, a state of psychological balance (Festinger 1957).

CURRENT THEORIES OF POLITICAL CULTURE: A CRITIQUE

Scholars of political culture agree that people's orientations should be studied in order to understand political decisions. But they disagree on other issues, such as which specific orientations to focus on, at what level, and how such orientations impact decision making. This section briefly reviews the major approaches to political culture studies and identifies the problems associated with each.[10]

The social character approach borrows concepts from anthropological studies of personality and from the study of national character in political science (Adorno et al. 1950; Almond and Verba 1963; Banfield 1958; Bell 1996; Goldhagen 1996; Inkeles 1983; Inkeles and Smith 1974; Metzger 1977; Pye 1985, 1992; Sun et al. 2005). The conceptualization of culture in this approach is exactly right: culture is defined as a complex of mental properties that assign meanings to social actions and that vary from one society to another. Cultures differ, among other ways, in how people view authority relations, in their members' commitment to particular religious or ideological views, and in the content and salience of their historical memories.

But the social character approach suffers from three problems. First, although defining culture as a collective property, it normally examines culture empirically at the level of the individual, ignoring the fact that culture may also influence individuals' choices at a group level, through social interaction (Aronoff 1988, xv–xvi). In this way the social character approach in practice becomes a study of individual psychology. Second, when the approach was developed in the 1950s, scholars pursuing it did not possess the empirical and statistical tools that would allow them properly to identify culture and test its impacts on people's behavior. Third, the theory does not clearly specify or test the causal mechanisms attributed to culture (Dickson 1992).

The civic culture school is the most influential approach to the study of political culture, and it explicitly incorporates the orientations proposed by Parsons and Shils. Unfortunately, the conceptualization veered off course when Almond and Verba tried to decompose culture into separate cognitive, affective, and evaluative domains. Rather than viewing these orientations as parts of a unified mental process that jointly determines actors' responses to situations, *The Civic Culture* treated them as if they play separate roles in a sequence of mental processes that lead to

---

[10] For a comprehensive review of cultural theories, see Wilson (2000).

Political Culture Theory and Regime Stability

different political behaviors. This confusion created several problems for political culture studies.

First, the approach moved political culture theory away from its focus on the meaning of social action toward the idea of knowledge of information. Almond and Verba defined cognitive orientation as the knowledge political actors have (1) of their nation and its political system, (2) of the structures and roles of their government, and (3) of the downward flow of policies from government. This definition transforms the concept of cognitive orientation into cognitive ability. The former refers to the predispositions that influence people's decoding of information; the latter refers to actors' knowledge and understanding of the political arena. The idea of culture as a distinctive normative rationality disappeared from their conception of political culture.

Second, in studying the impact of culture on political processes, Almond and Verba confined their inquiry to its effects on political participation. They tried to explore how an individual's psychological orientation influences his or her decisions regarding whether and how to participate in politics. Followers of the civic culture approach tend to ignore the impact of culture on other aspects of politics.

Third, the civic culture school fails to deal properly with the problems of level and unit of analysis. In Parsonian action theory, orientation is conceptualized as an individual phenomenon with social attributes. Almond and Verba used the national society as the unit of analysis and defined political culture as the distribution of alternative orientations in a country. This approach implicitly assumes that the political process in a society is determined by the orientation held by the majority of people and that those of minorities can be neglected. This commits, in effect, the "ecological fallacy" of inferring individuals' characteristics from the aggregate statistics of the group to which they belong. It causes scholars to neglect the political struggles generated by and around culture.

A third school of political culture studies focuses on the study of symbols, rituals, and myths. It explores how the socially constructed nature of knowledge shapes people's behavior. This approach defines culture as a set of collective meanings that groups create, share, and symbolically express. Although this definition of culture follows the Weberian concern with the meanings of social action, the way its adherents employ the idea generates several problems.

First, since symbols, rituals, and myths may be interpreted in different ways, it is difficult for scholars to identify clearly a determinate "meaning of action" behind a given cultural icon or to specify how such a symbol assigns meaning to people's political behavior. The causal linkage between culture and politics offered by this school is usually quite weak. Second, the school tends to confuse social objects that express culture with culture itself; this makes it difficult for scholars to identify the causal mechanisms by which culture influences politics. Third, given that there is usually more than one set of symbols and myths in a society, scholars taking this approach have difficulty choosing which symbols to study when trying to analyze a given society's culture.

The culture theory approach developed by Mary Douglas and Aaron Wildavsky defines culture as "social bias." In *Risk and Culture*, Douglas and Wildavsky argue, "Since an individual cannot look at all directions at once, social life demands organization of bias. People order their universe through social bias. By bringing these biases out into the open, we will understand better which policy differences can be reconciled and which cannot." To these scholars, the "organization of bias" is socially constructed. Social biases consist of both affective and evaluative components. These biases influence people's perceptions of risks, which, in turn, influence their choices of action (Douglas 1982, 1973; Douglas and Wildavsky 1982; Ellis 1993; Wildavsky 1987; Wilson 2000, 252).

Although this approach preserves the idea of meanings of action, the theory deduces culture from people's behavioral patterns, a method that creates several problems. First, although culture should indeed influence behavioral patterns, and we may therefore infer the nature of cultural attributes from our observation of individual and social behaviors, as a matter of theory culture should not be equated with behavioral patterns. Meanings cannot be assigned to actions by patterns of behavior; they can be assigned only by a culture that lies behind patterns of behavior. This confusion about the relationship between culture and behavior prevents scholars of this school from identifying the causal mechanisms by which culture influences social behavior.

Second and relatedly, if behaviors are used as the measure of culture, it becomes impossible empirically to assess the impact of culture on social behavior because a single measure cannot be used as both an independent and a dependent variable in the same equation. Third, the Douglas-Wildavsky approach believes that different behavioral patterns can be arranged along a single cultural dimension.[11] But culture is more properly seen as consisting of different dimensions that govern different kinds

---

[11] Social biases are said to range from apathetic, to intense concern for hierarchy, to competitive, to egalitarian, and finally to autonomous (Douglas and Wildavsky 1982).

Political Culture Theory and Regime Stability

of social interactions, as I will try to show in the empirical chapters of this book.

Social constructivism in international relations, the most recent approach in studies of political culture, has brought normative issues back to the study of international politics. The behavioral revolution in the middle of the last century shifted researchers' attention away from norms, mainly due to methodological reasons – normative and ideational phenomena were notoriously difficult to measure. But persistent puzzles that could not be resolved by the analysis of social-structural and institutional variables prompted international relations scholars to return to the study of norms and ideation in the 1980s.[12] Those scholars made the central claim that the behavior of transnational actors is influenced by ideas (Keohane and Nye 1977). As states are embedded in dense networks of international social relations, state actors' perceptions of the world and of their own roles are socialized by international society (Finnemore 1996). For this reason, scholarship on international regimes in the 1980s and theorizing about social constructivism in the 1990s directed scholars back to the role of norms in international relations (Lapid 1997).

The focus on norms highlighted two points of importance for the study of culture. First, unlike other kinds of ideas, which may be held privately, norms are collectively held ideas about behavior: they must be shared by a group if they are to function as norms. They are not just subjective but intersubjective; they must be understood as social. Second, while values and ideas may or may not have behavioral implications, the existence of behavioral consequences is part of the definition of norms: norms that have no impact on behavior can be considered aspirant or defunct norms, but not functioning norms.[13]

In trying to explain state behavior, social constructivism explores the normative orientations of subnational units and individuals within the state. Rather than assuming that the normative orientation held by

---

[12] For a discussion of this shift, see, among others, Finnemore and Sikkink (1998, 889). The shift was first associated with the regime project and later with constructivists led by Ruggie, Kratochwil, Wendt and others (Adler 1997; Dessler 1989; Krasner 1983; Kratochwil 1989; Kratochwil and Ruggie 1986; Wendt 1987).

[13] See Finnemore (1996, 22–23). There are additional differences between social constructivism and other approaches to culture studies. First, whereas the dependent variables in most other approaches to political culture are the political behaviors of individuals, the dependent variables in this approach are the political behaviors of states. Second, for social constructivists, the institutional environment facing all state actors is that of anarchy. This anarchy allows scholars to hold the international environment constant in order to explore the impact of normative conflicts on the behavior of state actors,

the majority determines the impact of culture, social constructivists examine the political struggles generated by alternative orientations within a society on both the behavior of individuals and the political processes of society. Social constructivists are also more methodologically rigorous than other cultural theorists. They clearly specify causal mechanisms and chains when making arguments about norms, culture, and ideas. They consider the micro foundations on which their theoretical claims rest, and they evaluate various claims in the context of carefully designed research.[14]

As evident from the foregoing review, the debate among scholars of political culture focuses on three issues. First, although all culturalists agree that the object of cultural study is people's orientations, they disagree about the structure of orientations, how different orientations are linked to the outside world, and about what specific orientations they should focus upon. Second, the approaches are divided over the proper level and unit of analysis to be used in cultural studies. Third, culturalists do not concur on the mechanisms through which culture influences the political behavior of individuals and political processes in a society. The following sections seek to address these areas of disagreement and to provide some resolutions.

ON WHICH ORIENTATIONS SHOULD STUDENTS OF CULTURE FOCUS?

For Weber, the distinctiveness of social action is that human beings "take a deliberate attitude towards the world to lend it significance" (Weber 1947, 72). He reminded social scientists to explore not only the instrumental rationality associated with actions but also the normative understanding of their own purposes that are held by individuals and/or groups. Thus, for Weber, the primary objective of cultural study was to explore the normative rationality of social action. To do this, researchers need to focus on orientations that assign "meaning" and "purpose" to the

---

whereas other schools of culture studies have to deal with the confounding effects of varying institutional environments on differences in behavior. Third, social constructivism does not borrow from theories developed in other fields, such as sociology and anthropology, to the same extent as other approaches. As a result, it retains a more theoretically consistent perspective on its subject than the other approaches (Finnemore and Sikkink 1998; Ruggie 1998, 856).

[14] Clear propositions are generated with regard to three aspects of norms in particular – their origins, the mechanism through which they exercise influence, and conditions under which norms will be influential.

Political Culture Theory and Regime Stability

political actions of individuals and to the political processes of society. The most important of these orientations are norms.

Political culture has often been seen as a unified system of mental attributes that includes values, norms, attitudes, and beliefs. But these mental attributes are not all the same. Research by social psychologists suggests that values and norms, on the one hand, and attitudes and beliefs on the other are different psychological dispositions that have separate origins and roles. Values and norms are internal standards that specify proper behavior. Attitudes and beliefs are orientations toward or convictions about particular objects.[15] The *norm* that a person should respect his or her father, for example, defines the proper way for people to treat their fathers. The *attitude* of a person toward his father, however, is shaped by the interaction between the norm that person subscribes to and the actual behavior of the father.

A person's psychological orientation may be thought of as consisting of three layers. At the core lie values. Values are desired or preferred states of the world.[16] The middle layer represents norms, which are shaped by values. Norms assign meaning to actions and guide people's choices of behavior.[17] The outer layer consists of attitudes toward specific objects produced by the interaction between values, norms, and the behavior of the objects themselves.

Values have some key characteristics:

1. They are mental constructs;
2. They provide actors with criteria for assessing what is right or wrong with various possible choices of ends. In helping people to select the ends of their actions, they define a core element of what actors regard as rational – that is, of people's subjective rationality;

---

[15] Culturalists sometimes use the terms "core values" and "core beliefs" interchangeably (Feldman 1988; McClosky and Zaller 1984). I use the word "values" to represent both of these concepts. Some scholars use terminology that confuses norms and beliefs. For example, Goldstein and Keohane use the term "principled beliefs," which "specify criteria for distinguishing right from wrong and just from unjust" (Goldstein and Keohane 1993, 4). Principled beliefs in this sense are norms rather than beliefs.

[16] Parsons defined values as "an element of a shared symbolic system which serves as a criterion or standard for selection among the alternatives of orientation which are intrinsically open in a situation" (Parsons 1968 [1937], 11–12). Kluckhohn, an anthropologist, defines values as "a conception, explicit or implicit, distinctive of an individual or characteristic of a group, of the desirable, which influences the selection from available modes, means, and ends of action" (Kluckhohn 1951, 395).

[17] For a discussion of conditions that can lead to changes of values and norms see Chu (1976) and Parry and Moran (1994).

3. As a primary or core element of thinking, values influence other orientations;
4. Values do not directly produce attitudinal or behavioral outputs but function by shaping norms, which are then applied to features of the actor's real-world environment to produce attitudes and behaviors. Because the effects of values are mediated, the values themselves must be inferred from attitudes or behavior;
5. Values may be either an individual or a social property;
6. Values are relatively few, thus unspecific in their guidance. The same values can be activated differently in different situations and lead to contradictory behaviors. For this reason, it is difficult, if not impossible, for students of political culture to establish empirical linkages between values and behavior.

Attitudes are important psychological properties, but they have improperly occupied a central position in studies of political culture. Almond and Verba defined political culture as "attitudes toward the political system and its various parts, and attitudes toward the role of the self in the system" (Almond and Verba 1963, 13). In response, Eckstein pointed out that "orientations are not 'attitudes': the latter are specific, and the former are general dispositions" (Eckstein 1988, 789). Located in the outer layer of one's mental system, attitudes differ from values and norms in several important ways. Attitudes always involve specific objects, but values and norms may not. Values set general principles for how actors should engage with the outside world and thus govern a broad range of issues. Norms have a larger boundary than attitudes, as they usually govern a category of events or a group of people. Attitudes, however, have specific targets. The target of regime-based trust, for example, is one's government, and the targets of incumbent-based trust are government officials. Attitudes are not only narrower in scope but less emotion-laden than values and norms (Abramson 1983, 35).

Second, attitudes – unlike values and norms, which are shaped primarily through socialization – are shaped by the interaction of norms and the behavior of the attitude's target. For example, a student's attitude toward his or her teacher is shaped jointly by social norms that regulate student-teacher relationships and by the behavior of the teacher. Even if a student acquires the social norm requiring respect for a teacher, if a teacher does not behave properly over time, the student may develop a negative attitude toward that teacher.

Third, social structure and political institutions have different impacts on values and norms, on the one hand, and attitudes on the other. Since

Political Culture Theory and Regime Stability

values and norms interact with the outside world via attitudes, attitudes help cushion values and norms, making them more sustainable in the face of structural and institutional changes. Attitudes, however, directly interact with political objects and are thus more sensitive to environmental changes than values and norms. When the behavior of a political object causes an attitudinal change, the change may not quickly, or ever, lead to a concomitant change in the inner layers of one's mental system.

Fourth, the causal pathway through which attitudes influence behavior is different from that of norms. Attitudes influence choices through a "logic of expected consequences" that helps actors to assess how various objects in their environment will respond to actions that they take.[18] Norms influence action through a "logic of appropriateness" that tells actors whether certain actions are socially legitimate (Finnemore and Sikkink 1998; March and Olsen 1998). While individuals' attitudes may influence their understanding of outside stimuli, shape their response toward such events, and constrain the means they choose to pursue their goals, the attitude of a particular individual may not be shared by others in a community. Thus, attitudes cannot legitimate an individual's choices at the societal level. A man who hates his father, for example, may refuse to ever see him, but his hatred does not legitimate his decision in the eyes of society. Only norms can assign meaning to actions and determine the social legitimacy of actions.

Similarly, policy makers may choose actions based on their expectation of the utilities associated with alternative courses of action. But this is only part of the story. Ethics and virtues can also shape their choices. In many situations, actors may attend less to material benefits than to ethical consequences. Rather than being motivated by instrumental considerations – getting what they want – actors may choose to do something because they believe such behavior is good, desirable, or appropriate.

The comparative advantage of political culture studies, as compared to studies using various versions of the theory of instrumental or rational choice, lies in its focus on the logic of appropriateness and this logic's influence on behavior. As this logic is defined by values and norms and directly guides people's behavior through norms, political culture studies should focus on how norms affect political behavior in different ways in different societies.

Norms play a more critical role than either values or attitudes in shaping behavior, yet they are largely ignored by scholars of political culture

---

[18] Although normative considerations may be embedded in attitudes, these considerations do not play a critical role when attitudes shape the behavior of political actors.

(with the exception of social constructivists). Parsons defined a norm as a "verbal description of the concrete course of action that is regarded as desirable combined with an injunction to make certain future actions conform to this course" (Parsons 1968, 75). More recently, international relations constructivists defined norms as "shared expectations about appropriate behavior held by a community of actors" (Finnemore 1996, 22; see also Katzenstein 1996, 5; Klotz 1995, 22). Jack Gibbs noted that all definitions of norms have three common attributes. A norm is: (1) a collective evaluation of behavior in terms of what it ought to be; (2) a collective expectation as to what behavior will be; and (3) a set of reactions to behavior, including attempts to apply sanctions or otherwise induce a particular kind of conduct (Gibbs 1965).

Norms and values both provide actors with criteria for evaluating social and political phenomena. However, two differences between them make norms the better focal point for cultural studies. First, whereas values identify generically desired end-states, norms prescribe or proscribe specific behaviors for specific actors in specific situations (cf. Coleman 1990, 246–47). This gives them a direct impact on behavior that makes them particularly suited to be a focus of the study of political culture.[19]

Second, norms are social phenomena. As individual mental constructs, values reflect individual psychology. An individual's mental construct can be considered a norm only when it is accepted by a group. James Coleman pointed out that "a norm is a property of a social system, not of an actor within it." Norms are:

ordinarily enforced by sanctions, which are either rewards for carrying out those actions regarded as correct or punishments for carrying out those actions regarded as incorrect. Those subscribing to a norm, or ... those holding a norm, claim a right to apply sanctions and recognize the right for others holding the

---

[19] This important difference is shaped, in turn, by the way actors acquire norms. Values are not transferred directly between generations. They are taught via certain carriers, such as norms, attitudes, and behavior, during the socialization process. It is up to recipients to derive values from those carriers. After values have been derived, the recipient also needs to establish a linkage between values and norms. The process of extracting values from their carriers and establishing the link between values and norms is similar to cooking: a slight difference in ingredients may lead to significant differences in flavor. Even if similar ingredients are used, the sequences of putting them in the wok may lead to different flavors. For instance, patriotism is an important value, but it does not directly provide actors with behavioral guidance. When actors extract this value from its carriers, some may interpret it as blindly following the government; others may interpret it as promoting democracy. As a result, the same value may have different behavioral consequences. Depending on the type and sequence of norms acquired by individuals, both the components of their values and the relative importance of those components can be different.

Political Culture Theory and Regime Stability

norm to do so. Persons whose actions are subject to norms (who themselves may or may not hold the norm) take into account the norms, and the accompanying potential reward or punishments, not as absolute determinants of their actions, but as elements which affect their decisions about what actions it will be in their interests to carry out. (Coleman 1990, 242–43)

This is exactly what we expect culture to be. Political culture exerts its influence on individuals' choices at two levels rather than one. At the individual level, actors' normative orientations guide their behavior.[20] But their normative orientations alone may not have the social characteristics that can define them as culture. Only when normative orientations are shared within a certain social group can they render shared behavioral guidance in a society. "The concept of a norm," argued Coleman, "existing at the macro social level and governing the behavior of individuals at a micro social level, provides a convenient device for explaining individual behavior" (Coleman 1990, 241).

In light of the above, political culture will be understood in this book as a body of norms that set standards of appropriate behavior for a group or category of people and that distinguish them from other groups or categories of people. It constitutes socially shared guidance to accepted and expected patterns of conduct for a particular social group. For its

---

Chapter 7, which deals with democratic values, presents empirical evidence to support this argument (see section entitled "How Cultural Norms Shape People's Understandings of Democracy").

Unlike values, norms can be directly transferred between generations by socialization. Children learn norms from observing how parents deal with outside stimuli. In this process, not only are norms and their jurisdictions transferred, but the hierarchy among norms can also be transferred. For example, loyalty to country and filial piety are two norms that represent core values in Chinese culture. Yet, two norms may provide conflicting guidance to individuals. If that happens, the rank order of these norms would become crucial. When the state needs a single child of aging parents to fight a war, what should the person do? Which norms should the person follow? The answer lies in the rank order between them.

Continual socialization also plays an important role in shaping norms for individuals. Since social groups differ in the ways they rank norms, social sanctions not only enforce the norms but also their rank order. As a result, individuals in the same group usually assign the same rank orders to specific norms. Of course, there is no guarantee that the younger generation will automatically accept the norms of the older generation. There is a window period in the socialization process during which social structures and institutions can influence the formation of norms. Therefore, we may expect people belonging to the same generation to have more similar norms and more similar normative rank orders than people from other generations because they grew up in a similar economic, social, and political environment.

[20] The term "normative belief," or "normative orientation," is best reserved for mental constructs in the mind of the individual. Norms are properties of social systems.

carriers, it defines the appropriate means to achieving desired ends – what I call their normative rationality.[21]

This definition departs from previous definitions in several ways. First, it sets aside attitudes, beliefs, and values in order to focus on norms. Because attitudes and beliefs are shaped by the interaction between values acquired in one's early life and the performance of political objects, they can be influenced by changes in institutions. This leads scholars who define culture as attitudes and beliefs to treat culture as an intervening variable between institutional change and behavioral change (Barry 1970; Jackman and Miller 1996a, 1996b). The independent causal impact of culture is thereby obscured. This difficulty is avoided if one focuses on values and norms, which change less readily. Since values influence behavior only by way of norms, the most rewarding focus for political culture studies is norms.

Second, I do not define political culture as a separate body of norms specialized for interactions with politics and government. Instead, I assume that the norms that shape people's social behavior also shape their political behavior. Even when people hold several conflicting values, such as freedom and respect for authority, it is not because they hold one value for the social sphere and another for the political sphere. Rather, the contradiction encompasses both spheres. Artificially dividing the norms that people apply to social issues from those they apply to political issues prevents researchers from properly understanding the mechanisms by which culture influences choices made in the course of political action. For this reason, my empirical strategy for identifying respondents' norms in survey research avoids the use of words like "politics" and "government." I ask about general social norms and then explore how people's commitment to such norms affects their political behavior.

LEVEL AND UNIT OF ANALYSIS PROBLEMS IN CULTURAL STUDIES

One of the major debates in political culture studies centers on the location of culture. Both Weber and Durkheim held that certain obligatory norms exist in societies to guide people's behavior, but they disagreed on where those obligatory norms are located. The difference comes from their theoretical orientation. Weber was an action theorist and Durkheim

---

[21] As Hofstede puts it, because culture is programmed in early life, it can be seen as nonrational, but "we ... subjectively feel our own to be perfectly rational!" (Hofstede 2001, 6).

Political Culture Theory and Regime Stability

an interaction theorist (Eckstein 1996, 485). Weber argued that all developed societies were built around expectations that actors have of other actors. When they become reliable and fixed, these expectations serve as the nervous system of societies. As a methodological individualist who believed all social phenomena were reducible to individual atoms, Weber claimed that culture or expectations existed only in the minds of individuals. He therefore chose individuals as the unit of analysis in his study of culture.

Durkheim, by contrast, viewed culture as a collective property.[22] He believed that there exists a collective consciousness that originates outside the individual and exists independently from individuals. Realizing that collective consciousness may vary across and within societies, he chose both whole societies and sub-populations as units of analysis in his studies of culture (Eckstein 1996, 482).

The level-of-analysis problem continues to puzzle students of political culture. Most scholars agree that culture is a social phenomenon; the challenge is how to operationalize this collective property. Some empirical scholars have equated culture with the orientations of individuals, using it to explain individual behavior.[23] The problem with this approach is that when culture becomes individualized, it is no longer a collective property; it becomes individual psychology. Other scholars have treated the distribution of individual orientations in a society as an aggregate quality called "political culture" and have used this aggregate to explain both individual behavior and political processes (Hofstede 2001, 15). The civic culture approach used the differing distributions of certain orientations in different societies to explain the differing degrees of stability of democratic regimes (Hofstede 2001). Inglehart used the distribution of what he labeled post-materialist values in different societies to explain both the prevalence of unconventional forms of political participation and the political transformation of societies as wholes (Inglehart 1997). But there are several problems with treating culture as an individual attribute or a societal distribution of individual attributes.

---

[22] Summarizing Durkheim, Eckstein states, "We [individuals] may not perceive that reality as concretely as individual persons, but it must 'really' exist because it is logically necessary that this be so, and logical necessity is incontrovertible" (Eckstein 1996, 481).

[23] For example, some scholars refer to civic orientation as "political culture" and use it as a proxy of culture to explain political participation. See, among others, Verba and Nie (1972) and Verba, Nie, and Kim (1978). Others use political interest, political knowledge, political efficacy, political tolerance, and political trust as cultural variables and study their impacts on people's political behavior (Dalton 1996).

First, these approaches make it difficult, if not impossible, to say how the cultures of different societies differ. How do we know that the culture in country A is different from that in country B? How much difference in the distribution of particular orientations is necessary before we can claim one culture differs from another? Finding the cutoff point is an impossible mission. There is no convincing theoretical argument to specify for researchers what percentage of difference is necessary to delimit cultures. There is no reason to claim, for example, that a society in which 55 percent of the people have a democratic orientation is more likely to transition to a democracy than a society in which 45 percent of the population have such an orientation.

Second, political actors are nested in social environments and regularly interact with other people in their social groups. When culture is defined as the distribution of orientations in a society, researchers are limited to using the dominant orientations to represent a society's culture (as is done, for example, by Inglehart 1977, 1990, 1997; Inglehart and Welzel 2005). This assumes that each person in society has an equal influence over politics and that only the culture of the majority influences the behavior of individuals and the political processes in a society; in effect, the culture of the minority can influence neither the behavior of others nor the society's politics as a whole.

Yet the operations of culture are more complicated than this. For example, let us assume that an actor with a high level of political efficacy (the belief in his own ability to influence politics) lives in a country where most people have high efficacy. The culture at both levels prompts him to participate in politics. If he now moves to country B where most people are apathetic, the culture at the social level may lower his level of participation even if his personal sense of efficacy does not change. This suggests that a combination of orientations at different levels can affect people's behavior. Unfortunately, the current approach to culture allows researchers to concentrate their inquiry on only one level. To understand fully the impacts of culture, researchers need to study them at both levels and to explore how cultural norms at different levels interact with one another to shape political behavior.

Because culture defines what is right and wrong, we may assume that whatever clashing norms exist in a society compete for influence. There is no reason to assume that the norms that stand in a majority at a particular point in time will continue to dominate indefinitely. For example, studies of democratic transition show that the democratic culture held by a minority can significantly influence a society's political evolution. To

Political Culture Theory and Regime Stability

understand how cultural norms held by a minority can prevail, we need to study how different norms in a society interact with one another to shape the political behavior of individuals and the political processes of the society. This raises another problem for students of political culture: What unit of analysis should be used in cultural studies?

People are usually embedded in different layers of social environments. An actor may be nested in the normative environments of successively larger geographically based social units such as a village, township, province, and country as well as in social groups such as a church, temple, or classmate association and in functional organizations, such as a factory or company. We cannot assume that the normative environment at the national level always has a greater impact on an individual than the normative environment in his or her local organization or community. Indeed, we should assume that the closer the normative environment to an actor, the greater its impact on the individual. Since political actors are in daily contact with other members of their groups and communities, the collective consciousness of their smaller and more local associations should impact them more strongly than the cultural environment of their society at large.[24]

When the degree of cultural homogeneity is high in a society, we may identify culture at the national level. But when the degree of heterogeneity is high, researchers should examine the impacts of cultural environments in relevant subunit social groups (potentially including geographic regions, professions, gender groups, age groups, and others) to identify the sources of struggles over culture and the influences of such struggles on behavior. Even to study the impacts of culture at the national level, one may need to analyze the impacts of cultural environments in subnational units.

This analysis suggests that the primary collective unit of analysis for studying a culture's impacts on the behavior of individuals should be an actor's immediate social environment. It further implies that at any level of analysis scholars should not assume that the majority's norms fully determine the cultural environment. Instead, analysts should examine how competing orientations within a community interact with one another and how these interactions influence individuals' choices.[25]

---

[24] Even for the study of democratic transition, the collective consciousness in certain groups, such as elites, intellectuals, and journalists, may play a more important role than the general cultural environment in the society.

[25] Some previous studies, for example, Brown (1984), have attended to the role of subcultures in a society. Since ideology also defines normative rationality, ideological studies

34   *Theory of Political Culture*

Finally, political culture scholars need to study the simultaneous impact of cultural norms at different nested levels of the society.

In short, to capture how culture affects individual behavior and political processes, researchers need to identify: (1) how norms influence choices made by actors via individual psychology; (2) how norms exert influence through the local social environment; and (3) how norms at these two levels – individual and community – interact to shape individual behavior and collective political processes.

CAUSAL MECHANISMS IN CULTURAL STUDIES

The effects of cultural norms on social action take place in five steps:

(Step 1) *Cultural norms influence how actors interpret the meaning of social action.* Facing an outside stimulus such as a governmental decision, an actor must interpret the decision and comprehend its meaning before he or she decides how to respond. This is the process identified by Parsons and Shils (1951) as "cognitive decoding." A psychological device known as "framing" offers perspective and manipulates the relevance and importance of information to influence the judgment of political actors. Cultural norms may influence framing through three mechanisms: they provide standards for evaluating others' behavior; they allow people to interpret other actors' motivations; and they provide guidance for how to seek, filter, and arrange information to simplify information processing. When operating under the condition of incomplete information, a person may assume that another actor shares and is following the same norms. Thus a person's cultural norms may affect how she or he codes others' behavior.

People may also try to seek out and evaluate additional information to help them decode the meaning of an event. Their decisions (usually unconscious) on what and how much information to seek are shaped by cultural norms. For many, the primary purpose is not to find alternative facts but to seek evidence to validate their predispositions in order to avoid the unpleasant state of cognitive dissonance.

(Step 2) *Cultural norms provide standards against which people evaluate the behavior of other actors.* As established earlier, because these standards vary, two people may reach different conclusions about the same behavior by a political actor. An observer whose norms are

can also be categorized as cultural studies, and studies of ideological struggles frequently use subnational groups as their units of analysis.

Political Culture Theory and Regime Stability

satisfied by the behavior of a political actor will evaluate that behavior as norm-compliant, whereas another observer may evaluate the same behavior as noncompliant.

(Step 3) *Cultural norms provide sources of affect toward other actors.* Just as different norms require people to use varying standards to evaluate political actors and actions, the same object may give rise to different emotional responses as well. When an event damages a person's private interests, cultural norms do not automatically authorize the individual to feel resentment or antagonism. Likewise, norms may not mandate gratitude or loyalty in return for a positive action. An individual who receives a benefit from someone else but learns it was acquired by means he or she disapproves of may not feel positive affect toward the person who helped provide the benefit; an individual who is harmed for reasons he or she regards as legitimate similarly may not feel resentment.

(Step 4) *Cultural norms define the goals actors can legitimately pursue in a particular circumstance.* In a given situation, persons holding different cultural norms may feel authorized to pursue dissimilar goals. For example, when the normative relationship between individuals and authority is defined as reciprocal, people are likely to oppose their government when the government fails to provide them with a desired service. When the citizen-government relationship is normatively modeled on familial relations, the same government failure may not constitute a legitimate reason to withdraw support. Instead, if the government's intentions are perceived as good (that is, its failure to deliver is not perceived as an act of malice), the norm of hierarchy authorizes people to remonstrate with rather than to oppose their government. Similarly, different cultural norms define different ideal political systems. Although "democracy" has been used to describe all ideal forms of political system, the ways in which people in different societies define democracy are shaped by their cultural norms.

(Step 5) *Cultural norms constrain the means actors can legitimately use to pursue their goals.* Studies of political culture have focused primarily on the impact of political culture on the frequency of political participation while neglecting the fact that culture also shapes the forms of political action that actors deem permissible. Although all cultural norms allow people to engage in some disruptive political activities (often labeled "unconventional participation") under certain circumstances, different cultural norms may not define the same thresholds for doing so.

At each of these last four steps, norms exert a causal effect because they are enforced by sanctions at both the individual and the social levels.

These sanctions take the form either of rewards for carrying out actions regarded as correct or of punishments for carrying out actions regarded as incorrect (Coleman 1990, 242).[26] The rewards and punishments are both internal and external. When a norm is internalized, a sense of shame develops that punishes norm subscribers who either violate the norm or fail to carry out the actions that it prescribes. At the same time, individuals who internalize a norm are accepting the right of others to punish them if they violate that norm.

Studies of self-regulation and self-esteem in social psychology help explain how norms control norm holders' behavior. E. Tory Higgins found that people have three selves: (1) the "actual self," which refers to the attributes a person thinks he actually possesses; (2) the "ideal self," or mental representation of the attributes a person would ideally like to possess; and (3) the "ought self," the attributes the person believes he should or ought to possess (Higgins 1989). The ideal self is defined by norms held by people connected to the actor, while the ought self is defined by the actor's own internalized norms.

According to Higgins, people in their daily lives are motivated to reach a state in which the actual self matches both the ideal self and the ought self. This is because self-regulation, in which people seek to match their performance to the standards held in the community and to their own expectations, has emotional consequences: the closer the match among their three self-concepts, the better people feel about themselves (see also Pelham 1991). Thus, both the ideal self and the ought self serve as behavioral guides. When there is a good match between the actual self and ideal self, people experience feelings of security. This mechanism can be called the *external policing system of norms*. When there is a good match between the actual self and ought self, people experience feelings of self-esteem. This mechanism can be called the *internal policing system of norms*.[27]

Discrepancies among the three selves lead to negative emotions. To reduce the pain caused by negative emotions, people strive to close the

---

[26] To say that there is an effective sanction does not imply that the sanction is always effective or effective for all targeted actors but that it is effective for at least some target actors some of the time. See Coleman (1990, 266). Note that the same principle can also be applied to law, in that it is not always obeyed.

[27] This set of causal mechanisms has been ignored even by many culturalists. For example, both Putnam and Coleman rejected altruistic explanations of norm adherence. Neither scholar has seriously considered the possibility that people follow norms because they believe that it is the right thing to do (Coleman 1990; Putnam 1993). Their explanations

Political Culture Theory and Regime Stability

gap between the actual self and the other self-guides. Thus, the desire to avoid negative feelings can deter actors from violating the guidance of norms. A person might be deterred from stealing from a store, for example, not necessarily by the probability of being caught, but by the psychological pain associated with norm violation. Since the level of commitment to a given norm varies among actors, the pain created by mismatches among the above three selves varies for different people with respect to a given norm.

The internal policing system is effective to varying degrees in controlling individual behavior. The more deeply an actor internalizes a norm (even unconsciously), the more painful it is to violate that norm. This does not mean that norms always trump material cost-benefit calculations: rather, the strength of a norm determines the threshold at which an actor will abandon that norm for a contradictory material interest. The deeper the internalization, the more likely a person is to be willing to sacrifice material interests to abide by the norm because the emotional consequences of a violation will outweigh the pleasure brought about by material gain.[28] Conversely, if a norm is only weakly internalized, the actor may take norms into consideration but allow material interests to outweigh principles.

A given person may internalize multiple norms. Since norms are situation-specific, the choice among relevant norms to apply to a given situation is defined by the internal rank order of norms. For example, two widely accepted norms in China are that one should be loyal to the country and one should be loyal to the family. How will an actor choose between country and family in case of a conflict, for example, if the state requires him to join the army and go to war when his father is dying? For most Chinese today, the rank order of the norms requires loyalty to country to take precedence over loyalty to the family.

> of norm following do not really conform to most people's experiences with norm adherence. Many of us can think of situations in which we extended trust or reciprocity to another person even though we did not expect that person to return it in kind.
>
> [28] This process can be complicated. Research in social psychology suggests that even people with high self-esteem blend positive and negative aspects in their self-conceptions. For example, C. Showers has found that a negative thought in one's self-conception usually triggers a counterbalancing positive thought (Showers 1992). This means that when people fail to follow norm guidance in one instance, they may feel compelled to release the tension of their failure to follow the guidance of their ought self. For example, they should be more likely to follow norm guidance in another instance or to become a stricter norm follower in a similar situation. In this way the impact of norms is cumulative: the more norms a person subscribes to, the stronger the impact of norms on his or her behavior. This is one reason why norms are stable and difficult to change.

Norms are also enforced by the external policing system. James Coleman found that when someone spits on the street or fails to mow their lawn, neighbors or people passing by may confront and blame the offender on behalf of the community. Coleman calls such an act a "heroic sanction" (Coleman 1990, 279). Imposing a heroic sanction requires the sanctioner to pay costs (albeit usually low ones) that will not be fully compensated by the direct personal benefits of the act. And if the norm violator reacts defensively, unpleasantness will ensue for the sanctioner. This might lead us to expect community members to "free ride" – to stand by and let others take on the costs of imposing community sanctions. Despite these risks, the opposite of free riding – an excess of zeal – does occur frequently. Coleman identified the puzzle that "there are many empirical situations in which just the opposite of free-rider activities [seem] to occur, even though the circumstances are those in which free riders would be predicted to abound" (Coleman 1990, 273).

The answer, he suggested, is that sanctioners paradoxically often enjoy implicit support from norm violators. When a norm becomes social, sanctioners can reasonably assume that the norm violator knows that his behavior is wrong, and that he will acknowledge the right of others to impose sanctions on him. A norm violator's feelings of guilt will reduce the costs incurred by those who impose sanctions on him.

In addition, sanctioners may be rewarded by a community norm that disapproves of shirking and approves of working toward common goals. When people jointly pursue certain outcomes, each has an incentive to reward others for working toward the mutual goal. The heroic sanctioner may be rewarded from two sources. First, demonstrating one's good qualities to others, by helping the community for example, may generate self-esteem, thereby increasing the internal benefits associated with heroic action. Second, when a norm becomes social, observers may reward heroic sanctioners with esteem – an external reward.[29] The combination of these two rewards can outweigh the costs of heroic sanctions.[30] Because praise can come only from people with the same normative rationality as

---

[29] The expectation of the sanctioner is contingent upon the social relations between the sanctioner and other holders of the norm because the establishment of the norm and the vesting of the right to sanction can be achieved only by some form of collective decision, implicit or explicit. See Coleman (1990, 283).

[30] This line of analysis leads Coleman to argue that the rationality of free riding and the rationality of zeal arise from the same structure of interests. The expectation of rewards from others may change the cost-benefit calculation of zeal and prompt the person to invest time and energy in punishing violators.

Political Culture Theory and Regime Stability

the sanctioner, homogeneity of norms in a community increases the likelihood that heroic sanctions will occur.[31]

Norm enforcement is not an isolated one-time event but unfolds through a gradual chain of incremental sanctions that can lead the community collectively to impose more powerful punishments of norm violators, such as social isolation. The process of incremental sanctions often involves three phases. The first is the circulation of information about an event or action. The second is the formation of some consensus about the moral meaning of that event – how it is to be interpreted and which rules are to be applied. The third phase is the implementation of the consensus, the transformation of shared opinions into some form of action. The action can range from individual acts of snubbing to collective decisions to expel (Merry 1984, 279).

Gossip plays an important role, helping first to form a consensus that a certain norm is applicable to the action in question and later to forge consensus on a collective decision either to expel the offender and cut off communications with him or her or to support heroic sanctions applied by other individuals (Zablocki 1980). Böckenholt and van der Heijden found that the decision to comply was influenced not only by one's personal beliefs about complying with the law but also by the expected evaluative reactions of friends and family, that is, social sanctions (Böckenholt and van der Heijden 2007). In a review article, Robert Cialdini and others point out, "what's surprising, given the unambiguity and strength of the evidence, is how little note people take of this potent form of influence" (Cialdini, Petty, and Cacioppo 1981).

The cumulative effect of incremental sanctions on violators can be significant (Coleman 1990, 278). The potential for such unpleasantness can

---

[31] This is neither the structure of interests that characterize most situations – where the interests of different persons are complementary and realized through some kind of social exchange – nor a structure in which interests are opposed so that one person's interests are realized at the expense of another's. It is a structure of common interests, that is, the interests of all are realized by the same outcome. An example of such a structure is a situation in which a legitimate government exists. This line of reasoning helps explain a phenomenon noted by Lily Tsai in *Accountability without Democracy* (Tsai 2007). She observes, "The more that a solidary group encompasses all the citizens in a particular local governmental jurisdiction and the more that [it also] embeds local officials in its activities, the more effective it is at enabling citizens to hold local officials accountable for public goods provisions." Officials in such situations feel an enhanced incentive to contribute to the good of the group. I would argue that the source of this incentive comes from the interaction between the internal and external policing systems of norms. The local officials have internalized certain norms, and external policing increases the incentive for them to comply with them.

40   *Theory of Political Culture*

dissuade norm violators from continually engaging in proscribed acts and lead them to modify their behavior. A popular Chinese saying, *zhongnu nanfan* ("It is risky to offend the community"), alludes to this situation.

CONCLUSION

Self-regulation and social regulation interact. When culture in a society is homogeneous, sanctions from the internal and external levels push an actor in the same direction, encouraging certain choices and prohibiting others. Since the pressures from the two levels reinforce one another, the effects of self-regulation and social regulation are cumulative: the internal policing system provides actors with guidance on what choices are right, and the external policing system constitutes a feedback loop that rewards prescribed behavior and punishes proscribed behavior. In this way, norms come to have a powerful impact on behavior.

Observing this phenomenon, Lu Xun, the famous Chinese writer of the early twentieth century, wrote in his short story "A Madman's Diary" that Confucian doctrine (*li*), the powerful source of China's enduring traditional norm system, killed many people. Speaking through the voice of the Madman, he claimed that the history of Confucianism could be summarized in one phrase: *chiren* (eat people). Many of the best-selling novels in early twentieth-century China carried a common theme of battles between young protagonists who engaged in heroic crusades against the traditional norms defined by the dominant, traditional culture. Most of the protagonists initially ignored pressure (heroic sanctions) from their parents, extended family, and acquaintances in order to pursue liberty and happiness. Yet nearly every story ends with the failure of the main character in the face of mounting social pressure (incremental sanctions). Even without the action of formal legal institutions backed up by material force, cultural norms have the powerful mechanism of social sanctions to enforce their rules. The foregoing discussion of how norms work to influence social behavior lays the groundwork for understanding the theory of political culture proposed in the following chapters.

2

Cultural Norms East and West

This chapter identifies four key cultural norms that influence political behavior in China and the West and focuses on two of them for a deeper analysis of the causal mechanisms by which norms influence behavior. To illustrate how dominant Western and Chinese beliefs about the four norms differ, I will contrast the ways in which two central traditions – social contract theory in the West and Confucianism in China – addressed a core issue in social thought: what can move human beings from a disorganized, pregovernmental state to a governable society. The norms articulated by these two intellectual traditions have demonstrated their staying power despite centuries of social and institutional change. Rather than change rapidly along with social structures and political institutions, they have proven relatively enduring.

Political philosophers in both eighteenth-century Europe and ancient China (circa 700 BCE) addressed the issue of how to make a cooperative social life possible. Their points of departure, however, were different. In the Western social contract tradition, Hobbes and Locke proceeded from the belief that the existing political institutions could not resolve the problems of motivating cooperation. The Chinese philosophers Confucius and Mencius assumed that the existing political institutions of the Zhou dynasty and the feudal system had the capacity to resolve the problems of social cooperation but had failed to achieve the desired goals. From these differing points of departure the two philosophical traditions moved toward different solutions. For Hobbes and Locke, the question was how to build institutions to foster cooperation. For Confucius and Mencius, the question was how to make the existing institutions work effectively.

41

The challenge facing both sets of thinkers was similar to what scholars of social movements today call the "collective action problem" – that is, that an interest in the collective good is a necessary but not sufficient condition for social cooperation. The larger the group, the more likely it is that people will "free ride," that is, act in their own interest to the detriment of the collective interest. This problem can be overcome either externally or internally. An external solution would involve a leader imposing constraints on members of the group to force them to cooperate. An internal solution would entail manipulating actors' values so they perceive collaboration as intrinsically rewarding (Olsen 1965, 51).

Western social contract theory resembles the external solution to the collective action problem, whereas the philosophy of Confucius and Mencius is in line with the internal solution. The two sets of solutions are based on different assumptions about human nature, rely on different means to achieve their goals, grant different rights to individuals, and assign different obligations to the government and its subjects. The theories of Hobbes, Locke, and Rousseau rely on a sovereign to externally impose common rules and regulations, thus constraining the pursuit of private interests. Confucius and Mencius tried to change actors' payoff structures by indoctrinating them with certain norms to constrain their choices. Each set of theories was grounded in a distinctive set of values and norms – a culture – that would enable its preferred type of system to work properly.

SOCIAL CONTRACT THEORY AND LIBERAL NORMS

The social contract theories developed in the seventeenth and eighteenth centuries defined what we would today call the "collective action problem" (discussed above) as the problem of bringing man out of the state of nature to a state of civil society. The challenge was managing man's selfish nature so as to avoid a constant state of war and make cooperative social life possible (Hobbes 1996 [1651], 72). Thomas Hobbes based his solution on three assumptions: (1) humans are fundamentally and irrevocably selfish beings (Smith 1982 [1759], 349); (2) pursuing self-interest is a natural, inalienable right; and (3) self-interest can be a beneficial force for society (Hirschman 1997). Order was the overriding goal for Hobbes. The sovereign's absolute power can be justified because it offers people the only way to escape from a state of nature. Any order is better than none; providing order was the sovereign's only political obligation; and the best sovereign to achieve order was an authoritarian

Cultural Norms East and West

monarch. Hobbes did not explore how people expressed the consent to partially transfer their natural rights to a sovereign or the political responsibilities of rulers to their people beyond providing order.

John Locke perceived the relationship between individuals and the political authority as a more conditional exchange. He agreed with Hobbes that rational individuals possessing the natural right to pursue their interests must surrender some of those rights when they enter into a social contract to form a political order. A rational man would not do so unless he stood to receive something more desirable than what he was giving up. As with Hobbes, the benefit to the individual is that others are also bound by the same restrictions that he is. Going beyond Hobbes, however, Locke argued that a government is legitimate only if it seeks to achieve the common good (Locke 2000 [1728], 99). If the sovereign becomes a tyrant, people have the right to rebel and to replace the regime with a different one. Locke's definition of the ideal relationship between an individual and authority has been categorized by some scholars as a "liberal monarchy."

Jean–Jacques Rousseau outlined a version of social contract theory based on popular sovereignty. Like Hobbes and Locke, Rousseau argued that to move beyond a state of nature, man must enter into a contract with others. In this social contract, everyone is free because all forfeit the same amount of freedom, and the same duties are imposed on all. Rousseau believed that liberty is possible only where there is direct rule by the people as a whole; popular sovereignty must be indivisible and inalienable. He believed it illogical for any man to surrender his freedom for slavery; participation in the social contract must be voluntary. Although a contract imposes new laws, especially laws safeguarding and regulating property, a person must be able to exit it at any time and return to a state of natural freedom. Thus, the social contract is not permanent, and the civil rights it endows are not natural rights. Rather, the contract is a means to an end – the benefit of all. The contract is legitimate only to the extent that it meets the general will of the people in a society. When failings are found in the government, people should be able to renegotiate its form. Rousseau's theory has provided the theoretical groundwork for liberal democracy and republicanism.

The solutions offered by these three European philosophers have the following common characteristics: (1) as individuals enjoy a natural right to pursue self-interest, giving up one's natural rights to a public authority must be voluntary; (2) as sovereignty is based on the people's consent, the system must build institutional arrangements by which people can express such consent or withdraw support from authority; (3) the authority established through a social contract should act for all by imposing rules and laws to impartially regulate private interest articulation; (4) because each actor stands a chance of being worse off than if he were to act alone, and man's innately selfish nature may prompt him to defect, public authority needs to possess the monopolistic right legitimately to use force to facilitate cooperation.

These theories implicitly assumed the existence of at least four key norms that would enable such a system to work properly. The first two, which are the focus of this study, are discussed in greater detail toward the end of this chapter. All four norms have been fundamental to the Western liberal concept of democracy (see Chapter 7).

Idiocentric Definition of Self-Interest: The social contract solution to the state-of-nature problem allows people to use the self as the unit of analysis in making calculations of their interests. ("Idiocentric" here means centered on the individual.) They are normatively allowed to pursue self-interest in any way that is not prohibited by law. Subscribers to the social contract are not required to take the interests of others into account when pursuing self-interest. The individual is allowed to view other individuals either as enemies or as rivals.[1]

Reciprocal Orientation toward Authority: The social contract solution requires people to transfer part of their natural rights to the government on a conditional basis; they also have the right to withdraw their support from the authority. In societies based on social contract values, we can expect this norm to make political support contingent on the ability of a regime to protect the rights and serve the interests of individual citizens.

Acceptance of Conflict: Because the solution assumes that the pursuit of self-interest is a natural right, it allows and encourages competition in private interest articulation within the limits defined by mutually accepted rules and laws. Conflicts are perceived as not just unavoidable but as a driving force of development. We expect a norm that defines conflict as a normal way of life to gain legitimacy under such an institutional arrangement.

Procedural Justice: Social contract theory requires the authorities to adjudicate in a neutral manner between competing private interests. So rules and procedures must be developed to regulate interest competition, and the law becomes the overriding factor for evaluating claims by political actors. The resulting norm in a society where law has become supreme

---

[1] While Hobbes characterizes "others" as the enemy, Locke characterizes them as rivals.

Cultural Norms East and West

is that actors are expected to evaluate the legitimacy of competing claims based on whether the claim accords with rules and procedures defined by established institutions.

Working together, these four norms play important roles in creating political systems based on the theory of the social contract. Because these norms are widely accepted in advanced industrial democracies, scholars of comparative politics in these societies tend to take them for granted. Scholars who compare only advanced democracies can ignore culture because the cultural norms in these societies are unlikely to vary. Students who compare societies across cultural regions, however, do not have the luxury of ignoring culture; for them, ignoring culture will result in omitted variable problems, which can lead to incomplete or erroneous conclusions.

CONFUCIAN THEORY AND GUARDIANSHIP NORMS

Confucius (551–479 BCE) and his major disciple, Mencius (372–289 BCE), saw a different solution to the problem of living in society. While they preceded the Western philosophers discussed in this chapter by about 2,000 years, they grappled with a similar question about how to make citizens cooperate for the collective good. At the time of Confucius, the Zhou dynasty had set up what has been called a "feudal" network, in which enfeoffed (*fengjian*) sons of Zhou were assigned to rule fifty or more vassal states (Fairbank and Goldman 1998, 39). Rather than bringing peace and prosperity to the land, however, the competing vassal states created chaos. Not only did the vassal lords constantly fight one another for land and people, but officials within the vassal states also frequently launched coups to usurp the power of the vassal lords. Confucius took the existence of a sovereign as a given. The issue he faced was how to bring peace under the rule of the existing sovereign (McKown and Kauffman 1974, 81). His solution anticipated one of the central findings of contemporary theories of social movements and collective action.

Theorists of social movements and collective action have found that people participate in social movements "not only as the result of self-interest, but because of deeply held beliefs, the desire to socialize with others, and because they ... understand the Olsonian dilemma" (i.e., that it is necessary to rise above self-interest to gain the benefits of cooperation) (Kertzer 1988, 104). In effect, culture can assist even a very large and disparate group to act together (Tarrow 1994, 19).

Collective action requires people to feel simultaneously aggrieved about some aspect of their lives and optimistic that they can jointly address the problem at hand. "Lacking either one or both of these perceptions, it is highly unlikely that people will mobilize even when afforded the opportunity to do so" (McAdam, McCarthy, and Zald 1996b, 5). These perceptions are formed through the framing process, described in Chapter 1, section titled "Causal Mechanisms in Cultural Studies." Meanings and ideas play a critical role in helping actors overcome the collective action problem and facilitate cooperation (Lynch 1999; Snow et al. 1986).[2]

Confucius' theory anticipated such ideas. In his effort to find ways to promote social cooperation under the Zhou rulers, Confucius introduced cultural variables as early as 500 BCE. He believed that the transaction costs that came with facilitating cooperation through externally enforced solutions were too high for any sovereign to bear. He complained that if one "lead[s] them by means of regulations and keep[s] order among them by punishments, people will evade them and lack any sense of shame" (Confucius 1999, *Analects* 2:3). Instead, he proposed manipulating norms to foster cooperation from within. "Lead them through virtue and the rites," he wrote, and "they will have a sense of shame and thus correct themselves" (Confucius 1999, *Analects* 2:3). Shifting the transaction costs from the government to the people themselves would reduce the sovereign's burden to facilitate cooperation.

How does one make an individual behave according to the role defined by his status and lead him to incorporate concern for collective interests into his behavioral goals? For Confucius, education was the answer. Confucius believed that social-mindedness, which he called benevolence or *ren*, was socially constructed rather than inherent (Confucius and Mencius 1992, 43). Building an "inner sense of sincerity" among the populace would be the most effective way to facilitate cooperation. For this reason, norm transfer through education and socialization was central to Confucius' solution to the state-of-nature problem.

Throughout Chinese history, the state has taken an active role in inculcating norms among the people. Over centuries of indoctrination,

---

[2] Cooperation may be facilitated through the mechanism of "repeated games" whereby people learn from experience that cooperation produces worthwhile results. However, repeated games by themselves do not guarantee cooperation. No apparent equilibrium is associated with solutions through repeated games. For this reason, students of collective action assign meanings and ideas a prominent place in their theories. Some even describe culture as the "third solution" to the collective action problem (McAdam, McCarthy, and Zald 1996a, 5).

Cultural Norms East and West

ordinary people internalized the Confucian codes of conduct that regulated social, economic, and political life, deeply rooting them in Chinese society. Education influences people's choices through two channels. At the individual level, education socializes people voluntarily to maintain norm-defined codes of conduct. At the group level, education assigns norm holders an obligation to enforce its rules; it stipulates the collective punishment of norm violators. As a result, education not only makes incremental sanctions more likely to occur but also increases the pain that sanctions impose on norm violators.

There are three major ways in which Confucianism differs from Western social contract theory. First, instead of viewing human nature as unalterably selfish, Confucius and his disciples believed that the virtues and vices of human beings are socially constructed.[3] They viewed children as innocent at the time of birth (*ren zhichu xing benshan*) with virtue or vice acquired through socialization.[4] Second, Confucius saw social hierarchy as natural and expected each actor to behave according to the role defined by his status (Confucius and Mencius 1992, 15).

Third, Confucius believed that ideas could be manipulated to facilitate cooperation. If people can be socialized to identify their personal interests with groups to which they belong, the likelihood of cooperating with other members of the group will increase (Confucius and Mencius 1992, 13). When people know that values and norms have been internalized by others in the community and can predict that others are likely to cooperate, cooperation becomes more likely. When such norms are

---

[3] Confucius did not give a clear-cut answer to the question of the basic quality of human nature. He did talk about *ren* (benevolence) and made a sharp distinction between righteousness and profit. Mencius argued that all people are clearly good by nature. Xunzi, in the next generation of Confucian scholars, argued differently. Eventually the Mencian solution to this problem became dominant in Confucianism (Mote 1989, 49).

[4] According to *The Works of Mencius*:

The philosopher Gao said, "Man's nature is like water whirling around in a corner. Open a passage for it to the east, and it will flow to the east; open a passage for it to the west, and it will flow to the west. Man's nature is indifferent to good and evil, just as the water is indifferent to the east and west." Mencius replied, "Water indeed will flow indifferently to the east or west, but will it flow indifferently up or down? The tendency of man's nature to good is like the tendency of water to flow downwards. There are none but have this tendency to good, just as all water flows downwards. Now by striking water and causing it to leap up, you may make it go over your forehead, and, by damming and leading it, you may force it up a hill. But are such movements according to the nature of water? It is the force applied which causes them. When men are made to do what is not good, their nature is dealt with in this way" (Confucius and Mencius 1992, *The Works of Mencius*, 11.2).

Confucius said, "By nature, men are nearly alike; by practice, they get to be wide apart" (Confucius 1971, *Analects* 17:2).

48 *Theory of Political Culture*

widespread in society, sanction by others in the community can deter wrong behavior.[5] In effect, by making the behavior of others predictable, norms can facilitate cooperation among strategically rational actors (Mote 1989, 43).

Confucius' ideas are based on four norms that contrast with those embedded in Western social contract theory. Because his ideas were accepted by the rulers of the Han dynasty and reinforced by rulers in every succeeding dynasty, they exerted a lasting influence on Chinese political culture. Today, they underlie a view widespread in China of democracy as a form of regime in which an elite takes care of the people's collective interest, which I term "guardianship democracy" (see Chapter 7).

Allocentric Definition of Self-Interest: Confucius saw individuals as embedded in a community. ("Allocentric" here means "community-minded.") Self-interest for an individual could never be separated from group interests. A person's sense of self must arise from, and intertwine with or be embedded in certain groups, such as the family, lineage and/or clan, community, race, and nation. By blurring the boundaries between the self and others, Confucius hoped to socialize people to use a "larger self" as the base of their interest calculations. Over time, socialization shaped individuals' identities along this line and created societal norms that required people to use such a "larger self" as the unit of analysis in their interest calculations (Pye 1988, 59).

I follow Triandis in using the terms *allocentric definition of self-interest* and *idiocentric definition of self-interest* in order to avoid more broadly defined terms like collectivism and individualism (Triandis 1995).[6] Despite the blurring between personal goals and the goals of the collective found in the allocentric definition of self-interest, the norm does not call for people to ignore their personal interests. Instead, it simply encourages them to incorporate their self-interest into that of a larger group, such as the family, community, or state. By contrast, the idiocentric definition legitimizes the pursuit of personal goals separate from those of any group, even when personal goals are in conflict with those of groups to which the individual belongs.

---

[5] In the same chapter, Confucius also argued that "from the loving example of one family, a whole State becomes loving, and from its courtesies, the whole State becomes courteous, while, from the ambition and perverseness of the one man, the whole State may be led to rebellious disorder – such is the nature of influence" (Confucius and Mencius 1992, 13).

[6] However, in contrast to the study of personal and social psychology, I emphasize here that the differences in people's definition of self-interest are socially constructed. For traditional studies of individualism vs. collectivism, see among others: Hofstede (2001); Kim and Han'guk Simni (1994); Triandis (1995); and Vinken, Soeters, and Ester (2004).

Cultural Norms East and West

Hierarchical Orientation toward Authority: Confucius described five key relationships in a society: (1) father and son, (2) brother and brother, (3) husband and wife, (4) neighbor and neighbor, and (5) ruler and subject. Each pair represents an important link in society; taken together, they constituted the key social relations in traditional patriarchal society. Confucius saw them as hierarchical in nature: parents were superior to children, elder brothers to younger brothers, and so on (Confucius and Mencius 1992, 39–41). If actors in each pair of relationships – both the superior and the inferior – conducted their "proper behavior according to status" (*li*), the result would be social harmony (*hexie*).

There are three important differences between hierarchical and reciprocal orientations toward authority. First, whereas reciprocal orientation sees explicit consent from the people as a prerequisite for government legitimacy, under a hierarchical orientation, the authority's mandate comes from the natural order of things (in traditional Chinese discourse, "Heaven"), and citizens' obligation to obey is not contingent upon consent. Second, for those with a reciprocal orientation, how a regime acquires power is a crucial basis for its legitimacy, whereas for those with a hierarchical orientation, legitimacy is based chiefly on the substance of a regime's policies. People holding a hierarchical orientation expect that those in power will take care of the people's interests. This is expressed in the Confucian ideal of humane governance, or the rule of the "Sage Kings" and "noble men" (de Bary 1991). Third, with a reciprocal orientation, the ability to withdraw support from government is seen as a basic right under the social contract, whereas a hierarchical orientation takes rebellion as a privilege granted by Heaven rather than a right inherent in the individual.[7]

Conflict Avoidance: As the unconstrained pursuit of self-interest was perceived as potentially harmful to the interests of everyone, Confucian philosophers discouraged actors from confronting others to articulate their interests. Instead, collaboration was encouraged, even if it meant that one party had to sacrifice certain interests for the sake of society. Even with the sacrifice of private interests, an actor would still be better off than if he defected from the group.

---

[7] In the more than two thousand years of Chinese history, people involved in rebellions have always claimed that they were acting on behalf of Heaven (*titian xingdao*). This suggests that even the individuals who were actively engaged in rebellion did not think it was their natural right to rebel against despotic rulers. The right to punish despotic rulers, even in the mind of rebels, belonged to Heaven.

TABLE 2.1. *Two Normative Traditions*

Issue	Social Contract Tradition	Confucian Tradition
How interest should be defined	idiocentric	allocentric
How the relationship with authority should be defined	reciprocal	hierarchical
How conflict should be handled	legitimate	avoided
How justice should be defined	procedural	substantive

Substantive Justice: Because authorities are superior in status, they are perceived to be in a better position to evaluate the merits of competing claims made by different people. Moreover, because the theory arranges interests in a hierarchical order, the authorities are able to resolve conflicts among interests according to this order. As a result, procedural validity is not the prime criterion on which political actors evaluate claims by others. For Confucius, the substantive justice of a decision was more important to its legitimacy than how the decision was made.

Table 2.1 summarizes the four differences between the two normative traditions.

HOW TWO CRITICAL NORMS REGULATE INDIVIDUALS' CHOICES

I argued in Chapter 1 that norms influence individual behavior in five ways and that they do so through both individual-level and social processes. They affect how people decode information, how they evaluate other actors' behavior, their emotions (affect) toward other actors, and the goals and the means that they consider appropriate. This section illustrates how these five processes work to enable two norms – *orientation toward authority* and *definition of self-interest* – to regulate people's behavior.

Norms influence how actors decode the meaning of social action. People decode the same information differently, and according to the norms they follow. For example, when the orientation toward authority differs, the same information about government behavior may be interpreted in divergent ways. The protests in Tibet on March 14, 2008, offer an example. While most of the media and people in the United States tended to decode the events as the Chinese government's brutal suppression of

Cultural Norms East and West

peaceful demonstrators, most Chinese interpreted the actions as a rightful restoration of law and order. Most scholars have attributed the difference to the Chinese regime's control of the media, which prevents people in China from seeing the truth. Although this interpretation may help to explain the way people within China decoded information, it can hardly explain why many educated Chinese outside of China with regular access to Western media also decoded the information in the same way. I argue that the difference in event decoding was shaped by cultural norms.

This is not to suggest that people with hierarchical orientations never challenge public authority. Chinese people challenged the government in Tiananmen Square in 1976 and 1989. But their threshold for challenging public authority is higher than that defined by the reciprocal orientation. Under the hierarchical orientation, people are expected to give public authority the benefit of the doubt. Unless sufficient evidence shows that the government is abusing power or failing to take care of its people, the hierarchical orientation requires people to assume that the intentions of the authorities are good. Holders of a hierarchical orientation were therefore more likely to frame the Tibet issue in terms of the rationale given by the government. Because the government in Tibet is not democratically elected (no explicit consent has been expressed by the Tibetan people), observers under the influence of reciprocal orientation were more likely to see the government as having no legitimate right to rule Tibet and to see the demonstrators' burning and looting as responses to the regime's political suppression. It appeared to them that the regime had used brute force to suppress the Tibetan people's legitimate right to revolt in order to maintain its own rule.

Likewise, definition of self-interest guides actors to interpret the same information differently. Actors with an idiocentric definition of self-interest will evaluate government policy on the basis of its impact on their self-interest, whereas those with an allocentric definition will evaluate it based on the impact on the interests of groups to which they belong. Actors tend to project their own normative orientation on the government and assume that officials will follow the guidance of the same definition of self-interest. Those with allocentric definition can thus be expected to assume that government officials are trying to help the people rather than pursue their own private interests. On the contrary, people holding an idiocentric definition would assume that, without proper restraints, government officials would pursue their own private interests.

For example, in 2002 when I interviewed people in Shenyang, the largest city in northeastern China, about their views on state-owned enterprise reform, most of the people holding an allocentric definition of self-interest told me that the government promoted state-owned enterprise reform to develop the national economy, whereas most people holding an idiocentric definition told me that the government officials promoted this reform in order to steal money from the state.[8]

Norms guide people in their search for additional information to comprehend complex phenomena, especially government behavior. In this process, norms shape people's perceptions about what constitutes "relevant" information for decoding political events through priming.[9] Often such searches are not aimed at fact-finding; instead their aim is to validate an actor's previous predisposition or refute unpleasant contradictory information to eliminate cognitive dissonance.

To reduce the discomfort of cognitive dissonance, an actor with a hierarchical orientation, when confronted with information about official corruption, for example, may: (1) discredit the information as a rumor; (2) blame others (a greedy merchant for trapping an innocent official, for instance); and/or (3) interpret the event as an isolated case that does not represent the bureaucracy as a whole.[10] Actors with reciprocal orientation would not face cognitive dissonance when presented with such information. As a result, we can expect people with a hierarchical orientation to be more "generous" toward their government when decoding information about its performance than would people with reciprocal orientation toward authority.

The norms that are prevalent at the social level can also influence individuals' cognitive decoding through small group interaction (Shirk 1982; Townsend 1969). Facing complexity and uncertainty, individuals are likely to seek cues and get help from other actors with whom they have close interactions. Lazarsfeld et al. found that information transfers usually involve intermediation (Berelson, Lazarsfeld, and McPhee 1954;

---

[8] Interviews in Shenyang, Liaoning province, conducted in August 2002. The survey conducted by Wenfang Tang shows that people in that area supported the reforms no less than did people in other parts of the country even though their region contained a high concentration of state-owned enterprises whose workers' interests would be hurt by the reforms (Tang 2005).

[9] "Priming" in psychology refers to the influence of an earlier stimulus on the response to a later stimulus (Kolb and Whishaw 2003, 453–54, 457). Priming can be perceptual or conceptual. Perceptual priming is based on the form of the stimulus and is enhanced by the match between the early and later stimuli. Conceptual priming is based on the meaning of a stimulus and is enhanced by semantic tasks.

[10] According to Festinger, actors may (1) rationalize away the inconsistency; (2) change attitudes toward a particular government; and (3) change their own normative belief system to reduce cognitive dissonance (Festinger 1957).

Magalhães 2007). Framing, as discussed in Chapter 1, is the psychological process that orders and ranks the relevance and importance of information, which helps form perspective and perceptions. From a political perspective, framing has widespread consequences. Frames reduce complexity by setting the vocabulary and metaphors through which participants can comprehend and discuss a complicated issue. They form an inherent part, not just of political discourse, but of cognition as well (Goffman 1986).

For this reason, intermediaries play a critical role in shaping people's reading of events. They receive information first, decode it, and then pass the interpreted information to the general public. Since opinion leaders' cognitive decoding of political information is influenced by their normative orientations, intermediaries' orientation toward authority can indirectly influence how their audiences decode information. As a result, how others in a community decode information can have a significant impact on the decoding performed by an individual in the community.

Two separate mechanisms are at work: (1) the decoding of other actors in the community can be borrowed directly; and (2) when an actor's interpretation of a particular event differs from that of the majority in a community, the actor may feel pressure to change his or her own interpretation or risk possible social isolation. For this reason, a person with reciprocal orientation, who happens to live in a community in which a majority of people hold a hierarchical orientation, may be under silent social pressure to adapt his or her view to that of the majority.

Norms at the community level may cause people to assign different weights to the same information or to prefer information from different sources. As a general rule, people in hierarchical social environments can be expected to assign more weight to information from opinion leaders, authorities, elders and/or from government. People living in communities dominated by a reciprocal orientation, however, will likely assign more weight to information from independent sources, especially nongovernmental organizations (NGOs).[11]

---

[11] Beyond norms, institutional environments can also have an important influence on how people decode events. This is because institutions determine whose decoding is more likely to be accessed by people in a community. In traditional institutional settings, the opinions of elders and those of other traditional authorities are more accessible to people in that community. Their decoding of events will then have more influence on the overall decoding of events than that of others in the community. With the introduction of modern communication, the opinions of the central authorities, intellectuals, and civil society have become more accessible to people in a community. In this kind of setting, the cognitive decoding of individuals may not only be influenced by the orientation toward authority of the elites in the community, but also by that of elites beyond their previous reach.

Norms provide standards against which people evaluate the behavior of other actors. After actors decode information, they need to evaluate the behavior of others. For example, people under the influence of the hierarchical orientation toward authority expect the government to take care of their interests, as parents do for their children, without the need to vigilantly guard it (de Bary 2004). People under the hierarchical orientation toward authority, therefore, can be expected to (1) have higher expectations of their government than those with a reciprocal orientation; (2) be more likely to trust their government; and (3) evaluate public authority on whether it can provide people with substantive benefits, rather than on how it acquired political power.

Those holding a reciprocal orientation, by contrast, tend to evaluate the performance of their government based on four specifications: (1) whether it provides them with good policy; (2) whether it allows ready access to the government; (3) whether government officials are seen as uncorrupt (Fenno 1978); and (4) whether the government acquired power through legitimate procedures.

Likewise, people with an idiocentric definition of self-interest perceive political acts aimed at pursuing interests for a particular group as normatively acceptable, but people with an allocentric definition might disapprove of such behavior. Unless the activities of a special interest group are packaged as benefiting certain "larger selves," people with allocentric attitudes are likely to perceive them as illegitimate.

This helps explain the puzzle of why so few workers laid off in China's reform of state-owned enterprises rebelled against the state. Most Western scholars blamed the workers' fear of suppression. The theory proposed here provides an alternative interpretation, that is, a policy jeopardizing the private interests of certain actors in the society may not have been enough to trigger people with an allocentric definition of self-interest to rebel. As long as the government can frame the issue as a policy that, while harmful to the private interests of certain people, is beneficial to "larger selves," the allocentric definition deprives actors of the normative authority to revolt. This also helps to explain why, in survey after survey in China, NGOs received the least support among different institutions. In China, NGOs have been perceived as pressure groups pursuing the narrow interests of specific sectors. They are not yet seen as unselfish fighters for the general good. This makes it hard for them to gain the support of people influenced by allocentric DSI.

Norms provide sources of affect toward other actors. A hierarchical orientation toward authority injects affective components into the relationship between the individual and the state such that an attitude of approval toward authority is easily developed and does not easily fade. Simple dissatisfaction toward government does not lead to a withdrawal of emotional approval, just as small rejections by parents do not give children sufficient reason to oppose them.

For people with a reciprocal orientation, by contrast, for whom the relationship between individuals and government is a formal exchange, there are few affective components built into the relationship. This is not to suggest that approval cannot develop, but approval in exchange relationships must be earned by the government through its acts and policy, and there is no normative compunction about abandoning one government in favor of another.

Different definitions of self-interest also affect the emotional tie of citizens to government. When the private interests of people with an allocentric definition are jeopardized by government policy, the norm does not automatically grant them normative power to resent the regime. By the same token, when a policy fails to take the interests of larger groups into consideration, even if it can further a citizen's private interests, it is defined as wrong behavior according to the norm and may alienate even the benefited citizen from authority.

Instrumental utility also plays a role in the affective process, but it is conditioned by normative rationality. When the allocentric definition of self-interest compels people to sacrifice the interests of their "smaller self" for that of the "larger self," the sacrifice may actually tie them more closely to public authority in emotional terms. This kind of effect, which may seem counterintuitive to people within other political cultures, is precisely why students of comparative politics must treat culture as a precedent variable in their studies of the political behavior of individuals and the political processes in different societies. Unless we understand the normative rationality of people defined by culture, we cannot understand their behavior.

Norms define the goals actors can legitimately pursue in a particular situation. Hierarchical orientation does not authorize people to withdraw support merely because the government fails to provide desired services. Even if a policy is perceived as wrong, as long as the decision is not seen as due to malfeasance, and the intention of the government is seen as good, the norm requires people to remonstrate with rather than oppose their government. With reciprocal orientation, however, if the government fails to provide desired services, the norm authorizes people to withdraw support from the regime and replace it with a new one.

56   *Theory of Political Culture*

Norms constrain the means actors can legitimately use to pursue their goals. Culture designates certain kinds of behavior as permissible and others as violations. Although both orientations toward authority allow people to engage in both conventional and unconventional political activities, they define different thresholds for people to engage in unconventional political acts.

Orientations at the community level can also constrain people's political behavior. The community will reward prescribed responses to political stimuli and sanction proscribed responses. For example, suppose a person holding a reciprocal orientation toward authority wants to engage in acts of protest to express his opinion. If this person happens to live in a community where the majority of people subscribe to a hierarchical orientation, others in the community may believe that such acts are not justified. As a result, other actors in the community may impose sanctions against the person, an additional cost that will discourage him from acting. If the potential protester happens to live in a community where the majority of people subscribe to the reciprocal orientation, the same acts may trigger positive sanctions from fellow citizens, thus reducing the costs and increasing the benefits of such activities.

A NOTE ON GUILT AND SHAME

The discussion in the preceding section provides a new perspective on the contrast drawn by Ruth Benedict between guilt and shame cultures (Benedict 1989). In her classic study of Japanese behavior during World War II, Benedict found that guilt (or conscience) played a critical role in constraining the behavior of Westerners, whereas shame played a critical role in social control for the Japanese. Following this intellectual tradition, scholars have shown that "shame" and "face" still play important roles in Chinese politics today (Mann 1999). Although many students of Chinese politics have attributed this difference to culture, none have specified the mechanism through which culture makes shame a critical mechanism in Chinese politics.[12]

The difference between social control based on guilt and social control based on shame lies in the requirement for a third party to elicit the latter. Guilt is produced by the internal policing system of norms described in Chapter 1. As such, control over one's behavior by guilt is exercised

---

[12] Here it is important to differentiate causal and constitutive effects. Following Wendt, causal arguments presuppose that the explanandum or consequence (identities and

Cultural Norms East and West

without requiring the involvement of a third party. Shame, on the other hand, requires an actor to partially transfer the right to judge his actions to others in a group. Shame works through the interaction between the internal and external policing system of norms. It is an individual's internal policing system of norms that makes the person take external sanctions seriously. Working together, the internal and external policing systems of norms can influence the behavior of individuals.

The two opposing definitions of self-interest assign different responsibilities to their holders. The idiocentric definition does not assign its holders the right to interfere in others' private business (as long as they are obeying the law), nor does it obligate people to take others' interests into consideration when making decisions. This is not to suggest that people holding the idiocentric definition never listen to others' opinions or impose sanctions on others. But the influence of others is channeled primarily through the actor's instrumental calculations of his own interests.[13] As a result, shame plays a smaller role in societies dominated by the idiocentric definition of self-interest; social control relies more heavily on guilt.[14]

---

interests) exist independently of the cause (explanans) and that interaction with the latter changes the former over time in a billiard-ball, mechanistic sense. The constitutive effects of culture show that identities and interests depend conceptually or logically on culture in the sense that it is only by virtue of shared meanings that it is possible to think about who one is or what one wants in certain ways (Wendt 1999, 276).

[13] To elaborate further, I am not trying to suggest that external sanctions are unimportant for people with an idiocentric definition of self-interest. They may also impose sanctions against their fellow citizens, but the motivation behind such acts is usually also self-interest. This argument is in line with the argument of rational choice institutionalists, whose arguments capture the behavior of people with an idiocentric definition of self-interest. For example, repeated games may change the way people define interests and make them take the possible responses of others into consideration.

[14] To make social control possible, religion plays a critical role in idiocentric cultural environments, as the religious norms help form the conscience that generates guilt. People holding an idiocentric definition of self-interest are also capable of feelings of shame, but the range of issues that generates such feelings is narrower. For example, in a study of college students in the United States and in China, respondents from both countries claimed that they would feel more guilty and ashamed if they were caught cheating on an examination than if their brother were caught cheating. Chinese claimed that they would feel more proud if their child were accepted into a prestigious university than if they, themselves, were accepted, whereas Americans claimed they would feel equally proud in these two circumstances. Americans had more positive attitudes toward expressing pride in personal accomplishments, and Chinese were more likely to claim that pride should be experienced only for outcomes that benefit others. These findings extend the notion of collectivism to include shared self-related emotions (Stipek 1998). See also Qian, Qi, and Xie (2000); Hong and Chiu make a clear distinction between guilt and shame. They argue that the antecedent conditions for the two emotional responses are different (personal inadequacy versus

58   *Theory of Political Culture*

Allocentric definition of self-interest, on the other hand: (1) grants actors in a group the normative power to interfere in the behavior of others within the group and (2) obliges an actor to take the interests and opinions of others into consideration when making decisions. The allocentric definition thus facilitates social control based on shame.[15]

The key to effective shame-based social control lies in socialization. In societies with an allocentric definition of self-interest, self-consciousness is shaped by self-improvement and self-perfection. The effort involves a process through which actors learn that society is interrelated and that one's behavior has an impact on others. Education in such a social environment deliberately seeks to establish social norms to make actors in the society sensitive to the interests of others and constantly concerned about how others perceive them.[16] People in societies embracing the allocentric definition of self-interest transfer part of their decision-making rights to others within the group to allow them to control their behavior.

CONCLUSION

This chapter has proposed a theory about the mechanisms by which two dimensions of culture – orientation toward authority and definition of self-interest – influence the behavior of individuals. Before this theory can be tested, we must establish whether the two dimensions of culture can be measured empirically. Chapter 3 addresses this challenge, using data from mainland China and Taiwan. It describes the measures that are

---

moral norm violation). They found that guilt emerged more frequently when subjects felt personally inadequate. Shame, by contrast, was more likely to emerge when individuals had violated a moral norm and held themselves responsible for their own conduct. The difference may be understood as the difference between the ways the internal policing system and the external policing system work (Hong and Chiu 1992).

[15] Confucius consistently reinforced the external policing system of shame. He reminded his disciples that the worst thing for a gentleman was to be blamed by his fellow citizens for anything. Since different people in a society are interrelated and everyone's activities must have an impact on others, people in the society should constantly take others' feeling into consideration. If one does not want to be ill treated by others, he or she should not ill-treat others.

[16] In an effort to understand shame in Chinese culture, researchers in psychology conducted an ethnographic study to examine parental beliefs and practices with respect to shame as well as young children's participation in shaming. The study involved the primary caregivers and longitudinal observations of spontaneous home interactions. It revealed that the socialization of shame was well underway by age two and a half. The child's rudimentary sense of shame was manipulated in order to teach right from wrong and to motivate the child to amend mistakes (Fung 1999). See also Bedford (2004) and Bedford and Hwang (2003).

Cultural Norms East and West 59

used, explores whether the two norms under study can be identified in these two societies, and analyzes whether their structure and configuration are the same in both societies.

A second challenge for an empirical test of culture theory is to establish whether cultural norms exert causal effects independent from those exerted by social structures and institutions. Modernization theorists and institutionalists are not the only ones to argue that culture is shaped by structure and institutions; as suggested in this chapter, some culturalists have made similar claims. If culture is not independent from structure and institutions, institutional analysis would be a more fruitful strategy for studying people's political behavior and political processes in different societies. In Chapter 4, the data gathered from mainland China and Taiwan are used to discover whether structural changes in China and institutional changes in Taiwan altered the cultural norms held by individuals and/or changed the composition of cultural norms in the society. The chapter shows that cultural norms persisted even as society and politics changed. Together, the two chapters clear the way for the empirical investigation of culture's effects on attitudes and behavior in Part II.

3

Measuring Cultural Norms in Mainland China and Taiwan

This chapter introduces six questionnaire items that I use throughout the book to measure the cultural norms that I call orientation toward authority (OTA) and definition of self-interest (DSI). The chapter presents statistical tests that seek to establish three points: (1) that these items are valid measures of the cultural norms they are designed to measure; (2) that the two norms are distinct from one another and not aspects of a single, more general norm; and (3) that culture – understood as people's commitment to these and similar norms – changes more slowly than do social structure and political institutions. On this latter point hangs the argument that culture is an independent force in the regulation of behavior, not a mediating variable that simply transmits the effects of social and institutional change from the environment to the individual's behavior. To begin, however, the chapter justifies the choice of mainland China and Taiwan as settings for the analysis.

WHY MAINLAND CHINA AND TAIWAN?

A major challenge facing cultural studies is that culture is intertwined with social structure and political institutions. We can show that culture (defined as norms) influences attitudes and behavior, but how do we know that culture does not itself simply reflect the impact of society's structural resources and political institutions, instead of exerting an independent causal effect? The ideal way to separate the effects of culture from those of social structure and institutions is to locate research sites with the same cultural traditions but different levels of economic development (and consequently different social structures) and different

Measuring Cultural Norms 61

kinds of political institutions. Mainland China and Taiwan, both under the influence of Confucian culture but separated for more than a century, present an excellent pair of cases through which to examine the relationships among social structure, political institutions, and culture.

Socioeconomic development varies widely between and within the two societies. At the time of the first survey in 1993, economic development in Taiwan was at least thirty years ahead of that in mainland China. At the time of the second survey in 2002, despite the changes that economic reform had brought to China, per capita GDP adjusted for purchasing power was only $2,881; by the time of the third survey in 2008 it was $5,302. The figures in Taiwan, by contrast, had reached $21,263 by 2002 and $31,891 by 2008.[1] Although economic development had minimized the urban – rural economic disparity in Taiwan, it was still a major problem on the mainland.

There were wide economic differences among regions in the mainland as well, which provided another variable for testing the cultural theory. The average level of education in Taiwan was also much higher than that of mainland China. If a person's normative commitments are shaped by the social and economic environment of his or her adolescence, as some cultural theories posit, the normative orientations of our mainland and Taiwan survey respondents would have diverged from one another well before our first survey (Eckstein 1975).

Political institutions in the two societies were likewise fundamentally different. Mainland China at the time of our surveys was under the rule of an authoritarian government. People enjoyed few civil liberties or political rights, and the media were under tight government control. The only elections were those of rural village committee members, and these elections were only semi-competitive. People in Taiwan, by contrast, enjoyed a broad range of civil liberties and political rights. In 1994, Taiwan held its first provincial election for governor; in 1996, the first general election was held for the presidency of the Republic of China (the name of the government in Taiwan); and finally in 2000 the opposition party won a presidential election, leading to a peaceful change of government. The fundamental differences in the political institutions in these two societies – and especially the institutional transformation that occurred in Taiwan between the first and the second surveys – provide ideal variation for examining the impacts of institutions on culture.

---

[1] World Economic Outlook Database, International Monetary Fund, http://www.imf.org/external/pubs/ft/weo/2008/02/weodata/index.aspx (accessed December 17, 2013).

62   *Theory of Political Culture*

Moreover, mainland China's political history allows us to test the impact of institutional change on culture by comparing cultural orientations across age groups. In order to remake the Chinese people into "new socialist men," Mao Zedong worked for nearly the first thirty years of the PRC to eliminate the influence of Confucian culture. The Thought Reform Campaign (1953–56) marked the beginning of government efforts to transform the minds of the public systematically. This was followed by significant institutional and structural transformations carried out through such programs as the People's Communes and the Great Leap Forward of the late 1950s. In 1966, Mao called for Red Guards to clean up the so-called "Four Olds" (old customs, old culture, old habits, old ideas) and encouraged people to rebel against the ruling Communist Party establishment. The campaign to criticize Lin Biao and Confucius in the early 1970s exemplified Mao's radical efforts to move Chinese society away from traditional culture. If culture is shaped by political institutions, a dramatic shift in cultural orientation should be found among those who came of age between 1966 and 1976 in China, the Cultural Revolution generation. If we find no significant cultural differences associated with the political experiences of various age groups, we may conclude that regime mobilization does not alter a society's political culture.[2]

THE DATA

The data used for this analysis of political culture come from the five surveys that were described in the Introduction. The first two (one each from mainland China and Taiwan) were part of the 1993 project "Political Culture and Political Participation in Mainland China, Taiwan, and Hong Kong."[3] The second two (again, one each from mainland China and Taiwan) were part of the 2002 first-wave Asian Barometer Survey (ABS I). Because the ABS grew out of the 1993 study, the two sets of surveys share many questions in common.

---

[2] Because communist regimes attempt to remake their societies' cultures, Almond argued that these systems provide researchers with the best cases for testing political culture theory (Almond 1983).

[3] The data are available at the China archive at Texas A&M University. It would have been helpful to use data from Hong Kong in this book, but because people's tolerance for surveys is lower in Hong Kong than in mainland China and Taiwan, the Hong Kong questionnaire was much shorter and did not include the questionnaire items used in this book.

Measuring Cultural Norms 63

The fifth source of data is a 2008 mainland China survey that formed part of the second-wave Asian Barometer Survey (ABS II). Including 2008 data in the analysis stretches the time interval of cultural change that we can study in mainland China from nine to fifteen years. However, some changes in the questionnaire make it impossible to use this data set for a full comparison with the first four data sets. Five of the six questions in the 2008 survey designed to measure culture are identical to those used in the previous surveys, but the wording of the sixth question – one of three used to measure orientation toward authority – is somewhat different, which makes it impossible to construct an OTA scale that is fully comparable to the one used in the first four datasets. Furthermore, some dependent variables examined in the second part of this book are missing from the 2008 survey. The 2008 data therefore are used here in limited ways: in this chapter to illustrate the extent of continuity and change in people's answers to questions about normative beliefs, and in Chapter 4 to test for the impact of structural and institutional changes on DSI. It was not possible to use the 2008 Taiwan data because four of the six questions used to measure OTA and DSI were not asked in the 2008 Taiwan survey.

Reliability is a problem for survey research in all settings, but it may seem more serious in the authoritarian setting of mainland China. I used five methods to ensure that we got honest answers in China. First, I used retired high school teachers as interviewers. Teachers in China retire at age 55, and most of them are healthy and available to take part-time jobs. Their experience working with students makes them willing to listen to different opinions, and they tend to be more trusted than people from other professions. Their previous teaching experience equips them with good interpersonal communication skills. I found that respondents tended to trust schoolteachers and were more willing to talk frankly to them than to other fieldworkers.[4] I encouraged our interviewers to tell respondents that they were retired schoolteachers. For further details about how the interviewers were trained, see Appendix A. Second, I placed questions on socioeconomic status at the end of the questionnaire so as to increase respondents' sense of anonymity during the bulk of the questioning. Third, the questionnaire refrained from asking highly sensitive questions, especially questions on people's perceptions of national leaders, so as to avoid creating unnecessary anxiety for respondents as well as to avoid interference in the conduct of the survey from the

---

[4] In fact, the worst interviewers were professional interviewers, because they knew how to cheat.

government. Fourth, we asked interviewers to assure respondents of confidentiality and anonymity before the interviews and to insist on conducting interviews one-on-one at the respondents' homes. Fifth, certain internal checks were written into the questionnaires so as to identify people who answered inconsistently. Appendix A gives further details about the survey design and implementation.

There are various indications that the answers we received were reliable. First, the questionnaire included an item for the interviewer to fill out, reporting whether he or she believed that the respondent had answered honestly, and most interviewers said yes. Second, the questionnaire included several items asking people to evaluate the political atmosphere in China. An overwhelming majority of respondents said that China was much freer than it was previously in terms of civil liberty and political rights, a perception that would encourage honesty in the respondents (Shi and Lou 2010b). Although respondents' subjective evaluation does not necessarily reflect the reality of Chinese society, people would more likely be deterred from telling the truth by their own evaluation of political reality than by objective assessments from experts. To the extent that respondents think the political atmosphere in China is relatively free, they are likely to answer survey questions frankly.

Third, we have evidence that political fear did not prevent our respondents from giving candid answers. To monitor our interviewers' behavior, before dispatching them to the field we sent a letter with a self-addressed envelope to prospective respondents, notifying them of the survey and asking them to evaluate the performance of our interviewers afterward. In 1993, we received more than 1,500 letters back from our respondents. Among them, more than 1,000 included an additional letter reporting political, social, or economic problems in their localities, either addressed to us or asking us to transfer the letter to a higher authority. If political fear had been a major issue in China, few respondents would have sent such letters to our office, as they would have feared that the authorities would be able to trace the letter back to them.

Finally, two questions were built into the surveys to ask respondents whether they believed political fear was a problem in China. Although some said that it was, the analyses in Appendix B indicate that political fear did not influence the way respondents answered the questions used to measure cultural orientations or those measuring political attitudes and behaviors. Other survey researchers based in the West have reached similar conclusions on the reliability of answers from respondents in China (Chen 2005; Manion 1994; Tang 2005). In light of all

Measuring Cultural Norms

these positive indications, I believe that the survey answers from China can be trusted.

MEASURING CULTURE: ORIENTATION TOWARD AUTHORITY AND DEFINITION OF SELF-INTEREST

To find out what norms people subscribe to, it is less effective to ask them to agree or disagree with abstract normative statements (since most respondents will agree with most socially appropriate abstractions) and more effective to pose a series of concrete decision situations. This allows researchers to identify the general principles underlying the choices respondents say they would approve. From a methodological point of view, we treat the norm as a "latent construct" that is measured through "observable variables." But which observable variables should be used, and how do we define the relationship between them and the latent constructs?

In the 1993 and 2002 surveys, three questions served as the observable variables to gauge people's orientations toward authority. Respondents were asked whether they strongly agreed, agreed, disagreed, or strongly disagreed with the following statements:

- If a conflict should occur, we should ask senior people to uphold justice. (OTA 1)
- Even if parents' demands are unreasonable, children should still do what they ask. (OTA 2)
- When a mother-in-law and a daughter-in-law come into conflict, even if the mother-in-law is in the wrong, the husband should still persuade his wife to obey his mother. (OTA 3)

These items were designed with several considerations in mind. First, political referents were avoided, so that later in the analysis we could assess how general attitudes toward authority influence attitudes toward politics in particular. A finding that normative orientations toward authority in general have influence on people's interactions with government would support the hypothesis that culture affects people's political attitudes and behavior.

Second, the questions were designed to steer respondents to answer clearly in terms of norms rather than other motives that might influence action. For example, an individual may obey his parents because he loves them, wants their money, or fears the consequences of disobedience. We were interested in the logic of appropriateness in the minds of the respondents. To make sure they understood this, we used "should" in

66   *Theory of Political Culture*

the wording of the questions and instructed our interviewers to emphasize it when reading the survey questions in the interviews.

Third, the questions were framed to require respondents to choose only one of two possible norms governing the given social relationship. This is because an individual cannot simultaneously subscribe to two norms that govern the same social relationship, as that would provide him or her with contradictory guidance.

Three questions were similarly used to measure definition of self-interest. Respondents were asked whether they strongly agreed, agreed, disagreed, or strongly disagreed with the following statements:

- A person should not insist on his/her own opinion if people around him/her disagree. (DSI 1)
- Various interest groups competing in a locale will damage everyone's interests. (DSI 2)
- The state is like a big machine and the individual is only a small cog and thus should have no independent status. (DSI 3)

These questions refer to sequentially wider collective groups to assess the size of the circle of others with which the individual identifies. As defined earlier, whereas the allocentric definition of self-interest requires actors to ground their identity in certain groups, the idiocentric definition empowers them to ground their identities in the self. An allocentric definition does not prevent people from pursuing their own interests, but it guides them to see their interests as overlapping rather than conflicting with the collective interest. With this distinction in mind, we designed the questions to ask respondents whether they prioritized the isolated self or the socially embedded self in their interest calculations. Rather than asking respondents directly whether they embedded their private interests within those of a group, we asked whether they were prepared to sacrifice their personal interests to those of the group. I designed the questions in this way in order to avoid socially acquiescent easy answers. In societies where the norm of allocentric DSI dominates, I expected respondents to give the easy, socially compliant answer if the question allowed them to do so; by forcing a harder choice I wanted to push them to reveal their real beliefs.

Table 3.1 displays the frequency of respondents' answers to these questions in different surveys. Because we are interested in cultural change – throughout the book, we want to explore how many people abandon the traditional norms of hierarchical OTA and allocentric DSI and why they do so – our entries here, as in other tables, display the percentages of people who hold attitudes consistent with reciprocal OTA and

TABLE 3.1. *Reciprocal Orientation toward Authority and Idiocentric Definition of Self-Interest in Mainland China and Taiwan*

	Mainland China					Taiwan		
	1993	2002	2008	% Change[a]		1993	2002	% Change[a]
				2002	2008			
Orientation toward authority (reciprocal)								
OTA 1. If a conflict should occur, we should ask senior people to uphold justice.	16.6 (547)	26.5 (845)	15.1 (521)	9.9	−1.5	24.2 (340)	29.6 (419)	5.4
OTA 2. Even if parents' demands are unreasonable, children should still do what they ask.	63.6 (2,097)	64.2 (2,040)	46.7 (1,606)	0.5	−16.9	72.8 (1,021)	73.7 (1,004)	0.9
OTA 3. When a mother-in-law and a daughter-in-law come into conflict, even if the mother-in-law is in the wrong, the husband should still persuade his wife to obey his mother.	41.8 (1,377)	43.7 (1,391)	32.7 (1,126)	1.9	9.1	43.9 (615)	48.3 (683)	4.4
Definition of self-interest (idiocentric)								
DSI 1. A person should not insist on his/her own opinion if people around him/her disagree.	34.0 (1,119)	26.5 (844)	33.7 (1,158)	−7.5	−0.3	46.8 (656)	34.1 (483)	−12.7
DSI 2. Various interest groups competing in a locale will damage everyone's interests.	29.3 (965)	18.8 (599)	17.9 (618)	−10.5	−11.4	27.2 (382)	34.0 (481)	6.2
DSI 3. The state is like a big machine, and the individual is only a small cog and thus should have no independent status.	14.9 (491)	21.2 (674)	14.3 (491)	6.3	−0.6	28.9 (404)	35.9 (508)	7

[a] Change in percentage from 1993 to the year given.
Note: Entries are the percentages of respondents giving negative answers to the question.
Source: 1993 Survey of Political Culture and Political Participation in Mainland China, Taiwan, and Hong Kong; 2002 China and Taiwan surveys, Asian Barometer Survey I; 2008 China Survey, Asian Barometer Survey II (China 1993 N = 3,287; 2002 N = 3,183; 2008 N = 5,098/Taiwan 1993 N = 1,402; 2002 N = 1,415).

68   *Theory of Political Culture*

idiocentric DSI. These people disagreed with the conventional Confucian norms presented in the questionnaire.[5] The numbers in the parentheses are the Ns. For example, when answering OTA1 in 1993, 547 respondents, or 16.6 percent of the population, said that they disagreed with the statement.

The table shows that the distributions of normative beliefs in mainland China and Taiwan are similar. Despite fundamental differences in social structures and political institutions, minorities in both societies had abandoned Confucian cultural norms. Although higher percentages of respondents in Taiwan than in China subscribed to reciprocal OTA and idiocentric DSI, the differences between the two societies were small.

Comparing the data over time, the distribution of responses in each society changed little from 1993 to 2002. Contrary to convergence theory, which argues that socioeconomic development and institutional change make people adopt norms that are more modern, our data indicate a mixed direction of change in both norms, with responses to different questionnaire items increasing or decreasing by small amounts from one survey to the next. The data from Taiwan were similarly mixed. The largest change in China was a drop of 17 percent in the number of people who disagreed that children should do what unreasonable parents ask. In Taiwan, the largest change was a decline of 12.7 percent in the number of respondents who disagreed with the norm that a person should yield to the opinion of his or her neighbors.

Comparison with mainland China data from 2008 provides further evidence that structural and institutional changes in China had only limited impacts on people's normative orientations. Although people's answers changed from survey to survey, the pattern of responses swings around a center. This suggests that random rather than nonrandom errors were at least partially responsible for the fluctuations we observe, whereas underlying attitudes remained essentially stable.

CREATING INDEXES OF ORIENTATION TOWARD AUTHORITY AND DEFINITION OF SELF-INTEREST

To reduce the impact of such random fluctuations on our ability to measure real changes in norms, I use the six questionnaire items to create

---

[5] Here and elsewhere in the book, we have coded people who disagreed with the questionnaire prompts as 1 and all others (those who agreed as well as those who did not answer) as 0.

Measuring Cultural Norms

two multi-item indexes, one for each of the two norms. To do so, I use confirmatory factor analysis based on item response theory (IRT), also known as latent trait theory.[6] I show, first, that OTA and DSI are indeed separate norms – that is, in factor analysis terms, that they constitute separate dimensions. This is important because I will show later that each of these norms has distinct implications for political behavior and that each changes differently in response to changes in the social and political environment. Second, I show that each of the three questionnaire items designed to measure each norm does in fact measure it – that is, that the standardized coefficient indicating the strength of each variable's association with the latent construct is statistically significant. Third, I show that the factor structure is valid across my four datasets (China 1993 and 2002 and Taiwan 1993 and 2002). Finally, in Chapter 4, I combine the three questionnaire items that belong to each factor to build a score for each respondent on each of the two cultural variables.

For the first step, I conducted a confirmatory factor analysis using the 1993 mainland China data. I imposed a two-factor structure on the data and assigned the three questions about orientation toward authority (OTA1 through OTA3) to the first factor and the three questions about definition of self-interest (DSI1 through DSI3) to the second factor. The results are presented in Table 3.2.

Three statistics displayed at the bottom of the table confirm that the two-factor model provides a good fit with the data.[7] The first two fit statistics compare the given model with an alternative model. Confirmatory Fit Index (CFI) is the comparative fit index, which varies from 0 to 1.[8] A CFI close to 1 indicates a very good fit. In our case, CFI = .977 which indicates that the model fits very well. The second fit statistic is the TLI

---

[6] For a comparison of CMT and IRT, see Appendix C.

[7] The Chi-square statistic is also displayed for consistency with convention, but it can be disregarded. A statistically significant Chi-square may indicate an unsatisfactory model fit. But the larger the sample size, the more likely the Chi-square is to be significant, leading to the risk that a Type II error (rejecting something true) will occur. In very large samples, even tiny differences between the observed model and the perfect-fit model may lead the Chi-square to be statistically significant. For this and other reasons, many researchers argue that with a reasonable sample size (> 200) and good fit as indicated by other tests (such as CFI, TFL, and RMSEA), the significance of the Chi-square test may be discounted. Since more than 3,000 cases are used in this table, the result of the Chi-square test is not informative.

[8] CFI is also known as the Bentler Comparative Fit Index. It compares the existing model fit with a null model, which assumes the latent variables in the model are uncorrelated (the "independence model") (Fan, Thompson, and Wang 1999).

70   *Theory of Political Culture*

TABLE 3.2. *Confirmatory IRT Model for 1993 Mainland China Data*

Observable Variables	Standardized Coefficient[a]	Difficulty[b]
Orientation toward authority (reciprocal)		
OTA 1. If a conflict should occur, we should ask senior people to uphold justice.	0.638	0.925
OTA 2. Even if parents' demands are unreasonable, children should still do what they ask.	0.745	−0.351
OTA 3. When a mother-in-law and a daughter-in-law come into conflict, even if the mother-in-law is in the wrong, the husband should still persuade his wife to obey his mother.	0.704	0.177
Definition of self-interest (idiocentric)		
DSI 1. A person should not insist on his/her own opinion if people around him/her disagree.	0.802	0.428
DSI 2. Various interest groups competing in a locale will damage everyone's interests.	0.269	0.560
DSI 3. The state is like a big machine, and the individual is only a small cog and thus should have no independent status.	0.444	1.133

Estimation method: WLSMV
CFI = .977 TLI = .966 RMSEA = .041
Covariance between OTA and DSI = .788
Chi-Square (8) = 52.002 P-value = .0000

[a] All standardized coefficients are significant at the .01 level.
[b] Difficulty is the measure of how unlikely it is that respondents will disagree with a questionnaire item.
Note: Mplus is used for the estimation. For binary variables, the result from Mplus is identical to the results from other IRT estimates.
Source: 1993 Survey of Political Culture and Political Participation in Mainland China, Taiwan, and Hong Kong (N = 3,287).

(Tucker-Lewis Index). Similar to CFI, a TLI close to 1 indicates a good fit. In our case, TLI = .966.

Other things being equal, more complex models always generate a better fit than less complex models. Another goodness-of-fit test, Root Mean Square Error of Approximation (RMSEA), incorporates the discrepancy function criterion (comparing observed and predicted covariance matrices) and the parsimony criterion. If RMSEA is less than or equal to .05, the model fit is generally considered good. If RMSEA is less than or equal to .08, the model fit is considered adequate. In our case, RMSEA is .041, which tells us that the model fits extremely well. Altogether, the statistical

Measuring Cultural Norms

tests of the model confirm my hypothesis on the structure of people's normative orientation in mainland China: there are indeed two dimensions in people's normative orientations, and OTA can be clearly distinguished from DSI.

Second, we see that each of the standardized coefficients in Table 3.2 is statistically significantly correlated with the underlying construct at the .01 level. In IRT analysis, in contrast to classical measurement theory (CMT), this measure of statistical significance, rather than the size of the standardized coefficient, assures us that the observable variable has been assigned to the correct latent variable. The size of the standardized coefficient, meanwhile, tells researchers how *strongly* a variable correlates with the latent constructs and *how much* it should contribute to the IRT score compared with other variables. (See Appendix C for a more detailed discussion of the benefits of IRT analysis versus CMT for studying culture.) In Table 3.2, all coefficients are statistically significant, which indicates that all of them contribute something to the score. The "difficulty" of each item is a measure of how unlikely it is that respondents will disagree with the question. In IRT, a higher difficulty score means that the item is weighted more heavily in the combined scale.

As a third step in building indexes of the two cultural norms, I show in Table 3.3 that the factor structure identified in the 1993 China data set also appears in the other three data sets. It is important in particular to establish whether people in Taiwan subscribe to the same cultural norms as people in China. Some people believe that the century-plus-long separation of Taiwan from mainland China fundamentally transformed political culture there – that although people in Taiwan were influenced by Confucianism in the past, economic development, and more importantly, democratic transition and consolidation brought about fundamental cultural changes. They argue that whereas political culture in mainland China remains authoritarian, political culture in Taiwan has become democratic.[9] However, the claim that political culture in Taiwan has changed has either been deduced from the fact that it successfully accomplished democratic transition or imputed on the basis of changes in Taiwanese people's political attitudes rather than from the direct study of their normative orientations.

---

[9] See *The China Quarterly*, Special Issue: Elections and Democracy in Greater China, no. 162, June 2000. Many studies of democratic transition make this claim. See among others Diamond et al. (1997) and Guang (1996).

The impacts of structural and institutional changes on culture, however, are more complicated than current political culture theory suggests. In Chapter 4, I develop a new theory of cultural change. Here, I examine whether the variables designed to measure people's normative orientations in mainland China perform in the same way and with equal efficiency in measuring cultural norms in Taiwan.

To carry out this analysis, I merged the four data sets and treated them statistically as subsamples representing the same population. On this dataset I conducted an IRT confirmatory factor analysis conditioned by three constraints. First, I imposed the same two-dimensional factor structure as in Table 3.2; second, I assigned the same three variables to each of the two latent constructs as in Table 3.2; and third, I imposed the constraint that the difficulty level for each indicator should be the same across the four subgroups. If the structures of cultural norms differed across the four subgroups, or if the observable variables were not related to the same latent constructs in every subgroup, the standardized coefficients that express the relationships between latent constructs and observable variables for different subsamples would be significantly different or the fit statistics for the overall model would be poor. If, on the other hand, the structure of norms in Taiwan is similar to that in mainland China, we should see similar standardized coefficients for each variable in each subsample and strong overall fit statistics.

Table 3.3 confirms that the six variables performed equally well in measuring people's normative orientations in mainland China and in Taiwan at different times. The structure of cultural orientations matched across the two societies and remained stable over time. The fit statistics are also excellent: the model CFI is .965 and TLI is .944. The RMSEA equals .048.

Data from mainland China in 2008 were also examined to determine whether cultural shifts occurred after 2002. The same three constraints as in Table 3.3 were imposed on the model using the three China data sets. Again, as shown in Table 3.4, the factor structure proves robust across the three data sets. The observable variables are associated with the latent constructs in the same way as in the previous tables, and the model generates strong goodness-of-fit statistics. If structural and institutional changes had altered people's cultural orientations between 2002 and 2008, the relationship between latent constructs and observable variables for different subsamples would have been significantly different, and the fit statistics would have been weak.

TABLE 3.3. *Confirmatory IRT Model for Combined Mainland China and Taiwan Data*

Observable Variables	Standardized Coefficient[a]				Difficulty[b]
	Mainland China		Taiwan		
	1993	2002	1993	2002	
Orientation toward authority (reciprocal)					
OTA 1. If a conflict should occur, we should ask senior people to uphold justice.	0.638	0.606	0.367	0.459	0.925
OTA 2. Even if parents' demands are unreasonable, children should still do what they ask.	0.745	0.720	0.766	0.607	−0.351
OTA 3. When a mother-in-law and a daughter-in-law come into conflict, even if the mother-in-law is in the wrong, the husband should still persuade his wife to obey his mother.	0.704	0.682	0.719	0.658	0.178
Definition of self-interest (idiocentric)					
DSI 1. A person should not insist on his/her own opinion if people around him/her disagree.	0.802	0.638	0.475	0.658	0.428
DSI 2. Various interest groups competing in a locale will damage everyone's interests.	0.270	0.198	0.475	0.388	0.550
DSI 3. The state is like a big machine, and the individual is only a small cog and thus should have no independent status.	0.444	0.464	0.507	0.464	1.133

Estimation method: WLSMV
CFI = .965 TLI = .944 RMSEA = .048
Covariance between OTA and DSI for 1993 Mainland China Data = .788
Covariance between OTA and DSI for 2002 Mainland China Data = .763
Covariance between OTA and DSI for 1993 Taiwan Data = .739
Covariance between OTA and DSI for 2002 Taiwan Data = .935
Chi-Square (31) = 197.96 P-value = .0000

[a] All standardized coefficients are significant at the .01 level.
[b] Difficulty is the measure of how unlikely it is that respondents will disagree with a questionnaire item.
Note: Mplus is used for the estimates. For binary variables, the results from Mplus are identical to the results from other IRT estimates.
Sources: 1993 Survey of Political Culture and Political Participation in Mainland China, Taiwan, and Hong Kong; 2002 China and Taiwan surveys, Asian Barometer Survey I (China 1993 N = 3,287; 2002 N = 3,183/ Taiwan 1993 N = 1,402; 2002 N = 1,415).

TABLE 3.4. *Confirmatory IRT Model for Combined Mainland China Data*

Observable Variables	Standardized Coefficient[a]			Difficulty[b]
	1993	2002	2008	
Orientation toward authority (reciprocal)				
OTA 1. If a conflict should occur, we should ask senior people to uphold justice.	0.638	0.864	0.480	0.926
OTA 2. Even if parents' demands are unreasonable, children should still do what they ask.	0.745	0.920	1.919	−0.350
OTA 3. When a mother-in-law and a daughter-in-law come into conflict, even if the mother-in-law is in the wrong, the husband should still persuade his wife to obey his mother.	0.704	0.682	0.849	0.177
Definition of self-interest (idiocentric)				
DSI 1. A person should not insist on his/her own opinion if people around him/her disagree	0.802	0.272	0.767	0.428
DSI 2. Various interest groups competing in a locale will damage everyone's interests.	0.269	0.112	0.169	0.560
DSI 3. The state is like a big machine, and the individual is only a small cog and thus should have no independent status.	0.444	0.465	0.378	1.133

CFI = .968 TLI =.939 RMSEA = .050
Covariance between OTA and DSI for 1993 Mainland China Data = .788
Covariance between OTA and DSI for 2002 Mainland China Data = .764
Covariance between OTA and DSI for 2008 Mainland Data = .861
Chi-Square (24) = 254.91 P-value = .0000

[a] All standardized coefficients are significant at the .01 level.
[b] Difficulty is the measure of how unlikely it is that respondents will disagree with a questionnaire item.
Notes: Mplus is used for the estimates. For binary variables, the results from Mplus are identical to the results from other IRT estimates.
Source: 1993 Survey of Political Culture and Political Participation in Mainland China, Taiwan, and Hong Kong; 2002 China and Taiwan surveys, Asian Barometer Survey I; 2008 China Survey, Asian Barometer Survey II (1993 N = 3,287; 2002 N = 3,183; 2008 N = 5,098).

CONCLUSION

Despite the long separation between mainland China and Taiwan, the dramatic political changes in Taiwan, the rapid pace of social and political change in both societies, and the differences in the developmental levels they have attained, the structure of normative orientations remained remarkably similar in both and stable over time. Two separate norms could be empirically identified in both societies, and questions designed to capture people's orientations toward the two norms did a good job of capturing them. These findings enable us to go on in Chapter 4 to construct scores that reflect where people stand and to begin to analyze how and why people's orientations toward norms change.

4

Culture, Social Structure, and Political Institutions

Social-structural and institutional theories are the major rivals of the theory of political culture. Structural theory argues that socioeconomic development will lead to cultural shifts in society, and institutional theory suggests that culture is shaped by institutions. For both theories, culture is merely an intervening variable with no independent effects. Culturalists do not deny that structure and institutions have important impacts on culture but argue that changes in structure and institutions do not necessarily bring about immediate cultural shifts. Culture can have a significant and independent impact on people's political behavior. Ignoring culture may create the "omitted variable" problem for comparative politics discussed in the Introduction.

This chapter begins with a critical review of the literature on cultural change and argues that the dynamics of cultural change are more complicated than previously realized. I offer a new theory to explain the mechanisms of cultural change. Data collected from mainland China and Taiwan are used to test the impacts of changes in social structure and political institutions on culture. The analyses reveal that between 1993 and 2002 (and in the mainland, extending to 2008), some people in both societies did change their positions on key cultural norms, but the direction of change was contrary to the predictions of current theories.[1] Rather than causing people to convert to more modern orientations, structural and

---

[1] Some may argue that the nine-year interval between the two surveys is too short a time over which to study cultural shifts. But because this was a period of rapid and dramatic economic and social change in both societies, I believe the nine years provide an adequate interval.

76

Culture, Structure, Institutions

institutional changes led them to re-embrace traditional norms. Further analysis shows that the way in which people respond to structural and institutional change is influenced by their education. While less educated people are more likely to update their normative orientations to conform to new incentive structures, more educated people are more likely to respond to social change by re-embracing traditional norms. The chapter concludes with an explanation of these findings and discusses their implications for culture studies.

SOCIAL STRUCTURE, POLITICAL INSTITUTIONS, AND CULTURE: COMPETING THEORIES

Three theories have been advanced to explain cultural shifts. Modernization theory holds that economic development leads to rapid increases in the general level of education in a society. Education, in turn, increases people's ability to understand politics, which psychologically mobilizes them and increases their belief that they can understand and influence politics (that is, it increases their political efficacy) (Deutsch 1961; Diamond 1992; Inkeles 1974; Nie, Powell, and Prewitt 1969a, 1969b). Moreover, as modernization is usually accompanied by an expansion of government activities, it increases the interaction between state and society and consequently people's interest in politics. When the government is responsible for collecting more taxes and issuing more permits, for example, people have a greater incentive to participate in politics (Huntington and Nelson 1976, 44). The experience of participating in politics further changes people's psychological orientations.[2] For modernization theorists, social-structural changes dramatically alter a society's culture.

Institutionalists have contributed a second theoretical approach. Some argue that culture is shaped by institutions, and others claim that culture itself is a part of institutions.[3] The first group asserts that changes in institutions alter the incentive structure for political actors and that actors will update their normative orientations accordingly (DiMaggio and

---

[2] See among others Huntington (1968); Huntington and Nelson (1976); and Moore 1(966). Huntington and Nelson also predict a shift from patron-client politics to class and party politics correlated with increased economic development (Huntington and Nelson 1976, 55).

[3] Jackman and Miller (2004). For a summary see Knight (1992). Knight's claim that "social institutions affect strategic decision-making by establishing social expectations" is a way of saying that culture is part of social institutions. The point is discussed in more detail in Knight (1992, 48–83).

78   *Theory of Political Culture*

Powell 1991; March and Olsen 1984; North 1990, 1996; Weir 1992). According to the second group, when institutions change, so by definition does culture (Gambetta 1993; Hirschman 1984; Jackman and Miller 1996a, 1996b, 2004; Knight 1992). Both structural and institutional theories endogenize culture – that is, they treat culture as an intervening variable with no independent effect on people's political attitudes and behavior.

Cultural theory holds that people acquire cultural values and norms in their adolescence and typically carry them throughout their lives. People's cultural values thus usually reflect the social, economic, and institutional environments in their society at the time they came of age. The social environment may vary, and thus impact cultural norms differently, from one generation to the next. In this way generational replacement may gradually alter the culture in a society over time. For culturalists, culture is at least partially independent from structure and institutions, so that social and institutional change do not quickly bring about corresponding changes in culture (Barnes et al. 1979; Eckstein 1970, 1996; Inglehart 1977, 1990, 1997; Inkeles and Levinson 1997; Kaase and Kohut 1996).

Some works in cultural theory have been criticized for their lack of a strong theory of change (Rogowski 1974). The assumptions that underlie cultural theory lead to an expectation of continuity, even in the case of changes in the social, economic, and political environments (Eckstein 1988, 792). However, as Eckstein explained, "if changes in cultural patterns and themes were categorically excluded, political cultural theory would immediately be dismissed as nonsense, for political cultural change in some societies does still occur" (Eckstein 1988, 792). As Inglehart correctly pointed out, culturalists should not claim that culture does not change but that cultural changes take place slowly and are brought about primarily by generational replacement.[4]

---

[4] Eckstein argued that traumatic social discontinuities – such as rapid industrialization, civil wars, major economic and political crises, and defeat in war – can have cultural consequences (Eckstein 1988; Werlin and Eckstein 1990). Lipset argued that rapid economic development is associated with political extremism (Lipset 1981). Huntington made the same argument (Huntington 1968). Examples of changes caused by economic trauma include the rise of Nazism in Germany in the 1930s and communism in China in the 1940s. The Democracy Wall movement in China in 1979 also arguably belongs to this category since it was triggered at least in part by inflation. The embrace of democracy and the abandonment of authoritarianism in Taiwan in the 1980s can also be explained by a traumatic political event – the shifting of U.S. diplomatic recognition from the Republic of China to the People's Republic of China.

Culture, Structure, Institutions 79

A CRITIQUE OF CURRENT THEORIES OF CULTURAL CHANGE

Culturalists are themselves at least partially responsible for the confusion about the dynamics of cultural change. First, the current theory of culture fails to make clear distinctions among various orientations, especially between values and norms on the one hand and attitudes and beliefs on the other. As I have emphasized, because values and norms are more fundamental elements of the belief system, they are less easily influenced by changes in the environing society. Attitudes and beliefs, by contrast, are relatively sensitive to such changes. The failure to distinguish clearly between different psychological properties is partly responsible for the misapprehension that culture is endogenous to structure and institutions.

A second problem comes from the way in which current cultural theory defines change. A cultural shift is defined as a change in the distribution of various psychological orientations in a society. This way of conceptualizing cultural shifts is too simple. Culture's major function is to regulate people's behavior so as to make social interaction possible. Cultural shifts should be understood as changes in the ability of particular cultural norms to regulate interactions in a society. Although the change in the distribution of orientations toward a particular norm may influence that norm's effectiveness, the relationship between this change and that norm's overall effectiveness at regulating social interactions may not be linear as implicitly assumed by current theories of cultural change.

As described in Chapter 1, culture constrains the choices of political actors through two "policing systems," one internal and one external. Both of these and the interaction between them play a part in shaping people's behavioral choices. When individuals change their orientation toward a given cultural norm, their internal policing system will push them to follow the guidance of the new normative orientation. But if the majority of people in their community still hold to the traditional orientation that they used to hold, the normative social environment will press them in a different direction. In such a situation, their choices will be shaped by the interaction between the internal policing system associated with their new cultural orientation and the external policing system in their community with its traditional orientation. Changes at the individual level alone do not necessarily have an effect on behavior.

There is no theoretical reason, for instance, to believe that culture can more effectively control people's behavior in a society in which 80 percent of people hold a hierarchical orientation toward authority than in one in which only 60 percent subscribe to it. In both cases, the norm is socially dominant and may govern at the external level even as it commands fewer people's support at the internal level. In other words, the external policing system's ability to regulate people's behavior may not be linearly associated with the percentage of dominant norm holders in a population, as is implicitly assumed by current theories of cultural shifts. It is when deviating norm holders pass a certain threshold, which has to be empirically investigated, that the external policing system may collapse. Researchers studying cultural shifts must therefore look at the impacts of structural and institutional changes on the effectiveness of both the internal and the external policing systems of culture, as well as on their interactive effects in controlling people's political attitudes and behavior.

A third problem with the current theory of cultural change is that it overlooks the differences among kinds of change in people's normative orientations. To remedy this, Eckstein proposed to differentiate three types of cultural change (Eckstein 1988, 793–98):

1. *Pattern-maintaining change*, defined as applying existing norms directly to new situations so that the norms are preserved. The norm does not change in the abstract, but it is extended to a new situation in a way that justifies behavior that would previously have been interpreted as unjustified. As an example, Eckstein points out that when, in the nineteenth century, the British Tories yielded to the rise of the working class by extending the vote and creating the beginnings of a welfare state, they justified their actions by invoking the traditional norms of upper class care for the lower classes and lower class deference. The function of pattern-maintaining change "is to keep cultural patterns in existence and consonant."

2. *Cultural flexibility*, which means reinterpreting the norms in a more generalized way so they can be applied to novel situations. In modern societies where the situations that actors face are constantly changing, cultural norms are reformulated in more abstract ways so that they can be applied to constantly changing situations. In this way the norms are maintained at a general level, but their application and hence specific content shifts in response to the frequent and rapid changes that are endemic in modern societies.

3. *Cultural discontinuity*, or a rapid reorientation of norms, when changes in the social and political environments are so extensive that neither pattern-maintaining change nor cultural flexibility is possible. Rapid industrialization, war, inflation, economic depression,

Culture, Structure, Institutions

revolution, decolonization or other traumatic upheavals may produce a breakdown in people's ability to apply the old norms (anomie[5]), followed by a painful and slow effort to develop and learn new norms.

Eckstein's distinctions were a major theoretical breakthrough. (For further discussion of the three types of cultural change, see Appendix D.) But like other cultural theorists, he ignored the fact that cultural change occurs at both the individual and the community levels, so changes on one level may affect cultural norms at the other level and may affect the overall effectiveness of cultural regulation of behavior. And he did not specify empirical methods for distinguishing the three kinds of change.

To take advantage of Eckstein's insights while addressing the shortcomings in his and other theories reviewed above, I propose to conceptualize a cultural shift as a change in the way in which dominant cultural norms guide, constrain, and regulate social interactions. This conception incorporates the different types of culture change proposed by Eckstein and resolves the level of analysis problem. It mandates that researchers examine cultural changes at both levels and assess how changes at one level influence the effectiveness of cultural norms at that and the other level so as to estimate culture's total regulatory effects on social interaction. In the next section I propose a fuller theory of cultural change and ways to measure its elements empirically.

A THEORY OF CULTURAL CHANGE

Changes at the Individual Level

All three of Eckstein's forms of cultural change can occur at the individual level. First, when a traumatic event occurs, some actors may abandon the norms they acquired in early socialization and convert to new norms that provide different behavioral guidance.[6] This kind of change, which

---

[5] Emile Durkheim described anomie as a state of relative normlessness or a state in which norms have been eroded. A norm is an expectation of how people will behave, and it takes the form of a rule that is socially rather than formally enforced. Thus, in structural functionalist theory, the effect of normlessness, whether at a personal or societal level, is to introduce alienation, isolation, and desocialization. As norms become less binding for individuals, they lose a sense of what is right and wrong. See Durkheim (1952 [1897], 1964 [1893]).

[6] This is different from the pattern whereby group norms change as younger cohorts enter the population and over time become the majority. In this pattern, individuals are not

82   *Theory of Political Culture*

Eckstein calls cultural discontinuity, is analogous to the type of profound, paradigmatic shift described by Thomas Kuhn with regard to science.[7]

A traumatic event capable of altering the normative orientations of an individual or a group may have different effects on other people or groups, leading to a different effect for the society as a whole. For example, the deaths of thousands of schoolchildren in the 2008 Wenchuan earthquake in Sichuan province was a traumatic event that appears to have triggered many parents of the victims to convert from hierarchical to reciprocal OTA and from allocentric to idiocentric DSI. But the same event seems to have had a different impact on the population outside the area. Television footage of premier Wen Jiabao's personally risky trip to the center of the earthquake area and his direction of the rescue mission seems to have reinforced many people's commitment to hierarchical OTA and allocentric DSI. At the aggregate societal level, the effects of the trauma on different sectors of the population appear to have canceled each other out. Cultural discontinuity at the aggregate social level can occur only when the traumatic event produces systematic change in the orientations of a sufficient number of people to dominate the entire population.

Cultural change at the individual level may also take the form of pattern-maintaining change. As society changes, pattern-maintaining change may either reduce or enlarge the scope of issues governed by a given norm. Individuals may adhere to their original norms but alter in some way the roster of actions or the features of actions to which they apply them. I will refer to this as changing their understanding of the norms' boundaries of jurisdiction. In terms of the functions ascribed to norms in Chapter 1, we can define pattern–maintaining change as adjustments either to the standards for evaluating others' behavior, to the goals that can be legitimately pursued in a given situation, and/or to the means that can legitimately be employed to pursue a goal. When this type of change occurs, acts proscribed by the norm in the past may become legitimate. For example, directly confronting government leaders is strictly prohibited by the hierarchical OTA, but when pattern-maintaining change occurs, such behavior may become acceptable under certain conditions that had not been encountered before.

---

changing their normative orientations but are keeping them as they pass through the life cycle.

[7] Kuhn describes significant scientific breakthroughs as changes in paradigm and argues that after members of the scientific community convert to the new paradigm, they see the world in an entirely different light (Kuhn 1970).

Culture, Structure, Institutions   83

Individual-level cultural change may also take the form of cultural flexibility. We can understand cultural flexibility as changes in the scope of violations that trigger external sanctions from society. This is a social phenomenon, but it begins with changes at the individual level because, as discussed in Chapter 1, social sanctioning requires the cooperation of individuals.

Two possible changes at the individual level can result in cultural flexibility. First, holders of traditional norms may no longer be willing to impose sanctions against certain norm violations that were punishable in the past. For example, traditional norms may have held that it was inappropriate under any circumstances to criticize government. However, when cultural flexibility occurs, people may still sanction those who blame their government in front of foreigners, but they may tolerate those who criticize government in front of their fellow citizens. People may either hold back from imposing sanctions against such a person or refuse to join others when mobilized to do so. The second way in which social change originates from individual change occurs when changes in the social environment make sanctions impossible or ineffective, even though the dominant norm holders are willing to impose them. Once a certain number of people in a community have converted to new norms, holders of the traditional norm can no longer assume that the violator recognizes the sanctioner's right to impose sanctions. This can prevent them from imposing sanctions against (that is, socially isolating) that person.[8]

Changes at the Group Level

The causal mechanisms for changes at the group level that influence culture's effectiveness are more complicated than those at the individual level.[9] Traditional investigations of cultural change have focused on

---

[8] Cultural flexibility at the social level and pattern-maintaining change at the individual level do not usually move in tandem. Actors' responses to changes in the social environment vary. Some may be carried along by the tide (*suibo zhuliu*), that is, they abandon cultural norms acquired in their early lives to accept the guidance of new ones, which would lead to cultural discontinuity for them. Others may decide to conduct themselves virtuously (*dushan qishen*) by ignoring the responses of others to change in the social environment and preserving their moral standards. These people may refrain from imposing sanctions on norm violators, but they, themselves, still strictly follow norm guidance.

[9] There is another important conceptual distinction that I will not pursue here, between cultural shifts at the community level and cultural shifts at the level of the whole society. The sources, processes, mechanisms, and consequences of cultural shifts at the community level may differ from those at the societal level.

84   *Theory of Political Culture*

cultural discontinuity. But scholars also need to look at pattern-maintaining change and cultural flexibility, both of which occur before cultural discontinuities. All three types can significantly reduce norms' ability to regulate social behavior.

Pattern-maintaining change at the individual level may not necessarily lead to pattern-maintaining change at the group level. As long as the jurisdiction of a norm for a large number of people in a society remains unchanged, the external policing system of traditional culture may force actors to observe the traditional norm boundaries. Pattern-maintaining change of cultural norms at the group level occurs when the collective definition of the jurisdiction of a cultural norm in a community changes.

Cultural flexibility at the group level may be triggered by the accumulation of three different kinds of individual-level cultural changes: (1) pattern-maintaining changes at the individual level may make previously prohibited behavior possible; (2) cultural flexibility at the individual level may alter the boundaries of norms collectively defined by people in a community – people may now tolerate certain violations and refrain from imposing sanction against violators even though they may still observe the norms' guidance themselves[10]; and (3) when a certain number of people in a community convert to new norms, traditional norm holders may no longer be able effectively to punish norm violators. Even if traditional norm holders do not hesitate to impose sanctions against norm violators, these sanctions may no longer be able to deter norm violators as before. As such, the jurisdiction of the external policing system of traditional culture may change.

Cultural discontinuity at the societal level occurs when traumatic events produce system-wide shifts in people's normative orientations. In China, the Opium War of 1840, the May Fourth Movement of 1919, the Communist victory of 1949, and the Cultural Revolution (1966–76) all fall under this category.[11] Generational replacement may also lead to a cultural discontinuity at the social level. As more and more young people socialized into new cultural norms enter into a population and replace

[10] The reason for this kind of change in a given community, I would argue, comes from the dominant norm holders' rational calculations based on their assessment of changes in that community.

[11] For the impact of the Opium War, see Fairbank (1983, 1986) and Spence (1999). For the impact of the May Fourth Movement of 1919, see among others Bianco (1967) and Chow (1967). For the impact of victory of the Communist Revolution, see Schram (1973).

Culture, Structure, Institutions

older generations, the composition of cultural norms in a society will gradually change.[12]

Cultural norms' effectiveness at regulating people's social behavior can be significantly reduced not only by cultural discontinuity but by pattern-maintaining change and cultural flexibility as well. Although changes in the distribution of cultural norms do influence culture's effectiveness at controlling social interaction, culture's effectiveness is not *necessarily* determined by the distribution of alternative norms in a community. Distributive changes have no predictable effects. For example, even if the distribution of a cultural norm in a community remains stable, its power to control social interaction in a community may have vanished. On the other hand, even if the distribution of a specific cultural norm changes, its ability to control people's choices in a community may continue to be strong.

Given the complexity of these mechanisms, the study of cultural change requires researchers to go through three steps of analysis, only the second of which is the standard procedure of comparing the distribution of alternative cultural norms over space and time. First, researchers need to find out whether structural and institutional changes in a society have altered cultural norms' scope of jurisdiction. Empirically, this can be done by analyzing the structure of cultural norms at the individual level over time and/or across societies and/or groups.

I demonstrated a way to do this in Chapter 3 by using factor analysis. Cultural norms govern many aspects of social relationships. Survey researchers ask various questions to measure cultural norms, which are designed to tap different issue areas. When culture's jurisdiction changes, it changes the relationships between the survey questions designed to measure a particular cultural orientation and the latent construct those questions are designed to measure. In Chapter 3 we found that the structure and dimensionality of the two cultural norms OTA and DSI remained stable in mainland China and Taiwan over the period of study. In the

---

[12] As I have pointed out previously, structural and/or institutional changes may lead to cultural flexibility in a society. When cultural commitment becomes looser, actors refrain from imposing external sanctions against norm violators. Basically, when an individual begins to doubt whether or not to abide by a norm, he or she would not be expected to make efforts requiring others to follow the guidance of the same norm. Norm flexibility therefore should reduce the pressure for people to conform to the prescription of dominant norms through its impact on the external policing system. The interaction between cultural flexibility at the individual level, and the consequent relaxation of external pressures on actors to conform to dominant norms, reduces for younger people the overall risks of taking on deviating norms.

86   *Theory of Political Culture*

terminology introduced in this chapter, the jurisdiction of the two norms remained stable. Despite the occurrence of social-structural and institutional changes in these two societies, cultural change had not occurred (not even pattern-maintaining change) with respect to these two norms.

The second step is to find out whether cultural discontinuity has occurred by analyzing the distribution of various cultural norms in a society across geographic regions within the culture area and/or over time. I undertake this analytic step in the next section of this chapter.

Third, because the relationship between the distribution of cultural norms and their effectiveness in a society are not linearly associated, we need to explore whether norms' effectiveness at regulating social behavior has changed. Only then can we judge whether cultural flexibility or cultural discontinuity has occurred.[13] In Appendix D, I illustrate changes in the effectiveness of the external policing system of culture using two cases that occurred in China. The first case shows how powerful the external policing system of cultural norms can be when punishing a norm violator, and the second case documents how cultural flexibility can destroy the impacts of the external policing system of culture on people's behavior even while the distribution of cultural norms remains largely unchanged. This last step of analysis requires researchers to find out if the impacts of cultural norms at different levels on people's political attitudes and behavior remain stable. I give an example of how this problem can be investigated empirically in Chapter 5. Unless researchers go through all three steps, their inquiry into the impacts of structural and institutional changes on culture will be incomplete.

CULTURAL CHANGE IN CHINA AND TAIWAN

This section undertakes the second of the three steps outlined above, an analysis of changes in the distribution of the alternate orientations toward the two norms in China and Taiwan between 1993 and 2002.

The ideal way to track changes in the distribution of norms is to use panel data (data collected in interviews conducted at intervals with the

---

[13] Cultural flexibility may come either from changes in the scope of norm violations that would trigger sanctions by others in the community or from changes in the composition of alternative cultural norms in a community that make it no longer possible to socially isolate norm violators. Although I am not able to specify theoretically how a different distribution of norms in a group influences the effectiveness of norms as a system of social control, I posit that the relationship between the distribution of norms in a community and its effectiveness as a system of social control is not linear.

Culture, Structure, Institutions

same individuals). This allows researchers to compare the orientations of the same individuals at different times. But this type of data is not available from mainland China and Taiwan. I therefore rely here on cohort analysis, which uses cohorts of persons born in a given time period as units of analysis. With cohort analysis, researchers track some feature of the distribution (usually the mean value) of selected variables for a group of people born in a certain span of years as that group advances in age. Because the interval between my two surveys was nine years, I use nine-year intervals to define the age cohorts for this analysis. This allows us to see whether the normative orientation of each cohort changed over the nine-year interval (1993–2002) between the surveys.

If we find that the mean values of cultural orientations for some cohorts changed over time, we can distinguish among three different explanations. One would attribute changes in a cohort's normative orientations to social-structural and/or institutional changes. In mainland China and Taiwan between 1993 and 2002, for example, rapid modernization and political change might have caused people to update their normative orientations to adapt to the new incentive structures. If so, we would expect the normative orientations of all age cohorts to adjust in more or less the same way over the same period of time. If changes in the social and political environment cause norm change, then in a modernizing society the orientations of all age cohorts will become more liberal over time, and the gap between adjacent cohorts will remain stable.

A second cause of normative change could be life-cycle effects, that is, the effects on people's preferred norms that are created by the shifting responsibilities, opportunities, and needs that come with age. People may become more liberal or more conservative with age, or the relationship between age and orientations can even be curvilinear. But the most common pattern is that people's orientations become more traditional as they become older, up to a certain point, and then remain stable. If life-cycle effects explain cultural change, we will find that the normative orientations of younger people are consistently more liberal than the orientations of older people, but that each cohort grows more traditional as it ages (although at the higher ages the rate at which norms shift in the traditional direction may slow down).

We might also observe a third pattern of change that would be less consistent, whereby different age cohorts experience different patterns of normative change. This would suggest generational effects, whereby people in a given cohort undergo an important common experience at an

88   *Theory of Political Culture*

impressionable age that shapes their attitudes in a similar way.[14] If this happens, the distribution of cultural norms in this particular cohort will be different from those in adjacent older and younger cohorts but will tend to remain stable as the affected cohort ages. If generational effects cause norm change, we will notice one or more cohorts whose norms are markedly different from those of adjacent cohorts, and the norms of the affected cohort(s) will remain relatively stable as their members age.

Each of the three patterns of change carries a different implication for the aggregate distribution of cultural norms in a society. If norm change is an adaptation to change in the social environment, then the culture as a whole will move in a more liberal direction as society modernizes. With life-cycle effects, each age group changes its orientations over time but the population's overall normative orientation remains stable as younger and older groups continue to balance each other out. If generational effects cause a shift, the overall population mean will be pulled in the direction of the affected cohorts' normative preferences during the time that those cohorts are moving through the population.

We saw in Table 3.1 that at the level of the aggregate populations, people's normative orientations remained essentially stable between 1993 and 2002 or 2008 in both mainland China and Taiwan. The distribution of orientations toward specific questionnaire items moved up and down, but not in patterns that produced marked overall changes in the norms of the whole society. Beneath the surface, however, changes were occurring in population subgroups that tended to cancel one another out. Cohort analysis can help us to identify these patterns of change and their causes. To do this, I compare the mean scores of OTA and DSI of different age cohorts in mainland China and Taiwan.[15]

[14] A generation is usually defined as a group of birth cohorts whose combined length is approximately twenty-two years. In this analysis, no prior generational boundary is assumed. Instead, I empirically identify possible political generations in these two societies (Delli Carpini 1986; Loeb 1994).

[15] In complicated multistage sampling, design effects (DEFF) can severely contaminate the results of the statistical inferences, as the standard errors (SEs) of the estimates are larger than would be obtained from simple random samples of the same size. The design effect is defined as the true variance of a statistic under the actual design divided by the variance that would have been obtained from a simple random sample of the same size. DEFF represents the cumulative effect of design components such as stratification, unequal weighting, and clustering. The data used in this study were collected by complicated samples and thus DEFF may be a significant source of sampling errors. Traditionally, survey researchers adjust sampling error by weighting, that is, ensuring the key features of the sample are statistically no different from those of the overall population (Kish 1965). Although this method can help researchers correct certain errors when making point estimations,

Culture, Structure, Institutions   89

As described in Chapter 3, these scores are computed on the basis of item response theory. The computer program MPlus generates the scores, allowing variables that have higher standardized coefficients and higher difficulty levels to make larger contributions to the score. Because of my interest in norm change, I have chosen to code each respondent's position on the two scales with the "modern" normative position scored as high and the Confucian or traditional position scored as low. Thus, a high score on OTA indicates a commitment to reciprocal OTA, and a low score represents a commitment to hierarchical OTA; a high score on DSI represents a preference for the idiocentric position and a low score a preference for the allocentric position. Each scale is calibrated in such a way that the mean level of commitment to that norm across the given population is set at zero, and the standard deviation within the population is set at one. For each respondent, therefore, a positive value on a given scale implies an above-average commitment to the more modern version of that norm, and a negative value implies an above-average commitment to the more traditional version of the norm.[16]

Tables 4.1 through 4.4 present cohort analyses of OTA and DSI for various age cohorts in mainland China and Taiwan in 1993, 2002, and 2008. In each table, the upper section compares younger people with older people at the time of each survey, to measure whether the pattern of difference between the young and the old changed from the time of one survey to the time of another. The lower section tracks the normative orientation of each nine-year cohort of people across the surveys to see whether people in any age cohorts converted from one orientation to another during the time between the two surveys.

weighting cannot effectively address the issue of usually underestimated standard errors associated with those estimates. Thus, significance tests and other statistical inferences relying on estimated standard errors could be biased, if only weighting is used for analyzing complex survey data. This is because most statistical software assumes the data analyzed comes from simple random samples (SRS), despite the fact that much more complicated sampling strategies are usually adopted when collecting data. See among others Kish (1965); Kish and Frankel (1970); Lee and Forthofer (2006); Lehtonen and Pahkinen (1995); and Shao and Tu (1995).

To cope with DEFF in multistage samples, researchers have developed a method that incorporates complex sampling information in estimating SEs of the parameters of interest. The method divides sampling information into primary sampling units (PSUs), secondary sampling units (SSUs), and tertiary sampling units (TSUs) and uses finite population correction (FPC) for each stage of the sampling process to adjust for DEFF (Korn and Graubard 1999). I used the method to adjust for DEFF in the analyses reported here.

[16] In order to maximize the variance in scores across subjects, I recalculated the standardized coefficients one dimension (three variables) at a time instead of retaining the standardized coefficients displayed in the tables in Chapter 3.

TABLE 4.1. *Reciprocal Orientation toward Authority by Age Group and Cohort in Mainland China*

| Age at Time of Survey | 1993 | | | Age at Time of Survey | 2002 | | | |
	Mean[a]	SE[b]	N		Mean[a]	SE[b]	N	P-value
Younger versus Older Age Groups at a Given Time								
18–26	0.06	0.02	472	18–26	0.09	0.02	302	0.33
27–35	0.01	0.02	733	27–35	0.00	0.02	652	0.70
36–44	−0.02	0.02	831	36–44	−0.03	0.02	767	0.93
45–53	−0.03	0.02	447	45–53	−0.07	0.02	663	0.12
54–62	−0.07	0.03	374	54–62	−0.06	0.02	378	0.69
63+	−0.16	0.02	430	63+	−0.13	0.03	421	0.38
Age at Time of Survey	**Mean**	**SE**	**N**	**Age at Time of Survey**	**Mean**	**SE**	**N**	**P-value**
Change as People Age[c]								
18–26	0.06	0.02	472	27–35	0.00	0.02	652	0.04
27–35	0.01	0.02	733	36–44	−0.03	0.02	767	0.18
36–44	−0.02	0.02	831	45–53	−0.07	0.02	663	0.06
45–53	−0.03	0.02	447	54–62	−0.06	0.02	378	0.31

[a] Entries are mean values of the IRT scores of reciprocal OTA. The data are adjusted for design effects of multistage sampling.
[b] Entries are robust standard errors.
[c] Data are juxtaposed.
Source: 1993 Survey of Political Culture and Political Participation in Mainland China, Taiwan, and Hong Kong; 2002 China Survey, Asian Barometer Survey I (1993 N = 3,287; 2002 N = 3,183).

Culture, Structure, Institutions

The top section of Table 4.1 shows that the mean values of the normative orientations for different age groups did vary in a meaningful way in both survey years. Reading down the columns that record the mean scores, we find that in both 1993 and 2002, each older age group was less reciprocally oriented than the next younger age group. The 18–26 and 27–35 age groups had mean reciprocal OTA scores above the total population mean, whereas each of the older age groups had mean scores that were to increasing degrees below the population mean. The gap between the youngest and the oldest groups was .22 in both 1993 and 2002, nearly one-quarter of a standard deviation of the normalized IRT score for the population as a whole. Reading across the rows, we find that the difference in the mean score of any given age group between the first survey and the second is small – in most cases, less than the standard error (SE of the difference in the table). The p-values show that none of these differences were statistically significant (a p-value less than .05 would indicate statistical significance).

So far, the pattern is consistent with life-cycle theory – each young group that enters the population starts with more modern attitudes and becomes steadily more traditional as it ages. The lower section of the table gives some support to this interpretation, although it is not decisive. (We had to drop two groups from this part of the analysis: (1) the people between 18–26 years of age from the 2002 survey because they were not eligible respondents in 1993; and (2) the people who were 63 and older in the 1993 survey because a substantial percentage of them had died between the two surveys.) A comparison of the mean values for each cohort at two points in time shows no significant change over time for three of the four cohorts. Only one of the p-values is statistically significant: the one for the youngest cohort, which moved from a reciprocal OTA score of .06 above the population mean to a score exactly at the population mean. This tells us that a substantial number of people in this age group became more hierarchically oriented between 1993 and 2002. This finding seems to be most consistent with the life-cycle explanation: people in this youngest age cohort became more hierarchically oriented as they aged. But without more data points, the finding is not conclusive.

Table 4.2 presents a similar analysis for definition of self-interest in China. The pattern is similar to that of orientation toward authority. As all the questions designed to measure DSI were also used in the 2008 survey, however, we are in a position to extend this analysis to a longer time frame. The upper section of the table shows that people tended to move

TABLE 4.2. *Idiocentric Definition of Self-Interest by Age Group and Cohort in Mainland China*

	1993				2002					2008				
Age at Time of Survey	Mean[a]	SE[b]	N		Age at Time of Survey	Mean[a]	SE[b]	N	P-value	Age at Time of Survey	Mean[a]	SE[b]	N	P-value
Younger versus Older Age Groups at a Given Time														
18–26	0.09	0.01	472		18–26	0.09	0.02	302	0.96	18–26	0.08	0.02	498	0.67
27–35	0.02	0.01	733		27–35	0.05	0.01	652	0.11	27–35	0.05	0.01	639	0.18
36–44	0.00	0.01	831		36–44	0.01	0.01	767	0.35	36–44	0.02	0.01	1,241	0.13
45–53	−0.02	0.01	447		45–53	−0.01	0.01	663	0.50	45–53	−0.01	0.01	939	0.20
54–62	−0.03	0.01	374		54–62	0.00	0.01	378	0.15	54–62	−0.02	0.01	875	0.73
63+	−0.06	0.01	430		63+	−0.06	0.01	421	0.87	63+	−0.04	0.01	850	0.27
Age at Time of Survey	Mean	SE	N		Age at Time of Survey	Mean	SE	N	P-value	Age at Time of Survey	Mean	SE	N	P-value
Change as People Age[c]														
18–26	0.09	0.01	472		27–35	0.05	0.01	652	0.00	33–41	0.026	0.011	1,120	0.00
27–35	0.02	0.01	733		36–44	0.01	0.01	767	0.25	42–50	0.003	0.011	1,019	0.14
36–44	0.00	0.01	831		45–53	−0.01	0.01	663	0.43	50–59	−0.019	0.009	928	0.22
45–53	−0.02	0.01	447		54–62	0.00	0.01	378	0.17	60+	0.036	0.01	118	0.34

[a] Entries are mean values of the IRT scores for idiosyncratic DSI. The data are adjusted or design effects of multistage sampling.

[b] Entries are robust standard errors.

[c] Data are juxtaposed.

Source: 1993 Survey of Political Culture and Political Participation in Mainland China, Taiwan, and Hong Kong; 2002 China Survey, Asian Barometer Survey I; 2008 China Survey, Asian Barometer Survey II (1993 N = 3,287; 2002 N = 3,183; 2008 N = 5,098).

Culture, Structure, Institutions 93

toward a more traditional cultural position as they aged. The lower section shows no statistically significant changes in DSI for age groups over time, except that some people in the youngest age group abandoned their idiocentric DSI to convert to an allocentric definition. Apart from this age cohort, contrary to modernization and institutionalist arguments, the dramatic structural and institutional changes during the fifteen years between 1993 and 2008 in China did not change the way most people normatively defined their relationships with other actors. Nor was there any sign of generation effects. As with OTA, the pattern of change in DSI was most compatible with the life-cycle explanation.

Comparing the patterns of cultural change in mainland China to those in Taiwan allows us to probe further for the effects of institutional change. Like mainland China, Taiwan is under the influence of Confucian culture; unlike mainland China, however, by 1993 Taiwan had already experienced key changes in political institutions. If institutional change makes people adapt their cultural norms to new incentive structures, people in Taiwan should have become more reciprocally and idiocentrically oriented between the two surveys.

Tables 4.3 and 4.4 address the changes in OTA and DSI in Taiwan from 1993 to 2002. (Because the youngest respondents in the Taiwan data sets were 21, the composition of the age cohorts is slightly different from that for China.) The upper part of Table 4.3 shows that younger cohorts in Taiwan, like their mainland Chinese counterparts, were more reciprocally oriented than older cohorts, and this was true for both 1993 and 2002. Also as in mainland China, people in a given age range in 2002 had a statistically identical level of reciprocal OTA as the people who were that age in 1993. The lower part of the table shows that the normative orientation for three of the four cohorts changed over time, a pattern unlike that in mainland China. However, remarkably similar to mainland China, people in each of these groups in Taiwan became more hierarchically oriented between 1993 and 2002.

The fourth cohort serves as an example. In 1993, when they were 48–56 years old, the mean value of reciprocal OTA for this cohort was –.05. When the same group reached the age range of 57–65 in 2002, the mean value of their reciprocal OTA dropped to –.13, indicating a significant change both statistically and substantively in the average orientation of this group from more reciprocal to more hierarchical during the nine years between the two surveys.

Largely similar patterns appear in Table 4.4. The upper section shows that the definition of self-interest for the two youngest age groups changed

TABLE 4.3. *Reciprocal Orientation toward Authority by Age Group and Cohort in Taiwan*

1993				2002				
Age at Time of Survey	Mean[a]	SE[b]	N	Age at Time of Survey	Mean[a]	SE[b]	N	P-value
Younger versus Older Age Groups at a Given Time								
21–29	0.054	0.014	303	21–29	0.065	0.018	246	0.621
30–38	0.015	0.014	356	30–38	0.016	0.014	357	0.943
39–47	0.000	0.018	247	39–47	−0.001	0.014	362	0.964
48–56	−0.052	0.022	155	48–56	−0.048	0.017	189	0.897
57–65	−0.109	0.018	187	57–65	−0.134	0.022	108	0.380
66+	−0.138	0.019	154	66+	−0.190	0.021	153	0.060
Age at Time of Survey	Mean	SE	N	Age at Time of Survey	Mean	SE	N	P-value
Change as People Age[c]								
21–29	0.054	0.014	303	30–38	0.016	0.014	357	0.055
30–38	0.015	0.014	356	39–47	−0.001	0.014	362	0.410
39–47	0.000	0.018	247	48–56	−0.048	0.017	189	0.055
48–56	−0.052	0.022	155	57–65	−0.134	0.022	108	0.008

[a] Entries are mean values of the IRT scores for reciprocal OTA. The data are adjusted for design effects of multistage sampling.
[b] Entries are robust standard errors.
[c] Data are juxtaposed.
Source: 1993 Survey of Political Culture and Political Participation in Mainland China, Taiwan, and Hong Kong; 2002 Taiwan Survey, Asian Barometer Survey I (1993 N = 1,402; 2002 N = 1,415).

TABLE 4.4. *Idiocentric Definition of Self-Interest by Age Group and Cohort in Taiwan*

	1993				2002			
Age at Time of Survey	Mean[a]	SE[b]	N	Age at Time of Survey	Mean[a]	SE[b]	N	P-value
Younger versus Older Age Groups at a Given Time								
21–29	0.161	0.022	303	21–29	0.103	0.014	246	0.028
30–38	0.114	0.026	356	30–38	0.021	0.011	357	0.001
39–47	−0.011	0.026	247	39–47	−0.008	0.018	362	0.920
48–56	−0.051	0.028	155	48–56	−0.063	0.018	189	0.716
57–65	−0.158	0.019	187	57–65	−0.145	0.018	108	0.610
66+	−0.179	0.023	154	66+	−0.187	0.017	153	0.755
Age at Time of Survey	Mean	SE	N	Age at Time of Survey	Mean	SE	N	P-value
Change as People Age[c]								
21–29	0.161	0.022	303	30–38	0.021	0.011	357	0.000
30–38	0.114	0.026	356	39–47	−0.008	0.018	362	0.000
39–47	−0.011	0.026	247	48–56	−0.063	0.018	189	0.106
48–56	−0.051	0.028	155	57–65	−0.145	0.018	108	0.005

[a] Entries are mean values of the IRT scores for idiocentric DSI. The data are adjusted for design effects of multistage sampling.

[b] Entries are robust standard errors.

[c] Data are juxtaposed.

Source: 1993 Survey of Political Culture and Political Participation in Mainland China, Taiwan, and Hong Kong; 2002 Taiwan Survey, Asian Barometer Survey I (1993 N = 1,402; 2002 N = 1,415).

96   *Theory of Political Culture*

to a statistically significant degree between the two surveys. The lower part shows that three of the four cohorts underwent statistically significant change. All of these changes were in the opposite direction from that predicted by both modernization and institutionalist theories: those groups who shifted their normative commitments did so not to reject but to re-embrace traditional cultural norms. The change of cohorts in a more conservative direction as they age is consistent with the theory of life-cycle effects.

CULTURAL BACKLASH AS A RESPONSE TO SOCIAL AND INSTITUTIONAL CHANGE

That cultural change in democratic Taiwan resembled that in authoritarian mainland China suggests that cultural change cannot be attributed to the effect of institutions. What, then, is the relationship between social-structural and institutional changes and the shift within certain subgroups in these two societies to re-embracing traditional cultural norms? The answer requires an analysis of the mechanism through which structural and institutional changes influence culture. According to culture theory, actors can have two different responses to changes in the social environment: adjust or resist. They can either update their normative orientations or refuse to make changes. The data we have just examined reveals a third possible response: actors may re-embrace traditional culture.

The theory presented in Chapter 3 helps to explain how this can happen. Before actors can formulate a response to changes in their society, they must first decode stimuli from their environment to understand their meanings and implications. Such cognitive decoding is influenced by an actor's cultural norms. Norms also provide actors with standards for evaluating the behavior of other actors and with assumptions that help them predict the possible responses of others to their behavior. In all these ways norms constrain actors' choices of responses to change. If actors perceive change as the source of unwelcome phenomena such as social anomie or lawlessness that traditional norms are unable to control, they may convert to new cultural norms. Alternatively, if their cultural predispositions lead them to blame anomie or lawlessness on others' failures to follow norm guidance, the perceived solution will be a reassertion of traditional culture.

Institutionalists correctly argue that actors are subject to bounded rationality – that is, when facing a problem, rather than comprehensively

Culture, Structure, Institutions 97

searching for a solution, actors usually focus on a limited set of solutions based on the information available to them while ignoring other potential solutions. Culturalists agree but add that an actor's search for solutions is systematically biased by the culture into which the actor was socialized. While institutionalists focus on the limitations of an actor's cognitive capacity to explain such a phenomenon, culturalists attribute the limitations to constraints in people's mindsets as defined by culture.

Even when actors realize that structural and institutional changes have altered the incentive structures in society, internalized cultural norms may prevent them from converting to new cultural norms. To avoid the discomforting phenomenon of cognitive dissonance, actors may ignore choices that require norm conversion and refuse to update their normative orientation. They may find it easier to blame violators in their society for social anomie and to believe that a restoration of traditional culture will resolve the problem. I name this argument the "cultural backlash hypothesis."

Chinese history offers plenty of examples of such phenomena, from as early as 500 BCE. Confucius blamed the decline of virtue, rather than changes in social conditions, for the problems he saw in his era – constant war among countries and kings in China proper, as well as numerous coups within different states. The solution he offered was *keji fuli* (overcome selfish desires and restore traditional virtues), which called for revitalizing traditional culture. Similarly, Dong Zhongshu in the Han dynasty saw returning to Confucian tradition as the solution to the chaotic situation in Chinese society at his time.

Public intellectuals across 2,000 years of Chinese history have repeatedly claimed that *renxin bugu* (public morality is not what it used to be) and called for the restoration of traditional virtues, that is, Confucian cultural norms, as the primary answer to China's problems. This was true of the Ming restorationists in the second half of the nineteenth century, neo-Confucian scholars in the first half of the twentieth century, and the communists in the 1983–84 Anti–Spiritual Pollution Campaign. An emerging social movement advocating Confucianism as the solution to social ills facing China today is the most recent example (Kang 2008).

Similar cultural backlash movements can be found in other parts of the world. These include the emergence of a fundamentalist movement in Iran and other parts of the Middle East in the 1970s, as well as the revival of communist parties in Eastern European countries after 1990. Samuel Huntington correctly observed that increasing the interaction between different cultures does not necessarily mean an embrace of Western norms as suggested by structural and institutional theorists. Huntington wrote:

Increasing interactions intensify civilization consciousness and awareness of differences between civilizations and commonalities within civilizations ... that in turn, invigorates differences and animosities stretching or thought to stretch back deep into history ... The processes of economic modernization and social change ... are separating people from longstanding local identities ... In much of the world religion has moved in to fill this gap, often in the form of movements that are labeled "fundamentalist." ... In the past, the elites of non-Western societies were usually the people who were most involved with the West ... and had absorbed Western attitudes and values. At the same time, the populace in non-Western countries often remained deeply imbued with the indigenous culture. (Huntington 1993b, 25–27)

Huntington observed that in the East, unlike in the West, the elites rather than the masses often gave rise to movements against Western norms and in favor of the restoration of indigenous cultures. In many non-Western countries, people who were active in fundamentalist movements were young, college-educated, and professional. It was among the masses that Western – usually American – cultures, styles, and habits became popular.

It is reasonable to suggest that the more strongly an actor is committed to a cultural norm, the more heavily he or she is influenced by that norm when interpreting and responding to changes in the social environment. The less committed a person is to a particular cultural norm, by contrast, the more likely it is that he or she will update his or her normative orientation to correspond to the new incentive structure. We can test this effect with the data from mainland China and Taiwan.

In the analysis that follows, we will use level of education as a proxy for the individual's level of commitment to traditional norms. In theory, level of education might affect cultural change in two contradictory ways. On the one hand, level of education is positively associated with cognitive capacity and thus a person's ability to understand changes occurring in society; this awareness can lead people to the realization that the only way to cope with a problem is to update their normative orientations. On the other hand, level of education is also positively associated with more intensive socialization in a society's existing norms; this may strongly bias how actors decode information and more powerfully constrain their choices of means for resolving problems. When faced with the choice of updating norms to match new incentive systems and violating traditional norms in the process, the psychological pain triggered

Culture, Structure, Institutions 99

by norm violations may be higher for people with education. Although some educated people may readily update their normative orientations, and some may even serve as "norm entrepreneurs," on the average they may be more likely, at least in early stages of transformation, to see the restoration of traditional culture as the solution to problems caused by structural and institutional changes in their society. People with lower levels of education, by contrast, are less likely to be deeply socialized into traditional cultural norms, so that conversion to new cultural norms may create less cognitive dissonance for them than it does for educated people. This line of thought suggests the following hypothesis, which we can test with our data:

H1: *If structural and institutional theories of cultural shifts are correct, more educated people are more likely than people with less education to abandon traditional cultural norms and convert to new cultural norms.*

H2: *If cultural theory is correct, people with less education, despite being less cognitively sophisticated, are more likely than educated people to abandon traditional cultural norms and convert to new ones.*

Table 4.5 follows the format of previous tables in this chapter but introduces a comparison between people with the highest and lowest levels of education. It looks at changes between our two surveys in mainland China in idiocentric DSI in each age group and cohort with the educational variable added to the analysis.[17] In the upper part of the table, only two of the cell entries are statistically significant (that is, with a p-value below .05), and these show change away from the idiocentric orientation among the more educated people in the two youngest age groups. In the lower part of the table four cells are significant. Three of them, likewise, show change in the direction of allocentric DSI among highly educated people in the three youngest cohorts. One shows change in the more idiocentric direction among people in the most senior cohort, those who were 45–53 years of age in 1993 and reached 54–62 years of age in 2002. The data, then, support the culturalist theory of how education affects cultural change: the more highly educated people tended to see the restoration of traditional culture as the answer to social anomie. It seems that people indoctrinated by traditional culture were constrained by it.

Table 4.6 carries out the same analysis for Taiwan. Similar to mainland China, educated people in the three youngest age groups were

---

[17] I only analyzed the changes and continuity of DSI because the previous analysis shows that OTA in both societies was rather stable.

TABLE 4.5. *Changes in Idiocentric Definition of Self-Interest by Level of Education in Mainland China*

Age at Time of Survey	Elementary and Lower Difference between 1993 and 2002[a]	SE[b]	P-value	Age at Time of Survey	College and Higher Difference between 1993 and 2002[a]	SE[b]	P-value
Changes in DSI for Different Age Groups over Time							
18–26	−0.025	0.031	0.421	18–26	−0.122	0.042	0.005
27–35	0.029	0.020	0.154	27–35	−0.114	0.043	0.009
36–44	0.025	0.017	0.151	36–44	−0.059	0.040	0.139
45–53	0.023	0.016	0.158	45–53	−0.059	0.055	0.289
54–62	0.024	0.017	0.156	54–62	−0.052	0.072	0.472
63+	0.002	0.016	0.888	63+	−0.065	0.066	0.336

Age at Time of Survey	Elementary and Lower Difference between 1993 and 2003[c]	SE	P-value	Age at Time of Survey	College and Higher Difference between 1993 and 2003[c]	SE	P-value
Change in DSI as People Age							
27–35	0.022	0.022	0.930	27–35	−0.192	0.036	0.000
36–44	0.004	0.020	0.836	36–44	−0.137	0.045	0.003
45–53	0.007	0.016	0.635	45–53	−0.150	0.044	0.001
54–62	0.035	0.016	0.027	54–62	−0.025	0.063	0.689

[a] Mean value for cohort in 2002 minus the mean value for that age group in 1993.

[b] Entries are standard errors corrected for complex sampling.

[c] Mean value of the cohorts in 2002 minus the mean values for the same age group in 1993. People who were 27–35 years old in 2002 were 18–26 years old in 1993. Thus we substracted the mean value of the 27–35 cohort in 2002 by the mean value of the 18–26 cohort in 1993.

Source: 1993 Survey of Political Culture and Political Participation in Mainland China, Taiwan, and Hong Kong; 2002 China Survey, Asian Barometer Survey I (1993 N = 3,287; 2002 N = 3,183).

TABLE 4.6. *Changes in Idiocentric Definition of Self-Interest by Level of Education in Taiwan*

Changes in DSI for Different Age Groups over Time

	Elementary and Lower			College and Higher		
Age at Time of Survey	Difference between 1993 and 2002[a]	SE[b]	P-value	Difference between 1993 and 2002[a]	SE[b]	P-value
21–29	0.230	0.074	0.009	-0.190	0.037	0.000
30–38	0.857	0.054	0.000	-0.192	0.035	0.000
39–47	0.046	0.035	0.185	-0.178	0.055	0.002
48–56	0.013	0.038	0.725	-0.094	0.073	0.203
57–65	0.045	0.027	0.095	-0.038	0.112	0.736
66+	-0.006	0.027	0.839	-0.058	0.144	0.691

Change in DSI as people age

	Elementary and Lower			College and Higher		
Age at Time of Survey	Difference between 1993 and 2002[c]	SE	P-value	Difference between 1993 and 2002[c]	SE	P-value
30–38	0.022	0.083	0.790	-0.197	0.039	0.000
39–47	0.77	0.040	0.000	-0.231	0.039	0.000
48–56	0.022	0.039	0.571	-0.149	0.060	0.016
57–65	-0.015	0.033	0.646	-0.237	0.095	0.019

[a] Mean value for the age group in 2002 minus the mean value for that age group in 1993.

[b] Entries are standard errors corrected for complex sampling.

[c] Mean value of a given age group in 2002 minus the mean value of the same age group in 1993. People who were 30–38 years old in 2002 were 21–29 years old in 1993. Thus, we substracted the mean value of the 30–38 cohort in 2002 by the mean value of the 21–29 cohort in 1993.

Source: 1993 Survey of Political Culture and Political Participation in Mainland China, Taiwan, and Hong Kong; 2002 Taiwan Survey, Asian Barometer Survey I (1993 N = 1,402; 2002 N = 1,415).

more allocentrically oriented in 2002 than in 1993. The two youngest age groups among less educated Taiwanese moved in the opposite direction, becoming more idiocentrically oriented. Among cohorts, the changes were in the same directions: five entries were statistically significant; among them, all four cohorts of the most highly educated became more allocentric and one cohort among the less educated became more idiocentric.

In neither Table 4.5 nor Table 4.6 is there any statistically significant cell entry indicating norm change in a direction contrary to that predicted by the culturalist theory in H2. More highly educated people in both mainland China and Taiwan were less likely than people with low levels of education to update their cultural norms; they tended instead to re-embrace traditional cultural norms. Less educated people were less likely to be biased by traditional culture and more likely to update their normative orientation in response to environment changes in their society. Although educated people are more cognitively sophisticated than people without education, their decoding of outside stimuli and their choices of responses to the change were more constrained by their cultural norms and cultural environment.

The findings suggest that culture is to some extent self-maintaining. Cultural norms impact cognitive decoding as if actors view and understand the outside world through a prism of norms. Norms color their interpretation of the meaning and implication of changes and constrain their choice of responses to new challenges. In some cases structural and institutional changes in a society may, at least in their initial stages, trigger some people to re-embrace traditional culture. This finding provides a micro foundation for understanding the mechanism of cultural stability and change.

Elites in every Chinese dynasty and in many other parts of the world have seen the restoration of traditional culture as the answer to problems facing their societies. Political scientists and historians have tended to interpret restoration movements as regime-engineered efforts to resist change. They have pointed to the communist regime, for example, for the emergence of neo-Confucianism in early twentieth-century China and the restoration movement led by the New Left at the turn of the twenty-first century. The findings here suggest that these movements have a much broader social base. But do they reflect temporary or more stable changes? More data will be required to fully understand the nature of these changes.

Culture, Structure, Institutions

CONCLUSION

Chapters 3 and 4 have demonstrated the essential stability of cultural norms in mainland China and Taiwan from 1993 to 2002. Despite the occurrence of rapid and dramatic social and political change, and despite changes within certain age groups and cohorts, the aggregate distribution of norms in the two societies was stable. But this evidence pertains to the internal policing system of culture, without telling us whether change occurred in the external policing system or the interactive effects of the internal and external policing systems. Without addressing these additional mechanisms, our evidence is inconclusive, for two reasons. First, the effectiveness of the external policing system of norms may not be linearly associated with norm distribution in a society. Second, cultural flexibility is produced by the interaction of both internal and external policing systems of culture. Thus, changes at the societal level may influence the effectiveness of culture at the individual level. As discussed earlier, the probability that people in a society will impose sanctions against norm violators depends, in part, on their ability to assume that the violator shares their normative orientation (and thus gives tacit permission to be sanctioned). When the distribution of alternative cultural norms changes in society, so do the calculations of potential sanctioners and the likelihood that they will impose sanctions. Even if the overall distribution of a norm in society is stable, the existence of a strong group of nonconforming extremists can undercut the ability of the external policing system of norms to work effectively.

Our next task, therefore, is to determine whether culture's effectiveness at controlling social interaction changed over time in the two societies. Specifically, it must be determined whether changes in the distribution of alternative cultural norms at the societal level influenced the ability of norms at the individual level to influence people's political attitudes and behavior. This question is addressed in Part II.

PART II

CULTURE'S IMPACT ON POLITICAL ATTITUDES AND BEHAVIORS

5

Culture's Impact on Political Trust

Political trust – people's belief that government works for the people's interests – is one of the most consequential attitudes in the political system because it has a strong influence on regime stability. Dominant theories hold that political trust is shaped chiefly by people's evaluations of government performance. But if this book is correct in arguing that culture shapes the way in which people decode and evaluate information, we should find that culture also has an impact on political trust. This chapter explores whether that is indeed the case.

The analysis is divided into five parts. The first reviews how political trust has been conceptualized. The second looks at variations in the determinants of political trust in different world regions. Most theories assume that political trust responds to government performance and that people in different regions use the same standards to evaluate the performance of their governments. But if culture defines interests and costs for actors, people's differing normative commitments should influence how they understand and evaluate the costs and benefits of government's actions. The third part of the chapter therefore applies this book's cultural theory to generate hypotheses about how the cultural norms under study in this book should affect political trust.

The fourth section tests these hypotheses using data from mainland China. Because my theory argues that culture influences a person's political attitudes and behavior through two channels – the internal policing system of norms and the external policing system of norms – it is necessary to separately estimate the impacts from each channel and at the same time explore whether cultural impacts from different channels interact to shape people's attitudes toward public authority. This can be accomplished

108 *Impact on Attitudes and Behaviors*

by using the technique of hierarchical linear modeling (HLM). I show that orientation toward authority and definition of self-interest have statistically significant and independent impacts on political trust at both the individual and the group levels and further that the impacts of culture at the two levels interact as suggested by my theory.

The final part of the chapter brings in the case of Taiwan. Some may argue that both the content of culture and cultural impacts on political trust in China are determined by the presence of authoritarian institutions. To rule out the possibility that cultural impacts on political trust are endogenous to institutions, I show that similar causal mechanisms operate in the very different institutional setting of Taiwan. The findings confirm that cultural norms have an independent impact on political trust.

CONCEPTUALIZING POLITICAL TRUST

Political trust – sometimes referred to as "institutional trust" or "trust in political institutions" – refers to people's belief that their political system, or some part of it, will produce preferred outcomes even if left untended (Braithwaite and Levi 1998; Citrin and Muste 1999; Fukuyama 1995; Hardin 2000; Jennings 1998; Li 2004; Manion 2006; Mishler and Rose 1997; Nye, Zelikow, and King 1997; Shi 2001; Tyler 1998; Uslaner 2002; White 2005). Political trust is a critical determinant of regime stability because it is a component of "political support," the set of attitudes that give a political regime room to maneuver when it encounters difficulties in performing its political tasks. Lack of political trust in authoritarian societies has been theorized as a major reason for democratic transitions (Linz 2000).

Political trust used to be conceptualized as a one-dimensional phenomenon. An important debate in the 1970s, however, between Miller and Citrin, challenged that understanding. Miller argued that a dramatic decline of political trust in the United States meant that people no longer trusted the political system and that the democratic system itself was in danger. Citrin reanalyzed the data and found that Americans made clear conceptual distinctions between the political system, a political regime, and individual officials. Even when trust in particular officials and in a particular regime declined significantly, this could not be interpreted as a generalized alienation from democratic institutions (Citrin 1974; Miller 1974b). Distrust in incumbent officials could be differentiated from distrust in the political system.

This multidimensional approach was influenced by the work of Easton and Dennis. They theorized that political trust had three dimensions

Culture's Impact on Political Trust

based on the political objects in which people imbue trust (Easton and Dennis 1969, 58–59):

1. Trust in the political community, an "aspect of a political system that we can identify as a collection of people who share a division of labor";
2. Trust in the regime, the "constitutional order in the very broadest sense of the term ... that arranges who is to do what in the system";
3. Trust in the authorities or incumbents, referring to "those members of a system in whom the primary responsibility is lodged for taking care of the daily routines of a political system."

Subsequent empirical studies found that although incumbent-based trust can be empirically distinguished from regime-based trust, the latter cannot be empirically distinguished from system- or community-based trust (Craig, Niemi, and Silver 1990). Accordingly, the analysis in this chapter is limited to two dimensions of trust – incumbent-based and regime-based.

Each of these two dimensions of trust can be thought of as having a "specific" and a "diffuse" component. These concepts were introduced by Easton and Dennis in the context of their discussion of two kinds of "support" for government (Easton 1975, 1965). They defined "specific support" as an attitude of approval or disapproval that responds to specific behaviors and outputs of government, such as a particular policy or decision. "Diffuse support" is "generalized trust and confidence that members invest in various objects of the system as ends in themselves" (Easton and Dennis 1969, 62–63).

Scholars of democratic political systems have tended to assume that trust in the incumbents and in the regime is always "specific" because it responds solely to the incumbents' or the regime's policy performance and outputs, whereas "diffuse" trust is directed exclusively at the political system or community as an expression of convictions about the rightness or validity of that system or community. In this way the concepts of specific and diffuse are absorbed into the distinction among different objects of support – incumbents, regime, and community. It is more useful, however, to conceive of all dimensions of political trust as having specific and diffuse components.

Can the conceptual framework for political trust developed from democratic societies be applied to authoritarian societies and more specifically to China? Easton and Dennis asserted that people's conviction in the rightness of a democratic system could prevent distrust toward incumbents from spilling over to distrust in the regime or community. When incumbent-based trust declines in democratic societies, people are mobilized to participate in politics. As a result, the regime removes unpopular government officials and changes policy, or people vote unpopular leaders out of office and replace them. Incumbent-based trust bounces back, and trust at the regime and system levels are protected from the spillover effects of distrust toward incumbents (see also Newton and Norris 2000; Pharr and Putnam 2000).

If diffuse support in democracies comes from conviction in democracy itself as a form of government – and specific support depends mainly on whether the government provides good policy and access and on whether government officials are seen as "good men and women" – where does diffuse support come from in nondemocratic societies (Fenno 1978, 240–41)? Many scholars believe that authoritarian governments may enjoy short-term legitimacy (for example, utopian or revolutionary legitimacy, legitimacy based on nationalism, or on the restoration of order). However, because authoritarian institutions do not allow people to transfer from short-term support to moral conviction, authoritarian governments cannot enjoy diffuse support from their people (Linz 2000).

An obvious problem with that argument is that it assumes that moral conviction in regime legitimacy can be elicited only by democratic institutions. But this assumption may not hold water. More than one hundred years ago, Weber reminded us that governmental legitimacy can be based on different foundations, which he called traditional, charismatic, and legal-rational (Weber 1947, 324–90). Presumably each kind of system was capable of enjoying its own kind of diffuse support based on its own type of legitimacy. Similarly, years ago Lucian Pye challenged conventional views on authoritarianism and legitimacy by arguing that both specific and diffuse support can exist in authoritarian societies in Asia. He argued, in fact, that authoritarian regimes were the most legitimate ones in Asia (Pye 1985, 1992). Many scholars have criticized this assertion. The problem with these debates is that the arguments on both sides are based on theoretical claims and deductions. Neither side has provided empirical support. This chapter will show that cultural differences generate different levels of political trust for different kinds of objects.

REGIONAL VARIATIONS IN DETERMINANTS OF POLITICAL TRUST

To lay the groundwork for that demonstration, this section describes regional differences in the determinants of political trust. The Global Barometer Surveys (GBS) allow researchers to empirically assess

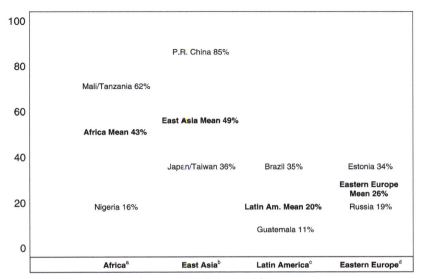

FIGURE 5.1. Institutional trust around the world, 2001–2005.
[a] 2002–2003 Africa: 16 countries.
[b] 2001–2003 East Asia:, 8 regions and countries.
[c] 2003 Latino Region: 17 countries.
[d] 2004–2005 Eastern Europe: 11 countries.
Note: Entries represent mean trust in institutions. Percentages are weighted means of the total sample for each country.
Source: Global Barometer Surveys (www.globalbarometers.org).

variations in political trust on a global scale.[1] The surveys asked people on four continents about their trust in each of the following political institutions: the army, police, courts, parliament, and the current ruling political party.[2] The data allow us to answer two questions. First, do Asians trust their governments more than people on other continents do? Second, does institutional trust exist in nondemocratic societies? To find out, I calculated the mean of each country and each region for the five questions on political trust. The results are presented in Figure 5.1.

[1] For more information on the Global Barometer Surveys, see http://www.globalbarometer.net/background.htm.
[2] Since interviews are conducted in more than three dozen languages, the exact wording of questions must vary, but the meaning is the same. The data used in this chapter are from the 2004–2005 New Europe survey in eleven countries; the 2003 Latino survey in seventeen countries; the 2001–3 East Asian survey in eight regions and countries; and the 2002–3 Africa survey in sixteen countries.

The figure identifies significant cross-continental variations in political trust. The general level of political trust was lowest in Latin America, whose mean value of political trust was 20 percent. New Europe was slightly higher at 26 percent. The mean level of political trust in Africa was 43 percent, and the mean value of political trust in East Asia was 49 percent. At the same time, there were substantial intra-continental variations in political trust. The difference between the most trusting and least trusting countries in East Asia was 49 percent, Africa 46 percent, Eastern Europe 15 percent, and Latin America 24 percent.[3]

The percentage of people in mainland China reporting that they trusted political institutions may seem suspiciously high. However, as reported in Chapter 3 and Appendix B, I ruled out the possibility that these results were a consequence of political fear. The data, therefore, show that it is possible for an authoritarian regime to enjoy a higher level of political trust than many democratic governments.

Why do Asians and Africans trust their governments more than people in other parts of the world? According to current theory, political trust is shaped primarily by regime characteristics, government performance, and social resources that help actors understand the implications of government policy for their interests. To see whether these theories apply equally well in all regions, I examined the bivariate relationship between variables deemed by current theory to be important in shaping political trust and the mean regional scores of political trust acquired from the GBS. Three groups of variables were used in this analysis:

1. The first measured the effect of regime characteristics, using the 2003 Freedom House scores of civil liberty and political rights[4];
2. The second group measured government performance. For market economies, gross domestic product (GDP) per capita was used to measure government performance in the economic arena. For nonmarket economies, I also included per capita GDP adjusted for Purchasing Power Parity (PPP). I also used the corruption perception index provided by Transparency International,[5] and economic growth rates;

---

[3] The countries that possess the lowest levels of political trust are all located in Latin America: Bolivia (14 percent), Ecuador (12 percent), and Guatemala (11 percent).

[4] Freedom House scores countries from a low score (freer, more democratic) to a high score (less free, less democratic). Here and elsewhere in the book I invert these scores to provide a more easily interpretable result.

[5] The Corruption Perception Index acquires its data by asking third parties about their perceptions of corruption in a particular country rather than by surveying citizens of that country. The Asian Barometer Survey includes some questions on citizens' perceptions of corruption in their own countries, and I use these data elsewhere in the book.

TABLE 5.1. *Correlations of Structural and Institutional Variables with Political Trust*

	Civil Liberty[a]	Political Rights[a]	Corruption Perception Index[b]	GDP per Capita	GDP per Capita Adjusted for PPP	GDP Growth	Rural Population in Total Population	Internet Use	Telephones per 100 Households
Global Barometer	−0.280	−0.304	0.096	−0.250	−0.175	0.288**	0.526***	−0.128	−0.198
New Europe	0.365	0.424	0.459	0.108	0.058	0.286	0.086	0.509	−0.049
Africa	0.124	−0.137	0.195	−0.178	−0.164	−0.351	0.574**	−0.348	−0.408
Latin America	0.493	0.477	0.660***	0.485**	0.482**	−0.134	−0.564**	0.563**	0.671***
East Asia	−0.923	−0.828	−0.378	−0.510	−0.565	0.893***	0.552	−0.612	−0.389
East Asia without China	−0.664	−0.424	−0.341	−0.494	−0.516	0.784**	0.379	−0.660	−0.540

*** $p < .01$; ** $p < .05$; * $p < .1$

[a] The Freedom House scale for Civil Liberty and Political Rights runs from 1 (totally free) to 7 (totally unfree), but the scale is inverted here to provide a more easily interpretable result.

[b] Corruption Perception Index scale ranges from 1 (extremely corrupt) to 10 (no corruption).

Source: Data on Civil Liberty and Political Rights are from Freedom House 2003 (www.freedomhouse.org). The Corruption Perception Index is from Transparency International (http://www.transparency.org/policy_research/surveys_indices/cpi). The remaining data (on GDP per capita, GDP per capita adjusted for PPP, GDP growth, Internet usage, rural population in the whole population, and telephones per 100 households) are from the World Bank online data bank.

114 *Impact on Attitudes and Behaviors*

3. The third measured the population's social resources. The percentage of Internet users per 100 households and the number of telephone lines per 100 households measure people's access to political information, serving as a proxy for their political knowledge. The percentage of rural population provides a rough measure of the level of modernization of the society.

The results of the analysis are shown in Table 5.1. At the global level, government performance played a critical role in shaping political trust. Both economic performance and modernization were found to have positive impacts. Although absolute levels of development played no role in shaping political trust, economic growth rates were positively correlated with political trust. However, urbanization reduces political trust (countries with larger rural populations had higher levels of political trust).

Political information played no role in shaping political trust – neither Internet usage nor telephone availability had any impact. Corruption also had no impact on political trust. The bigger surprise, however, was that although civil liberties and political rights had significant impacts on institutional trust, the direction of the relationship was the reverse of what most scholars would predict. Institutional trust is lower in countries where people enjoy more civil liberties and political rights than in countries where people enjoy fewer liberties and rights.

The global pattern, however, masks important regional variations. In Eastern Europe, none of the variables examined could predict institutional trust. In Africa, the only variable that had a statistically significant impact on political trust was the proportion of rural population. At the other extreme, in Latin America, nearly every variable derived from current theory was significantly correlated with political trust, with all the correlations in the direction predicted by theory. Greater civil liberties and political rights in Latin American made people trust their government more; corruption reduced the level of political trust; economic vitality as measured by GDP per capita, with or without adjusting for PPP, was positively correlated with trust; information played a significant role; and Latin American countries with larger rural populations had lower levels of political trust than those with larger urban populations.

The pattern in East Asia was different in several ways from those in other parts of the world. First, while GDP growth had no impact on political trust on the other three continents, it had a statistically significant and positive impact on political trust in East Asia. Second, while more extensive civil liberties and political rights made Latin Americans trust their governments more, the same variables showed a negative correlation with trust in East Asia. Finally, while corruption caused people in Latin American to distrust their political institutions, it had no impact on institutional trust in East Asia. The East Asian findings are essentially the same when the data from mainland China – the only fully authoritarian state among the eight Asian systems included in the survey – are removed. GDP growth continues to influence political trust, followed by one of the two measures of regime characteristics, civil liberties. (With the China data removed, political rights cease to influence political trust.)

How do we explain these cross-continental variations? Why does governmental performance play a different role in influencing political trust in East Asia than it does in other continents? The answer lies in culture.

CULTURAL IMPACTS ON POLITICAL TRUST: THEORY AND HYPOTHESES

Conventional theory, influenced by the rational choice perspective, explains political trust in terms of the calculations of material interests made by political actors (Riker 1990). People's attitudes toward government are shaped by its performance, their positions in society, and their cognitive capacity to understand the impact of government policies on their interests. Following this logic, scholars argue that trust is either knowledge-based or possible when an actor perceives his interaction with others as a repeated game. For example, Yamigishi and Yamigishi suggest that trust depends on information (Yamigishi and Yamigishi 1994). Offe asserts that trust results from past experiences (Offe 1999, 50). Hardin has claimed that "my trust of you must be grounded in expectations that are particular to you, not merely in generalized expectations" (Hardin 2000, 10). If interactions are perceived as a repeated game, the incentive to defect may be overcome by the threat of punishment, leading to the possibility of a cooperative outcome. To these scholars, trust is essentially strategic.

However, a second line of theorizing argues that trust is founded in moral values, which are part of culture. Conceptually, according to this view, the problem with the rationalist theoretical framework is that strategic trust presupposes risk (Misztal 1996; Seligman 1997). When person A trusts person B, A puts himself in a dangerous position, as he cannot tell if B will be trustworthy. If B violates his promise, say by defaulting on a loan, A will lose. Second, Uslaner points out that strategic trust can lead to cooperation only among people who have gotten to know one another, so it can explain trust only at the individual level and not on a larger scale (Uslaner 2002, 20). Third, rationalist theories have been challenged by empirical findings that trust in government is "independent of outputs and performance in the short run" (Patterson, Wahlke, and Boynton 1973, 273).

Summarizing the theories of several political trust scholars, Uslaner argues that trust on a larger scale must be based on "some sort of belief in the good will of the other."[6] What he calls "moralistic trust" comes from the belief that others will not try to take advantage of us (Uslaner 2002, 14–50). He stresses that moralistic trust is not a prediction of how others will behave; moral values require people to behave as if others could be trusted, whether they turn out to be trustworthy or not. Trust, in Uslaner's understanding, therefore has ethical roots.[7] "If trust connects us to our community and helps us solve collective action problems, it must be moralistic trust that does the job." He continues:

Unlike strategic trust, moralistic trust is not primarily based upon personal experiences .... Moralistic trust is not about having faith in particular people or even groups of people. It is a general outlook on human nature and mostly does not depend upon personal experience or upon the assumption that others are trustworthy, as strategic trust does. (Hardin 2000, 14, 174)

Instead, moralistic trust is a commandment to treat people as if they were trustworthy (Uslaner 2002, 17, 18).

Similarly, David Easton pointed out that instrumental calculations of interest cannot fully explain diffuse support which, he said, is "a kind of support that a system does not have to buy with more or less direct benefits [in exchange] for the obligations and responsibilities the member incurs" (Easton 1965, 273). Except in the long run, diffuse support is independent from specific support. According to Easton, diffuse support can have three sources: legitimacy, common interest, and identity. But what makes people perceive a regime as legitimate? Easton argued that legitimacy has three possible components: ideological legitimacy (moral convictions about the validity of a regime), structural legitimacy (belief in the validity of the government structures that make up the regime), and personal legitimacy (belief in the personal qualities of an incumbent or incumbents who occupy leadership positions in the regime) (Easton 1965). The "moralistic trust" to which Uslaner refers or Easton's "moral

---

[6] Yamigishi and Yamigishi (1994, 131); Seligman (1997, 43 in Uslaner [2002]).

[7] See further Uslaner (2002, 20) for citation of other authors who argue that trust has moral sources.

Culture's Impact on Political Trust

conviction about the validity of the regime" clearly must be shaped by culture.

The argument that culture influences political trust is therefore not new. What I hope to contribute is a new theory of the mechanisms through which culture influences political trust. Building on the theory presented in Chapter 2, I argue that cultural norms help political actors decode the meaning of information; shape the expectations of government that people use as a standard for evaluating government performance; and define the proper responses political actors can take toward governmental behavior under different situations.

Specifically, I propose the following hypotheses about how the two cultural norms analyzed in this book influence regime-based trust and incumbent-based trust. The analysis begins at the individual level. Under reciprocal orientation toward authority, the contractual nature of the relationship between the individual and the state compels people to keep suspicious eyes on their government and to distrust public authority. The paternalistic nature of the hierarchical OTA, on the other hand, not only leads people to assume that the government will take care of their interests, but also obliges them to trust their government. I therefore hypothesize that people under the influence of hierarchical OTA are more likely to trust their government than people under the influence of reciprocal OTA. People holding hierarchical orientations might decide to withdraw support from their government, but the threshold at which they would do so is higher than that set by the reciprocal orientation. Thus:

H1. *An individual who believes in hierarchical OTA is more likely to trust political institutions than one who believes in reciprocal OTA.*

Like orientation toward authority, definition of self-interest also helps people to decode information, shapes their expectations toward public authority, and influences their responses to authority. Public policies seldom benefit everyone equally; policies benefitting certain groups of people usually jeopardize the interests of others to some extent. The idiocentric definition of self-interest authorizes people whose private interests are threatened to withdraw support from government. Under the allocentric definition of self-interest, on the other hand, as long as the government can frame its policy as benefitting the majority of people in the society, people do not have the legitimate power to withdraw support from authority. Thus:

H2. *An individual who believes in allocentric DSI is more likely to trust political institutions than one who believes in idiocentric DSI.*

A second set of hypotheses flows from considering how cultural norms influence political trust through social interactions. I argue that they do so in two ways. First, as noted earlier, politically relevant information is received and decoded with the help of various intermediaries, such as mass media, fellow members of secondary associations, and face-to-face contact within personal networks. An individual's decoding of political information will be influenced by the intermediaries' normative orientations. Thus:

H3. *People living in a social environment dominated by hierarchical OTA are more likely to trust political institutions than people living in a social environment dominated by reciprocal OTA.*

H4. *People living in a social environment dominated by allocentric DSI are more likely to trust political institutions than people living in a social environment dominated by idiocentric DSI.*

Cultural norms at the societal level may also influence people's political attitudes and behavior through their impact on the individual's instrumental cost–benefit calculations. Through the external policing system of norms, dominant norm holders in a community may force deviating norm holders to comply with the dominant norms to avoid painful social isolation.

In the past, scholars have used the percentages of people holding a particular cultural orientation or the mean values of an orientation in a community to assess what cultural orientation is dominant in the community. This makes sense when assessing how the cultural environment influences political trust through the impact of norms on decoding information (hypotheses 3 and 4): the greater the proportion of people holding a particular norm in a community, the more likely the norm can influence how each individual decodes information. But when assessing how effectively the social environment influences political trust through the external policing system of culture, we should focus on whether there is a sizeable social group willing and able to support norm violators. If there is, the fear of social sanctions is less likely to deter norm violators.

Thus:

H5. *If the cultural environment influences political trust through its external policing system, the level of political trust in a community will depend on whether there exists a sizeable group of deviating norm holders: communities with a sizeable group of deviating norm holders will have a lower level of political trust.*

EMPIRICAL TESTS: CHINA

The proper statistical tool to test these five hypotheses is a technique called hierarchical linear modeling (HLM). This is a form of regression analysis that simultaneously models the impact on a given dependent variable of: (1) attributes characterizing the individual respondents and (2) attributes characterizing the social units to which the respondents belong. Conventional regression assumes that the values of the variables recorded for each case in the data set are independent. HLM takes into account the nested structure of the variables – that is, the fact that the second-level variables assume the same value for all members of the given collective unit.

I used data from the 2002 survey in mainland China for these analyses. The survey was conducted in 138 randomly selected counties and county-level municipalities[8] (for simplicity, I will use "county" to refer to this level of analysis). The county serves as the second-level unit in the models in this and subsequent chapters.[9]

The dependent variables in this analysis are the two types of political trust, regime-based and incumbent-based. They are constructed from the six variables displayed in Table 5.2. Respondents were asked to rate their level of trust on a scale of 1 (complete distrust) to 6 (complete trust) toward five political objects: the central government, the local government, the ruling Chinese Communist Party, the National People's Congress (parliament), and "the typical government official" (*yiban zhengfu guanyuan*). In addition, the questionnaire contained an item with a four-point scale asking whether "most government officials" could be "trusted without constant oversight."

A factor analysis, presented in Table 5.2, shows that in China these six variables express two underlying dimensions of political trust that correspond to the concepts of regime-based trust and incumbent-based trust. Trust in the CCP, the central government and the NPC grouped together

[8] *Xianji shi* – municipalities occupying the same administrative level as counties in the Chinese administrative system.

[9] The convention in hierarchical analysis is that one needs at least thirty second-level units and, in each unit, at least thirty cases (Kreft 1996; Maas and Hox 2005). Ideally a smaller unit, such as the rural village or urban work unit, would be used for the second level of analysis in HLM. Because the sample was not originally designed for a hierarchical model, however, there were not sufficient cases in the sub-county units. Using a larger community as a second-level unit will cause us to underestimate rather than overestimate the impact of the cultural environment on individuals' choices. Counties can legitimately be used as second-level units, as this will provide more conservative estimates.

TABLE 5.2. *Exploratory Factor Analysis of Political Trust in Mainland China*

Trust Variable	Regime-Based Trust	Incumbent-Based Trust
Trust in Chinese Communist Party	0.89	
Trust in National People's Congress	0.89	
Trust in central government	0.85	
Trust in the typical government official		0.85
Trust in local government		0.82
Trust in most government officials		0.63
Eigenvalue	2.93	1.21
Total variance explained	48.87	20.10

Source: 2002 China Survey, Asian Barometer Survey I (N = 3,183).

to form one factor, and trust in local government, the typical official, and most officials formed a second factor. In many societies, trust in local government is grouped with variables measuring regime-based trust (Li, Wang, and Fischer 2004). The fact that it aligns with incumbent-based trust in China makes sense because local governments in China have no autonomous decision-making power but act as implementers of decisions made by authorities at higher levels. In the eyes of citizens, local governments are distinguished not by their structures or policies but by the qualities of the local officials. I recoded the six variables so that positive scores indicated trust, and negative scores indicated distrust. "No opinion" was coded as 0.[10] I added the scores on questions measuring regime-based trust together to form a regime-based political trust scale and added the scores on incumbent-based trust to form an incumbent-based political trust scale.

The model uses four clusters of independent variables representing three different intellectual traditions. (Many of the variables are also used in subsequent chapters.) The first cluster measures government performance to test the extent to which actors' instrumental calculations play a role in shaping political trust. The following variables were used to measure government performance.

---

[10] To test the robustness of my finding against the coding of missing values, I have also tried list-wise deletion in regression analysis. The results are basically the same.

Culture's Impact on Political Trust

A long tradition of scholarship argues that citizens evaluate government performance largely on the basis of its perceived economic achievements (Fiorina 1981; Key and Cummings 1966). Many sinologists attributed the stability of the communist regime in China to its economic performance (Gilley 2004; Nathan 2003; Pei 2006). Since citizens attribute the economic success of the country to the regime, rather than to individual officials, a retrospective evaluation of economic performance should increase regime-based trust but not incumbent-based trust. Three variables were used to measure respondents' retrospective evaluation of economic performance. The first question asked, "How would you describe the change in the economic condition of our country over the past five years?" The second question asked, "How would you compare the current economic condition of your family with what it was five years ago?" The response categories were "much worse," "worse," "remains the same," "better" and "much better." The third item referred to a major issue in China at the time of the survey, the state-owned enterprise (SOE) reform, which had laid off millions of workers. The question asked whether any members of the respondent's family had been laid off. Since the policy to reform SOEs was made by the central government and implemented by local officials, those whose family members had lost their jobs might have blamed both the regime and/or individual officials for their economic misfortunes.

People who perceive the government as responsive to their demands are found to trust the government more than people who think otherwise (Abramson 1972; Craig 1979; Hayes and Bean 1993). Even though people in China cannot elect national leaders, channels of access exist for them to communicate with government officials, especially at the local level (Falkenheim 1978; Shi 1997). Reforms in people's congresses have provided people with additional institutional means through which to express their opinions (O'Brien 1990a, 1990b, 1994a). Semi-competitive elections were introduced into rural China in the late 1980s, allowing peasants to remove from office officials they did not like (Li and O'Brien 1999; O'Brien 1994b; O'Brien and Li 2000; Shi 1999). Therefore it makes sense to include this variable in the model.

Two approaches have been developed to measure the perceived responsiveness of government (also sometimes referred to as "external efficacy"). The one developed by Almond and Verba in *The Civic Culture* asks respondents whether they think the government treats them equally when they approach it for help. The method developed by University of Michigan scholars directly asks people to assess government responsiveness to their demands (Almond and Verba 1963; Craig and Maggiotto 1982; Craig et al. 1990). Scholars of Chinese politics have used both methods.

However, these methods are vulnerable to the criticism that respondents in China may interpret the questions in different ways than people in Western societies.[11] To address this problem, I designed two new sets of questions to measure respondents' evaluation of their political access in China. In each set, the first question tapped the normative orientation of respondents toward political participation, the second asked them how likely they would be to participate in politics given the situation specified in the first question, and the third asked them to assess the possible response of government to their acts. Using government policy as a lead-in, the first set of questions started by asking, "If a policy made by the government is harmful to your interests, should you participate in politics to influence its decisions?" The second set used respondents' personal matters as a lead-in: "If you have a personal matter that needs to be resolved by the government, should you make demands on government officials?" In each set, the second question was, "If such a situation occurs, would you participate in politics to influence government decisions?" And in each set, we asked those who gave positive answers whether they expected their participation to bring them their desired results. The answers to these last two questions were used to represent the perceived responsiveness of government. As a third question on government responsiveness, we asked people if they agreed that the "power of government in our country is concentrated among a few individuals and people have no effective say." The three questions on responsiveness were factor-analyzed, and one factor emerged. I added them together to form an index of external efficacy.

---

[11] Gary King and his collaborators argue that, due to China's institutional constraints, traditional measurements of political efficacy cannot be used in China because they will provide researchers with biased information. Scholars have long attempted to address these problems, with uneven success, by using approaches designed to reduce incomparability, such as writing more concrete questions. King et al. suggested an alternative approach – via respondents' assessments of hypothetical individuals described in short vignettes. Because the actual (but not necessarily reported) levels of the vignettes are invariant over respondents, variability in vignette answers reveals incomparability (King et al. 2004). The Asian Barometer Survey did not use King's method for two reasons. First, King's method ignores institutional effects on people's political behavior and consequently on their feelings of efficacy; second, further tests of King's method have found that it performs no better than traditional methods in measuring political efficacy in both mainland China and Taiwan.

Political corruption is one of the main reasons for the erosion of political trust. In democratic societies, corruption is a clear violation of the social contract and thus constitutes a reason for people to withdraw their support for the political regime (Anderson and Tverdova 2003; Seligson 2002). Many political scientists attribute the dramatic decline of political trust in the United States to the long-lasting effects of Watergate (Citrin 1974; Inglehart 1997; Miller 1974a, 1974b, 1974c; Pharr and Putnam 2000). Corruption is likewise seen in China as a violation of the role assigned to rulers. I hypothesize that perceived corruption reduces both incumbent-based and regime-based political trust in China. I measured perceived corruption with the question, "In your opinion, is corruption a widespread problem in the area where you live?"

The second cluster of variables measured respondents' socioeconomic resources. As in most survey research, the primary measure of individual-level socioeconomic resources is education. To measure education, I used the number of years of formal schooling.[12] Scholars have argued that education reduces political trust in three ways[13]: (1) Education raises actors' level of interest in politics, which prompts them to search for political information. The more information a person in an authoritarian society has, the more likely the person will distrust authority; (2) education increases people's aspirations and encourages actors to adopt self-expressive values (Inglehart 1997). As Pharr and Putnam note, "Increases in the heterogeneity of public desires make it more difficult for government to identify any feasible set of policies to satisfy its constituencies." Furthermore, as "public demands on government aspire insatiably upward, satisfaction could fall even if performance remains unchanged" (Pharr and Putnam 2000, 23–24); and (3) education reduces the role of norms for people to formulate their attitudes toward public authority. As educated people are better informed about politics and government affairs, they are less likely to rely on cultural norms to deduce the meanings and the implications of government policies. Gender, age, and urban residence were used as control variables.

---

[12] In the process of model building, I tried to code education in different ways; findings were essentially the same whichever coding method was used.

[13] Education used to have a positive impact on political trust in the United States, but that relationship disappeared after the 1970s. Stokes reported that when questions designed by the Survey Research Center of the University of Michigan were first used, "the disposition of the individual to take a favorable stance toward government seems to depend somewhat on the extent of his education" (Stokes 1962, 65). In recent years, however, education has been found to have a negative impact on political trust.

124 *Impact on Attitudes and Behaviors*

The third cluster of variables measured institutional effects. The first such variable is fear of regime repression. This was measured with two questions: "If you criticize the government, are you worried that someone might snitch on you?" and "If you criticize the party and national leaders, are you worried that someone might snitch on you?" The two variables were coded so that reported political fear was 1 and all other answers were 0. The answers were added together to form a political fear index.

Three questions were used to measure people's access to media. I asked respondents how often they followed political news on television, how often they read newspapers, and how often they listened to the radio. These questions were factor-analyzed to confirm their consistency and then summed to form a media access index.[14]

Many scholars have attributed the decline of political trust in democracies in recent years to "media malaise" (Gerbner et al. 1994; Sabato 2000). The increase of information on politics and government affairs is thought to make people increasingly distrust both the regime and the incumbents. Early theories of the impacts of media on political trust emphasized the quantity of information – the more information on politics and government one had, the less one trusted the government. More recently, scholars of political communications argue that it is the content of information carried by the media that reduces political trust. In China and other authoritarian systems, however, the media play a fundamentally different role from the media in the West. The Chinese media are designed to serve as the regime's mouthpiece, and the regime uses them to feed people with positive information and to "educate" (Lynch 1999). Theories developed in liberal democracies about media impacts on political trust do not automatically apply. If regime propaganda in China is successful, access to official media should increase the level of regime-based trust. It may, however, have the opposite impact on incumbent-based trust. The regime has come to realize that in order to prevent people from becoming overly dissatisfied with rampant corruption in recent years, it needs to use the media to monitor the behavior of its agents. Thus the CCP has changed its propaganda strategy; rather than preventing the reporting of all negative news, it exposes the corruption of selected cadres in official media, although it portrays them as isolated incidents. Stories of corruption in the Chinese media are always accompanied by comments praising

---

[14] For each of the three questions the respondent could give an answer ranging from "less than once a week" to "several times a day," creating a five-point scale. The index is created by summing the points on the three answers.

Culture's Impact on Political Trust

the CCP for its determination to eliminate corruption. If this strategy is successful, access to official media should raise people's trust in the regime but lower their trust in government officials.

I also created a variable to measure people's access to unofficial information channels. People in China seek information outside the officially controlled media through so-called "small-street news" (*xiaodao xiaoxi*), which I translate as "grapevine rumors." (At the time of the 2002 survey, Twitter-like services, blogs, and other social media were not yet a factor in mainland China.) Unlike the official media, grapevine rumors rarely carry positive news, and their contents are often similar to (although less reliable than) those of free media in liberal societies.[15] I therefore hypothesize that information from unofficial channels should reduce both incumbent-based and regime-based trust. Two questions measured people's exposure to information through unofficial channels. The first question asked respondents whether they had heard any grapevine rumors concerning the government and/or public affairs in the month prior to the survey; the second asked whether they had discussed these rumors with others during the same period. Positive answers to both questions were coded as 1 and all other answers were coded 0. The answers were summed to form an index of access to unofficial information.

Another variable related to political institutions is membership in the Chinese Communist Party. In democracies, joining a party usually means that the person has accepted its standard beliefs and policies as a general summary of his/her own political views and preferences (Campbell et al. 1960, 185). If the party with which an individual identifies is in power, the person should be more likely to trust the regime and the incumbents. Party membership represents something different in China. People join the Chinese Communist Party for multiple reasons. While some may accept the party platform, others join for the instrumental benefits associated with membership, such as career advancement and material privileges

---

[15] Although information transferred through grapevine rumors can hardly be verified, ordinary people tend to believe in such information for three reasons: (1) although the information cannot be independently confirmed, it cannot be easily refuted either; (2) the regime in China is reluctant to deny the rumors because it may trigger people's curiosity, cause the release of more information, and possibly cause a chain of events beyond its control. To avoid such trouble, the CCP usually ignores grapevine rumors, but people usually interpret the CCP's lack of response as a confirmation of the rumors; and (3) knowing such a dynamic, dissidents and dissatisfied people in China may deliberately make up various rumors and use them as an important weapon in politics. In fact, some student leaders in 1989 confessed to the author that they used a strategy of disinformation to mobilize the general populace to participate in the student movement.

(Shirk 1982, 90–91). For those who join the CCP because they identify with its platform, party membership should make them more likely to trust the government. For those who join the party to pursue instrumental benefits, membership should be either negatively correlated to or have no impact on political trust. Since we have no measure of the reason why a respondent joined the CCP, we are unable to test this hypothesis directly. But indirectly, it implies that party membership will have no statistically significant relationship with political trust since the two kinds of motives will cancel each other out.

The last cluster of variables, and the one in which we are most interested, measures political culture. The model uses the IRT scales of OTA and DSI described in Chapter 3 to represent individuals' cultural norms.

Finally, I include life satisfaction in the model to test an alternative theory of how culture affects trust that has been presented by Inglehart. He has argued that the most important cross-cultural difference is the diffuse feeling that a public can have toward its government, a feeling built up and stabilized over the course of a country's history. This diffuse feeling can play a critical role in helping a regime overcome various difficulties it may face. The best indicator of such a feeling is "whether one is satisfied with the way things are going in one's life" (Inglehart 1988, 1205). This question measures a diffuse attitude that is not tied to the current performance of the economy, the authorities currently in office, or to any specific aspect of society. Inglehart argues that a person's satisfaction with life will spill over onto his or her satisfaction with government. When people are satisfied with their lives, they view problems with their government as temporary glitches that will eventually be resolved.[16] This contrasts with my argument that culture influences political trust through normative definitions of an ideal government and definitions of interests and costs. Life satisfaction was measured by asking respondents: "If 1 means completely dissatisfied with your life and 10 means completely satisfied, how satisfied are you with your life?"

Model building in HLM proceeds in three steps. First, to confirm that multilevel modeling is appropriate, one must find out how much variance there is in the dependent variable across the second-level units and whether that variance is statistically significant. For this purpose I used a hierarchical ANOVA model. The analysis, not shown here, demonstrated that

---

[16] Inglehart suggests that "these feelings in turn may reflect economic and other successes that one experienced long ago or learned about second-hand as a part of one's early socialization" (Inglehart 1988, 1205).

Culture's Impact on Political Trust

87 percent of the variance across counties in incumbent-based trust can be attributed to differences at the individual level, and 13 percent can be attributed to differences at the county level. This means that some mechanism at the county level affects the incumbent-based trust expressed by individuals living in that county, even after the differences among those individuals have been taken into account. The Intra-Class Correlation Coefficient (ICCC) was .13 for incumbent-based trust. The ICCC was only .03 for regime-based trust, showing that there are also some level-2 effects for this dependent variable, but they are substantively small.[17] The results indicate that HLM should be used for the analysis of determinants of incumbent-based trust but not necessarily for regime-based trust.

The second step of the analysis explores the effects of selected individual-level variables on both dimensions of political trust. The results of a hierarchical OLS regression are displayed in Table 5.3.

The table shows that most indicators of government performance had a positive impact on one or both dimensions of political trust as per conventional expectations. As in other societies, both economic performance and government responsiveness increase people's trust both in agents of the regime and in the political institutions of the country. The finding that government responsiveness had a greater impact on incumbent-based trust than on regime-based trust is to be expected because political participation in China is primarily aimed at changing the way local officials interpret and implement policies made by the central government rather than at influencing how decisions are made by the central government. While people who saw local government officials as corrupt distrusted both regime agents and the regime itself, people who perceived those in the central government to be corrupt tended to distrust the political institution in the country overall.[18] In all, despite the authoritarian nature of Chinese society, government performance does have a significant impact on political trust among Chinese people.

---

[17] The finding suggests that little of the variance in regime-based trust in mainland China is attributable to variable features of the counties. This, in turn, implies that people in China do not blame the central government for the performance of local officials. Corruption in China can be assumed to vary from county to county. If corruption of local officials causes people to withdraw support for the regime, the level of regime-based trust should be lower in counties and cities where corruption is more serious. Since this is not the case, it seems that regime-based trust in China is not based on citizens' calculation of the instrumental benefits they receive from the regime.

[18] This finding contradicts some of the previous research in China, which has reported that people tend not to blame the central government for problems found among local officials.

128 · Impact on Attitudes and Behaviors

TABLE 5.3. *Effects of Individual-Level Variables on Political Trust in Mainland China*

	Incumbent-Based Trust		Regime-Based trust	
	Coefficient[a]	SE[b]	Coefficient[a]	SE[b]
Fixed components				
Intercept	1.19***	0.05	4.20***	0.02
Government performance				
Country economic situation	0.26***	0.04	0.13***	0.03
Family economic situation	−0.05	0.03	−0.02	0.02
Family members laid off	0.00	0.09	−0.10*	0.06
Corruption in local government	−1.21***	0.07	−0.16**	0.04
Corruption in central government	−0.11	0.12	−0.60***	0.11
Responsiveness of government	0.34***	0.04	0.07**	0.02
Institutional effects				
Political fear	0.02	0.04	0.03	0.02
Media access	−0.01	0.02	0.00	0.01
Grapevine rumors	−0.19***	0.04	−0.04	0.03
Party membership	−0.03	0.09	−0.01	0.05
Structural effects				
Urban	−0.01	0.10	−0.04	0.04
Education	−0.02	0.01	0.00	0.01
Gender	−0.15**	0.06	0.04	0.04
Age	0.01**	0.00	0.01***	0.00
Political cultural effects				
OTA (Reciprocal)	−0.44***	0.11	−0.03	0.06
DSI (Idiocentric)	−0.73***	0.19	−0.26**	0.12
Life satisfaction	0.10***	0.02	0.02**	0.01
Random components				
Intercept	0.23***		0.02**	
OTA (Reciprocal)	0.32**			
DSI (Idiocentric)	1.07**		0.56***	
Media	0.01**			
Responsiveness of government			0.009**	
Life satisfaction			0.003**	
Variance explained	30%		15%	

*** $p < .01$; ** $p < .05$; * $p < .1$
[a] Entries are restricted maximum likelihood unstandardized coefficients with HLM 6.06.
[b] Entries are robust standard errors.
Source: 2002 China Survey, Asian Barometer Survey I (N = 3,183).

Culture's Impact on Political Trust

By contrast, individuals' encounters with specific institutions have a limited impact on political trust. The fact that political fear had neither a positive nor a negative impact on either incumbent-based or regime-based trust reinforces the finding that our measures of political trust are not distorted by a fear factor. (See also Appendix B.) The fact that party membership has no impact on either dimension of political trust supports the idea suggested earlier that a substantial number joined the CCP not because they identify with the party's platform or ideology but because they were motivated by the instrumental benefits associated with membership. The fact that access to the regime's official media neither increased nor decreased political trust suggests that CCP propaganda has neither achieved its intended goals nor created the backlash suggested by some media scholars. It is possible, however, that without the efforts of the controlled media, people would distrust their government more than they do. There is some support for this interpretation in the table. As grapevine rumors normally carry negative news, this channel can be considered a proxy for uncontrolled media. The table shows that uncontrolled information does reduce incumbent-based trust although it has no impact on regime-based trust. The finding suggests that media control does help the regime because without it, incumbent-based political trust would further decline.

Individual socioeconomic resources have a limited impact. Neither urbanization nor education had an independent effect on either dimension of political trust. When OTA and DSI are removed from the model, however, education has a statistically significant negative impact on both dimensions of political trust. This reinforces the earlier suggestion that the mechanism by which education influences political trust is by altering the normative standards actors use to evaluate government performance.

Female respondents trusted regime agents more than males did, but there was no statistically significant gender difference in regime-based trust. Age played a significant role in shaping both dimensions of political trust. The older the respondent, the more likely he or she was to trust both government officials and the regime. Because the cultural variables were controlled in the model, the relationship between age and trust is best understood as the product of life-cycle effects, as discussed in Chapter 4. The analysis also confirms Inglehart's argument that life satisfaction has a positive impact on both dimensions of political trust.

After all other effects are taken into account, both OTA and DSI have independent effects on political trust. Reciprocal OTA makes people less likely to trust government officials but has no independent impact on regime-based political trust. Idiocentric DSI has strong negative impacts on both incumbent-based and regime-based trust. People holding the allocentric DSI are more likely to trust their government as they tend to tolerate policies that are harmful to their private interests as long as these policies are perceived as benefiting the majority in the society.

At the bottom of Table 5.3, the random components show that there are several variables whose impacts vary across counties. Some of these variables are features of the county-level environment and are reflected in the random component associated with the intercept, which is significant for both dependent variables. Others are differences in the makeup of different counties in terms of the characteristics of their individual residents and are shown in the statistically significant random components associated with the coefficients for certain individual-level variables. Since the difference across counties in regime-based trust was identified in the ANOVA model as no more than 3 percent, we know it will not be promising to unravel this puzzle using HLM.

But for incumbent-based trust, the way is open for the use of HLM. Not only did the ANOVA model show that counties vary significantly in their levels of incumbent-based trust, but the statistically significant intercept coefficient in Table 5.3 shows that a substantial proportion of this variance across counties is associated with county-level attributes. We therefore undertake in Table 5.4 an HLM analysis of the effects of county-level attributes on incumbent-based trust when the effects of individual-level determinants are also taken into account.

In order to do this, we must select on theoretical grounds certain county-level variables to test. First, government performance varies by county, which may lead to differences in people's attitudes toward government officials. For example, the level of incumbent-based trust in counties where officials are perceived as more corrupt might be lower than in counties where officials are seen as less corrupt. The level of economic development in a county may also influence the level of political trust in that county. As people still hold the government responsible for economic development, people living in developed counties might be more likely to trust government officials than people in the less developed counties.

Second, although the level of education of respondents had no impact on political trust at the individual level of analysis, the overall level of education in different counties might influence people's attitudes toward their government. There are two contradictory possibilities about how this influence might work. On the one hand, since opinion leaders are usually among the better educated, and since the cognitive capacity

Culture's Impact on Political Trust

shaped by education may help opinion leaders to become aware of problems with government officials and policy, we might expect people in more educated counties to trust the government less than people in less educated counties. On the other hand, education at the aggregate level might increase the level of political trust by opening people more thoroughly to government-directed socialization. Schoolchildren in China are told that the CCP is the only force capable of leading the country to modernization.

Such socialization may influence the views of educated people and, through them, the attitudes of less-educated people. In addition, to buy the political support of intellectuals and silence their criticism, the CCP has increased salaries and benefits for educated people and made large investments in schools of higher education. Although the long-term effects of such policies remain to be seen, scholars have identified a trend toward conservatism among educated people in China. If the regime's efforts to buy political support are successful, people in more highly educated counties should be found to trust their government more than people in less educated counties.

Finally, my theory predicts that the cultural environment in a community should have an independent impact on people's attitudes toward government. A key innovation in the analysis presented in Table 5.4 is the comparison of two different measures of culture at the county level, which aims to clarify the difference between two possible mechanisms by which the cultural environment might influence people's attitudes toward government officials. These are designated as Model I and Model II.

The population mean of cultural variables (Model I) tests the theory that the cultural environment influences individuals' choices through normative channels, especially through the influence of pervasive norms in a community on the way in which individuals decode information. If this mechanism is at work we should see a linear relationship between the prevalence of a particular value and its impact on attitudes. Model II tests the alternate theory, that the cultural environment shapes actors' choices through what I have called the external policing system of norms. As argued previously, the external policing system's ability to impose sanctions on norm violators is prone to breaking down when a group emerges that is willing and able to provide deviating norm holders with critical social support. If this mechanism is at work, we would expect to see our dependent variable affected, not by the mean level of the population's adherence to dominant norms in the community, but by the presence or absence of a minority of strongly committed deviating norm holders.

Deviating norm holders in China are those adhering to reciprocal OTA and idiocentric DSI, because as shown in Chapter 3 (Table 3.1), the mean position for the population as a whole on these two norms is hierarchical and allocentric. How big the deviating minority has to be to undermine the effectiveness of external sanctions is an empirical question to which there is no clear theoretical answer. Therefore, I did not define this threshold in advance. In this and subsequent chapters, I coded as holders of extreme reciprocal OTA or extreme idiocentric DSI those respondents who disagreed or strongly disagreed with the hierarchical answers to all three questions measuring OTA or with the allocentric answers to all three questions measuring DSI.

The section headed "County-Level Effects" in Table 5.4 shows that the cultural environment of the county does have a statistically significant impact on the propensity of county residents to express incumbent-based trust. But this is true only when the cultural environment is measured as the percentage of strongly committed deviating norm holders and not when it is measured by the county mean. That is, Model II provides a more accurate account of culture's effects on trust than does Model I.[19] The higher the percentage of holders of extreme reciprocal OTA or idiocentric DSI, the lower the level of incumbent-based trust in a county. The findings confirm H3 and H4 – cultural environments have a significant effect on incumbent-based political trust – as well as H5, which states, in effect, that when the cultural environment is relatively homogenous dominant cultural norms can effectively control people's attitudes. Along with socialization through education, the promotion of consensus on cultural norms is a key tool that the regime can use to promote trust in its officials.

Aside from culture, the only other county-level variables that influence trust are political efficacy (responsiveness of government) and the percentage of college graduates. Although statistically significant, the influence of education was small, suggesting some support for the hypothesis that higher levels of education expose residents to higher levels of regime socialization. The perceived economic situations of the country and of the respondents' families do not explain cross-county variations in incumbent-based political trust. Nor does the county-level difference in the proportion of people who perceived corruption as a serious problem.

---

[19] Although Model II is more accurate than Model I, it does not produce a higher proportion of explained variance because the substantive impact of the cultural environment on incumbent-based trust is limited, compared with the impacts of individual-level features.

Culture's Impact on Political Trust

This finding does not mean corruption has no effect on whether people trust their government because, as seen in the lower section of the table, it has an effect at the individual level: that is, persons who see corruption as a serious problem are less likely to trust the incumbents than those who do not. But apparently corruption erodes incumbent-based political trust through individual attitudes rather than via the social environment.

At the individual level, the table confirms the earlier findings about the impacts of government performance, institutional effects, and structural variables. With respect to the influence of culture at the individual level, we already knew from Table 5.3 that persons holding idiocentric and reciprocal norms were less likely to express incumbent-based trust, and this finding is replicated in Table 5.4.

Finally, the bottom section of the table, headed "Random Components," informs us that neither model fully explains the sources of incumbent-based trust. Although the hierarchical model incorporating both individual-level and county-level variables explains 46 percent of the individual-level variance instead of the 30 percent explained in Table 5.3, there remain statistically significant county-level differences that are not explained by the variables in the table. This is shown by the fact (not illustrated here) that the slopes of regression lines between allocentric DSI and incumbent-based trust are markedly different for different counties in the sample. It is also shown by the fact that the random components of both norms, as shown at the bottom of Table 5.4, are statistically significant.

The final step of the analysis is to build a full HLM model to find out why the independent variables at the individual level play different roles in different counties. The question, addressed in Table 5.5, is whether any individual-level variable played different roles in different counties. To find this out it is necessary to examine whether cross-level interactions exist for any independent variables at the individual level. In HLM, each county has its own regression equation with an intercept and a slope. Cross-level interaction is indicated by the variations just noted in the slopes of the regression lines.[20]

Due to possible problems of multi-collinearity, cross-level interaction terms can introduce instability into the model (Aiken, West, and Reno

---

[20] To identify cross-level interaction one can manipulate centering methods and error terms in the process of model fitting. For each independent variable in the model, I center them around group means and open the error term to find out whether the random component of the variable is statistically significant. For discussion, see (Raudenbush and Bryk 2002, chapter 4).

TABLE 5.4. *Hierarchical Intercept Model of Cultural Environment's Effects on Incumbent-Based Trust in Mainland China*

	Model I		Model II	
	Mean Values of OTA and DSI in Different Counties		Percentage of Strongly Committed Deviating Norm Holders[a]	
	Coefficient[b]	SE[c]	Coefficient[b]	SE[c]
Fixed components				
Intercept	1.20***	0.05	1.20***	0.05
County-level effects				
OTA (reciprocal)	−0.01	0.13	−0.01**	0.00
DSI (idiocentric)	−0.14	0.17	−0.06**	0.02
Education (percentage of college graduates)	0.01**	0.00	0.01**	0.00
Country economic situation (mean)	0.25	0.18	0.06	0.16
Family economic situation (mean)	−0.03	0.15	0.03	0.16
Corruption in local government (mean)	0.00	0.00	0.00	0.00
Corruption in central government (mean)	0.00	0.01	0.00	0.01
Responsiveness of government (mean)	0.05	0.08	0.06	0.08
Individual-level effects				
Government performance				
Country economic situation	0.25***	0.04	0.25***	0.04
Family economic situation	−0.05	0.03	−0.05	0.03
Family members laid off	0.01	0.09	0.00	0.09
Responsiveness of government	0.33***	0.04	0.33***	0.04
Institutional effects				
Political fear	0.02	0.04	0.02	0.04
Media access	−0.01	0.02	−0.01	0.02

Grapevine rumors	−0.18***	0.04	−0.18***	0.04
Party membership	−0.04	0.09	−0.04	0.09
Structural variables				
Urban	−0.03	0.11	−0.01	0.11
Education	−0.02*	0.01	−0.02*	0.01
Gender	−0.14**	0.06	−0.15**	0.06
Age	0.01**	0.00	0.01**	0.00
Political culture				
OTA (reciprocal)	−0.43***	0.11	−0.43***	0.11
DSI (idiocentric)	−0.73***	0.19	−0.74***	0.19
Life satisfaction	0.10***	0.02	0.10***	0.02
Random components				
Intercept	0.22***		0.17***	
OTA (reciprocal)	0.33**		0.32**	
DSI (idiocentric)	1.06**		1.02**	
Responsiveness of government	0.02**		0.02**	
Variance explained	46%		46%	

*** $p < .01$; ** $p < .05$; * $p < .1$

[a] Strongly committed deviating norm holders are respondents who "disagree" or "strongly disagree" with the hierarchical or allocentric position on all three questions designed to measure OTA or DSI respectively.

[b] Entries are restricted maximum likelihood unstandardized coefficients with HLM 6.06.

[c] Entries are robust standard errors.

Source: 2002 China Survey, Asian Barometer Survey I (N = 3,183).

1991). To avoid the problem, the model has to be parsimonious; only a limited number of interaction terms can be tested. To be included in the full model, the interaction term must satisfy two conditions in addition to theoretical importance: statistical significance and improved overall fit. I have selected two interaction terms to model the impact of culture on trust: county-level mean media access and county-level mean efficacy (perceived government responsiveness). The rationale is as follows.

My theory argues that the impacts of cultural norms on people's choices should be inversely correlated with information. When actors possess sufficient information about politics and government, they do not need to rely as much on cultural norms to understand the meanings and implications of government behavior. Without sufficient information, actors are more likely to project their own normative orientation onto others and assume that others follow the guidance of the same norms. Thus, the theory suggests that information on politics and governmental affairs reduces the impact of cultural norms on people's attitudes toward their government. Since the major sources of political information in China come from officially endorsed media, the impacts of cultural norms should appear to interact with media access. Thus:

H6. *The greater the access to official media in a county, the smaller the role of OTA in shaping people's attitudes toward the government.*

Similarly, my theory proposes that the cultural environment in counties where officials are perceived as more responsive will reinforce the commitment to allocentric norms of residents who hold allocentric DSI, strengthening the external policing system of norms in favor of placing trust in government officials. Thus:

H7. *Idiocentric DSI plays a smaller role in shaping people's attitudes toward government officials in counties where people are more efficacious (government is perceived as more responsive).*

Table 5.5 presents the full HLM model. The analysis confirms H6: the impact of reciprocal OTA on incumbent-based political trust is lower in counties where the level of exposure to official media is higher. When political actors have more information on politics and government, they rely less on cultural norms to formulate their attitudes toward public authority. H7 is also confirmed. The greater the mean level of political efficacy in a county, the less the impact of idiocentric DSI on incumbent-based political trust. Finally, I found that the impact of perceived government responsiveness on political trust interacts with both idiocentric DSI and

Culture's Impact on Political Trust

TABLE 5.5. *Full HLM Model of Incumbent-Based Trust with Cross-Level Interaction in Mainland China*

	Coefficient[a]	SE[b]
Fixed components		
Intercept	1.777***	0.05
County-level effects		
Country economic situation (mean)	0.084	0.16
Family economic situation (mean)	0.016	0.16
Corruption in local government (mean)	0.000	0.00
Corruption in central government (mean)	0.001	0.01
Responsiveness of government (mean)	0.071	0.08
Percentage of strong reciprocal OTA holders	−0.011**	0.00
Percentage of strong idiocentric DSI holders	−0.060**	0.02
Education (percentage of college graduates)	0.008**	0.00
Individual-level effects		
Government performance		
Country economic situation	0.234***	0.04
Family economic situation	−0.048	0.03
Family members laid off	0.001	0.09
Corruption in local government	−1.213***	0.07
Corruption in central government	−0.143	0.13
Responsiveness of government		
Intercept	0.316***	0.04
Idiocentric DSI (mean)	0.155*	0.09
Life satisfaction (percentage of people claiming satisfaction)	0.004*	0.00
Institutional effects		
Political fear	0.015	0.04
Media access	−0.008	0.02
Grapevine rumors	−0.178***	0.04
Party membership	−0.045	0.09
Structural variables		
Urban	−0.012	0.11
Education	−0.013	0.01
Gender	−0.151**	0.06
Age	0.006**	0.00
Political culture		
OTA (reciprocal)		
Intercept	−0.462***	0.12
Media access (county mean)	0.173**	0.08
DSI (idiocentric)		
Intercept	−0.812***	0.17
Political efficacy (county mean)	1.023**	0.37
Life satisfaction	0.097***	0.02

(continued)

138 Impact on Attitudes and Behaviors

TABLE 5.5. (continued)

	Coefficient[a]	SE[b]
Random components	Variance of slope explained	
Intercept		
OTA (reciprocal)	23%	
DSI (idiocentric)	16%	
Responsiveness of government	5%	

*** $p < .01$; ** $p < .05$; * $p < .01$
[a] Entries are restricted maximum likelihood unstandardized coefficients with HLM 6.06.
[b] Entries are robust standard errors.
Source: 2002 China Survey, Asian Barometer Survey I (N= 3,183).

life satisfaction: both idiocentric DSI and life satisfaction strengthened the impact of political efficacy on incumbent-based political trust.

To summarize, the analysis presented in the full model confirms that cultural norms play critical roles in shaping people's attitudes toward government. At the individual level, both reciprocal OTA and idiocentric DSI can significantly reduce regime-based and incumbent-based trust. At the group level, reciprocal OTA and idiocentric DSI can reduce the level of incumbent-based political trust. The impacts of cultural norms on political trust cannot be fully explained by changes in structure and institutions or by variations in governmental performance. Culture exerts an independent effect.

The analyses also revealed the mechanism through which cultural norms at different levels influence political trust. While OTA and DSI at the individual level shape people's attitudes toward government through their definition of normative rationality, the cultural environment influences political trust primarily through the external policing system of norms, by increasing the costs of defection. Finally, the analysis also confirms that cultural norms interact with information: cultural norms play a more important role in shaping people's attitudes toward government when people have less information.

TAIWAN AND THE ROLE OF INSTITUTIONS

The foregoing analysis confirms that OTA and DSI play critical roles in shaping people's attitudes toward authority in mainland China but leaves unanswered whether these patterns are unique to the institutional environment of mainland China. An institutionalist might argue that

Culture's Impact on Political Trust

the impacts of cultural norms on political trust revealed in China could simply reflect the communist regime's success at securing the compliance of ordinary citizens "by influencing, shaping or determining their very wants, and controlling their thoughts and desires" (Lukes 1974, 21–24). China's political culture and its impacts on political trust might be considered products of China's authoritarian institutions, reflecting patterns that do not hold in other institutional settings.

An analysis of the Taiwan case will enable us to see whether this is the case. I have already shown in Chapter 3 that despite the democratization of Taiwan's political institutions, many people in Taiwan still share common cultural norms with their compatriots in China. Chapters 3 and 4 showed that institutional changes in Taiwan between 1993 and 2002 had not brought about a cultural shift in that society as predicted by institutionalist theory.

This section will address a different question: whether cultural norms influence political attitudes in Taiwan through the same mechanisms as they do in mainland China. The analysis begins with an examination of the structure of the dependent variable, political trust, in Taiwan. Six questions were used to measure political trust in Taiwan. To find the dimensionality of political trust, I subjected the answers to these questions to an exploratory factor analysis. The results are shown in Table 5.6. Two factors emerged from the analyses – trust in the military, the police, and government in general grouped together to form one factor; and trust in the Legislative Yuan (legislature), political parties, and government officials formed another factor. The structure of political trust in Taiwan is not similar to that in mainland China or to that in other countries. Although items designed to measure regime-based trust grouped in a way similar to that found in other societies (trust in the military, police, and government in general), the two questions traditionally measuring trust in political institutions – trust in the Legislative Yuan and trust in political parties in general – grouped together with trust in government officials to form another dimension of political trust.

Why does the structure of political trust in Taiwan deviate from that in other societies? I suspect that the variation is produced by culture. Traditional Chinese culture expects public authorities to act like parental figures and take care of people's interests. The political institutions in the first group are all designed to represent the interests of all people in Taiwanese society. Institutions belonging to the second group, however, are both designed and perceived to represent special interests (this is true of government officials because they are elected as members of political

TABLE 5.6. *Exploratory Factor Analysis of Political Trust in Taiwan*

Trust Variable	Trust in State Institutions	Trust in Partisan Institutions/Agents
Trust in military	0.81	
Trust in police	0.70	
Trust in government	0.60	
Trust in Legislative Yuan		0.73
Trust in political parties		0.71
Government officials in general		0.66
Eigenvalue	2.21	1.01
Total variance explained	36.80	16.90

Source: 2002 Taiwan Survey, Asian Barometer Survey I (N = 1,415).

parties). The factor loadings suggest that people in Taiwan distinguish between political institutions that serve the common interest and political institutions that serve special interests.

To test whether OTA and DSI play the same role in shaping political trust in Taiwan as they do in mainland China, I used the same four groups of predictors in the models. Since the social structures and political institutions in the two societies differ, I removed and added some independent variables to make the models functionally equivalent in both societies. As political fear is no longer a major problem in Taiwan, that question was not included in the survey. Similarly, when the media in Taiwan became free and open after democratization, people in Taiwan became unlikely to rely on grapevine rumors to acquire political information, so that question was not asked in the survey. As a working democracy, Taiwan has two major political tendencies called Pan Blue and Pan Green. The former is organized around the Kuomintang (KMT), and the latter is organized around the Democratic Progressive Party (DPP). At the time of the 2002 survey, Pan Green was the incumbent, and Pan Blue was the challenger.[21] One can easily surmise that political trust in Taiwan

---

[21] Parties in Taiwan are divided, and often deliberately constructed, along ethnic lines. While most Pan Green supporters are "Taiwanese," having immigrated to Taiwan before 1949, Pan Blue consists in significant part of "mainlanders," those who escaped to Taiwan around or after 1949 when the KMT was defeated by the CCP in mainland China. Both parties see their struggle with the other party as zero-sum in nature. For supporters of Pan Blue, DPP victory threatens the future of the political community it identifies as consisting of the larger China. For Pan Green, KMT victory threatens its dream of establishing an independent Taiwan.

Culture's Impact on Political Trust

varies with party identification – for instance, DPP supporters would be more likely than KMT supporters to trust both the state institutions and partisan institutions/agents when their own party is in power, as it was in 2002. I created two dummies, Pan Blue and Pan Green, and used people without party affiliation as the base category in the model. Finally, since the early days of Taiwan's democratization, the DPP has used identity politics to mobilize political support. Such efforts may also have influenced people's attitudes toward authority. I added the ethnic identity of respondents to the model to test whether DPP's mobilization efforts had any impact on political trust.

As with my analysis of mainland China, I started model building for Taiwan by analyzing the individual-level determinants of both dimensions of political trust. Table 5.7 presents the results of a hierarchical OLS regression. Since they are self-explanatory, I will not discuss them in detail. The most important finding for cultural theory is that cultural norms in Taiwan play a role similar to the role they play in mainland China, despite fundamental differences in both political institutions and levels of economic development. Even after controlling for the impacts of socioeconomic resources, political institutions, and government performance, cultural norms still have an influence on political trust in Taiwan. While reciprocal OTA makes people less likely to trust both state institutions and partisan institutions/agents, idiocentric DSI has this effect with respect only to the partisan institutions/agents.

Are there also mechanisms at the group level through which culture influences trust in Taiwan? In mainland China, counties were used as the second-level unit in the hierarchical model. This was possible because the sample included a sufficient number of county-level units (more than 130) and respondents (25 to 35) in each county. The county was used as the primary sampling unit in Taiwan as well, but there are not enough counties in the sample (only 21) to allow for hierarchical modeling. There are, however, a sufficient number of secondary sampling units – electoral districts – in the Taiwan sample to construct a hierarchical model. There were more than thirty such units with more than thirty respondents each. Electoral districts in Taiwan are geographical blocks with sufficiently distinct cultural environments to allow us to assess whether the cultural environment played a role in shaping people's attitudes toward government.

Table 5.8 presents the full HLM model for political trust in Taiwan. As in mainland China, I did not find significant cross-district variation in trust in state institutions in Taiwan; therefore Table 5.8 is limited to the

142　　　　　　　　　　　　　　　　　　*Impact on Attitudes and Behaviors*

TABLE 5.7. *Effects of Individual-Level Variables on Political Trust in Taiwan*

	Trust in Partisan Institution/Agents		Trust in State Institutions	
	Coefficient[a]	SE[b]	Coefficient[a]	SE[b]
Fixed components				
Intercept	−1.30***	0.05	0.15**	0.05
Government performance				
Country economic situation	0.07**	0.03	0.02	0.04
Family economic situation	0.04	0.04	0.08**	0.04
Corruption in local government	−0.14**	0.05	−0.17**	0.06
Corruption in central government	−0.25***	0.05	−0.28***	0.06
Responsiveness of government	0.03	0.05	0.02	0.04
Institutional effects				
Media access	−0.07**	0.02	−0.02	0.02
Pan Blue	0.10	0.08	0.22**	0.09
Pan Green	−0.12	0.09	0.28**	0.11
Structural effects				
Urban	−0.28**	0.14	−0.02	0.15
Education	−0.05***	0.01	−0.02**	0.01
Gender	−0.03	0.07	−0.05	0.09
Age	0.00	0.00	0.01**	0.00
Ethnic identity	−0.04	0.05	−0.11	0.07
Political cultural effects				
DSI (Idiocentric)	−0.35**	0.14	−0.02	0.14
OTA (reciprocal)	−0.68***	0.15	−0.40**	0.14
Random components				
Intercept	0.06***		0.04**	
OTA (reciprocal)	0.15**			
Age	0.00**			
Country economic situation			0.03**	
Variance explained	30%		15%	

*** p < .01; ** p < .05; * p < .1
[a] Entries are restricted maximum likelihood unstandardized coefficients with HLM 6.06.
[b] Entries are robust standard errors.
Source: 2002 Taiwan Survey, Asian Barometer Survey I (N = 1,415).

analysis of variations in trust in partisan institutions/agents. The table shows that the cultural environment has similar impacts on both societies. I measured the cultural environment in the same way as it was measured in Model II in Table 5.5, that is, as the percentage of strongly

Culture's Impact on Political Trust

TABLE 5.8. *Full HLM Model for Trust in Partisan Institutions/Agents in Taiwan*

	Coefficient[a]	SE[b]
Fixed components		
Intercept	−1.300***	0.04
County-level effects		
Country economic situation (mean)	−0.226**	0.11
Family economic situation (mean)	0.320	0.24
Corruption in local government (mean)	0.000	0.00
Corruption in central government (mean)	−0.001	0.00
Responsiveness of government (mean)	0.569**	0.17
Percentage of strongly committed deviating OTA holders[c]	−0.001	0.00
Percentage of strongly committed deviating DSI holders[c]	−0.014**	0.00
Education (percentage of college graduates)	−0.001	0.00
Individual-level effects		
Government performance		
Country economic situation	0.078**	0.04
Family economic situation	0.039	0.04
Corruption in local government	−0.140**	0.05
Corruption in central government	−0.255***	0.05
Responsiveness of government	0.016	0.05
Institutional effects		
Media access	−0.064**	0.02
KMT membership	0.081	0.08
DPP membership	−0.111	0.09
Structural variables		
Urban	−0.230	0.14
Education	−0.040***	0.01
Gender	−0.054	0.07
Age	0.005*	0.00
Ethnic identity	−0.043	0.05
Political culture		
OTA (reciprocal)		
Intercept	−0.704***	0.15
Media access (county mean)	−0.182	0.24
DSI (allocentric)	−0.308**	0.14

*** $p < .01$; ** $p < .05$; * $p < .1$

[a] Entries are restricted maximum likelihood unstandardized coefficients with HLM 6.06.

[b] Entries are robust standard errors.

[c] Strongly committed deviating norm holders are respondents who "disagree" or "strongly disagree" with the hierarchical or allocentric position on all three questions designed to measure OTA or DSI, respectively.

Source: 2002 Taiwan Survey, Asian Barometer Survey I (N = 1,415).

committed deviating norm holders. After accounting for the impact of individual-level variables, government performance, and structural and institutional differences at the group level, an idiocentric environment defined in this way still had a statistically significant impact on trust in partisan institutions/agents. The higher the district's percentage of strongly committed holders of idiocentric DSI, the less likely people were to trust partisan institution/agents.

Unlike in mainland China, however, the hierarchical environment in Taiwan did not have a statistically significant impact on people's attitudes toward partisan institutions and government officials, despite the substantial number of people there still subscribing to hierarchical OTA. Orientation toward authority plays a significant role in shaping people's attitudes at the individual level but has no significance on the county level. This finding echoes my argument in Chapter 4 that cultural shifts may not be linearly associated with the distribution of alternative cultural norms in a community. Slight changes in the distribution of various cultural norms in a community may result in the collapse of the dominant culture's external policing system. When that happens, a cultural shift occurs in the society. Although hierarchical OTA at the individual level can still influence people's attitudes toward political institutions, the hierarchical environment has lost its ability to do likewise.

CONCLUSION

The findings in this chapter reinforce the point that current theories of cultural change, which concentrate on changes in the distribution of cultural norms in a society, do not fully capture the process of cultural change. As revealed in the empirical analyses of Taiwan, a small change in the distribution of cultural norms in a community can destroy the cultural environment's impacts on people's choices, even while cultural norms at the individual level continue to influence people's behavior. In order to study cultural shifts, students of political culture should examine not only changes of cultural norms at the individual level and changes in the impacts of those norms at the individual level but also changes in cultures' external policing systems, since their collapse can mark the beginning of a cultural shift.

This finding also helps us understand the dynamic of East Asian authoritarianism in general and authoritarian resilience in mainland China in particular. As dominant cultures in East Asia define the relationship with authority differently from Western cultures, people under the

Culture's Impact on Political Trust

influence of these cultures would (1) hold different expectations toward their governments and (2) use different standards to evaluate government performance. A large number of people in East Asia still believe their relationship with authority should be hierarchical and that individuals are obligated to sacrifice their personal interests to collective ones. This means that their level of tolerance for the government could be higher than that in parts of the world where different norms prevail. They trust their government more and are less likely to withdraw political support at any given threshold of dissatisfaction. The political trust shaped by culture, I would argue, constitutes a critical reserve of support that East Asian regimes can draw on if their performance flags. This suggests that democratic transitions and regime changes should be less likely to occur in societies under the influences of hierarchical OTA and allocentric DSI; the strength of these norms helps to diffuse pressure from society.

The prevalence of these cultural norms can also help to explain other Chinese puzzles: the tendency of the newly emerging bourgeoisie and deputies to the local and national-level people's congresses to identify with the regime rather than trying to challenge the authorities, and the responsiveness of village officials in some places to their people even without democracy.

Finally, if and when democratic transitions occur, culture in East Asia may have a positive impact on democratic consolidation. Traditional culture – which requires people to defer important decisions to political leaders and consider their interests in line with those of society – could significantly ease the pressure on a newly established democratic regime by providing critical "breathing space" for consolidating power while making the necessary changes from authoritarianism to democracy.

Even if people become dissatisfied with a new government's policy, cultural norms compel them to give political leaders the benefit of doubt, rather than quickly withdraw political support. Since the cultural norms give both authoritarian and democratic leaders more space and freedom to maneuver, the same cultural variable can explain why democratic transition in this region is rarely propelled by popular forces but is instead brought about primarily by elites. It can also explain why, once democratic transition has occurred, no democratic reversal has occurred in this region.

Of course, such cultural norms also pose a special danger to a newly democratizing regime. In the absence of cultural shifts toward more reciprocal and idiocentric norms, elites may face relatively little popular resistance if they turn the clock back and reinstall an authoritarian government.

In this case, traditional cultural norms would also make people tolerate such a change. For these reasons, I agree with the statement made by Almond and Verba that "the development of a stable and effective democratic government depends upon the orientations that people have to the political process" (Almond and Verba 1963, 498). Nonetheless, the mechanism by which culture influences political stability, identified by my theory, is different from that specified by Almond and Verba more than half a century ago.

6

Cultural Impacts on Political Participation

Previous research on political participation, like that on political trust discussed in Chapter 5, focused on the instrumental rationality of political actors. Following the work of Anthony Downs, scholars have theorized that the decision to participate in politics is shaped primarily by a cost-benefit calculation: actors participate if they expect that the benefits of participation will exceed the costs (Downs 1957). This has led students to concentrate on variables such as education, income, occupation, political interest, and efficacy, which can reduce the costs and/or increase the perceived benefits of participation. Empirical research based on data from the United States and other Western countries confirms that these sociological and psychological variables significantly influence the likelihood that people will participate in politics (Verba and Nie 1972).

When applying sociological and psychological models to the study of political participation in different countries, however, scholars have found that the explanatory power of socioeconomic status and psychological resources varies from country to country. To explain this Verba, Nie, and Kim sought to explore the effect of institutions (defined as political parties and voluntary associations) in mobilizing or demobilizing people for participation. Institutions, they surmised, could affect actors' ability to convert sociological and psychological resources into political activities. Institutions can mobilize political activities (for example, by exposing people to politically relevant stimuli, such as discussions about politics or social issues); provide opportunities for political activities (developing skills and expectations that can be generalized to political activities); and sometimes centralize control over the channels of political activities

148 *Impact on Attitudes and Behaviors*

such that unaffiliated persons cannot participate (Verba, Nie, and Kim 1978, 81).

Since institutions in different societies affect participation in different ways, the impacts of socioeconomic status on participation vary from country to country (Verba et al. 1978, 80). Empirical evidence from surveys conducted in seven countries confirms that political parties and voluntary associations do interact with sociological resources to influence people's decisions to participate in politics.

What puzzles students of comparative politics, though, is that even when the effects of institutional differences are taken into account, there are still major cross-national variations in the impacts of sociological and psychological variables. For one thing, dramatic increases in the general level of education in the West failed to produce similarly dramatic increases in participation in those societies. Moreover, socioeconomic status has little impact on the level of participation in Japan, despite the similar, if not identical, nature of the regimes and in patterns of institutional involvement in Japan and other, Western democracies (Flanagan et al. 1991). Similarly, social resources such as education and income in Taiwan were found to have little impact on people's propensity to vote (Shyu 2009).

Some scholars attribute these variations to political culture. Most studies of cultural impacts on political participation, following the pioneering work of Almond and Verba, characterize culture as a combination of political interest, efficacy, information, and civic orientation. These variables, they argue, can have significant impacts on people's political behavior (Campbell et al. 1960; Milbrath and Goel 1982; Verba and Nie 1972; Verba et al. 1978, 1993; Verba, Schlozman, and Brady 1995; Wolfinger and Rosenstone 1980). Although it is true that instrumental cost-benefit calculations can play a critical role in shaping people's participation, I argue that culturally defined normative rationality plays an equally, if not more, important role. Understanding its impacts is vital to an accurate understanding of the process by which people become politicized to participate in politics.[1]

---

[1] Culture also plays a role in Downs's argument. He used normative rationality to explain the "paradox of voting." Because a single vote cannot change the results of an election, the benefits of voting can never exceed the costs of voting based on instrumental interest calculation. To resolve this problem, Downs introduced the concept of nonmaterial expressive interests. That is, people may choose to vote to show their support to a democratic system or because they want to avoid being blamed by other people (Downs 1957).

Cultural Impacts on Political Participation

Unlike theories that assess how cultural variables increase the perceived benefits and reduce the costs associated with participatory activities, my theory investigates how culture influences participation by *defining* the costs and benefits of actions. Rather than simply influencing whether an actor participates, norms as defined by culture influence the whole process by which people respond to outside stimuli. In this process, as discussed in Chapter 1, actors need to make three decisions. First they need to decode information to understand its meaning and implications and assign responsibility. Unless they hold the government responsible for dealing with a problem, they would not think of responding by participating in politics. Second, actors need to decide how to respond – they may choose "voice" (participation) or "exit" (trying to avoid the problem) (Hirschman 1970). Third, if actors decide to use "voice," they must choose a particular political act to express their opinion. This chapter explores the impacts of cultural norms on each of these decisions.

THE CULTURAL THEORY OF POLITICAL PARTICIPATION AND THE CHINESE CASE

Prominent theories of political participation usually assume, albeit implicitly, that political actors all use the same standards to evaluate government performance and to define political goals and actions. My theory instead argues that the standards individuals use for these purposes differ in a systematic way for people holding different norms. Building on the theory developed in Chapter 2, I expect culture to influence participation in the following ways. First, norms define the proper role of government and thus shape people's expectations toward authority and standards for evaluating performance and behavior. For example, when state-owned enterprise (SOE) reforms cause people to lose their jobs, the policy may be decoded in different ways depending upon one's definition of self-interest. Those influenced by the allocentric definition may deem the policy legitimate, even though they may lose their jobs, as long as it can benefit the society as a whole in the long run. People holding the idiocentric definition, on the other hand, may oppose the policy on the grounds that it jeopardizes their private interest. A survey by Wenfang Tang revealed that people in Shenyang who lost their jobs due to SOE reform responded to the policy in different ways: some cursed the reform and the government, while others said they supported the policy even if it had deprived them of their jobs (Tang 2005). Similarly, people holding different orientations toward authority hold government responsible for different issues. As a general rule, people with a hierarchical orientation consider their government responsible for a broader array of issues than those defined by reciprocal orientation.

Second, culture defines the goals actors can pursue in their responses to government. Students of political participation typically assume that a person will participate in politics if he or she has the resources and ability to link a personal need to government policy. My theory argues, however, that even when people's material interests are jeopardized by the government and they have the sociological and psychological resources to participate in politics, their cultural norms may deny them the normative authorization to do so. For example, allocentric DSI does not give the laid-off SOE worker the option of pursuing the goal of opposing the reform policy. The exception is when government officials are found to have promoted a policy for personal gain, but even then the main purpose of political participation is to convey society's desires to the government, rather than press for policy change per se. The guidance provided by idiocentric DSI does give the worker the option of pressing for policy change and, if the government fails to respond favorably, to oppose the government and to seek its replacement.

Finally, cultural norms define the legitimate means people can choose to pursue their goals under different situations. An actor may choose to make an appeal to government officials, reach up the ladder of the bureaucracy to persuade higher level officials to intervene on his or her behalf, contact the media to expose the wrongdoings of local officials, or engage in unconventional political acts to protest. For rational choice theorists, the reason actors chose one action and avoid another lies purely in resources (Verba et al. 1995). While I do not deny that resources matter, I argue that culture plays an equally, if not more, important role in shaping such decisions.

The dramatic changes in China between our two surveys in 1993 and in 2002 provide a rare opportunity to demonstrate culture's independent impacts on political participation. As noted in Chapter 1, many scholars who agree that culture has some influence over people's political behavior argue that these impacts are endogenous to social structure and/or political institutions. They believe that when society modernizes or institutions change, culture adjusts, so that its impact on behavior merely transmits the causal effects of structure or institutions rather than exerting an independent effect. To establish the plausibility of my theory, I need to show that culture can influence people's participatory behavior independently of the influence of structure and institutions.

Cultural Impacts on Political Participation

I showed in Chapter 4 that dramatic changes in China and Taiwan between 1993 and 2002 had limited impacts on the distribution of cultural norms in the two societies. This rules out the hypothesis that cultural norms quickly adapt to changing circumstances. But even if the distribution of norms in a society remains relatively stable, structural and institutional changes might alter the functioning of either the internal policing system of norms or the external policing system of norms (Chapter 4). Changes of the type Eckstein called pattern-maintaining change and cultural flexibility might occur even if the distribution of norms changes little. Such a finding would show that cultural forces are, after all, endogenous to social and political forces as causes of action.

The situation in China constitutes a nearly perfect quasi-experimental setting for examining these issues. Between 1993 and 2002, both social structures and institutions underwent dramatic changes while culture remained stable. If cultural impacts on political participation are endogenous to structures and/or institutions as those theories assume, the impacts on participation should vary significantly, or even vanish, between the two surveys. Alternatively, if structure and institutions have undergone a dramatic change, but cultural impacts on political participation remain stable, this would strengthen my theory that culture is exogenous to institutions and structure and has independent impacts on political behavior.[2]

In both the 1993 and 2002 surveys, respondents were asked to report their engagement in both electoral and non-electoral participatory activities. I decided to exclude electoral participation from my inquiry for three reasons. First, electoral participation, especially voting, requires less initiative from participants than non-electoral participation, as asserted by Verba and Nie: "A voter does not choose the agenda; he doesn't choose the issues that divide the candidates, nor does he usually have much voice in choosing the candidates themselves" (Verba and Nie 1972, 106). Second, mobilization often plays an important role in shaping people's decisions to vote, creating a causal pathway to participation that is different from

---

[2] One of the major effects of institutions on participation is that institutions shape the means available for people to participate in politics in different societies. Because mainlanders cannot vote for national leaders, but people in Taiwan enjoy that right, the means available for mainlanders to participate in politics are different from those in Taiwan. Thus, including Taiwan in the study would create an irresolvable problem in the comparison: if we found, for example, that people in Taiwan were less active in, say, appeals than people in mainland China, we would not know whether the difference was caused by culture, structure, or institutions. To avoid such complications, I decided to rely on data collected from China to test the cultural theory of political participation.

152   *Impact on Attitudes and Behaviors*

the one I wish to investigate here (Rosenstone and Hansen 1993). Third, the development of electoral reform is uneven in China. Although most rural residents can choose village officials through competitive elections, urban dwellers still do not enjoy that right, so many of the subjects in my data set have no voting opportunity to report. Given these considerations, I decided to concentrate my inquiry on non-electoral participatory activities.

Table 6.1 presents the percentage of people who reported participating in a variety of political acts in 1993 and 2002. The table also shows the difference and rate of change for each item between the two surveys. Despite increases both in people's need for government help during a time of turbulent reform and in their resources for participation as a consequence of economic growth and social development, the level of participation declined in most categories. There was some increase in participatory activities directed to levels beyond the work unit or community (the people's congresses, newspapers, and complaint bureaus), but this was outbalanced by declines in participation within the grassroots unit.

To identify the role of cultural factors in this decline requires analysis of the whole process by which actors become politicized and participate in politics. Political scientists have traditionally been concerned only with the final decision made by political actors to participate or not. However, as suggested above, actors actually make three related decisions leading up to the act of participation. In the analysis that follows I seek to tease out the impacts of social structure, institutions, and culture on each of these decisions. First I examine the impact of culture on perceived government salience, that is, the likelihood people will see the government as relevant to problems they encounter. The second step is to explore the impact of culture on the likelihood that people will participate. Finally, I examine if and how cultural norms influence people's choices of political acts and goals by prescribing some participatory activities and proscribing others.

IMPACTS OF CULTURE ON PERCEIVED
GOVERNMENT SALIENCE

Perceived government salience for our purposes can be defined as the propensity for political actors to hold government responsible for solving the problems they encounter. Culture fundamentally shapes this decision. Even if a problem is caused, or could be solved, by a government policy, actors under the influence of certain norms may not hold the government

Cultural Impacts on Political Participation

TABLE 6.1. *Non-Electoral Participation in Mainland China*

Reported Political Act	1993		2002		Difference	Rate of Change
	Percent	N[a]	Percent	N[a]		
Contacted unit leader	39.9	1,361	30.9	983	−9.0%	−22.6%
Asked other leaders in the same unit to intervene	15.1	498	9.4	299	−5.7%	−37.7%
Sought help from those who could persuade leader	11.8	387	9.3	297	−2.5%	−21.2%
Complained to higher authority	12.7	419	9.5	303	−3.2%	−25.2%
Complained through various political organizations	2.3	76	2.1	66	−0.2%	−8.7%
Complained through People's Congress	2.7	88	2.8	89	0.1%	3.7%
Wrote letter to appropriate government office	3.7	121	2.9	91	−0.8%	−21.6%
Wrote letter to newspaper	0.8	28	1.1	37	0.3%	37.5%
Reported to a complaint bureau	1.3	41	1.4	44	0.1%	7.7%
Carried out a work slowdown	2.2	71	2.1	67	−0.1%	−4.5%
Organized colleagues to resist leadership's demands	3.6	119	2.9	91	−0.7%	−19.4%
Harassed the leader	1.4	46	0.8	24	−0.6%	−42.9%
Demonstration/ sit-in	0.1	5	0.2	8	0.1%	100.0%

[a] The raw frequencies in N columns do not add up to the sample sizes due to missing values.

Source: 1993 Survey of Political Culture and Political Participation in Mainland China, Taiwan, and Hong Kong; 2002 China Survey, Asian Barometer Survey I (1993 N = 3,287; 2002 N = 3,183). Data are weighted.

responsible for it. Alternatively, an actor can hold the government responsible for solving a problem that has nothing to do with government policy. For example, when an SOE employee is laid off, he can assign blame for his misfortune variously: he could blame himself, his manager in the enterprise, the local or central government, the CCP, and/or the political system. Only if the employee sees some level of government as responsible for the problem is he likely to think of participating in politics to get it solved.

Conventional theories of political participation presume that variations in perceived government salience are due to differences in citizens' socioeconomic and psychological resources (Goel 1975; Huntington 1968; Nie et al. 1969a, 1969b). Citizens are portrayed as knowledgeable, or not knowledgeable, about the impact of government on their daily lives and attentive or inattentive to government, depending on their cognitive capacity, political interest, and sociological resources.

But cultural norms also play an important role. Cultural definitions of the relationship between individuals and authority serve as a yardstick for assessing the government's responsibility for solving problems. Reciprocal OTA defines the government as an institution run by staff hired to manage public affairs. I hypothesize that people holding the norm of reciprocal OTA will resist governmental attempts to intrude on issues outside the explicitly public domain. Where hierarchical OTA is widespread, as in China, however, people consider the government to be the guardian of the people and as such responsible for a broad array of issues. Until the 1980s, for example, when a married couple could not resolve their conflicts, the neighborhood committee, trade union, or village committee was expected to send a representative to mediate. Another example is the one-child policy, under which government dictates how many children a couple can have. Under the influence of hierarchical OTA such an infringement on people's private lives is viewed as legitimate because of the claim that having too many children creates an extra burden for society.

Students of Chinese politics often argue that hierarchical OTA breeds dependency on the government and political passivity. This conceptualization is simplistic. Although it is true that hierarchical OTA creates a degree of dependency on government, rather than making people politically passive, it can actually make them more demanding. People under the influence of hierarchical OTA hold their government responsible for a much broader array of issues than those who subscribe to reciprocal OTA. As result, the government's failure to intervene on social issues may

Cultural Impacts on Political Participation

trigger people's political participation to demand that the government take responsibility. In addition, culture plays a role in helping people interpret political information. While reciprocal OTA holders assume that government officials will not protect people's private interests unless they are forced to do so by proper institutional constraints, hierarchical OTA leads people to expect that government officials want to take care of people's interests and that if they fail to do so it is because they are not aware of what the people need. Thus, we have:

H1. *People under the influence of hierarchical OTA hold government responsible for a broader array of issues than do people with reciprocal OTA.*

Idiocentric DSI provides people with the normative authority to blame their government if and when government policies jeopardize their interests. Since governments can never satisfy everyone's interests simultaneously, we should find that people with idiocentric DSI are more likely to express dissatisfaction with their government. Allocentric DSI, by contrast, deprives people of the normative authority to blame the government as long as government can claim its policies benefit a collective group with which the individual identifies. In interpreting government officials' motivations, citizens will commonly project their own values onto government actors. Those with allocentric DSI are likely to assume that government policies are motivated by collective interests, further depriving norm holders of the normative authority to blame government. Together, this leads to:

H2. *People holding idiocentric DSI are more likely than those holding allocentric DSI to hold government responsible for their problems.*

I explored the plausibility of these arguments in face-to-face interviews with workers in a Beijing factory during the severe acute respiratory syndrome (SARS) outbreak that took place 2002–3. Some respondents held the government responsible for the spread of the virus because it had withheld critical information from the public and believed it had done so for self-serving reasons – to guarantee the success of the annual National People's Congress meeting. But others believed the government had handled the situation correctly, acting so as to protect the country's economic development. When I pointed out to the latter that the government's decision to hold back information had led to a larger outbreak, they defended the government, arguing that it had wanted to prevent unnecessary panic. One middle-aged worker argued: "If the government revealed information prematurely, foreign investors might have withdrawn from China.

What if it was a false alarm? Our country's economic development would have been jeopardized unnecessarily."[3] When I asked them what would have happened if they themselves had been infected, they replied that the government would have told them about the disease if necessary.

This second group of workers based their responses on two assumptions: (1) the government would take care of its people, so critical decisions could be deferred to it with confidence and (2) collective interests are more important than individual ones, and the government's decision to withhold information must be aimed at protecting the public interest. Whereas the first assumption is shaped by hierarchical OTA, the second is shaped by allocentric DSI. Since the motivations of policy makers could not be directly observed, the respondents projected their cultural norms onto government officials and assumed they were following the same guidance.

To demonstrate this effect of culture empirically, I tested whether the norms, OTA and DSI, had statistically significant impacts on the likelihood that people would consider the government responsible for helping them with an issue. In both the 1993 and 2002 surveys, interviewers were asked to read the following statement to respondents:

People sometimes need leaders' help when they run into personal or family problems, or if they disagree with a certain policy, or are dissatisfied with the unfairness with which a policy is implemented, or encounter cases of abuse of power by a particular leader.

Interviewers then asked respondents whether they had encountered any such problems during the three years prior to the survey. I classified those who said "yes" as showing an awareness of government's salience. This variable, labeled "government salience," differentiates those who reported having no problem needing government help (coded as 0) and those who reported having a problem needing government help (coded as 1). In 1993, 28.2 percent of respondents reported that they had not had any problems that required government intervention, and in 2002 that percentage dropped to 3.2 percent.[4]

---

[3] Respondent No. 7, a truck driver in his late fifties working in Beijing.

[4] Because previous analyses had already demonstrated that the distribution of cultural norms during the same period of time remained stable, this change cannot be attributed to cultural shifts in the society. Instead, the finding seems to confirm Huntington's theory that economic development enlarges the scope of government activities and enriches the sociological and psychological resources for people in a society so that they become more aware of the relevance of government policies to their private lives.

Cultural Impacts on Political Participation

The same four clusters of individual-level variables that I used in Chapter 5 – with some adjustments to account for standard theoretical expectations about the determinants of participation – are used in this chapter to predict dependent variables, beginning in this section with government salience. The first cluster of independent and control variables groups the sociological resources of education, income, urban residence, and gender. Education increases people's cognitive skills, which help them to understand and work with complex and abstract subjects. Schooling also imparts experience with a variety of bureaucratic relationships through processes such as learning requirements, filling out forms, waiting in lines, and meeting deadlines (Wolfinger and Rosenstone 1980). In short, education provides people with the skills necessary to process political information, link their problems to public authority, and calculate the costs and benefits of participation. Education was measured by years of formal schooling. Income is thought to be correlated with both the motives and the capabilities for participating in politics (Nie, Powell, and Prewitt 1969a, 373; Wolfinger and Rosenstone 1980). Income was measured by respondents' total family incomes. Urban residence may increase participation because the relationship between individuals and the government in urban areas is more intense and multifaceted than in rural areas, especially in China where, until the reform era, people working in urban enterprises were socially, economically, and politically dependent on their government-run work units.[5] Urban residence was measured by the respondent's type of household registration. Age and age squared were also included in the model to assess both the linear and the curvilinear relationships between age and participation.

The second cluster of variables assesses the psychological resources of respondents: this includes political interest and internal and external efficacy. People who are interested in politics pay more attention to government activities and would thus be more likely to understand problems as a function of government policies. Political interest can reduce the costs and increase the perceived benefits of political participation. Political interest was measured by the question "How interested are you in political and governmental affairs? Would you say you are very interested, somewhat interested, not very interested, or not interested at all?" Responses were coded from 4 (very interested) down to 1 (not interested at all).

Political efficacy, as discussed in Chapter 5, refers to a person's self-perceived ability to understand and influence politics and government.

---

[5] According to Walder, this involved wages as well as other social and economic needs: health insurance, medical care, pensions, housing, loans, and education. See Walder (1986).

Internal efficacy refers to a belief in one's own ability to understand and participate in politics, and external efficacy refers to the belief in the government's responsiveness to citizens' demands (Abramson and Aldrich 1982). Those who are internally and externally efficacious are expected to be more likely to call on government for help in resolving their problems. The two dimensions of efficacy were measured with widely used questionnaire items. To assess internal efficacy respondents were asked whether they agreed or disagreed with the following three statements:

- I think I understand major political problems facing our country well.
- Politics and government are too complicated for a person like me to understand.
- I consider myself capable of participating in politics.

People who agreed with the first and third questions and disagreed with the second were considered internally efficacious.

For external efficacy, respondents were asked whether they agreed or disagreed with the following statements:

- Government officials don't care much about what people like me think.
- In our country, people have many ways to influence government decisions.
- People like me do not have any right to speak about government policy.

People who agreed with the second question and disagreed with the first and third were considered externally efficacious. Factor analysis confirmed that the internal and external efficacy batteries measure separate dimensions of efficacy in China, as they do elsewhere. The indexes are created by adding the number of efficacious answers given in each battery.

The third cluster of variables measured the effects of institutions, focusing on the regime's suppression of dissent and control of information. Conventional wisdom holds that regime suppression makes people retreat to their private lives and avoid political activity. A plausible alternative view, however, is that repression generates resentment so that people are more likely to hold government responsible for problems. I used the index of political fear described in Chapter 5 to test for the impact of regime suppression. I used the measure of exposure to official media described in the same chapter to see whether praise of the CCP in official media may raise people's expectations of the government's competency

Cultural Impacts on Political Participation

and their general expectations of government, such that they are more likely to hold government responsible for a wider range of problems. To measure the impact of unofficial information sources, I use the index of grapevine rumors, also described in Chapter 5.

The fourth cluster of individual-level variables consists of the IRT scores of the two cultural norms (see Chapter 3).

I was also interested in seeing whether variation in the cultural environment at the county level had an effect on perceived government salience. If so, this effect would have to be measured using hierarchical linear modeling (HLM, see Chapter 5). I first used a hierarchical ANOVA model to determine whether there was enough cross-county variation in government salience to warrant the use of HLM. The results of that analysis, presented in Appendix E, Table E.1, indicated that the average government salience is near zero in some counties, but in other counties nearly everyone holds government responsible for their problems. The finding of significant cross-county variation confirms that HLM can be used to examine how culture impacts perceived government salience at the county level.

Table 6.2 displays the results of the HLM analysis.[6] Model I on the left side of the table looks only at individual-level effects.[7] Model II on the right side adds the county-level analysis.[8]

---

[6] I chose an intercept model because none of the random components of independent variables were found to be statistically significant, which indicates that no cross-level interaction was found.

[7] Since multistage PPS sampling was used in the survey, the traditional estimation technique, which assumes simple random sampling (SRS) as the data-generating mechanism, would tend to underestimate the standard errors (SEs) of regression coefficients. Such an underestimation may lead researchers to reach overoptimistic conclusions about the explanatory power of independent variables in the model. See among others Lee and Forthofer (2006); Lehtonen and Pahkinen (1995); and Skinner, Holt, and Smith (1989). To avoid this problem, I used SVY commands in STATA to incorporate complex sampling information when estimating standard errors of the independent variables. Following the specification of SVY commands in STATA, I included sampling information like the IDs of strata, PSUs, SSUs, and TSUs, as well as finite population correction (FPC) for each stage of sampling. Due to serious missing data problems for some SSUs, only IDs of strata and PSUs (as well as FPC for sampling at that stage), were included in the final analysis. I tried both linearization and jackknife methods for estimating standard errors, and they gave similar results. Sub-population command was also used to specify the domain of interest for the following analysis. For more information on technical issues, see Korn and Graubard (1999) and STATA manual for SVY commands. The results of the analysis were basically the same.

[8] In Model II, rather than using the proportion of extreme deviating norm holders to represent the cultural environment as I did in Tables 5.5 and 5.8, I used the mean values of the cultural variables at the county level. The mean value is a more appropriate measure when theory suggests that culture influences people's choices through information. The proportion of extreme deviating norm holders is the more appropriate measure when theory holds that the influence is exerted through culture's external policing system.

TABLE 6.2. *Cultural Impacts on Government Salience in Mainland China*

| | Model I | | Model II | |
| | Individual-Level Variables Only | | County-Level Intercept Effects | |
	Coefficient[a]	SE[b]	Coefficient[a]	SE[b]
Fixed components				
Intercept	1.553***	0.166	1.568***	0.166
County-level effects				
OTA (reciprocal)			−0.041**	0.020
DSI (idiocentric)			−0.017	0.013
Education			0.009	0.017
Individual-level effects				
Cultural norms				
OTA (reciprocal)	−0.557	0.357	−0.549	0.357
DSI (idiocentric)	1.824*	0.930	1.844**	0.932
Sociological resources				
Education	0.031*	0.018	0.031*	0.018
Income	0.000	0.000	0.000	0.000
Urban	0.305*	0.181	0.331*	0.183
Male	0.475***	0.113	0.476***	0.114
Age	0.066***	0.017	0.066***	0.017
Age squared	−0.001***	0.000	−0.001***	0.000
Psychological resources				
Political interest	−0.056	0.079	−0.054	0.079
External efficacy	−0.044*	0.026	−0.045*	0.026
Internal efficacy	0.012	0.032	0.011	0.032
Institutional effects				
Political fear	0.027	0.055	0.030	0.056
Media exposure	0.046*	0.026	0.046*	0.026
Access to grapevine rumors	0.295***	0.076	0.296***	0.077
Random components				
Intercept	3.242***		3.256***	

*** p < .01; ** p < .05; * p < .1
[a] Entries are restricted maximum likelihood unstandardized coefficients with HLM 6.06.
[b] Entries are robust standard errors.
Source: 1993 Survey of Political Culture and Political Participation in Mainland China, Taiwan, and Hong Kong (N = 3,287).

Cultural Impacts on Political Participation

In both models, most of the variables specified by social resource theory have statistically significant impacts. Better educated persons and those possessing urban household registration were more likely than their less educated or rural counterparts to hold the government responsible for problems they encountered. Males were more likely than females to hold government responsible. The relationship between age and government salience appears to be curvilinear – middle-aged people were more likely to hold the government responsible for their problems than either the young or the old.[9] This finding confirms the well-documented start-up and slowdown effects of age on political participation (Wolfinger and Rosenstone 1980). That is, younger people are usually busy with other activities and are less likely to be concerned about, or get involved in, politics; older people tend to gradually retreat from public life. Middle-aged people, however, are responsible for the issues facing their families and are more likely to attribute problems to their government. Income made no difference in government salience – the rich were no more or less likely to blame the government than the poor. The findings confirm that sociological resources play a critical role in raising government salience, which is a precondition for political participation.

The relationship between psychological resources and government salience seems counterintuitive. While political interest and internal efficacy had no impact on government salience, external efficacy made people less likely to look to government for solutions to their problems. This may be because people who see government as responsive to their demands believe that government has already done what it could to address their problems. Two of the three institutional variables had a significant impact on government salience. Access to both official and unofficial information made people more likely to view government as salient to their problems. Official media may foster the expectation that the government is an omnipotent force capable of solving any and every kind of problem, whereas information from unofficial channels may encourage people to blame government for problems. Political fear does not seem to prevent people from holding government responsible.

With all these variables accounted for, the table shows that cultural norms have statistically significant independent impacts on government salience. Idiocentric DSI at the individual level makes people more likely to hold government responsible for their problems. This finding confirms

---

[9] The curvilinear effect is captured by the statistically significant coefficients on both the variable "age" and its quadratic form, "age squared."

162   *Impact on Attitudes and Behaviors*

TABLE 6.3. *Comparing the Effects of Culture and Education on Government Salience in Mainland China*

Probability if Respondents Belong to	Marginal Effects	Differences between	
		Two Adjacent Categories	Lowest and Highest Categories
County-level effects			
OTA (reciprocal)			
Most hierarchically oriented counties	0.884		
Mean	0.872	−0.005	
Most reciprocally oriented counties	0.660	21.220	22.360
Individual-level effects			
DSI (idiocentric)			
Most allocentrically oriented people	0.832		
Mean	0.886	0.054	
Most idiocentrically oriented people	0.945	0.059	0.113
Education			
Illiterates	0.884		
Mean	0.901	0.017	
College graduates	0.933	0.033	0.050

Source: 1993 Survey on Political Culture and Political Participation in Mainland China, Taiwan, and Hong Kong (N = 3,287).

H2. Although OTA does not have a statistically significant impact at the individual level, its impact emerges at the county level in Model II. In an environment dominated by hierarchical norms, people are more likely to hold government responsible for a broader array of issues than in a place where reciprocal OTA is more influential. This confirms H1.

I also included the mean years of education for each county in Model II, to see whether a higher overall level of education in a community would increase the likelihood that people would perceive government as having an impact on their lives. This variable did not have a statistically significant impact.

Table 6.3 helps clarify the meaning of the coefficients in Table 6.2. The entries in Table 6.2 are unstandardized coefficients from a logit model. They represent the logged odds of the dependent variable for a one-unit change in the independent variable. For example, the coefficient of

Cultural Impacts on Political Participation

idiocentric DSI is 1.824, which means that one unit change in idiocentric DSI increases the logged odds of government salience by 1.824. Such a result has little intuitive meaning. It does not tell us whether idiocentric DSI plays a more or less important role than other variables in shaping government salience. To compare the impacts of my two cultural variables with that of education, Table 6.3 converts the coefficients of these variables from logged odds to probabilities. For each variable the table displays three values – people or counties with the highest and lowest scores of each independent variable, and people or counties in the middle (the mean value).[10]

The table shows that cultural norms play a more important role than years of education in shaping how people perceive government salience. The mean value of education for the Chinese population in 1993 was 5.81 years (primary-school level). People with only primary school education were 1.7 percent more likely than illiterates to attribute their problems to the government. College graduates were 3.3 percent more likely than people with only primary school education to hold government responsible. If we compare college graduates to illiterates, the difference is 5 percent.

By contrast, people holding the highest value of idiocentric DSI were 5.4 percent less likely than people holding the mean value of DSI to attribute their problems to the government, and people holding the highest level of allocentric DSI were 5.9 percent more likely than people holding mean values of DSI to perceive government as salient. If we compare those holding extreme values of allocentric DSI to people holding extreme values of idiocentric DSI, the difference in probability that they would see government as salient reaches 11.3 percent.

OTA at the societal level played an even larger role. The average level of perceived government salience in the most reciprocally oriented counties in China was 22.36 percent lower than in the most hierarchically oriented counties. The average level of government salience of the most reciprocally oriented counties was 21.22 percent lower than in counties where OTA was at the mean level.

---

[10] Because the relationship between the independent variables and probability in the logit model is nonlinear and nonadditive, it cannot be represented by a single coefficient. The calculation involves multiplying the logged odds of an independent variable by its exponent while holding constant other independent variables in the model. During the transformation, I fixed continuous variables at their means, binary variables at zero, and categorical variables at their medians.

Three conclusions can be drawn. First, culturally defined normative rationality plays a critical role in politicizing people. The way in which political actors decode information is determined not only by government behavior and individual socioeconomic resources, but also by the norms of the culture in which people have been socialized. Ignoring the impacts of culturally defined standards of government behavior on government salience would lead to an omitted variable problem and distort the picture of how people become politicized in different societies. Second, OTA and DSI influence government salience through different channels – DSI primarily through individual psychology and OTA through people's interactions with others in their community. When individuals rely on others to help them decode political information, the way those individuals interpret political information and assign responsibility is influenced by the dominant culture in the community. Finally, different dimensions of culture shape government salience in different directions. While allocentric DSI at the individual level makes people less likely to hold government responsible, hierarchical OTA at the communal level makes people more likely to hold government responsible. This is because allocentric DSI at the individual level requires people to take collective interests into consideration when they evaluate government policy, whereas a hierarchical environment creates high expectations of public authority.

CULTURE'S EFFECTS ON THE LIKELIHOOD OF POLITICAL PARTICIPATION

After perceiving government as having influence over a problem, actors must make a second decision – how to deal with this awareness. They can decide to participate in politics to express dissatisfaction and try to effect change, or they can decide to put up with the situation. As discussed at the beginning of this chapter, existing theories of political participation assume that actors base this decision on cost-benefit calculations. Sociological and psychological resources can reduce the costs and increase the perceived benefits of participation and thus are the major determinants of participation.

But people under the influence of different cultures do not necessarily define costs and benefits in the same way. Some interviews I held with unemployed workers in the city of Shenyang, Liaoning province, illustrate this. When I asked laid-off workers how they evaluated the government policy to reform SOEs, many of them expressed resentment. "I devoted my whole life to the factory," one former worker said, "but

Cultural Impacts on Political Participation

the CCP's policy encouraged the factory to abandon me without proper compensation. All the wealth we created over the course of our whole lives was stolen by the government officials. Of course, I am opposed to the current policy and would do anything I could to make their lives difficult." For this worker, the fact that the policy jeopardized his personal interests justified expressing his dissatisfaction through confrontational political acts, even if such acts could not achieve policy change.

But another unemployed worker in the same city approached the issue from a different perspective. "People should not be too selfish," he argued. "Everybody in our society should share the burden of our government rather than only being concerned with his own personal interests. You and I both know that the SOE reform is necessary. How can the current economic model continue if the SOEs do not make money? It is true that SOE reform hurt my interests, but the reform will benefit our country and our people as a whole in the long run. As a citizen of our country, I have an obligation to support such a policy, even if my personal interests are hurt by it." The two respondents defined the costs and benefits in different ways, and this shaped their divergent responses to the policy.

Contrary to conventional wisdom, I argue that hierarchical OTA makes people more politically active. As the previous analysis demonstrated, the dependency created by hierarchical OTA raises people's expectations of government. It gives people the expectation that the government will come to their rescue whenever they encounter any difficulties. If and when it does not, the norm grants the governed the authority to participate in politics. As the responsibility assigned to the public authority by reciprocal OTA is narrower than that of hierarchical OTA, people under the influence of reciprocal OTA are expected to be less politically active than people with hierarchical OTA. Thus, we have:

H3. *People under the influence of hierarchical OTA can be expected to be more active in politics than people with reciprocal OTA.*

Since idiocentric DSI legitimates the self as the unit of interest calculation, it encourages people to participate in politics to guard their private interests. People under the influence of idiocentric DSI define their own interest instead of accepting the government's community-centered definition of their self-interest. The norm allows people, in their cost-benefit calculations, to accord their own interests a higher priority than the interests of others or of society as a whole.

Taken together, these features suggest that people under the influence of idiocentric DSI should be more likely to participate in politics.

Allocentric DSI, on the other hand, requires people to give up their self-interest for collective interests when the two are in conflict.[11] The norm discourages people from participating in politics to pursue private interests, endorsing such participation only when the private interest is seen as compatible with the collective interest. Finally, since allocentric DSI obligates people to consider the impacts of any political acts on their society's collective interests, the norm increases the perceived costs of political activities. Therefore:

H4. *People under the influence of idiocentric DSI are more likely to participate in politics than people under the influence of allocentric DSI.*

To test cultural impacts on the likelihood of political participation, I created a new dependent variable – "participation." Within the category of those who reported having problems that the government could solve, this binary variable differentiates between those who participated in politics and those who did not. (People who reported that they had no problems to bring to the attention of government were dropped from the analysis. We included the remaining respondents: 2,379 interview subjects from the 1993 survey and 3,054 from the 2002 survey.) Those who engaged in any of the political activities listed in Table 6.1 were categorized as participant and scored as 1. Those who had a problem with the government but failed to engage in any participatory activities were categorized as nonparticipant and scored as 0.

The 1993 and 2002 China data sets were analyzed to answer the following two questions: First, do the two cultural norms affect the likelihood that people will participate in politics? Second, did social-structural and institutional changes between the two surveys alter culture's impacts on participation?

As with the analysis of perceived government salience above, the first step was to find out whether China possessed sufficient cross-county variation in the level of participation to warrant the use of HLM. I again used a hierarchical ANOVA model for the analysis. As mentioned above, the populations of the study include only those people who claimed that they had problems with the government. The results of the analysis are shown in Table E.2 in Appendix E. On average, around one-fourth (25 percent) of people in some counties participated in politics, but around 90 percent of people in other counties engaged in some political acts. These results

---

[11] Since collective interests can hardly be clearly defined, the government usually manipulates information to deny people the legitimacy to participate in politics.

Cultural Impacts on Political Participation   167

confirm the appropriateness of HLM as a tool for the task of analyzing political participation.

Accordingly, Table 6.4 displays the results of two statistical models for each of the two years.[12] The first model assesses the effects of individual-level variables on the likelihood of participation; the second adds an analysis of county-level variables.

At the individual level, none of the sociological resources – education, income, urban residence, or gender – had an independent effect on the likelihood that people would participate in politics in either 1993 or 2002. This does not mean that education and urban residency have no impact on political participation in China. However, as shown in Table 6.2, their impact is exerted through the perception of government saliency, whereas Table 6.4 shows that among those who saw government as salient to their problems, there is no additional impact of socioeconomic status on the decision of whether or not to participate.

Likewise, psychological resources play only a limited role in mobilizing people who perceive government as salient to participate. Among the three psychological resources examined in the model, only political interest had a positive impact on participation in both years. Given that people who reported no problems with their government were removed from the sample, the impact of political interest on participation cannot be attributed to cognition. Political interest may instead help people to acquire critical psychological resources that facilitate participation. In their study of "rightful resistance" in China, Kevin O'Brien and Lianjiang Li argue that people usually appeal to central government policies to defend their interests against local officials (O'Brien 1996; O'Brien and Li 2006). In doing so, actors borrow normative power from central government policies to change the balance of power between themselves and local bureaucrats (Shi 1997). Information on central government policies is therefore an important enabling resource for political participation, and people interested in politics would be more likely to acquire this information. This suggests that political interest increases the level of political participation by helping participants acquire the political ammunition to defeat local officials.

The relationship between political efficacy and participation, on the other hand, appears to be unstable. In 1993, internal efficacy made respondents more politically active. This effect disappeared in 2002. External

---

[12] Since none of the random components of independent variables for both years were statistically significant, I chose the intercept model for the analyses.

TABLE 6.4. *Cultural Impacts on the Likelihood of Political Participation in Mainland China*

	1993[a]				2002[b]			
	Individual-Level Variables Only		County-Level Intercept Effects		Individual-Level Variables Only		County-Level Intercept Effects	
	Coefficient[c]	SE[d]	Coefficient[c]	SE[d]	Coefficient[c]	SE[d]	Coefficient[c]	SE[d]
Fixed components								
Intercept	0.746***	0.089	0.756***	0.087	−0.249***	0.083	−0.229***	0.08
County-level effects								
Education			0.080	0.058			−0.117	0.06
OTA (reciprocal)			−0.264	0.201			0.151	0.21
DSI (idiocentric)			0.686***	0.233			0.319*	0.19
Individual-level effects								
Political culture								
OTA (reciprocal)	−0.424	0.287	−0.370	0.287	−0.572**	0.247	−0.550**	0.25
DSI (idiocentric)	1.850**	0.730	1.631**	0.740	1.832**	0.835	1.699**	0.84
Sociological resources								
Education	0.012	0.016	0.009	0.016	0.001	0.014	0.005	0.01
Income	0.000	0.000	0.000	0.000	0.000	0.000	0.000	0.00
Urban	0.096	0.148	0.001	0.152	0.115	0.117	0.203	0.12
Male	0.144	0.096	0.164*	0.097	0.326***	0.088	0.325***	0.09
Age	0.041**	0.017	0.041**	0.017	0.034*	0.018	0.033*	0.02
Age squared	0.000**	0.000	0.000**	0.000	0.000**	0.000	0.000**	0.00

Psychological resources								
Political interest	0.199**	0.079	0.194**	0.079	0.172***	0.036	0.168***	0.04
External efficacy	−0.005	0.026	−0.004	0.026	−0.053	0.029	−0.055	0.03
Internal efficacy	0.060**	0.030	0.060**	0.030	0.042	0.026	0.038	0.03
Institutional effects								
Political fear	0.093*	0.048	0.091*	0.049	0.113**	0.054	0.111**	0.05
Media exposure	0.033	0.027	0.032	0.027	0.040*	0.024	0.042*	0.02
Access to grapevine rumors	0.343***	0.075	0.340***	0.074	0.238***	0.056	0.239***	0.06
Random components								
Intercept	0.723***		0.653***		0.646***		0.637***	

*** p < .01; ** p < .05; * p < .1

[a] N = 2,379

[b] N = 3,054

[c] Entries are restricted maximum likelihood unstandardized coefficients with HLM 6.06.

[d] Entries are robust standard errors.

Note: This analysis is limited to those who perceived the government as salient.

Source: 1993 Survey of Political Culture and Political Participation in Mainland China, Taiwan, and Hong Kong; 2002 China Survey, Asian Barometer Survey I.

efficacy had no impact on political participation in either year. Political fear, rather than deterring people from political behavior, made participation more likely. The analyses also show that information acquired from official media sources had no impact on political participation among respondents viewing government as salient to their problems. This suggests that once the regime propaganda makes people assign more responsibility to public authority, it has no further impact on people's political behavior. Information from unofficial channels, however, had a constant and significant impact on political participation. Those who reported access to grapevine rumors were more likely to participate in politics than people without access in both 1993 and 2002.

Turning to the impact of culture, with all other variables controlled, in both years, idiocentric DSI at both the individual and the county levels had a statistically significant impact on the decision to participate. This finding not only confirms H4 but also tells us that structural and institutional changes between 1993 and 2002 did not eliminate culture's impacts on people's participatory behavior.

The situation for OTA is different. It had no effect in 1993, but this changed in 2002, when individuals holding hierarchical OTA became more likely to participate in politics than people with reciprocal orientation. I showed in Chapter 4 that there was an increase in the number of people adhering to the traditional norm of hierarchical OTA between 1993 and 2002. Here we identify an additional change, which is an increasing tendency for those who hold hierarchical OTA to participate in politics.

To compare the impact of cultural norms on participation with the impact of sociological and psychological variables, I converted the coefficients of education, political interest, and cultural norms from logged odds to probabilities and present the results in Table 6.5. During the transformation, I again divided people and counties into three groups – those with the highest and lowest values of each independent variable and those with the mean value.

I first calculated the impact of the most important psychological resource – political interest – on the probability that people would participate in politics. I found that people who were interested in politics had a higher probability of participating than those who were not interested in politics. In 1993 and 2002, the former were respectively 10.8 and 16.6 percent more likely than the latter to participate. Idiocentric DSI at the individual level, however, played a more important role in mobilizing people to participate than did political interest. In 1993, people

Probability if Respondents Belong to	1993			2002		
	Marginal Effects	Differences between		Marginal Effects	Differences between	
		Two Adjacent Categories	Lowest and Highest Categories		Two Adjacent Categories	Lowest and Highest Categories
County-level effects						
DSI at group level						
Most allocentrically oriented counties	0.573			0.511		
Mean	0.575	0.002		0.575	0.064	
Most idiocentrically oriented counties	0.778	0.203	0.205	0.695	0.120	0.184
Individual-level effects						
DSI						
Most allocentrically oriented individuals	0.614			0.429		
Mean	0.704	0.090		0.505	0.076	
Most idiocentrically oriented individuals	0.824	0.120	0.210	0.633	0.128	0.204

(*continued*)

TABLE 6.5. (*continued*)

Probability if Respondents Belong to	1993			2002		
	Marginal Effects	Differences between		Marginal Effects	Differences between	
		Two Adjacent Categories	Lowest and Highest Categories		Two Adjacent Categories	Lowest and Highest Categories
OTA						
Most hierarchically oriented individuals				0.591		
Mean				0.503	−0.087	
Most reciprocally oriented individuals				0.383	−0.120	−0.207
Psychological resources						
Individuals who are not interested in politics	0.697			0.422		
Mean	0.758	0.061		0.497	0.075	
Individuals who are interested in politics	0.804	0.046	0.107	0.588	0.091	0.166

Source: 1993 Survey of Political Culture and Political Participation in Mainland China, Taiwan, and Hong Kong; 2002 China Survey, Asian Barometer Survey (1993 N = 3,287; 2002 N = 3,183).

Cultural Impacts on Political Participation

holding the most extreme idiocentric DSI were 21.2 percent more likely to participate in politics than people holding the most extreme allocentric DSI. Compared with people in the middle of the DSI scale, those holding the most idiocentric DSI were 12.8 percent more likely to participate in politics, and those with the most allocentric DSI were 7.6 percent less likely to participate in politics.

Did structural and institutional changes in China between 1993 and 2002 bring about any pattern-maintaining changes in DSI? A comparison of the individual-level effects of DSI in 1993 and 2002 reveals that both the direction and magnitude of DSI's impact on political participation were quite similar. People holding the most extreme allocentric DSI in 2002 were 20.4 percent more likely, as compared with 21 percent more likely in 1993, to participate in politics than those with extreme idiocentic DSI. The dramatic social-structural changes in China between 1993 and 2002 did not change the impacts of definition of self-interest on people's participatory behavior.

OTA had no impact on participation in 1993, but the situation changed in 2002. Compared with people in the middle of the scale, people holding the most hierarchical OTA were 8.8 percent more likely to participate in politics, and people holding the most reciprocal OTA were 12 percent less likely to participate in politics. If we compare people with the most extreme hierarchical OTA to people with the highest score for reciprocal OTA, the difference reaches 20.7 percent.

To compare the impacts of county-level variables on the average level of political participation across counties, I converted the log odds of variables at the second level into probabilities. In 1993, the average level of participation in the most idiocentrically oriented counties was 16.3 percent higher than that in the most allocentrically oriented counties. In 2002, the figure rose to 18.4 percent.

Several conclusions may be drawn from the analyses in this section. First, culturally defined normative rationality has significant impacts on the decision to participate that are independent of the effects of social structures and institutions. Second, different dimensions of culture have different impacts on participation. While hierarchical OTA increases the likelihood that people will participate in politics, allocentric DSI decreases the likelihood. Viewing all traditional or all modern cultural norms as pushing behavior in the same direction is liable to conceal rather than reveal the ways in which culture affects political behavior.

Third, the relationships among social structure, political institutions, culture, and behavior are more complicated than previously understood.

Structural and institutional changes between 1993 and 2002 altered neither the distribution of DSI in China nor its effect on political participation. However, contrary to the expectations of modernization theory, social change intensified rather than weakened both the commitment of many Chinese to hierarchical OTA and the efficacy of hierarchical OTA in motivating participation. Rather than making people update their normative orientations to make them compatible with new incentive structures, structural and institutional changes induced people to re-embrace traditional cultural norms and at the same time reinforced the norms' impact on political behavior. Culture in China shifted in the opposite direction from that foreseen by Inglehart in his theory of cultural shifts (Inglehart 1990). This pattern of change belongs to the category of cultural shift identified by Eckstein as pattern-maintaining change.

CULTURAL IMPACTS ON PEOPLE'S CHOICE OF CONFRONTATIONAL ACTS

Once people perceive government as salient to the solution of a problem they face and decide to take an action (other than voting) to try to obtain a government response, they must then choose among political acts.[13] In China during the period under study, as shown in Table 6.1, the possible actions ranged from less confrontational to more confrontational. Contacting local officials, asking one's immediate leaders for help, and seeking help from friends when dealing with government officials are acts that generate little social conflict because they respect the order of authority within the work unit or local government. Through such acts a citizen remonstrates with officials to remind them of their obligations to serve the people. Attempts to enlarge the scope of conflict by dragging higher-level government, party, or people's congress officials into the issue are more confrontational because they present a challenge to the authority of local officials.[14] Even more confrontational are tactics that may damage the careers of officials involved, such as writing letters to expose local officials' wrongdoing to higher levels of the government, newspapers, and complaint bureaus. Going still further are acts

---

[13] If actors fail to achieve a goal through the acts they have chosen, they need to decide whether to choose another political act to pursue the same goal. If yes, another participatory act must be chosen. The cycle may continue until actors achieve their goal or decide to give up.

[14] Compare Schattschneider (1960). For application of the strategy in China, see Shi (1997).

Cultural Impacts on Political Participation

like organizing colleagues to resist, harassing leaders, and participating in demonstrations and sit-ins, which may create instability in communities and generate severe conflict within the society.

The choices people make are consequential for the political system as a whole. Transitions to democracy may be triggered by social movements and other confrontational political activities. If a cultural norm discourages people from involvement in political activities that generate conflicts, democratic transition is less likely to occur.

Research on the means people choose for participating in politics, like research on the decision to participate, has been dominated by the rational actor model. Verba and his colleagues, for example, argue that the choice is shaped by instrumental cost-benefit calculations: for example, people with money are more likely to make campaign donations, and people with time are more likely to engage in campaign activities (Verba et al. 1995). I agree that instrumental rationality plays a role in shaping people's choices of political acts, but I argue that normative rationality is more fundamental to these choices because it defines the very legitimacy of various acts.

My interviews with laid-off workers in Shenyang illustrate how cultural norms play a role in shaping people's selection of political acts. In response to being laid off, some made appeals to officials in their enterprises, others went up the bureaucratic ladder to seek help from higher-level officials, and others harassed their leaders or took to the street to protest. I asked those who confined their participation to their work units whether they thought more confrontational actions could bring them tangible benefits. Many told me that they believed they could. But why, then, did they refrain from choosing these more confrontational acts to pursue their goals?

Scholars of communist societies often attribute the avoidance of confrontational political activities to fear. To assess this explanation, I asked the laid-off workers whether they believed that such acts would be risky for them. Their answers were mixed: while some felt that such acts would trigger revenge from the regime, others argued that it was safe for them to engage in confrontational actions. For example, a worker in his forties told me that harassing an individual government official never triggers retaliation from the regime, even though the specific harassed official may retaliate. Furthermore, since the worst-case scenario – losing his job – had already occurred, revenge by individual officials was no longer a threat to him. Others told me that the government would not punish them for these acts because (1) protest requires the participation of many people, and the law cannot be used to punish a large group of people (*fa buzezhong*) and (2) past experiences had shown that local officials usually tolerated and tried to co-opt protesters if they confined their appeals to economic issues and avoided making any sort of political statement. These interviews suggest that political fear only partly explains why some people in China refrain from engaging in confrontational political acts.

Nor does the free rider problem fully explain such avoidance. Many respondents pointed out that local officials were sometimes forced to help people resolve their problems in order to avoid being continually harassed. These rewards were always selective, however, so that only those who harassed the leader got the rewards. Nonparticipants received no benefits. If respondents understood that protest could bring them desired benefits and perceived the risks of engaging in such acts as low, why did so many still avoid engaging in those acts? When I confronted the laid-off workers with that question, most of them told me that they refrained from harassing their leaders or getting involved in protest because it was not right to do so. A worker in Beijing put it this way:

When my personal interests are threatened by the reform, what should I do? Follow the leaders home for a meal and place to stay [i.e., camp out at the leader's house as a form of pressure on him], or go out on the street to protest like others? Not for me. If everybody in society only concerned themselves with their own interests, without taking other people or the society into consideration, our country could never develop. Of course, this doesn't mean I shouldn't let the government know my difficulties. I personally contacted officials at my workplace and went to the local government to ask people there for help. You and I know that lots of people ask the government for help, but the government can't help everybody. Even if the government can't give me the help I need, I still think it's improper for me to harass leaders or go on the street to protest like other people did.

Other respondents gave similar normative justifications for avoiding confrontational political acts. One unemployed worker told me that he refused to harass his leaders because that "would lower myself to the level of people who put their private interest above that of the country."[15] Another unemployed worker said, "I have no problem with making appeals to the government or going up the bureaucratic ladder to make appeals. But I understand that the government has its own difficulties.... As good citizens, we need to understand the government's difficulty, rather than *nao* [create trouble] as some people did."[16]

[15] Respondent No. 7, Shenyang, 2003.
[16] Respondent No. 13, Shenyang, 2003.

Cultural Impacts on Political Participation

When I asked people who had pursued confrontational political acts why they had done so, their rationale was quite different from that of the first group. Several told me that they had the natural right to confront government and to make their voices heard. If the government refused to respond to conventional means, they would not hesitate to engage in confrontational activities. When reminded that this could be disruptive to society, some told me that they had no obligation to consider whether their political acts threatened the interests of others or social stability. One unemployed female worker said, "I worked in this factory for my whole life. Now I am old and the factory that I devoted my life to kicked me out. Of course I have the right to do anything I can to defend my interests." Her response to the idea voiced by many others that the SOE reform was a necessary evil was that it was not her business. "My interests were jeopardized by the government and I cannot let this *wang-badan* [son of a bitch] government off the hook. ... I started with leaders in my work unit," she added. "When they didn't help me, I went to the local government, and the local government also refused to help me solve the problem. I couldn't follow the [work unit] leader home to stay [i.e., harass him at home] like some male employees, but I did join the street protests. The government still refused to help me resolve my problem, but at least I made their lives difficult."[17]

Norms prescribe legitimate responses under a particular situation; thus, the impact of culture on people's choices of political acts is situation-specific. Acts that are not justifiable in one circumstance may become justifiable in another. When I asked those who had chosen not to join protest activities what would compel them to protest, several said they would protest if and when the government threatened society's collective interests. When I pressed them for a few examples, they named inflation, large-scale corruption of government officials, and police abuse of power.

I hypothesize that cultural norms shape a person's choices of political acts in the following ways. First, I expect that people under the influence of hierarchical OTA will be more persistent in their activities than those under the influence of reciprocal OTA.[18] This is because (1) they define

---

[17] Respondent No. 21, Shenyang, 2003.

[18] *Bitter Love* (*Kulian*, 1979), a film script by Bai Hua later made into the movie *The Sun and the People* (*Taiyang yu ren*, 1980) best demonstrates this mentality. In the movie, since the participants have no intention of overthrowing the government, they usually expect favorable responses from the government. When they find out that the government has failed to respond to their political acts, which were aimed at helping the regime, they exhaust all means available to them to make their voices heard.

the purpose of their political activity as remonstrating with government, that is, helping government become aware of its obligation to resolve a problem and (2) their expectations of government are higher than those of people with reciprocal OTA. When people with hierarchical OTA project their normative orientation onto government officials, they assume that the officials will understand their benevolent intentions, and they expect them to respond to their political acts favorably. If the government fails to do so, people with hierarchical OTA are authorized to continue to make their voices heard and to use more strident tactics if their petitions go unanswered. People under the influence of hierarchical OTA may even escalate to confrontational measures with the understanding that their goal is the good of the government and society in general. Thus, we have:

H5. *Hierarchical OTA makes it more likely than reciprocal OTA that people will engage in confrontational political acts to pursue their goals.*

Second, as shown by H4, idiocentric DSI encourages people to participate in politics to guard their private interests. Having made this decision, they are less constrained in their choice of political means by the possible impact of their act on others or on society as a whole. By contrast, the allocentric definition of self-interest compels people to consider the impact of their acts on others and on society. Since confrontational political acts can generate conflicts among actors and create social unrest, people under the influence of allocentric DSI can be expected to avoid confrontational political acts, whereas idiocentric DSI gives normative permission for people to choose such acts. This leads to:

H6. *People under the influence of idiocentric DSI are more likely to engage in confrontational political activities to pursue their interests than people with allocentric DSI.*

To arrange political acts in China in hierarchical order based on their potential for generating conflict, I conducted a factor analysis of political acts. Four factors emerged, constituting an obvious hierarchy in degree of confrontation.[19] I scored the least confrontational acts 1, the next most

---

[19] The factors consisted of the following: Factor One – contacted unit leader, asked other leaders in the same unit to intervene, sought help from those who could persuade leader; Factor Two – complained to higher authority, complained through various political organizations, complained through People's Congress; Factor Three – wrote letter to appropriate government office, wrote letter to newspaper, reported problem to an appeals bureau; Factor Four – carried out a work slowdown, organized colleagues to resist leadership's demands, harassed the leader, participated in demonstration/sit-in.

	1993				2002			
	Model I		Model II		Model I		Model II	
	Individual-Level Variables Only		County-Level Intercept Effects		Individual-Level Variables Only		County-Level Intercept Effects	
	Coefficient[a]	SE[b]	Coefficient[a]	SE[b]	Coefficient[a]	SE[b]	Coefficient[a]	SE[b]
Fixed components								
Intercept	3.002***	0.124	3.002***	0.123	−3.306***	0.124	−3.293***	0.121
County-level effects								
Education (mean)			0.060	0.046			−0.095*	0.054
OTA (reciprocal)			−0.303**	0.141			0.091	0.203
DSI (idiocentric)			0.527***	0.183			0.377**	0.183
Individual-level effects								
Political culture								
OTA (reciprocal)	−0.360	0.231	−0.291	0.232	−0.524**	0.227	−0.493**	0.230
DSI (idiocentric)	1.672***	0.614	1.481**	0.622	1.846**	0.735	1.695**	0.739
Sociologial resources								
Education	0.021	0.012	0.019	0.012	0.000	0.013	0.004	0.013
Income	0.000	0.000	0.000	0.000	0.000	0.000	0.000	0.000
Urban	0.049	0.132	−0.005	0.139	0.130	0.112	0.202*	0.120
Male	0.160**	0.076	0.173**	0.077	0.336***	0.086	0.334***	0.087
Age	0.035**	0.015	0.035**	0.015	0.031*	0.016	0.030*	0.016
Age squared	0.000**	0.000	0.000**	0.000	0.000**	0.000	0.000**	0.000

(*continued*)

TABLE 6.6. (*continued*)

	1993				2002			
	Model I		Model II		Model I		Model II	
	Individual-Level Variables Only		County-Level Intercept Effects		Individual-Level Variables Only		County-Level Intercept Effects	
	Coefficient[a]	SE[b]	Coefficient[a]	SE[b]	Coefficient[a]	SE[b]	Coefficient[a]	SE[b]
Psychological resources								
Political interest	0.236***	0.064	0.233***	0.064	0.179***	0.035	0.175***	0.035
External efficacy	−0.033	0.022	−0.033	0.022	−0.062**	0.026	−0.063**	0.026
Internal efficacy	0.073***	0.023	0.071***	0.023	0.057**	0.023	0.053**	0.024
Institutional effects								
Political fear	0.090**	0.041	0.089**	0.041	0.093*	0.055	0.090	0.055
Media exposure	0.045**	0.022	0.045**	0.022	0.039*	0.023	0.041*	0.023
Access to grapevine rumors	0.340***	0.061	0.340***	0.060	0.276***	0.052	0.277***	0.053
Intercept 2	0.763***	0.090	0.761***	0.090	0.642***	0.064	0.642***	0.064
Intercept 3	1.833***	0.109	1.831***	0.109	1.564***	0.090	1.565***	0.090
Intercept 4	3.714***	0.124	3.715***	0.124	3.061***	0.110	3.064***	0.109
Random components								
Intercept	0.519***		0.483***		0.606***		0.593***	

*** $p < .01$; ** $p < .05$; * $p < .1$

[a] Entries are restricted maximum likelihood unstandardized coefficients with HLM 6.06.

[b] Entries are robust standard errors.

Note: This analysis is limited to those who perceived government as salient.

Source: 1993 Survey of Political Culture and Political Participation in Mainland China, Taiwan, and Hong Kong; 2002 China Survey, Asian Barometer Survey I (1993 N = 3,287; 2002 N = 3,183).

Cultural Impacts on Political Participation

confrontational acts 2, and so on up to a score of 4 for the most confrontational acts. In Table 6.6, I use ordered logit in HLM to test whether cultural norms influence people's choice of more confrontational political acts. The same independent variables used in the previous models were used here.

The traditionally important sociological resources – education, income, and urbanization – were found to have no impact on people's choice of more confrontational political acts. Gender made a difference: males were more likely to choose confrontational political acts to pursue their interests than females. The relationship between age and the choice of act appears to be curvilinear; middle-aged people were more likely to engage in more confrontational political acts compared with both the young and the old.

Psychological resources had some effect. Those who were interested in politics and those who believed themselves capable of understanding and participating in politics were more likely to choose confrontational acts. External efficacy had the opposite effect: the more a person saw the government as responsive to his or her demands, the less likely they were to choose confrontational acts. This finding makes sense: people who see the government as responsive to their demands are more likely to expect the government to take care of their needs without their having to take extreme actions. The three institutional variables, political fear, access to media, and grapevine rumors had positive impacts on the likelihood of taking confrontational actions.

For the purposes of this study, the most important finding is that culture has a statistically significant, strong influence over the people's choices of political acts, a finding that was true for both 1993 and 2002. Consistent with H5, hierarchical OTA increased people's propensity to engage in confrontational political acts, although it did so only at the county level and not at the individual level in 1993 and at the individual but not the county level in 2002. The high expectations shaped by hierarchical OTA encourage people to engage in political acts to make their voices heard, and the norm further condones using all political means available for the purpose of remonstrating. Consistent with H6, idiocentric DSI at both the individual and the county levels increased the likelihood that people would engage in confrontational political acts.

To compare the degree of impact of cultural norms and interest in politics on people's choices of political acts, I converted the coefficients of political interest and cultural norms from the logged odds into probabilities and present the results in Table 6.7.

TABLE 6.7. *Comparing the Effects of Culture and Political Interest on the Likelihood of Choosing Confrontational Acts of Participation in Mainland China*

Probability if Respondents Belong to	1993			2002		
	Marginal Effects	Differences between		Marginal Effects	Differences between	
		Two Adjacent Categories	Lowest and Highest Categories		Two Adjacent Categories	Lowest and Highest Categories
County-level effects						
DSI at group level						
Most allocentrically oriented counties	0.556	0.140		0.513	0.076	
Mean	0.696			0.589		
Most idiocentrically oriented counties	0.821	0.125	0.265	0.726	0.137	0.212
Individual-level effects						
DSI						
Most allocentrically oriented individuals	0.380	0.090		0.430	0.076	
Mean	0.470			0.506		
Most idiocentrically oriented individuals	0.623	0.153	0.243	0.634	0.128	0.204
OTA						
Most hierarchically orientated individuals				0.583	−0.078	
Mean				0.505		
Most reciprocally oriented individuals				0.397	−0.108	−0.174
Psychological resources						
People who are least interested in politics	0.462	0.093		0.419	0.079	
Mean	0.555			0.498		
People who are most interested in politics	0.634	0.079	0.172	0.592	0.094	0.173

Source: 1993 Survey of Political Culture and Political Participation in Mainland China, Taiwan, and Hong Kong; 2002 China Survey, Asian Barometer Survey I (1993 N = 3,287; 2002 N = 3,183).

Cultural Impacts on Political Participation

Those who were interested in politics in 1993 were 17.2 percent more likely, and in 2002, 17.3 percent more likely to engage in more confrontational political acts than those who were not interested in politics. DSI, however, appears to have an even larger impact. In 1993, people with the highest idiocentric DSI score were 24.3 percent more likely to choose confrontational political acts than people with the highest allocentric DSI score. In 2002, this gap in likelihood was 20.4 percent. The similarity of the two numbers shows that changes in social structures and political institutions in the intervening years had little effect on the impact of DSI on choice of political acts. The same is true for the impact of DSI at the group level. In 1993, the people living in the most idiocentrically oriented counties were 26.5 percent more likely to engage in more confrontational political acts than people living in the most allocentrically oriented counties, and in 2002 the difference was 20.4 percent. At both the individual and the collective levels, culture remained a strong factor influencing participation, and its influence persisted despite changes in the social and institutional environments.

CULTURE'S IMPACTS ON PROTEST POTENTIAL

Some students of comparative politics have analyzed a subset of political acts that they label "unconventional political participation." The category overlaps with but is not identical to the category of confrontational participation, which was analyzed in the preceding section. Unconventional participation consists of acts of public mobilization designed to dramatize demands and challenge the authorities outside the norms of everyday political life, and includes acts like strikes, protests, demonstrations, and riots (Barnes et al. 1979). Although such acts are rare in most societies most of the time, they are potentially important because unconventional participation can influence political stability. Social movement scholars have suggested that economic development can mobilize people to participate in politics, and an explosion in political participation may lead to democratic transition (Nie et al. 1969a, 1969b). Few transitions to democracy, however, have been triggered by explosions of voting, electoral campaign activity, lobbying, and contacting – so-called conventional political participation. Most bottom-up political transitions are sparked by the kinds of activities labeled unconventional political participation.

Rapid economic development and social change in China have led to a rise in social protest and an expectation among many that protest may increase even further. Before the reforms, the government designated work units and other grassroots organizations to distribute resources on behalf of the state. If one person in the organization received a particular state-controlled resource, the chance for other members to get the same resource was reduced proportionately. This institutional design confined most resource competition within grassroots organizations and fragmented the interests of people within a given organization so that large-scale collective action was unlikely to occur (Shi 1997). After market reforms, employee interests were no longer tied to the work units. Instead, people's interests became aligned roughly with social status. Access to jobs, housing, education, health insurance, and other social goods was now determined by government policies at the municipal, provincial, and central levels. Collective action became not only possible but also necessary for resource competition (compare the logic of Barnes et al. 1979, chapter 4).

Because different social groups change positions in a society over time, there are always interests that have not yet gained access to channels of influence, even in democratic societies. Those who have not been co-opted into the regular bargaining processes are thought to be more likely to resort to unconventional political acts to express themselves. Unconventional political actions, therefore, should be more likely to occur in transitional societies where interests are reorganizing (Barnes et al. 1979; Jennings and van Deth 1990). This line of reasoning by structural theorists predicted an increase in both the level and the scope of unconventional political acts in China.

Moreover, changes brought about by economic reform in Chinese society were destroying the traditional ways in which people participated in politics without establishing new channels of communication for the public to express their opinions and articulate interests. This inadequate representation of a substantial number of people, it was predicted, would push them to engage in unconventional political acts to pursue their interests (Falkenheim 1978, 1981, 1987; Shi 1997). This is the underlying reason why many scholars of Chinese politics predicted that a deepening of economic reform, especially SOE reform, would shake the foundations of the regime and possibly lead to its collapse.

There has been, in fact, a substantial increase in protests in China since the reforms began, and particularly since the turn of the century. In 1995, there were 10,000 collective mass incidents (a category used by the government to refer to such political acts as protests, riots, and mass petitioning). In 2004, this figure rose to 74,000 and in 2005 to 87,000 (Kahn 2006). Yet, given what the regime accomplished through SOE reform

Cultural Impacts on Political Participation

TABLE 6.8. *Protest Potential in Mainland China (Percent of Sample Approving)*

Do You Approve of People Doing the Following to Express Their Views?	1993		2002		Difference[b]	Rate of Change
	Percent	N[a]	Percent	N[a]		
Demonstration/sit-in	13	428	8.7	279	−4.3	−33.08%
Strike	9	283	7.4	234	−1.6	−17.78%
Carrying out a work slowdown	5.2	172	3.5	114	−1.7	−32.69%
Signing a petition	25.2	830	31.7	1,010	6.5	25.79%
Writing big character posters	11.1	366	10.6	338	−0.5	−4.50%

[a] The raw frequencies in N columns do not add up to the sample sizes due to missing values.
[b] All differences are significant at the .001 level.
Source: 1993 Survey of Political Culture and Political Participation in Mainland China, Taiwan, and Hong Kong; 2002 China Survey, Asian Barometer Survey I (1993 N = 3,287; 2002 N = 3,183).

over this period of time – laying off more than 20 million workers – the increases in the level and scope of protests seem relatively limited.

Scholars of social movements distinguish between objective and structural opportunities for unconventional political action and the subjective and cultural framing of those opportunities. Although culture does not create opportunities for action, it plays a role in the framing efforts that mediate between objective political opportunities and subjective psychological mobilization (McAdam et al. 1996b; McAdam, Tarrow, and Tilly 1997). If cultural norms in China reduce the likelihood of people choosing unconventional political acts, they may help to explain the unexpected stability and resilience of the authoritarian regime in China.

To test this possibility, I followed Samuel Barnes and Max Kaase in studying not unconventional political participation itself but the "propensity" to engage in such acts, which they label "protest potential." The reason for doing so is that actual participation in unconventional political acts is infrequent and episodic, but the willingness to consider engaging in such acts is a more stable and possibly more widespread attribute. To create this variable, a series of questions was posed, asking respondents whether they approved of people taking each of five unconventional political acts to express their views (following Barnes et al. 1979, chapter 3). People's attitudes toward unconventional political activities set the boundaries between endorsement and censure and provide us with a measure of their propensity or potential to engage in each form of protest.

The results are presented in Table 6.8. Approval of unconventional political acts was generally low across the population, ranging from 3.5 percent in favor of carrying out a work slowdown in 2002 to 31.7 percent in favor of signing a petition in the same year. Even more noteworthy was the overall decline in approval of unconventional political acts from the earlier to the later date. Except for a rise in the percentage of respondents who approved of signing a petition to express one's political views, approval of all other forms of protest activity declined.

What is the role of culture in shaping protest potential? I argued in this chapter that because hierarchical OTA defines the goals of participation as remonstration, people under its influence usually have no intention of overthrowing the government when they choose to engage in political activities but seek to the attention of government to inform and assist the authorities to do a better job, and that they are therefore willing to persist in remonstrating until they feel that they have been heard. I therefore hypothesize:

H7. People with hierarchical OTA are more likely to approve of unconventional political activities than people with reciprocal OTA.

Definition of self-interest can also positively influence the likelihood that people will approve of unconventional political activities. Most unconventional political activities lead to social unrest. In choosing political acts, people holding idiocentric DSI need only consider whether it can help them achieve their desired goals. Thus idiocentric DSI condones unconventional acts, even if they may pose a threat to social stability or others' interests. Allocentric DSI, on the other hand, requires actors to consider the impacts of their choices on others and on society as a whole. Even if a political act can help a person to achieve his or her goals, if the act may create societal turmoil, allocentric DSI would not authorize an actor to pursue that choice. We thus have:

H8. People with idiocentric DSI are more likely to approve of unconventional political acts for interest articulation than people with allocentric DSI.

It is reasonable to assume that unconventional political actions tend to cluster together: that a person who approves of demonstrations and sit-ins is more likely to approve of signing petitions and engaging in other unconventional participatory activities as well. A factor analysis of the

Cultural Impacts on Political Participation

five acts confirmed this supposition. One factor emerged from the model, confirming that all those acts belong to the same dimension. I added them together to create an index of protest potential and used it as the dependent variable in the following analysis.

I then used a hierarchical ANOVA model to partition protest potential, in order to find out if there exists sufficient cross-county variation to warrant HLM. The analysis, not shown here, shows that 90 percent of variance in the protest potential comes from individual level differences, and 10 percent of the variance comes from the county level. This is true for both 1993 and 2002. I thus chose HLM to analyze the data.

As independent and control variables to predict protest potential I used those already established and added two more – relative deprivation and social trust. The idea of deprivation as a motive for unconventional political activities can be traced to Aristotle. He believed that the principal causes of revolution were common people's aspirations for economic or political equality and the oligarchy's aspirations for maintaining and increasing economic and political inequalities. Much later, de Tocqueville linked the violence of the 1789 French Revolution to unfulfilled aspirations outpacing objective conditions, thereby increasing overall dissatisfaction and the pressure for change (Tocqueville et al. 1945 [1835, 1840]). Similarly, Marx saw personal dissatisfaction and the competition between the haves and have-nots as the driving force of history and the ultimate source of political revolt (Marx 1967 [1884]). The index of relative deprivation in this model was based on three questions:

- In light of your individual ability and work achievements, do you think your current income is reasonable or not?
- Do you think your ability and work get appropriate attention and acknowledgment from your unit leaders?
- Do you think your ability and work get appropriate respect and recognition in society?

Negative answers were coded as 1 and positive answers as 0. These questions were factor-analyzed and one factor emerged. I added them together to create the index of relative deprivation.

Unlike many conventional political acts, unconventional political actions always require collective effort. To draw the government's attention, actors need to mobilize others to work together. To do this, the organizers need to overcome the free rider problem (Diani and McAdam 2003; McAdam et al. 1996; McAdam, Tarrow, and Tilly 2001; Olsen 1965; Tarrow 1994). Scholars have found that social trust plays a critical

TABLE 6.9. *Cultural Impacts on Protest Potential in Mainland China*

	1993		2002	
	Coefficient[a]	SE[b]	Coefficient[a]	SE[b]
Fixed components				
Intercept	1.025***	0.024	0.634***	0.031
County-level effects				
Education	−0.007	0.016	0.041	0.021
OTA (reciprocal)	−0.083	0.055	−0.143	0.079
DSI (idiocentric)	0.178***	0.061	0.099	0.074
Individual-level effects				
Political culture				
OTA (reciprocal)	0.079	0.117	−0.242*	0.140
DSI (idiocentric)	0.839***	0.289	1.172**	0.507
Sociological resources				
Education	0.036***	0.006	0.007	0.006
Income	0.000	0.000	0.000	0.000
Urban	0.166***	0.051	0.010	0.059
Male	0.181***	0.037	0.097**	0.039
Age	−0.006***	0.001	−0.007***	0.002
Age squared				
Psychological resources				
Political interest	0.010	0.023	0.042***	0.015
External efficacy	−0.002	0.011	−0.067***	0.012
Internal efficacy	−0.027**	0.011	−0.006	0.014
Institutional effects				
Political fear	0.047***	0.016	0.062**	0.024
Media exposure	0.000	0.008	0.000	0.009
Access to grapevine rumors	0.041*	0.022	0.084***	0.025
Relative deprivation	0.237***	0.049	0.061	0.040
Interpersonal trust	−0.198***	0.038	−0.076**	0.038
Random components				
Intercept	0.050***		0.077***	

*** p < .01; ** p < .05; * p < .1

[a] Entries are restricted maximum likelihood unstandardized coefficients with HLM 6.06.
[b] Entries are robust standard errors.

Source: 1993 Survey of Political Culture and Political Participation in Mainland China, Taiwan, and Hong Kong; 2002 China Survey, Asian Barometer Survey I (1993 N = 3,287; 2002 N = 3,183).

role in helping to overcome this problem (Putnam 1993). To determine the impact of interpersonal trust on protest potential, I asked respondents whether they felt that most people could be trusted or that people should be cautious when dealing with others. Those who expressed trust were coded as 1. All the others are coded as 0. I included this variable in the model as a control.

Table 6.9 reports the results of parallel models for the data collected in 1993 and 2002. We find the sociological and psychological variables working largely as expected, although with some changes from 1993 to 2002. For the study of political culture, the most important finding is that, with all other variables controlled, idiocentric DSI had a statistically significant positive impact on protest potential in both years, as predicted in H8. In 1993, OTA was not found to have any impact; in 2002, consistent with H7, hierarchical OTA at the individual level increased people's inclinations for unconventional political methods. Structural and institutional changes that took place between the two surveys did not erode the impact of political culture on protest potential and, if anything, served to reinforce it.

However, there is some evidence of cultural flexibility (Chapter 4). The impact of DSI was statistically significant in 1993 but not in 2002. In 1993, those holding idiocentric DSI expressed themselves as more willing to protest, whereas those holding allocentric DSI were less willing. By 2002, the difference had disappeared. This means that those who held to allocentric norms had redefined the situation, so that their norms – which they still held – no longer constrained them to any greater extent than idiocentric norm holders from expressing approval of protest activities as a potentially appropriate form of action.

CONCLUSION

Political theories tend to assume that culture's impacts on political participation are unidirectional, that is, that traditional culture makes people more passive in politics, while modern culture mobilizes them to participate. This chapter showed that this was not the case in China. It is true that the traditional, allocentric definition of self-interest made people politically passive and encouraged them to refrain from confrontational and unconventional political acts. But hierarchical OTA made people more likely to blame their government, made them more active political participants, and made them more likely to engage in confrontational and unconventional political activities. Failure to differentiate the alternative impacts of different dimensions of traditional culture on people's political behavior can lead researchers to the wrong conclusions about cultural impacts on political participation.

These findings shed light on the puzzle of authoritarian resilience in China. People holding allocentric DSI are less likely than those with idiocentric DSI to hold government responsible for solving their problems, to participate in politics (even if their problems require government intervention), and to join confrontational activities, including social movements to oppose the government. The prevalence of this cultural norm gives the Chinese government valuable space for promoting policies that will jeopardize the interests of a substantial number of people but that are claimed to benefit society as a whole in the long run.

Another dimension of traditional culture, hierarchical OTA, confines the goals of participation to remonstration and sets the threshold extremely high for activism against the government. While the norm does not prevent people from engaging in unconventional political activities, the impacts of those activities, when aimed at remonstration, can be fundamentally different from the impacts they produce in other cultures. By providing the government more policy-making freedom, increasing the public's general tolerance of the government, and setting a higher threshold for opposition to the government, traditional culture makes a societal-led transition to democracy more difficult in China than elsewhere.

Even if traditional culture constitutes a barrier to democratic transition, some believe that both traditional culture itself and its impacts on people's political behavior will change as a consequence of social and economic development. This argument suffers from two problems. First, it assumes that structural and institutional changes make people update their cultural orientations according to a new incentive structure, that is, that a cultural process of "becoming modern" is inevitable, ignoring other possibilities. Second, it focuses exclusively on cultural discontinuity, ignoring pattern-maintaining change and cultural flexibility.

My analyses, however, call these assumptions into question. I found that culture, operationalized as norms, was more stable than previously conceived, even by political culture scholars. Rather than making people abandon traditional cultural norms, structural and institutional changes in China motivated a substantial number of people to re-embrace traditional culture. Moreover, culture's impacts on participation were not linear and one-dimensional. Instead, different dimensions of cultural norms had different impacts on people's participatory behavior. While idiocentric DSI encourages people to engage in various political acts, including unconventional ones, another dimension of modern culture – reciprocal OTA – discourages people from engaging in political acts to

Cultural Impacts on Political Participation 191

pursue their goals. Even if the modernization process can lead to a cultural shift, as suggested by structural and cultural theorists, it may not always lead to a participation explosion.

Finally, even when people with different cultural norms engage in the same political activities, their goals for those activities will usually be fundamentally different. People holding hierarchical OTA may pursue unconventional acts to remonstrate with their rulers, while reciprocal OTA authorizes unconventional political activities to oppose the government. The political consequences of each are likely to be fundamentally different. While social movements initiated by people with reciprocal OTA can be a major threat to the regime, the same activities by people with hierarchical OTA may not pose any danger. Until cultural norms change in China or alter the way in which they affect political behavior, democratic transition is unlikely to be triggered by pressure from below.

7

The Impact of Culture on Understandings of Democracy

After the Third Wave of democracy, which began in the 1970s and blossomed around the world in the following decades, democracy came to define people's aspirations for the ideal political system. But people had many different understandings of the meaning of democracy. Some associated democracy with individual freedom, others with institutional limits on government power, and still others with paternalistic government that takes care of the people's needs. Such divergent understandings shape people's expectations about their roles as citizens and the demands that they place on governments, influence the degree to which citizens feel satisfied with the kind of government they have, and hence have the potential to influence the stability of regimes.

What factors influence citizens' understandings of democracy? This chapter argues that while social and institutional factors are part of the answer, in China and Taiwan, individuals' cultural norms also have important effects on citizens' understanding of democracy.

Before probing the effects of culture, the chapter illustrates the diversity of views of democracy across Asia with data from Asian Barometer Survey I (2001–3). The second section then suggests two contrasting conceptions of democracy that contend for adherence in the Chinese cultural sphere, liberal democracy and guardianship or *minben* democracy. Adherents of the guardianship view of democracy are likely to identify democracy as government that produces good substantive results for the people rather than government limited by procedures that protect the rights of the people. In order to map citizens' views according to these ideal types, the third section analyzes the answers to an open-ended question asking people in China and Taiwan to use their own words to

192

Impact on Understandings of Democracy

describe what democracy means to them. A comparison of the answers from China and Taiwan reveals that the institutional differences between the two societies did not eliminate the convergence of their citizens' views on the nature of democracy. This suggests the persistent influence of culture. The fourth section explores how cultural variables affect people's willingness to form a view on the nature of democracy.

The fifth section offers a cultural theory to explain why people understand democracy in different ways. I argue that people in the Chinese culture area have had to decode the foreign concept of democracy with the help of their existing normative beliefs. I will suggest that persons committed to the norms of hierarchical OTA and allocentric DSI are more likely to understand democracy in terms of guardianship, whereas reciprocal OTA and idiocentric DSI predispose people toward a procedural understanding of democracy. I test this theory by empirically assessing the roles of socioeconomic factors, institutions, and culture in shaping people's understanding of democracy. Although socioeconomic resources help explain why people develop some understanding of democracy, they do not explain which understanding of democracy people adopt; those are shaped by the cultural norms into which people were socialized. These findings hold true for people in both mainland China and Taiwan. The chapter concludes with a discussion of the implications of the findings for authoritarian resilience in China and democratic reversal in East Asia.

DIVERSE VIEWS OF DEMOCRACY IN ASIA

"We live in a democratic age " Fareed Zakaria asserted. "Over the last century the world has been shaped by one trend above all others – the rise of democracy. In 1900 not a single country had what we would today consider a democracy: a government created by elections in which every adult citizen could vote. Today 119 do, comprising 62 percent of all countries in the world" (Zakaria 2004, 13). This trend is consistent with the modernization theory of political development, as described in Chapter 4, which predicts that the universal values of liberty and democracy will gradually conquer the world as modernization proceeds.

However, certain parts of the world seem to be exceptions to this pattern. Year after year the annual Freedom in the World reports have shown countries that are deemed "not free" to be concentrated in Eurasia, the Middle East, and central Africa.[1] In Asia, too, at the time of our 2002

[1] See, for example, the 2002 report, at http://www.freedomhouse.org/report/freedomworld/freedom-world-2002 (accessed December 17, 2013).

survey, Freedom House rated about half of the countries "free" and the rest "partly free" or "not free." Among the "not free" countries was China, which maintained its authoritarian political system despite abandoning a planned economy and undergoing rapid economic growth. Many surveys have shown that the majority of people in China are satisfied with the authoritarian regime, despite the fact that the regime still deprives its citizens of basic rights (Chen 2004; Shi 2001; Tang 2005).

In the rest of Asia as well, authoritarianism commands widespread prestige. According to Asian Barometer Survey I, in 2002 less than half the public in South Korea and Taiwan thought that democracy was the best form of government, and a majority of citizens supported a possible authoritarian alternative. The number of citizens who harbored reservations about democracy was significantly large in Thailand, the Philippines, Taiwan, and Mongolia. Even in Japan, the region's oldest democracy, citizens showed low support for the political system (Chu et al. 2008).

Citizens often gave seemingly inconsistent answers to survey questions. Average answers to the question "If 1 indicates entirely unsuitable, and 10 indicates entirely suitable, please tell us how suitable you think democracy is for your country?" ranged from 8.75 in Thailand to 6.67 in Taiwan (see Figure 7.1).

The high level of demand for democracy in China suggests that the citizens there are dissatisfied with their regime. Yet when asked, "What is the level of democracy in your country now on a scale from 1 to 10," Chinese citizens gave an average answer of 7.22 (see Figure 7.2), suggesting that their country was already nearly as democratic as they wanted it to be.

The scores from Taiwan were puzzling in the opposite way. The level of democracy desired, or demand for democracy, was the lowest among the countries surveyed, and the perceived level of democracy already achieved – the supply of democracy – was higher than the demand.

As a final illustration of the point, consider the correlation between the levels of democratic achievement reported by respondents in the Asian Barometer Survey and the same countries' Freedom House scores, which can be considered as objective outside assessments.[2] The Pearson's correlation coefficients (not shown here) between countries' Freedom House scores and their scores on the ABS democratic perception scale are not statistically significant. This suggests that the meaning of democracy in

---

[2] For Freedom House's coding methods, see http://www.freedomhouse.org/report/freedom-world-2008/methodology (accessed December 17, 2013). The scores range from 1 for "Free" to 7 for "Unfree" and are recoded in reverse order here to make the results more intuitively meaningful.

Impact on Understandings of Democracy

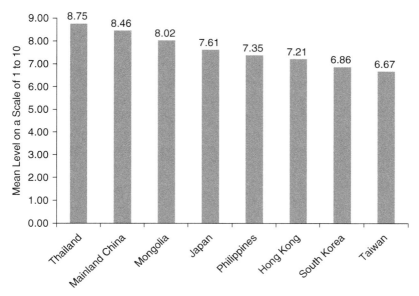

FIGURE 7.1. "How suitable is democracy for your country?"

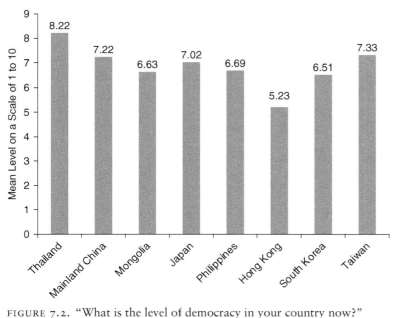

FIGURE 7.2. "What is the level of democracy in your country now?"

196 *Impact on Attitudes and Behaviors*

the minds of Asians is different from that in the minds of the experts who apply the Freedom House coding scheme to Asian countries.

What explains such puzzling responses in Asia to a range of questions about democracy? The problem arises from the fact that survey questions like these are built on the assumption that people around the world understand the meaning of democracy in the same way. The surveys assume that democracy is democracy; neither cultural, nor social-structural, nor institutional differences can influence how people in different countries understand it. But in fact, as suggested earlier, people under the influence of different cultures and different political institutions do not understand democracy in the same way.

ALTERNATIVE UNDERSTANDINGS OF DEMOCRACY

Once democracy became the key word symbolizing the ideal type of government, all regimes, including authoritarian ones, began to claim that they were a kind of democratic polity. If in the past the struggle was over whether democracy was the best form of government, it is now concentrated on the very definition of democracy.[3] In this process, the definitions and understandings of democracy have changed and evolved over time and in different places.

Two stylized understandings of democracy can help us classify the views of our respondents in China and Taiwan. In a view widely accepted among Western social scientists and democracy promotion organizations, democracy is a set of institutional arrangements that constrain the power of government. Open and competitive elections, in which people can choose government leaders, lie at the heart of this arrangement.[4] In order for democratic institutions to function properly, the system must allow a free flow of information so that people can make informed decisions when

[3] Even in its totalitarian stage, the regime in China claimed that the country was under the rule of the people's "democratic dictatorship" – democracy was extended to people while dictatorship was extended to enemies of the state. "Democracy is practiced within the ranks of the people, who enjoy the rights of freedom of speech, assembly, association, and so on. The right to vote belongs only to the people, not the reactionaries. The combination of these two aspects, democracy for the people and dictatorship over the reactionaries, is the people's democratic dictatorship" (Mao 1964, 418). After the Cultural Revolution, the word "dictatorship" was dropped from the label, and the regime began to claim that the country was in the process of building a socialist democracy.

[4] According to Huntington, "a modern nation-state has a democratic political system to the extent that its most powerful decision makers are selected through fair, honest, periodic elections in which candidates freely compete for votes and in which virtually all the adult population is eligible to vote" (Huntington 1993a, 28).

Impact on Understandings of Democracy

choosing government leaders through elections. The democratic system encourages people to participate in politics to press political leaders to adopt the policies they want. Consistent with the norm I have labeled reciprocal OTA, democracy legitimizes opposing one's government, that is, replacing it with a different one through established procedures. I label this concept "liberal democracy."

According to Robert Dahl, the "perennial alternative to democracy is government by guardians" (Dahl 1989, 52). Historically, the idea of guardianship has appealed to many different political thinkers and leaders around the world. "If Plato provides the most familiar example, the practical ideal of Confucius, who was born more than a century before Plato, has had far more profound influence over many more people and persists to the present day" (Dahl 1989, 54). Since 500 BCE, the theory of *minben*, or the Chinese concept of government by guardians, has profoundly influenced political thinking in China.

Minben doctrine and liberal democracy have two important features in common: both assign central status to the people's welfare as a purpose of governance, and both give political elites the responsibility for making decisions toward this goal. Unlike liberal democratic theory, however, *minben* doctrine invests elites with full authority to use their own judgment in policy making without influence from the people, limits the function of ordinary people's political participation to that of communicating information about local conditions, and sets a high bar for people to demand any change of government. The traditional Chinese *minben* version of guardianship is similar to the guardianship doctrine of Leninism, which assigns elites absolute power to make decisions for the people. Ever since the victory of the Chinese Communist Party (CCP), the official People's Republic of China definition of democracy has been built on the overlapping dual traditions of *minben* and Leninism.

There are four important differences between liberal democracy and guardianship democracy. First, they assign different methods for building the ideal government. For liberal democratic theorists, the ideal government can be achieved only by implementing procedural arrangements for people to choose their leaders through periodic elections. For guardianship democrats, only a body of "highly qualified people – guardians, if you like – can be counted on to possess both the knowledge and virtue needed to serve the good of everyone" (Dahl 1989, 55).[5] The ideal

---

[5] Robert Dahl, in *Democracy and Its Critics*, represents Plato's ideas on guardianship through a debate between "Demos" and "Aristo" over the question "Who is best qualified

government requires an institutional design that can select and train people with the knowledge and skills to make wise decisions for everyone in the society.

Second, the two theories use different standards to evaluate legitimacy. According to liberal theory, government legitimacy can be acquired only through open and fair elections. The *minben* doctrine, however, calls for assessing a government by the substance of its policy outputs; how political leaders acquire power is not as critical as whether the government can bring substantive benefits to its people. For example, the Tang dynasty emperor Li Shimin is considered one of the best rulers in Chinese history, even though he assassinated his brother and put his father under house arrest in order to usurp power. After his coronation, Li rapidly developed the economy of the country, accepted constructive criticism from his ministers, and successfully defended China from the Mongol invasion. He is esteemed by Chinese historians and ordinary people alike, despite the way he acquired power, because he brought his subjects tangible benefits and good governance. But this is not to suggest that *minben* doctrine does not hold political leaders to high standards. In fact, their claim to legitimacy could be considered even more fragile than that of democratic governments. Governments built on *minben* doctrine have to sustain their legitimacy through a constant flow of good policy outputs; in democratic systems, elections empower political leaders to rule for a fixed time period even if their policy performance is poor.

A third difference between these two conceptions has to do with the role of political participation. In liberal democratic theory participation is a basic right enjoyed by everyone. Consistent with the norm of reciprocal OTA, it includes the right to demand a change of government through established procedures. By contrast, although *minben* doctrine requires political leaders to listen to people's opinions in order to gather information and avoid unnecessary mistakes, it limits ordinary people's political participation in the normal political process to communication or remonstration.[6] According to Confucianism, harmony cannot be achieved by

---

to rule?" and the merits of democracy versus guardianship. This quotation from "Aristo" defends the guardianship concept as articulated in Plato's *Republic*.

[6] As mentioned in Chapter 2, this does not mean that rulers are unconstrained by their people and can thus make arbitrary and irresponsible decisions. If they lose the mandate of Heaven (as judged by policy outcomes), people are authorized to revolt against and overthrow their government. But the threshold at which people will demand a change of government is much higher than that defined in the liberal democratic tradition.

Impact on Understandings of Democracy 199

preventing people from expressing their views.[7] But because ordinary people are understood to be shortsighted and to lack the information to make wise decisions, political leaders are not required to follow common people's opinions. Instead, they are expected to make decisions based on their own expertise and judgment of society's collective interest.

These two different views of participation were expressed during interviews that I conducted in China. When I asked a villager in Hebei province about the meaning of democracy, he told me that it means the government allows people to express their opinions.[8] When I asked a college student in Beijing the same question, he replied, "Democracy means that ordinary people enjoy the right to participate in politics to elect their leaders and to replace their government."[9] Without clear theoretical guidance, both answers would be coded as "democracy means participation." However, the political connotations of these two answers are fundamentally different. For the Hebei villager, democracy means a benevolent ruler who gives people an opportunity to express their views rather than preventing them from speaking out. For the college student, democracy means that citizens enjoy the right to exercise influence over government to try to get it to adopt the policies they want. The behavioral consequences of these alternative definitions are different. For the college student, if the government fails to comply, he is empowered with political rights to "oppose" it, that is, to demand a change of government using normal democratic procedures. For the peasant, the rulers' failure to respond to his demands, in and of itself, does not give him the normative power to oppose his government.

Fourth, the two theories offer different understandings of freedom, a concept closely linked to democracy. Freedom in the liberal tradition is that area of individual action that the state does not limit by validly grounded laws. In *The Federalist Papers*, James Madison pointed out that a good government must be able to control the governed and at the same time control itself. To him, democracy meant order plus liberty (Hamilton et al. 2009 [1787–1788]). Huntington made a similar argument in *Political Order in Changing Societies* (Huntington 1968). To

---

[7] In the *Analects*, Confucius says that a ruler who finds pleasure in everyone agreeing with him will ruin the state (Confucius 1999, *Analects* 13.15). Mencius argued that "to take one's prince to task is respect; to discourse on the good to keep out heresies is reverence" (1992, *Book of Mencius*, 7.1/36/8).

[8] Respondent No. 6, interview conducted in Jixian County in Hebei province in the winter of 2002.

[9] Respondent No. 11, interview conducted at Peking University, Beijing, in the winter of 2002.

balance these two goals, the freedom of individuals must be constrained to achieve order. John Stuart Mill resolved the tension between freedom and order by defining freedom as the absence of social coercion (Mill 1993 [1859, 1863], 12–16). Isaiah Berlin differentiated positive liberty from negative liberty (Berlin 2002 [1969]).[10] To him, liberty in the negative sense defines the area within which people are, or should be, left to do what they want without interference by others.

Guardianship democracy values positive rather than negative freedom. According to Zhang Dongsun, "the Chinese from ancient times had nothing like the Western [liberal] concept of freedom." The concept of *zide*, or "getting [something] in, by, or for oneself" might seem to resemble this idea, but it actually referred to a kind of positive freedom that can be achieved only through a long process of self-cultivation to make one change for the better over time (Tan 2003, 167–75). Mao likewise argued that true freedom can be achieved only by a cumulative process of self-perfection. He believed that one is thoroughly free only when he or she no longer has the impetus to take negative social actions.

The two concepts of freedom were easily confused when the term "freedom" (or "liberty") was first introduced in China. Without proper words to describe the concept, the term was originally literally translated as "unrestrained."[11] Although people later adopted the term *ziyou* ("from oneself") to translate the concept of freedom, without the distinction between positive and negative liberty, *ziyou* carries a connotation more closely connected to anarchism than to the meaning of freedom in liberal theory.

My interviews confirmed that people in China understand freedom in these two different ways. For example, one state-owned enterprise (SOE) worker told me that democracy means *ziyou*, and he elaborated by saying, "Democracy means I can do whatever I want to do!" "Does *ziyou* mean you can ignore traffic lights?" I asked. "Of course, real *ziyou* means I can do whatever I want to do. Otherwise, what does *ziyou* mean and why would I want *ziyou*?"[12] A member of an NGO, however, who also told me that democracy means *ziyou*, explained, "When people are exercising

---

[10] The latter designates a negative condition in which an individual is protected from tyranny and the arbitrary exercise of authority, whereas the former refers to having the means or opportunity, rather than the lack of restraint to do things.

[11] Wilhelm Lobscheid's *English and Chinese Dictionary* (1866–1869) offers such a translation. See Xiong (2001, 69).

[12] Respondent No 2. Interview was conducted in the winter of 2001.

Impact on Understandings of Democracy

their freedom they should not infringe on the freedom of others." "Then how do you know if you infringe on other people's *ziyou*?" I asked. "The boundary is defined by law," he answered. The meanings of freedom in the minds of the two men were quite different: to one it meant the absence of all constraints; to the other it meant the right to do whatever one wants within the boundaries defined by law.

The differences between the liberal and guardianship concepts of democracy are often obscured in general discourse. The way in which the word "democracy" was translated into Chinese – *minzhu* – further complicates the issue. Xiong Yuzhi traced *minzhu* back to its origins in the Chinese classics and found that the original meaning of the word was "master of people" (Xiong 2001). Chen Pengren pointed out that when *minzhu* was used in *Shang Shu*[13] it referred to the ruler who made important decisions on behalf of his people (Chen 1989, 17). After the Han dynasty, the term *minzhu* was used as an abbreviation of *weimin zuozhu*, which means "rule for the people," or more specifically, decision making by government officials on behalf of the people to protect their interests. The term *weimin zuozhu* does not recognize the sovereignty of people or give people political rights, even though it requires government to protect their interests. In 1864, when W. A. P. Martin translated Wheaton's *Elements of International Law*, the word *minzhu* was used for the first time to translate the idea of a democratic political system (Xiong 2001, 74). The particular Chinese phrase chosen by translators, I would argue, leaves a lot of room for traditional culture to influence how people understand democracy.

The differences between democracy and *minben* lie in the means they designed to achieve good governance, the standards they use to evaluate governmental legitimacy, the roles they assign to people's participatory acts, and the ways they define the concept of freedom. The similarity between the two theories causes some people in Asia to understand democracy according to *minben*, whereas others understand it in ways that are consistent with the liberal tradition. Depending on which view a person holds, the meaning of "democracy" in the minds of Asian people can be fundamentally different from the understanding of democracy in the minds of Western experts.

---

[13] *Shang shu*, also known as the *Book of Documents*, is one of the five Chinese classics. It contains ancient historical records and speeches from Chinese officials, with the historical records purportedly reaching back to the emperors Yao and Shun.

HOW DO PEOPLE IN MAINLAND CHINA AND TAIWAN UNDERSTAND DEMOCRACY?

Although the political institutions in Taiwan reflect the principles of liberal democracy and those in mainland China reflect the principles of guardianship democracy, the Asian Barometer Survey found that institutional differences had only a limited impact on the way citizens in the two political systems understand democracy.

The Asian Barometer Survey examined this subject by asking an open-ended question: "What does democracy mean to you?" Interviewers were instructed to probe respondents twice after they gave the first answer. Ideally, the answers from all societies in the survey would be analyzed (they are summarized in Chu et al. 2008, 12). However, since I lack the language skills to pick up subtle differences in answers given in languages other than Chinese, I concentrated my analyses on data collected from mainland China and Taiwan. The data are presented in Table 7.1.

In both societies, people understand democracy in various ways. Many people linked democracy to freedom or liberty. When coding the data, I made a distinction between freedom and liberty. The understanding of respondents who only mentioned the word *ziyou* in their answer was coded as "freedom." If the respondent told our interviewers that democracy meant freedom within the boundaries defined by law, or that people enjoy the freedom to do what they want to do without infringing on other people's rights, I coded the answer as "liberty." It turned out that in both societies, among respondents defining democracy in terms of freedom or liberty, only about one-quarter added the proviso about not infringing on other people's rights.

Respondents who told our interviewers that democracy means elections and other institutional arrangements to constrain political power were put in another category. In the mainland, 10.2 percent of respondents perceived democracy as elections, checks, and balances, or the division of power among different branches of government. Despite Taiwan's fifteen years of democracy, a lower percentage of people – only 9.3 percent – defined democracy this way. In mainland China, 12.1 percent of respondents saw democracy as giving citizens the right to participate in politics, and another 11.7 percent believed it obliges government to listen to people's opinions. In Taiwan, the figures were 8.7 percent and 9.3 percent, respectively.

At the same time, the analyses show that a substantial number of people understand democracy according to *minben* doctrine. For 8.7 percent of

Impact on Understandings of Democracy

TABLE 7.1. *Understanding of Democracy in Mainland China and Taiwan*

What Does Democracy Mean to You?	Mainland China		Taiwan	
	Percent[a]	N	Percent[a]	N
Liberal conceptions of democracy				
Freedom and liberty	24.0		43.0	
Freedom	18.0	574	33.1	468
Liberty	6.0	192	9.9	140
Elections and rights-based participation	34.0		27.3	
Elections, checks and balances, division of power	10.2	324	9.3	132
Government has an obligation to listen to people's opinions	11.7	372	9.3	132
Rights-based participation	12.1	386	8.7	124
Minben conceptions of democracy	20.4		9.1	
Remonstration: government allows people to express their opinions	11.7	374	4.8	68
Guardianship: government takes people's interests into consideration	8.7	278	4.3	60
Others	44.7		39.7	
Government solicits/listens to people's opinion	16.3	520	4.7	67
Joint decision making, majority rule	17.4	554	7.9	112
Equality	6.3	202	7.1	101
Government provides people with a good life	1.6	52	7.8	110
Self-control			4.6	66
Chaos			7.6	108
Democratic centralism	3.1	98		
Don't know	41.8	1330	18.2	258

[a] Percent entries are percent of the total sample. Total exceeds 100 percent because multiple answers are allowed for each respondent.
Source: 2002 China and Taiwan surveys, Asian Barometer Survey I (China N = 3,183; Taiwan N = 1,415).

the people in mainland China, democracy means that a government takes people's interests into consideration when making decisions or brings tangible benefits (*shihui*) to its people. Another 11.7 percent felt it means that government officials allow people to express their opinions.[14] Similarly,

---

[14] To be included in this category, respondents had to have used words such as the government "allows" or "permits" people to express their opinions. The respondents' word choices suggest that they did not envision participation as a natural right of citizens but rather as a privilege bestowed by the authority.

4.3 percent of people in Taiwan considered a regime democratic as long as its policy making takes people's interests into consideration; 4.8 percent identified freedom of expression as the determining factor of a democracy. In all, 20.4 percent of people in mainland China and 9.1 percent of people in Taiwan understood democracy according to the *minben* tradition.

Beyond the answers outlined above, respondents also gave some answers that did not fit into the liberal-versus-*minben* classification. Some did not fit because they had elements of both theories – that is, that a good government is one that solicits and listens to people's opinions when making decisions, pursues joint decision making, aspires to ensure equality in society, and provides people with a good life. Others did not fit because they were not conceptual definitions but references to specific institutions. For example, for a long time, the CCP defined democracy as "democratic centralism" (the party listens to the people, then makes decisions, and the people obey). Although the regime stopped using this term more than two decades ago, we still find people who define democracy in this way. In Taiwan, some defined democracy in a negative way, referring to their disappointment with such phenomena as ethnic mobilization by the Democratic Progressive Party (DPP), fistfights in the Legislative Yuan, and widespread corruption.[15] They referred to these phenomena as "chaos" or some equivalent term or criticized them by saying that a proper democracy would demonstrate "self-control" or an equivalent term. Since these institutionally oriented responses do not reveal people's exact definitions of democracy, I put them in the "other" category.

Table 7.1 tells us something about the persistence of culture. If cultural norms adapt rapidly to new institutions, democratization in Taiwan should have caused people to abandon the more traditional *minben* understanding of democracy and adopt a liberal understanding. The persistence of *minben*-based conceptions in Taiwan shows that institutions have a limited impact on how people define democracy. To be sure, the percentage of Taiwanese (9.1 percent) who defined democracy according to the *minben* doctrine was lower than that of mainlanders (20.4 percent). But this does not necessarily show that the experience of living in a democratic regime in Taiwan has brought a strong switch to a liberal conception of democracy. Indeed, the percentage of people who adopted procedural understandings of democracy in Taiwan is still lower than that of mainland China.

---

[15] Despite living in an authoritarian society, no respondents in China attached negative meanings to democracy.

Impact on Understandings of Democracy 205

Another indicator of the persistence of *minben* culture is the sizeable number of people in Taiwan who attach negative meanings to democracy. When culture is congruent with institutions, it normalizes the acceptance of certain negative consequences associated with the institutional design and characterizes them as necessary evils. Liberal democratic theory assumes that along with the rights to participate in politics and elect leaders comes the possibility that voters may choose a bad leader; this is defined by a democratic culture as a necessary risk. If incompetent or malicious political leaders are elected, actors who have internalized a democratic culture would not question their political system. Instead, they would either start the recall process or wait for the next election to select a new leader. People who have internalized *minben* doctrine would not be as forgiving because viewing a bad leader as legitimate is not culturally acceptable. They might begin to challenge the validity of the electoral institutions that produced such a leader. Many people in China, for example, when facing problems generated by rural elections, began to doubt the validity of the electoral system. This seems also to have been the reaction of some people in Taiwan when the political class was perceived as behaving badly.

Ideological transformation can be a complicated and prolonged process. Unless a person under the influence of *minben* thinking is fully converted to liberal democratic ideology, he or she may accept the goals, the means, and other principles defined by liberal theory but may not view the possible negative consequences as acceptable costs of the new system. Thus, a new convert may evaluate the performance of the newly democratized political system according to the old standards defined by *minben* doctrine. After discovering that elections had produced a corrupt leader, the half-converted person would become dissatisfied with the new political system. Thus, the negative evaluation of democratic performance in Taiwan may not indicate that the new democracy does not work but that democracy in operation departs from people's expectations. If this hypothesis is correct, then the findings in Taiwan suggest that people were only partially converted to liberal democratic ideology. This may also help to explain the low evaluation of democracy given by people elsewhere in East Asia.

CULTURAL NORMS AND "COGNITIVE DIFFIDENCE" ABOUT DEMOCRACY

Table 7.1 revealed that many respondents in both mainland China and Taiwan gave a "Don't know" answer to the question "What does democracy mean to you?" "Don't know" answers can be interpreted as reflecting a lack of interest in or attention to the subject being asked about, a characteristic I label "cognitive diffidence." The opposite of cognitive diffidence might be termed "cognitive engagement." Cognitive diffidence may have different sources for different topics, such as a topic's complexity or sensitivity or its lack of salience to the respondent. As students of culture, our interest is in whether cultural factors play a role in preventing respondents from forming an understanding of what democracy means.

To explore the role of culture in shaping cognitive diffidence toward the meaning of democracy, I constructed a model with variables that will be familiar to the reader from previous chapters. Education, a primary sociological resource, increases people's cognitive capacity, equipping them with the ability to understand politics and governmental affairs, and should diminish cognitive diffidence. Income and urban residence should contribute to cognitive engagement, since economic development is accompanied by an expansion of government activities that brings more people in contact with political life. Males are more likely than females to be cognitively engaged with politics. Age is included in the model as a control.

Psychological resources, as discussed in Chapter 6, play a critical role in cognitive mobilization, leading some people to develop concern about their political system, which should lead them to acquire some knowledge of democracy. Three variables used in previous chapters are used here again to measure psychological resources: political interest, internal efficacy, and external efficacy. Institutions are also expected to influence people's cognitive engagement with the political system. If media control is successful, we should expect that access to official media would make people more likely to develop a certain understanding of democracy. People with regular access to grapevine rumors should also be more likely to become interested in the political system and develop an understanding of democracy. I included political fear in the model as a control variable.

Furthermore, people's interest in the characteristics of regime types might be influenced by the performance of government. If people feel that their current government is doing a good job managing public affairs, there is no need for them to rock the boat. Alternatively, if people believe their government is not doing its job, they may seek alternative political solutions. Thus, the likelihood that people will take an interest in the characteristics of different types of regimes might be negatively

Impact on Understandings of Democracy

correlated with the perceived performance of government. I used two questions to measure perceived government performance. The first question read, "In your opinion, is corruption a major problem here in your local area?" and the second, "In your opinion, how serious is corruption in the central government?"

I also hypothesize an important role for cultural norms. Hierarchical OTA requires people to defer political decisions to a group of qualified elites and follow their guidance, so they may not need to form an understanding of different regime types; in contrast, reciprocal OTA assigns people the responsibility to pay close attention to politics and government affairs. This suggests:

H1. *People under the influence of hierarchical OTA are less likely to develop an understanding of democracy than people under the influence of reciprocal OTA.*

Similarly, allocentric DSI discourages people from evaluating government policies purely on the basis of their impacts on their private interests, which gives government greater room to maneuver. Idiocentric DSI legitimizes evaluating government performance purely on the basis of its impact on one's private interests and should lead people to be more critical of public authority and more likely to think about alternatives to their current political system. Therefore:

H2. *People under the influence of allocentric DSI are less likely to develop views on the meaning of democracy than people under the influence of idiocentric DSI.*

The sources of cognitive diffidence may not be the same for all objects of cognition. I therefore compare the role of culture in encouraging "Don't know" answers to the meaning of democracy with "Don't knows" to another question that has a different referent: "How suitable is democracy for your country?" (Figure 7.1).[16] The referent of the *meaning* of democracy question is democracy in the abstract, as a regime type. The referent of the *suitability* of democracy is the respondent's country and its situation and political needs. For each dependent variable, I coded people giving any substantive answer as 1, and all "Don't know" and "Not applicable" answers as 0.

---

[16] Around 23 percent of respondents in the mainland reported that they did not know whether democracy fits China, and 41.8 percent told interviewers that they did not know the meanings of democracy. When asked about democratic suitability in their society, 15.2 percent of respondents in Taiwan said that they did not know the answer. To the open-ended question about the meaning of democracy, 18.2 percent told our interviewers that they did not know the answer.

TABLE 7.2. *"Don't Know" Answers in Mainland China*

	Don't Know the Meaning of Democracy		Don't Know Whether Democracy Suits China	
	Coefficient	SE	Coefficient	SE
Political culture				
OTA (reciprocal)	−0.415***	0.154	−1.040***	0.380
DSI (idiocentric)	−0.486*	0.284	−0.565***	0.174
Sociological resources				
Education	−0.154***	0.020	−0.094***	0.001
Income	0.000	0.000	0.000	0.000
Urban	−0.213	0.165	−1.628***	0.132
Male	−0.459***	0.116	−0.680***	0.116
Age	−0.028***	0.005	0.007	0.004
Psychological resources				
Political interest	−0.261***	0.072	−0.229***	0.076
External efficacy	0.029	0.038	−0.065***	0.047
Internal efficacy	−0.197***	0.049	−0.308	0.064
Institutional effects				
Political fear	−0.058	0.057	−0.022	0.071
Media exposure	−0.080***	0.025	−0.092***	0.025
Grapevine rumors	−0.141**	0.071	−0.124	0.092
Government performance				
Corruption of local government	−0.261**	0.116	−0.467***	0.115
Corruption of central government	−0.094	0.185	−0.368	0.248
Intercept	−0.868***	0.100	−1.629***	0.132

*** p < .01; ** p < .05; * p < .1
Source: 2002 China Survey, Asian Barometer Survey I (N = 3,183).

Since the dependent variables are binary, I chose the probit model. The results are presented in Table 7.2. As expected, most sociological and psychological resources increased the likelihood that people would provide substantive answers to both questions. Exposure to official channels of communication and grapevine rumors encouraged people to develop some ideas about democracy, but only the official channels and not grapevine rumors affected the likelihood of giving an opinion on the suitability of democracy. Perceived corruption in local, but not central, government was a factor that counteracted cognitive diffidence in both cases.

Turning to culture, the analyses show that OTA and DSI have statistically significant and strong impacts on the likelihood that people will

Impact on Understandings of Democracy

TABLE 7.3. *"Don't Know" Answers in Taiwan*

	Don't Know the Meaning of Democracy		Don't Know Whether Democracy Suits Taiwan	
	Coefficient	SE	Coefficient	SE
Political culture				
OTA (reciprocal)	−0.659*	0.358	−0.563	0.456
DSI (idiocentric)	−1.131***	0.487	−1.609***	0.535
Sociological resources				
Education	−0.192***	0.026	−0.105***	0.033
Urban	−0.144	0.246	−0.194	0.260
Male	−0.351*	0.191	−0.588**	0.271
Age	−0.032***	0.008	0.030*	0.180
Psychological resources				
Political interest	−0.477***	0.154	−0.094	0.176
External efficacy	−0.191*	0.105	−0.295	0.180
Internal efficacy	−0.120	0.132	−0.106	0.177
Institutional effects				
DPP membership	−0.372	0.225	−1.071***	0.348
Media exposure	−0.109*	0.062	−0.202***	0.069
Government performance				
Corruption of local government	−0.293	0.233	−0.210	0.275
Corruption of central government	−0.521**	0.260	−0.459	0.293
Intercept	−2.442***	0.131	−3.052***	0.198

*** p < .01; ** p < .05; * p < .1
Sources: 2002 Taiwan Survey, Asian Barometer Survey I (N = 1,415).

or will not develop both an understanding of democracy and a view on the suitability of democracy. As hypothesized, hierarchical OTA and allocentric DSI encourage respondents to express cognitive diffidence about both the meaning of democracy and its suitability for China.

By conducting a parallel analysis with the data from Taiwan, we can see whether this cultural effect is the same in a different institutional setting. The Taiwan model is presented in Table 7.3. The variables of political fear and grapevine rumors were removed from the model since they are not relevant to the situation in Taiwan. I added DPP membership as a control variable. Because the party was a major force behind democratic transition, membership in the DPP may have increased people's concern for the type of regime in Taiwan.

We find that sociological and psychological resources played a similar role in Taiwan in encouraging people to develop an understanding of democracy and a view on democratic suitability. In contrast to mainland China, however, urban residents in Taiwan were no more likely than rural residents to understand the meaning of democracy. This reflects the fact that economic development has largely eliminated the rural/urban differences there. In Taiwan, it was the perceived corruption of the central rather than the local government that influenced people's cognitive attention. This discrepancy reflects the fact that the central government has a more direct influence on the life of the average citizen in Taiwan than is the case in the much larger political system of mainland China.

The most important finding for this study is that cultural norms in Taiwan play important roles in the same way as they do in mainland China in shaping people's willingness to form views on political questions. After controlling for structural and institutional effects and government performance, hierarchical OTA and allocentric DSI in two societies with fundamentally different political institutions made people less likely to understand the meaning of democracy.

The findings in this section show that both modernization and culture influence the likelihood that people will develop views on some political issues relating to regime type. But we have not yet explored how culture may influence what views people adopt. Different understandings of democracy may have different consequences for political behavior and for political development in a society. Even if people want a regime change, those influenced by the *minben* tradition may not want a change to liberal democracy. Any conclusion about the impacts of economic development on political development, and particularly on regime change, would be misleading without an understanding of the impacts of structure, institutions, and culture on how people understand democracy.

HOW CULTURAL NORMS SHAPE PEOPLE'S UNDERSTANDINGS OF DEMOCRACY

The fact that democracy has become a universally accepted value does not mean that people everywhere accept the liberal conception of democracy prevalent in the West. Some people in mainland China and Taiwan do, whereas others understand democracy in terms of the *minben* doctrine or in other ways. Since the way in which people define democracy can have important consequences for individual behavior and the evolution of the political system, it is important to understand what factors influence the ways in which people understand democracy.

Impact on Understandings of Democracy 211

When people are exposed to a new idea, they need to decode the concept to understand its meaning and implications. Since the *minben* tradition is so influential in East Asia, it may influence the way in which the idea of democracy has been decoded as it has come into Asia from outside. In particular, OTA and DSI might influence people's cognitive decoding in two ways: (1) by shaping their expectations of the ideal type of government and (2) by providing standards for people to evaluate public authority.

I hypothesize that under reciprocal OTA, government's legitimacy depends on whether rulers are selected by ordinary people through established procedures. Under hierarchical OTA, people evaluate government's legitimacy on the substance of its policy outputs. This suggests:

H3. *While reciprocal OTA encourages people to define democracy as a political system with procedural arrangements for the election of leaders, hierarchical OTA encourages people to define democracy as a political system in which the government provides people with good policy.*

Reciprocal OTA obliges government to take people's views into account in policy making or else face opposition and replacement, whereas hierarchical OTA allows government to disregard the people's opinions when necessary for the greater interests of the majority. Hierarchical OTA encourages elites to listen to people's opinions, but it confines this function to information and fact-finding.

Thus:

H4. *Whereas people under reciprocal OTA perceive democracy as a system in which people enjoy the right to participate in politics and to oppose their government, people under hierarchical OTA deem a system to be democratic as long as it allows people to express their opinion.*

Definition of self-interest can also influence how people understand democracy. For people who believe in allocentric DSI, collective interests are ranked above the interests of individuals, giving government the normative power to make decisions on behalf of society. As with hierarchical OTA, governments are judged on the basis of the substance of their policies. Those who believe in idiocentric DSI, on the other hand, believe that government should provide a fair opportunity for each person to pursue his or her interests. Thus:

H5. *Idiocentric DSI leads people to define democracy as a set of procedural arrangements by which people can compete for power. Allocentric DSI guides people to define democracy as a government whose policies bring about tangible benefits for the people.*

Since idiocentric DSI defines the self as a legitimate unit of analysis in interest calculation, participation is seen as a right enjoyed by citizens in democratic institutions. Because allocentric DSI embeds private interests in the interests of collectives, government enjoys the right to ignore the interests of individuals in order to serve the interests of larger collectives or the whole society. Although allocentric DSI does allow people to express their opinions to authority, and encourages government officials to listen, as with hierarchical OTA, the norm limits the goal of these acts to information-gathering and communication. Thus:

H6. *Idiocentric DSI guides people to define democracy as a political system in which people enjoy the right to participate in politics. Allocentric DSI leads people to define a system as a democratic so long as the authorities provide people with opportunities to express their opinions.*

To test these hypotheses, I classified responses to "What does democracy mean to you?" into five types ("Don't know" answers were removed from the sample):

- *Liberty*. People who defined democracy as freedom under rule of law or as freedom without interfering with the rights of other people, were coded as 1, others as 0.
- *Rights-based participation*. People who understood democracy as a political system in which people enjoy rights to participate in politics, the right to express their opinions, and other human rights, were coded as 1, others as 0.
- *Elections/checks and balances*. People who perceived democracy as a political system in which people enjoy the right to elect political leaders and/or as a political system with checks and balances among different branches of government, were coded as 1, others as 0.
- *Allows people to speak*. People who defined democracy as a government that allows people to speak or as a government that solicits people's opinions when making decisions, were coded as 1, others as 0.
- *Government for the people*. People who described democracy as a political system in which the government takes people's interests into consideration when making decisions or as a government that is concerned about its people, were coded as 1, others as 0.

Scores of 1 on any of the first three variables indicated that the respondent understood democracy according to the liberal concept, and scores of 1 on either of the last two variables revealed that respondents understood democracy in terms of the *minben* doctrine or government by guardianship.

Impact on Understandings of Democracy 213

The same independent variables used in previous analyses were used to predict how people understand the meaning of democracy. The goal was to try and tease out the impacts of structural, cultural, and institutional variables. As cultural norms, according to the argument I proposed in Chapter 1, shape people's choices through both individual-level and community-level channels, I chose hierarchical linear modeling (HLM) for the analysis. Because the dependent variables are binary, I chose probit within HLM for the analyses. Each type of understanding of democracy is subjected to a separate regression. (Since respondents were allowed to give up to three answers to the question, a given respondent would appear in more than one of the regressions if he or she gave answers that fell into more than one category.) The results are presented in Table 7.4.

Although we found in Tables 7.2 and 7.3 that socioeconomic resources associated with modernization, psychological resources, and institutional effects all had some impact on people's propensity to form views on political issues, Table 7.4 shows that all these variables had only weak effects in moving people away from a guardianship conception of democracy toward a liberal understanding. Education caused Chinese to understand democracy in terms of liberty and the right to participate but did not reduce the likelihood that people would define democracy as a government that takes people's interests into consideration and/or one that allows people to express their opinions as part of the decision-making process. Urban residence, rather than fostering a Western liberal understanding of democracy, encouraged people to understand democracy in terms of the *minben* tradition. Youth tended to be more liberal and elders more devoted to a *minben* conception. Our standard measures of psychological resources showed no effect on the conception of democracy. The fact that access to the official media increased the likelihood that people would define democracy in terms of elections is initially puzzling but probably represents the success of regime propaganda in promoting the importance of village elections. Likewise, perceived government performance had a limited impact on how people understood democracy. Those who saw local government as corrupt were less likely to define democracy as a government that allows people to speak, whereas those who saw the central government as corrupt were more likely to define it in that way, which suggests that local government corruption did more to destroy the faith in guardianship democracy than did central government corruption.

Cultural norms played the largest roles in shaping how people in China understood democracy. The analyses confirm H3, H4, and H6. After controlling for social-structural, psychological, institutional, and performance variables, people with reciprocal OTA tended to understand

TABLE 7.4. *Cultural Impacts on People's Understanding of Democracy in Mainland China*

	Liberty		Rights-Based Participation		Elections/Checks and Balances		Allows People to Speak		Government for the People	
	Coefficient[a]	SE[b]	Coefficient[a]	SE[b]	Coefficient[a]	SE[b]	Coefficient[a]	SE[b]	Coefficient[a]	SE[b]
County-level effects										
Intercept	−2.555***	0.131	−1.971***	0.106	−0.758***	0.075	−1.304***	0.081	−0.201***	0.089
OTA (Reciprocal)	0.349*	0.020	0.227	0.184	0.269*	0.146	−0.133	0.164	−0.024	0.152
DSI (Idiocentric)	0.029	0.344	−0.028	0.294	−0.362	0.234	0.141	0.232	0.539**	0.258
Individual-level effects										
Political culture										
OTA (Reciprocal)	0.959***	0.291	2.886***	0.264	0.522***	0.161	−1.184***	0.206	−1.213***	0.240
DSI (Idiocentric)	0.781*	0.041	2.051	0.304	−0.018	0.226	−0.643**	0.285	−0.342	0.365
Sociological resources										
Education	0.047*	0.026	0.108***	0.022	0.021	0.015	0.010	0.018	−0.008	0.025
Income	0.000	0.000	0.000	0.000	0.000	0.000	0.000	0.000	0.000	0.000
Urban	−0.160	0.210	−0.287	0.185	−0.145	0.137	0.408***	0.151	−0.035	0.152
Male	0.066	0.150	0.226	0.130	0.153*	0.085	0.262	0.132	−0.052	0.133
Age	−0.107*	0.006	−0.011**	0.005	−0.004	0.003	0.013***	0.005	0.004	0.005

Psychological resources										
Political interest	0.127	0.102	−0.097	0.072	−0.033	0.063	0.021	0.064	0.216	0.153
External efficacy	−0.089	0.064	−0.096	0.068	−0.062	0.046	−0.017	0.046	−0.017	0.063
Internal efficacy	0.075	0.065	0.046	0.045	0.037	0.050	−0.096	0.055	0.031	0.063
Institutional effects										
Political fear	−0.047	0.110	0.024	0.077	−0.014	0.076	−0.042	0.080	0.105	0.092
Media exposure	0.019	0.039	0.050*	0.025	0.046**	0.022	0.018	0.023	0.014	0.031
Grapevine rumors	0.194	0.109	0.078	0.083	−0.051	0.068	0.041	0.080	−0.159*	0.083
Government performance										
Corruption of local government	−0.032	0.174	0.088	0.129	0.078	0.101	−0.330***	0.122	0.262*	0.153
Corruption of central government	0.472	0.297	−0.081	0.229	−0.182	0.195	0.464**	0.262	−0.442	0.328

*** $p < .01$; ** $p < .05$; * $p < .1$

[a] Entries are restricted maximum likelihood unstandardized coefficients with HLM 6.06.

[b] Entries are robust standard errors.

Source: 2002 China Survey, Asian Barometer Survey I (N = 3,183).

democracy in terms of procedural arrangements to constrain political power, the guarantee of liberty, and the right to participate in politics. People holding hierarchical OTA were more likely to understand democracy according to the *minben* tradition. The effect is seen at both the individual level and the county level. People living in a reciprocal environment are more likely to define democracy according to the liberal tradition than people living in a hierarchical social environment. Likewise, idiocentric DSI at the individual level led people to understand democracy as a political system guaranteeing people liberty and the right to participate in politics. Allocentric DSI, on the other hand, led to the notion that a democratic government allows people to express their opinions when it makes decisions.

However, no empirical evidence can be found to support H5. Definition of self-interest had no impact on how people define the democratic character of a regime. Taken together, the analyses confirm that hierarchical OTA and allocentric DSI encourage people to understand democracy in terms of minben doctrine. Reciprocal OTA, on the other hand, fosters a traditional liberal understanding.

To see whether the effects of culture on understanding of democracy are independent of the institutional setting, I looked again to the data collected from Taiwan. Table 7.5 shows the impacts of structure, institutions, and culture on people's understandings of democracy in Taiwan. Similar to mainland China, sociological and psychological resources had limited impacts on how people in Taiwan understood democracy. Despite the fact that democratic values have become a major subject of civic education in Taiwanese public schools, people with higher levels of education were not more likely to define democracy in liberal terms.

The most important finding for the purpose of this study is that cultural norms in Taiwan, a society with fundamentally different institutional settings, work the same way as they do in mainland China. While reciprocal OTA and idiocentric DSI made people in Taiwan more likely to understand the meaning of democracy according to liberal theory, hierarchical OTA and allocentric DSI made them more likely to understand the meaning of democracy in terms of guardianship.

The findings in Tables 7.4 and 7.5 are likely to be weakened by the fact that each of the five concepts of democracy is compared to a mixed bag of all other concepts. A clearer view of the impact of culture on conceptions of democracy can be obtained by classifying all respondents into three exclusive categories: those who gave all of their up-to-three responses to the question "What does democracy mean to you?" in the category of

	Liberty		Rights-Based Participation		Elections/Checks and Balances		Allows People to Speak		Government For the People	
	Coefficient	SE	Coefficient	SE	Coefficient	SE	Coefficient	SE	Coefficient	SE
Intercept	−0.479	0.072	−2.621***	0.121	−1.034***	0.079	−1.260***	0.080	−2.732***	0.160
Political culture										
OTA (Reciprocal)	−0.776***	0.265	3.951***	0.592	1.268***	0.280	−0.550*	0.290	−2.923***	0.560
DSI (Idiocentric)	−1.183***	0.291	2.937***	0.480	1.587***	0.376	0.317	0.369	−2.538***	0.464
Sociological resources										
Education	0.011	0.016	0.036	0.031	−0.005	0.006	0.038*	0.022	0.028	0.031
Urban	−0.057	0.143	−0.225	0.310	−0.216	0.173	0.353	0.231	0.474	0.333
Male	−0.134	0.140	−0.086	0.197	−0.097	0.147	0.534***	0.141	−0.090	0.257
Age	−0.011**	0.004	−0.004	0.009	−0.005	0.006	−0.006	0.007	0.014	0.010
Psychological resources										
Political interest	0.077	0.080	0.039	0.137	0.157	0.096	0.103	0.079	−0.070	0.151
External efficacy	−0.019	0.056	−0.176*	0.098	0.038	0.060	0.137**	0.059	0.120	0.109
Internal efficacy	−0.095	0.072	0.051	0.105	−0.057	0.076	0.075	0.083	0.240	0.142
Institutional effects										
Media exposure	−0.072*	0.039	0.107*	0.056	−0.031	0.044	−0.015	0.042	0.027	0.053
DPP membership	0.371**	0.165	0.071	0.248	0.031	0.169	−0.055	0.160	−0.083	0.267
Government performance										
Corruption of local government	−0.226	0.191	0.093	0.195	−0.195	0.160	0.234	0.174	0.050	0.298
Corruption of central government	−0.097	0.180	−0.392	0.246	0.245	0.155	−0.057	0.156	0.187	0.255

*** $p < .01$; ** $p < .05$; * $p < .1$
Source: 2002 Taiwan Survey, Asian Barometer Survey I (N = 1,415).

TABLE 7.6. *Different Understandings of Democracy (2002)*

Understanding of Democracy	Mainland China		Taiwan	
	Percentage	N	Percentage	N
Procedural	24.6	819	29.7	466
Minben	14.1	541	6.7	96
Mixed, others, and don't know	61.3	1,823	63.7	853

Source: 2002 China and Taiwan surveys, Asian Barometer Survey I (China N = 3,183; Taiwan N = 1,415). Data are weighted. Adapted from Tianjian Shi and Jie Lu, "The Shadow of Confucianism." *Journal of Democracy* 21, 4, October 2010, p. 128.

liberal-democratic answers, those who gave all of their responses in the category of *minben* answers, and all other persons (including those who gave mixed responses and those who gave "Don't know" responses). The numbers in each category are shown in Table 7.6.

The technique of multinomial regression allows us to compare the believers in liberal and *minben* concepts of democracy to all other respondents. The results are presented in Table 7.7.

The findings again highlight cultural norms as the single most consistent determinant of people's conceptions of democracy. Although structural, psychological, and institutional variables increase the likelihood that people will pay attention to the political system and develop an understanding of democracy, they have very limited impacts on how people understand democracy. Cultural norms alone have this effect among the variables we have examined.

CONCLUSION

The key findings of this chapter can be summarized as follows: most people in mainland China and Taiwan claim that they want democracy, but democracy means different things to different people. While sociological and psychological resources do cause people to develop some understanding of democracy, as suggested by social mobilization theory, the ways in which they understand democracy are shaped by the cultural norms they were socialized into in their early lives. Traditional culture in Chinese society does not prevent people from accepting democracy as ideal form of government, but it does help to define the particular meaning of democracy for political actors. The ideal type of government

TABLE 7.7. *Multinomial Analysis of Cultural Impacts on People's Understanding of Democracy (2002)*

| | Mainland China | | | | Taiwan | | | |
| | Liberty/Rights-Based Participation | | Allows People to Speak/ Guardian of People | | Liberty/Rights-Based Participation | | Allows People to Speak/ Guardian of People | |
	Coefficient	SE	Coefficient	SE	Coefficient	SE	Coefficient	SE
Intercept	0.097***	0.078	0.073	0.072	−0.913***	0.095	−0.258***	0.164
Political culture								
OTA (reciprocal)	0.913***	0.208	−1.419***	0.236	1.172***	0.281	−2.400***	0.600
DSI (idiocentric)	0.434	0.291	−0.204	0.322	1.421***	0.387	−2.496***	0.569
Sociological resources								
Education	0.031*	0.018	0.017	0.020	0.000	0.211	0.011	0.033
Urban	−0.038	0.141	0.157	0.137	−0.169	0.179	0.359	0.314
Male	0.174	0.113	0.234	0.129	−0.092	0.148	−0.051	0.286
Age	−0.003	0.004	0.011**	0.005	−0.003	0.005	0.013	0.011
Psychological resources								
Political interest	−0.046	0.062	0.076	0.086	0.155	0.099	0.062	0.155
External efficacy	−0.086	0.054	−0.077	0.050	0.061	0.064	0.186	0.116
Internal efficacy	0.061	0.051	−0.027	0.060	−0.032	0.079	0.269	0.149
Institutional effects								
Media exposure	0.050*	0.025	0.050*	0.027	−0.025	0.044	0.011	0.056
CCP membership	−0.358**	0.152	−0.164	0.019				
DPP membership					0.029	0.166	−0.182	0.259
Government performance								
Corruption of local government	0.069	0.132	−0.092	0.128	−0.178	0.165	0.067	0.030
Corruption of central government	−0.100	0.230	0.086	0.254	0.257	0.157	0.136	0.263

*** p < .01; ** p < .05; * p < .1
Source: 2002 China and Taiwan surveys, Asian Barometer Survey I (China N = 3,183; Taiwan N = 1,415).

defined by traditional culture significantly influences the way people in these two societies understand democracy. Studying people's aspiration toward democracy without carefully examining what democracy means to them would cause researchers to reach inaccurate conclusions about the relationship between people's support for democracy, regime change, and democratic consolidation.

The analyses also reveal that the institutional changes in Taiwan, rather than altering the relationship between traditional cultural norms and the way people there understand democracy, reinforced cultural impacts. Together, these findings provide a possible explanation for why Asians under the influence of Confucian culture appear to be outliers to the social mobilization theory that predicts that democratization will follow modernization.

The findings may also help explain popular support for the authoritarian system in mainland China and popular suspicion of the democratic system in Taiwan. Since many people in both societies define democracy according to *minben* doctrine, the standards they use to evaluate government legitimacy and performance must be different from those of liberal democrats. Because traditional *minben* culture bases government legitimacy on policy outcomes, depriving people of the right to elect public officials or ignoring requests made by certain people in the society does not jeopardize regime legitimacy. Even if people are not satisfied with a policy, their understanding of democracy does not include the right to try to replace the government. Policy conflicts are to be resolved by informing the existing leaders of the realities of people's lives. Thus, despite the survey results showing that an absolute majority of people in China claim they want democracy, the way Chinese people understand democracy leaves their government great space to maneuver. This space, I would argue, constitutes the micro foundation of authoritarian resilience in China.

Cultural variables may also help explain the decline of popular support for democracy and the presence of democratic reversals in Asia in recent years. Unless people in this region fully convert to liberal values, they may accept the goals defined by liberal democratic theory and even the means defined by liberal theory to achieve these goals, but they may not be able to accept the negative consequences associated with the new institutional design. Newly converted democrats, such as the people of Taiwan, may evaluate the performance of the democratized political system according to the standards defined by *minben* theory.

Conclusion and Theoretical Reflections

This book has been dedicated to solving some long-standing puzzles about the political attitudes and behavior of people in the Asia region. These include the resilience of the authoritarian government in China; the failure of economic development to bring about democratic transition in that country as predicted by modernization theory; and democratic disaffection and reversals in some Asian countries. In the process of analyzing the multiyear Asian political survey data on which this study is based, some further, related puzzles arose. People in China simultaneously expressed high trust toward the authoritarian government and high demand for democracy; people in Taiwan evaluated their government as more democratic than the level of democracy that they want.

The theory of culture I have developed to explain these phenomena differs from traditional theories of political culture in three major ways. First, I have defined culture as socially shared norms that set up standards of appropriate behavior in a given society. Conventional theory in political science defines culture as a kind of resource, which influences people's choices by reducing the perceived costs and/or increasing the perceived benefits associated with political actions. I view culture as a social property that exists in the minds of people in a community.

Second, the mechanisms I have identified by which culture influences people's choices are more complicated than those described by the standard theory of political culture. I argue that culture influences people's choices through two channels. At the individual level, culture influences behavior through its definition of normative rationality. It influences the decision-making process by which actors develop their responses to other actors, especially their government. Culture influences how actors interpret others' actions by providing guidance for seeking, filtering, and arranging information; provides the standards people use to judge others' behavior; and helps define the goals people will pursue in their responses. At the societal level, culture exerts its influence through both normative rationality (the internal policing system of norms) and instrumental rationality (the external policing system of norms). The mechanisms by which the cultural environment influences people's choices are different from those at the individual level and include defining acceptable behaviors and defining social sanctions for unacceptable actions. Conventional studies of political culture have focused on culture's impacts on levels of political participation, leaving out culture's ability to constrain the means actors choose to pursue their goals. Although all cultural norms allow people to engage in conventional and unconventional political activities under certain circumstances, cultural norms differ in the conditions under which they define varying political acts, especially unconventional ones, as appropriate. I have stressed that unless researchers can take into consideration the impacts of culture from both levels and the complexity of culture's causal workings, any theory of cultural impacts on people's political behavior will be incomplete.

Third, I have proposed a new way to measure culture. In conventional theory culture is measured either by individual psychology or by the distribution of certain orientations in a society. I have argued that neither approach can properly measure culture. To understand how culture influences people's choices, researchers need to measure not only the psychological orientation of individuals but also the cultural environment surrounding political actors. This is measured either by the mean culture in a community or by the existence of a group of strongly committed deviating norm holders, depending on whether the effect of community culture on individuals is exerted through its influence on the internal policing system of norms or the external policing system of norms.

The core argument advanced in this book – and the one that provides answers to the puzzles laid out above – is that different cultural norms endow people with different standards to evaluate government performance, define for actors different goals to pursue, and constrain the choices of means with which people feel normatively justified to pursue political goals. It makes sense, then, that the same government behavior will generate different responses from people with dissimilar cultural orientations and thereby produce different impacts on the political processes in a society. Understanding the determinants of people's political attitudes and behavior requires students of comparative politics not only

Conclusion and Theoretical Reflections

to explore the structural and institutional constraints facing people but also to carefully examine the impacts of culture.

The cultural norms I chose to focus on – orientation toward authority (OTA) and definition of self-interest (DSI) – illuminate the political questions laid out at the start. They inform people's ideas respectively about the proper relationship between individuals and the state and about the proper unit on which to base interest calculations. The norms I view as prevalent in the Confucian-influenced societies of Asia (hierarchical OTA and allocentric DSI) and those prevalent in societies influenced by Western European philosophical traditions (reciprocal OTA and idiocentric DSI) indicate societies at odds in the ways they see the role of leaders, the role and rights of citizens, and the relationship between citizens and the state.

After specifying how culture influences people's choices, I used survey data collected in mainland China and Taiwan at different times to test the impacts of culture on people's political attitudes and behavior. The empirical analyses in this book are divided into two parts. In the first part, culture is treated as a dependent variable, and the two key aims were: (1) to find out whether the cultural norms I identified exist in both societies; and (2) to discover whether they are independent from social structure and political institutions. The book's argument turned on this second objective, for if culture is endogenous to structure and institutions, then it would be merely an intervening variable with no independent effects, and there would be no need to study the effect of culture on politics.

To measure cultural norms in mainland China and Taiwan, I used the same variables to survey people in these two societies. With the aid of confirmatory IRT factor analysis, I showed that OTA can be distinguished from DSI, and that this is true for both societies, and at different times. A similar relationship exists in both societies between latent constructs and the observable variables we used to measure culture. After demonstrating that both cultural norms exist in the two societies, I examined the impacts on culture of structural and institutional changes between 1993 and 2002. The analyses showed that although some people in both societies converted to different cultural norms between the two surveys, the direction of change was opposite from the one suggested by current theories of cultural change. Structural and institutional changes caused some people to re-embrace traditional culture rather than to update their cultural orientations in line with new incentive structures. This finding confirmed that structural and institutional changes in these societies failed to bring about the concomitant changes of culture predicted by some theories.

Having established that culture is independent from structure and institutions, the second set of empirical analyses explored how these two cultural norms influence people's political attitudes and behavior. I began with an examination of culture's impact on political trust. Political scientists have commonly believed that people's attitudes toward government are shaped by its performance and by people's ability to understand the impact of government activities on their lives. This theoretical framework is built on the assumption that people everywhere use identical standards to evaluate government performance. My theory challenges this assumption. I argue that different cultures endow people with different standards for evaluating government behavior and achievements. Thus the same government behavior can trigger different responses in different cultures.

Testing for the impacts of culture on people's political behavior required me to choose an analytical tool that could estimate separately culture's impacts through the two different channels I had theorized – the individual and the social-environment channel – and which could at the same time reveal the interaction between these two causal pathways. For this I used hierarchical linear modeling (HLM). The empirical test of cultural impacts on political trust in China demonstrated that cultural norms influence trust through both individual psychology and the social environment, and that hierarchical OTA and allocentric DSI make people more likely to trust their government.

A key question for the analysis was whether the cultural impacts revealed by the data could be products of China's authoritarian institutions. Ruling out this possibility – the endogeneity of culture – required controlling for social-structural and institutional variables in order to isolate culture's impacts on political trust. While comparison cases are difficult to obtain, Taiwan offered an excellent comparison because it has a more modernized social structure and a more democratic set of political institutions than China but similar cultural variables. The data collected from Taiwan confirmed that the impacts of culture on political trust cannot be reduced to those of structure or institutions. I found the same patterns in Taiwan as in mainland China: people holding hierarchical OTA and allocentric DSI were more likely to trust their government than people holding reciprocal OTA and idiocentric DSI.

Having established culture's impacts on a key political attitude, I went on to test its impacts on political behavior. To study cultural impacts on

Conclusion and Theoretical Reflections

participation, I separated people's decisions to participate in politics into three stages: (1) deciding whether to assign responsibility to government for a problem; (2) if yes, deciding whether to address the problem; and (3) if yes, choosing a particular act of political participation. I tested each stage separately for the impact of norms. The analyses confirmed that cultural norms have statistically significant impacts on each of these decisions. Most important, a comparison of the impacts of cultural norms, structural resources, and institutional constraints showed that cultural norms have more significant impacts on people's participatory behavior than do social structure and political institutions.

The impacts of different cultural norms on participation, however, are more complicated than it would seem. Allocentric DSI makes people more politically passive, whereas hierarchical OTA makes people more active. Participatory acts under hierarchical OTA, however, including unconventional political responses, take on different meanings because the goal of the acts, as defined by this norm, are different from those authorized by reciprocal OTA. Hierarchical OTA limits almost all acts of political participation to those designed to remind the government of its responsibilities and/or inform it about situations that need its attention – that is, to acts of remonstration. Only in the most severe case – when the people believe the regime has lost the right to rule – are unconventional political actions intended to be acts of opposition. The combined impact of these two norms – which make people less likely to engage in unconventional political acts (allocentric DSI) and limit the goals of participation to remonstration (hierarchical OTA) – suggests that the kind of widespread social movement critical to democratic transitions is unlikely to occur in China so long as these cultural norms retain strong influence.

Finally, I tested the impact of culture on people's understanding of democracy. Our surveys revealed that a majority of people in mainland China and Taiwan showed a strong desire for democracy. Yet the empirical results also showed that: (1) a majority of people in authoritarian China believed that they enjoy high levels of democracy and (2) respondents in Taiwan believed the democratic supply in their societies exceeded their demand. I have argued that these findings can be explained by the way people understand the meaning of democracy. Specifically, people in these two societies may associate some features of guardianship with the popular but abstract word democracy.

But what makes people regard guardianship as a form of democracy? The answer, I proposed, lies in the fact that guardianship and liberal democracy share the same glorious goals: securing quality governance by reducing chaos, providing a stable environment for socioeconomic and political activities, serving the public interest, and increasing collective benefits for the whole society. In other words, the goals embraced by guardianship coincide with the way in which good government is represented in the concept of liberal democracy in today's political discourse.

But liberal democracy and guardianship democracy also display important differences. First, in the liberal tradition, a regime is democratic when it allows open, fair, and competitive elections to choose government leaders and when governmental decisions are made according to well-established procedures. In the guardianship tradition, the nature of the regime is assessed by the substance of government policies, especially whether these policies can provide tangible benefits to its people. Second, in the liberal tradition, the system must allow people to oppose their government, that is, to replace it with a different one if that is what they collectively prefer. Guardianship limits the function of participation to communication and allows people to oppose their government only in extreme conditions. Under guardianship theory, when people's policy opinions differ from those of their leaders, the rulers' discretionary power allows them to take a different policy path, if they think that following public opinion will jeopardize collective societal interest.

To find out how people in these two societies understand the meaning of democracy, I used an open-ended survey question that allowed people to explain the meaning of democracy in their own words. I coded the answers into categories; most of them could be classified as relating either to liberal democracy or to guardianship democracy. A substantial number of people in both societies understood democracy in terms of guardianship. I then tested for structural, institutional, and cultural impacts on how people understood democracy. The analyses confirmed that reciprocal OTA and idiocentric DSI make people more likely to understand democracy in liberal terms, while hierarchical OTA and allocentric DSI make people more likely to define democracy in guardianship terms. The finding is true for both authoritarian China and democratic Taiwan, which again indicates that it is not China's authoritarian institutions that lead many people to understand democracy in terms of guardianship.

The book seeks to offer four contributions to comparative politics in general and the study of Chinese politics in particular. First, by defining culture as norms, the book brings normative rationality back to the study of politics. The cultural theory advanced here argues that the attitudes and behavior of political actors toward their government are shaped not only by government performance and people's cognitive ability to understand

Conclusion and Theoretical Reflections

its meanings and implications. They are also significantly shaped by the standards people use to evaluate government behavior. While I acknowledge that instrumental calculation of interests can shape people's political behavior, I make a broader argument that culture assigns the very costs and benefits that enter into such instrumental calculations. This points to the need for students of comparative politics to understand the normative rationality of people in the societies they are studying in order to correctly understand the determinants of political attitudes and behavior in those societies.

Second, in contrast with previous theories of culture, this theory specifies clearer and more complex causal mechanisms by which cultural norms influence people's choices. I model cultural norms as systems of societal regulation that control people's behavior through internal and external policing systems and specify the interaction between these two levels. I operationalize this conception with appropriate methodological tools. In doing so I hope to show how researchers can use multilevel analysis to estimate separately the causal pathways from culture via individual psychology and the social environment as well as the relationship between the two.

Third, I show that culture's *effects* are more complicated than previously recognized. Rather than simply influencing the level of political participation, cultural norms define the ideal type of government, shape people's attitudes toward their government and the standards they use to evaluate it, and constrain their choices of political acts. The two traditional cultural norms examined in this book – hierarchical OTA and allocentric DSI – encourage people to trust their government more, make them less likely to engage in unconventional political activities, confine the goals of participation under normal circumstances to remonstration, and discourage people from opposing their government. These norms guide people to understand the meaning of democracy in terms of guardianship rather than liberal procedural arrangements for people to choose their leaders.

Finally, these findings point to answers to the questions posed at the beginning of the book. The traditional norms – hierarchical OTA and allocentric DSI – held by the majority of people in China make them more likely to trust their government, less likely to engage in unconventional political activities, and more likely to perceive democracy as government by guardianship. This gives the communist regime in China greater space to maneuver than its Western counterparts have, providing a safety valve for the authoritarian regime. Culture has contributed to the success of the costly state-owned enterprise reforms and other painful economic reforms and to the resilience of the regime.

Likewise, the troubles of Asian democracies arise partly from the lack of congruence between their liberal-democratic institutions and cultural norms widely held among their people. If modernization and institutional change had driven cultural change, such incongruence could have been easily resolved. But culture is persistent. As a result, liberal democracy has a long way to go before it can consolidate its position in Asia.

Appendix A

Sample Design for the Surveys

CHINA SURVEYS

Sample Design for the 1993 China Survey

The 1993 data for China come from the earliest of our surveys – Survey of Political Culture and Political Participation in Mainland China, Taiwan and Hong Kong – conducted in mainland China from September 1993 to June 1994 in cooperation with the Center for Social Survey of the People's University of China. The sample represents the population over 18 years of age residing in family households at the time of the survey, excluding those living in the Tibetan Autonomous Region.

To select the sample, we used a stratified multistage area sampling procedure with probabilities proportional to size measures (PPS). For primary sampling units (PSUs) we used counties (*xian*) for rural areas and cities (*shi*) for urban areas. Before selection, counties were stratified by region and geographical characteristics, and cities were stratified by region and size. A total of 49 counties and 85 cities were selected as the primary sampling units. The secondary sampling units (SSUs) were townships (*xiang*) for rural areas and districts (*qu*) or streets (*jiedao*) for urban areas. The third stage of selection was geared toward villages (*xingzheng cun*) in rural areas and neighborhood committees (*juweihui*) in urban areas; a total of 551 villages and neighborhood committees were selected. Households were used at the fourth stage of sampling. The data analyzed include all villages in the sample as well as neighborhood committees in urban areas where more than 50 percent of residents held rural household registrations.

230   *Appendix A*

The *National Population Databook* (Ministry of Public Security 1987) was used as the basic material for constructing the sampling frame in the selection of PSUs. The number of family households for each county or city was taken as the measure of size in the PPS selection process. For the successive stages of sampling, population data were obtained either from the Public Security Bureaus of the regions or from the Statistical Bureaus of local governments. At the village and neighborhood committee levels, lists of household registrations (*hukou*) were obtained from police stations in urban areas and villagers' committees in rural areas.

We employed retired high school teachers as interviewers for most surveys (see also Chapter 3). Although most people in China read and write standard Mandarin Chinese, people in many southern provinces speak varying dialects, some of which are extremely difficult for Mandarin speakers to understand. To deal with this problem, professional interviewers from the National General Team for Rural Surveys (*guojia nongcun diaocha zongdui*) who speak local dialects were hired to interview in seven largely dialect-speaking southern provinces. All interviewers were given formal training before the fieldwork.

Before the interviews began, letters were sent to all the sampling spots to check for address changes. Any invalid addresses were removed from our sampling frame, thereby eliminating the majority of noncontacts. Of the 3,425 sampled cases, 3,287 interviews were successfully completed, giving us a response rate of 94.5 percent.

Sample Design for the 2002 China Survey

The 2002 survey (part of the Asian Barometer Survey I) was conducted in mainland China from March to June 2002 in cooperation with the Institute of Sociology at the Chinese Academy of Social Sciences. It yielded 3,183 valid cases out of 3,752 sampled cases for a response rate of 84.1 percent (82.5 percent in urban areas and 86.5 percent in rural areas). The sample represents the population over 18 years of age residing in family households at the time of the survey, excluding those living in the Tibetan Autonomous Region. Again, we used a stratified multistage area sampling procedure with probabilities proportional to size measures (PPS) to select the sample.

The primary sampling units (PSUs) employed in the sample design were counties (*xian*) in rural areas and cities (*shi*) in urban areas. In province-level municipalities, districts (*qu*) were used as the PSU. Before selection, counties were stratified by region and geographical characteristics,

Appendix A 231

and cities or districts were stratified by region and size. A total of 67 cities or districts and 62 counties were selected as the primary sampling units. The secondary sampling units (SSUs) were townships (*xiang*) in rural areas and districts (*qu*) or streets (*jiedao*) in urban areas. The third stage of selection was geared to administrative villages (*xingzheng cun*) in rural areas and neighborhood committees (*juweihui*) or community committees (*shequ weiyuanhui*) in urban areas. We selected 249 administrative villages and 247 neighborhood or community committees in the third stage of the sampling process. A total of 496 tertiary sampling units (TSUs) were selected. Households were used at the fourth stage of sampling.

In selecting the PSUs, we used the *National Statistical Yearbook* (1999) as the basic source for constructing the sampling frame. The number of family households for each county or city was taken as the measure of size (MOS) in the PPS selection process. For the successive stages of sampling, population data were obtained from the All China Women's Association (ACWA); we used the sampling data the ACWA had collected in the year 2000 for a survey on women's status in China. For areas not covered by the ACWA survey, local ACWA chapters were asked to collect sampling data for us. Household registration (*hukou*) lists were obtained for all village and neighborhood committee levels. These lists were used as the sampling frame for the fourth stage of the sampling process.

Weighting variables for the sample were calculated along the three dimensions of gender, age, and educational level using the method of "raking." This method ensures that when the data are used in a statistical program it produces distributions on these dimensions consistent with the entire population.

We employed retired high school teachers as interviewers for the survey. Our collaborators in China contacted the association for retired high school teachers in the Dongcheng and Haidian districts in Beijing to ask for their help in identifying newly retired teachers. We sent the identified retired teachers (between the ages of 55 and 62) a letter informing them about the survey and asking them to apply for jobs as interviewers. Around 150 retired teachers applied, and we chose 67 of them to be our interviewers.

The teachers chosen for the job went through an intensive training program. The training began with a lecture on the basic concepts of social science research, survey sampling, and interview techniques and also familiarized them with the questionnaire to be used in the survey. After the lecture, interviewers-in-training were instructed to practice among themselves. Project leaders then brought them to a village in rural Beijing and asked them to find someone in the village to interview. Project leaders reviewed these interview results and met with student interviewers one-on-one to go over any problems. One project leader, in a lecture to the whole class of trainees, described the common problems that arose in the practice interviews. As a "final exam," we subjected each trainee to a rigorous test: to conduct an "interview" of each instructor. These allowed our examiners to evaluate whether the trainees understood the proper interview techniques. Those who passed were dispatched to different places in China to conduct interviews.

Two measures of quality control were incorporated in the survey. First, we sent letters to prospective respondents, informing them that an interviewer would come to his or her home to conduct an interview within a month. In the letter, we included a self-addressed envelope and an evaluation form asking respondents to (1) report whether someone had in fact come to his or her home and (2) evaluate the interviewer's attitude toward his or her job. We asked respondents to send the letter back after the interview or after one month in the case of a no-show. Second, we asked our field supervisors to randomly check 5 percent of respondents to evaluate the quality of the interviews. We informed interviewers about the control mechanisms before dispatching them to conduct interviews in order to deter them from cheating.

In most cases, Mandarin was used for interviews. In the case of respondents who did not understand Mandarin, interviewers could hire interpreters to assist them in the interview.

Sample Design for the 2008 China Survey

The 2008 survey (part of the Asian Barometer Survey II) was conducted in mainland China in cooperation with the Research Center for Contemporary China (RCCC) of Peking University. Again, the sample represents the population over 18 years of age residing in family households at the time of the survey, excluding those living in the Tibetan Autonomous Region.

As with the first two survey designs, to select the sample we used stratified multistage area sampling procedure with probabilities proportional to size measures (PPS). The primary sampling units (PSUs) were counties (*xian*) for rural areas and cities (*shi*) for urban areas. Before selection, counties were stratified by region and geographical characteristics, and

Appendix A

cities were stratified by region and size. A total of 135 PSUs were chosen based on location, geographic characteristics, and region size. Among them, 67 were in urban areas and 68 were in rural areas.

The secondary sampling units (SSUs) were townships (*xiang*) in rural areas and districts (*qu*) or streets (*jiedao*) in urban areas. The samples selected for the third stage were administrative villages (*xingzheng cun*) in rural areas or community resident communities (*shequ weiyuanhui*) in urban areas. We selected 352 administrative villages and 136 community resident committees in the third stage of the sampling process. A total of 488 tertiary sampling units (TSUs) were selected. Households were used at the fourth stage of sampling. The number of households in each county and city was determined by the probabilities proportional to size measures (PPS). Half a year prior to the survey, RCCC had sent letters to the selected village committees and urban community resident committees to verify changes in the population so as to obtain an updated list of the current residents in each place. We then removed all invalid addresses from the sampling frame. The new lists were used as the sampling frame for the last stage of sampling. The survey sampling selected 6,971 potential respondents and our interviewers successfully completed 5,402 interviews, giving us a response rate of 77.5%.

Because the geographical location of the 2008 survey was identical to that of the 2002 survey, we decided to use the same interviewers from our 2002 survey team when possible. When interviewers who worked for us in 2002 were unavailable, new interviewers were recruited and trained to replace them. The same training materials and process were used to train the new interviewers.

To retrain interviewers who had worked with us on previous surveys, we sent them a training lectures DVD, an interviewer's guide, and the questionnaire. We instructed them to watch the DVD and carefully study the questionnaire. Field directors of the RCCC then called each interviewer to examine his or her knowledge of the new survey.

Fieldwork commenced in December 2007 and concluded in June 2008. Before the survey was conducted, RCCC sent letters to the selected respondents to inform them of the forthcoming interview and request that they respond to an independent post-interview evaluation of the performance of the interviewers. These telephone assessments were carried out by four trained staff between March and May 2008. Fifteen percent of the successfully completed questionnaires from each interviewer were randomly selected for assessment.

234   *Appendix A*

TAIWAN SURVEYS

Sample Design for the 1993 Taiwan Survey

The survey was designed and carried out by a team at the National Taiwan University directed by Professors Hu Fu and Chu Yun-han. The target population was defined as Taiwan residents who were eligible voters in the year of the most recent election. The voting age in Taiwan is 20. Because elections in Taiwan take place in November or December of a given year and the surveys were carried out in the following year, the lowest age found in the survey data set was 21.

Because the target population for this research project included all eligible voters in Taiwan, we adopted a fairly complex multiple stage sampling method. Using a variety of research strategies – including probabilities proportional to size sampling (PPS), stratified sampling, systematic sampling, and double sampling – we attempted to the best of our ability to produce a sample that would reflect and represent the general voting-age population. The design of the sampling process included three main steps: the method of sampling, determination of the optimal sample size, and the actual sampling process.

According to sampling theory, the size of the sample and the size of the population to be studied are unrelated. In general, a sample size of between 900 and 1,600 will produce a confidence interval of an acceptable level of precision (e.g., within 3 percent in each direction), at a confidence level (e.g., 95 percent) that most scholars deem desirable. From the perspective of efficiency, a sample size of more than 1,600 is not necessarily superior to a smaller one. Increasingly larger sample sizes mean greater capital, human, and time costs but limited reduction of sampling error. If the sample is too small, the analyst may not be able to make confident inferences about the general population. After considering all relevant factors, we determined that a sample size of 1,400, or one out of every 9,500 eligible voters, was optimal for this study. Respondents were selected from the electoral registers compiled by county and city election commissions for the 1992 Legislative Yuan elections.

The first step in the actual sampling process was to divide the target population into several strata. The guiding principle of stratified sampling is that differences within the stratum should be as small as possible, and the differences between the strata should be as large as possible. In an effort to achieve this goal, we used multiple analysis of variance

Appendix A 235

(MANOVA) and cluster analysis to divide Taiwan's electorate into six strata according to the vote shares of party candidates for the Kuomintang and Democratic Progressive Party as well as independent candidates. The number of respondents to be interviewed from each stratum was fixed in proportion to each stratum's percentage of the total electorate. A total of 33 rural townships (*xiang*), urban townships (*zhen*), and districts or boroughs (*qu*) were sampled from the six strata. Finally, several polling stations were selected from each designated *xiang, zhen,* and *qu*. The total number of eligible voters was determined by each county and city electoral commission.

To ensure that there were enough eligible respondents to successfully reach the target of 1,400 successful interviews, double sampling was employed. To compensate for respondents who might have moved, refused to be interviewed, or could not be successfully interviewed for some other reason, we obtained a pool nine times the size of the original target sample. In the event of an unsuccessful interview, the original respondent was replaced by a person with a similar background from this supplementary pool. All respondents were chosen by systematic sampling with equal intervals.

Reliability of Interviews
During a period of two months, 1,402 respondents were successfully interviewed. To test the reliability of these interviews, the research committee decided to use a test–retest reliability test. Thus, we sampled a significant proportion of successfully interviewed respondents to be interviewed again.

When choosing the questions to be tested in the follow-up interviews, we selected more important and more sensitive questions. The two most important questions asked in these follow-up interviews were whether the respondent had voted and for which political party. With respect to whether respondents voted or not, replies in the initial and follow-up surveys were positively and significantly correlated (κ = 0.69218; result: substantial). Only 16 of the 311 respondents (5.9 percent) reinterviewed gave a different answer when asked whether they had voted. When asked which party they had voted for, there was again a positive and significant correlation between the initial and follow-up interviews (κ = 1.0000, a perfect result). Of 187 respondents reinterviewed, not a single one changed his or her answer to this question. In light of these results, the reliability of this survey should be regarded as acceptable (see Table A.1 and A.2).

236   *Appendix A*

TABLE A.1. *Test–Retest for Whether Respondent Voted*

		Follow-Up Interviews	
		Did Not Vote	Voted
Initial Interviews	Did Not Vote	9.7 (21)	1.5 (4)
	Voted	4.4 (12)	86.5 (237)

Note: Entries are percentages. Numbers in parentheses are Ns. Kappa = 0.69218 Result: substantial df = 1 N = 274.
Source: Post-Survey Interview, Taiwan Survey, 1993 Survey of Political Culture and Political Participation in Mainland China, Taiwan, and Hong Kong.

TABLE A.2. *Test–Retest for Respondent's Vote (Choice of Party)*

		Follow-Up Interviews	
		Voted for KMT	Voted for DPP
Initial Interviews	Voted for KMT	74.3 (139)	0 (0)
	Voted for DPP	0 (0)	25.7 (48)

Note: Entries are percentages. Numbers in parentheses are Ns. Kappa = 0.69218 Result: substantial df = 1 N = 274.
Source: Post-Survey Interview, Taiwan Survey, 1993 Survey of Political Culture and Political Participation in Mainland China, Taiwan, and Hong Kong.

Sample Design for the 2002 Taiwan Survey

As with the 1993 survey, the 2002 survey was designed and carried out by a team at the National Taiwan University directed by Professors Hu Fu and Chu Yun-han. The target population was again defined as Taiwan residents who were eligible voters in the year of the most recent election, and the lowest age found in the data set was 21. The target population was sampled according to the PPS method.

PPS Method (Probability Proportional to Size)

Sampling was divided into three stages: towns/counties, villages/*li* and individual voters. Taiwan was statistically divided into 359 districts in accordance with changes in vote share from the 1998 to 2000 national elections. Gary King's EI method was used to estimate the effect of both elections on vote share.

Using the PPS method, voters were stratified and leveled into eight divisions. Each division was systematically sampled. Within each division, four, six, or eight towns/counties were selected; from these, two villages/*li* were selected, and out of the villages, between thirteen and sixteen people were sampled. However, in the municipalities of Taipei and Kaohsiung, only *li* and individuals were sampled (see Table A.3).

Appendix A

237

TABLE A.3. *Population Division and Sample Breakdown*

Division	Townships	Number of Voters	Percentage of Total Voters	Expected Sample	Total Sample (Townships × Villages × Individuals)
1	38	2,486,529	16.10%	225	8 × 2 × 14 = 224
2	31	1,384,339	9.00%	126	4 × 2 × 16 = 128
3	73	1,729,024	11.20%	157	6 × 2 × 13 = 156
4	51	2,603,242	16.90%	237	8 × 2 × 15 = 240
5	48	1,889,900	12.30%	172	6 × 2 × 14 = 168
6	95	2,372,053	15.40%	216	8 × 2 × 14 = 224
7 (Taipei)	444*	1,914,915	12.40%	174	30 × 6 = 180
8 (Kaoshiung)	463*	1,042,117	6.80%	95	16 × 6 = 96
Total		15,422,119	100.10%	1402	1414

* Borough level (equivalent to township) was skipped in these two cities and *li* level (equivalent to village) was sampled directly.

Note: The Taiwan project did not have the authority to access the personal information required to select individuals to survey. That responsibility fell instead to the Academia Sinica.

Source: Sampling Information, Taiwan Survey, 1993 Survey of Political Culture and Political Participation in Mainland China, Taiwan, and Hong Kong.

TABLE A.4. *Checking Representativeness of Taiwan Survey Sample (Data before Raking)*

Variables	Values	Sample Values	Expected Population	Chi-Square	Significance
Gender	male	688	719	2.735	P = .098
	female	727	696		
Age	20–29	247	341	43.591	P = .000
	30–39	358	345		
	40–49	368	314		
	50–59	168	173		
	60+	234	243		
Education	elementary	374	413	116.959	P = .000
	junior high	172	283		
	high school	445	409		
	two-year college	178	163		
	university	246	148		

Source: Sampling Information, Taiwan Survey, 1993 Survey of Political Culture and Political Participation in Mainland China, Taiwan, and Hong Kong (N = 1,402).

Raking was used to weight the data in order to render the sample's gender, age, and education data consistent with the entire population (see Tables A.4 and A.5).

238   *Appendix A*

TABLE A.5. *Checking Representativeness of Taiwan Survey Sample (Data after Raking)*

Variables	Values	Sample Values	Expected Population	Chi-Square	Significance
Gender	male	719	719	0.00003	P > .05
	female	696	696		
Age	20–29	335	341	0.327	P > .05
	30–39	341	345		
	40–49	314	314		
	50–59	175	173		
	60+	249	243		
Education	elementary	414	413	0.006	P > .05
	junior high	282	283		
	high school	409	409		
	two-year college	162	163		
	university	148	148		

Source: Sampling Information, 1993 Taiwan Survey (N = 1,402).

Appendix B

Validity of Measurements

Respondents' concern about the confidentiality of their answers might affect the validity of data gathered in China. We adopted several measures to protect the identity of respondents.

First, no one had access to the lists of respondents except the interviewers. Only the interviewer who was going to conduct a particular section of the fieldwork was authorized to see the respective list of families to be interviewed.

Second, each interviewer was required to sign a "pledge of confidentiality" and to attend a basic lecture on professional ethics. Rules and regulations were given to the interviewers to ensure professional conduct. Furthermore, there was a strict rule that if anyone were to reveal a respondent's identity, he or she would be fired immediately.

Third, after the interviews, no information about the respondents' identities was kept at our Beijing headquarters. All information was moved to the United States. Anybody who had access to the original questionnaires was asked to sign a statement of confidentiality and warned not to reveal any information about the questionnaire.

Fourth, the interviews were conducted with the formal, voluntary consent of the respondents. Respondents could refuse to be interviewed or to answer any of the questions.

The respondents were also informed that their names would not be revealed to anyone.

Whether or not the above measures were capable of making people comfortable enough to give candid answers to sensitive political questions is an empirical issue. In this appendix, I examine the validity of

240   *Appendix B*

the measures of political trust and of the measure of people's subjective evaluation of democratic supply in China.

VALIDITY OF OUR MEASURES OF POLITICAL TRUST

The high level of regime-based trust in China calls into question the validity of the measures used to tap political trust in China's authoritarian environment. Do these measures reveal the true level of political trust in the society, or are they a proxy for political fear? We believe that those variables indeed measure political trust in China for the following reasons:

First, the findings revealed in this survey are not unique. Nearly every survey in China in recent years has reported that general political trust, and regime-based trust in particular, are extremely high (Chen 2004, 2005; Li 2004; Shi 2001; Wang 2005). For example, the World Values Survey shows that comparatively, the Chinese government enjoys the highest support from its people in the world (Wang, Dalton, and Shin 2006). A survey conducted by Wenfang Tang yielded similar results (Tang 2005, Chapter 3). In a more recent survey, Lianjiang Li reported that only 4 percent of peasants in rural China expressed "relatively low" or "very low" support for the regime (Li 2004).

As numerous surveys independently conducted by different scholars have reached similar conclusions, we know that these results cannot be attributed to random error. But could the findings have been produced by a nonrandom error? Did respondents lie to interviewers to hide their true feelings about the regime and avoid potential political persecution? To test this explanation, I first examined whether political fear was still widespread in China. I designed two questions to measure the extent of political fear. These two questions were used in both the 1993 and 2002 surveys, and I present the answers acquired from both surveys in Table B.1. As shown in the table, political fear is still a problem in China, but the level has declined. In 1993, more than 40 percent of people reported that they were somewhat afraid of being reported if they criticized the government or party and national leaders. In 2002, one-quarter of people in mainland China reported the same kind of political fear.

Is political fear a problem in other transitional societies? We are fortunate to have data collected from Taiwan in 1993, then a society in transition. Although at the time of the first survey, an opposition party had been established and martial law was already lifted, no island-wide election for provincial leaders or national leaders had been

Appendix B

TABLE B.1. *Political Fear in Mainland China and Taiwan: Changes and Continuity*

Responses	Mainland China				Taiwan	
	1993		2002		1993	
	Percent	N	Percent	N	Percent	N
If You Criticize the Government, Are You Worried that Someone Might Snitch on You?						
No Fear at All	2.2	72	4.3	138	48.7	683
No Fear	47.5	1560	55.1	1753	20.4	286
Somewhat Fearful	38.7	1271	25.4	809	11.6	162
Very Fearful	3.3	108	2.1	66	2.8	36
Don't Know & Not Applicable	8.4	276	13.1	418	16.7	234
Total	100.1	3287	100.0	3184	99.9	1402

Responses	1993		2002			
	Percent	N	Percent	N		
If You Criticize Party and National Leaders, Are You Worried that Someone Mght Snitch on You?						
No Fear at All	2	67	4.4	141		
No Fear	45	1480	54	1721		
Somewhat Fearful	37.9	1246	20.8	663		
Very Fearful	4.5	149	2.6	81		
Don't Know and NA	10.5	345	18.1	578		
Total	99.9	3287	99.9	3184		

Source: 1993 Survey of Political Culture and Political Participation in Mainland China, Taiwan and Hong Kong; 2002 China Survey, Asian Barometer Survey I (China 1993 N = 3,287; 2002 N = 3,183; Taiwan 1993 N = 1,402).

held. Researchers on the Taiwan team thus included the first question in the survey, and I present the result on the right side of the table. The analysis shows that the percentage of people who claimed that they were very fearful of criticizing the government in Taiwan (2.8 percent) was similar to that of mainland China (3.3 percent); 11.6 percent of people in Taiwan also claimed that they were "somewhat fearful" of criticizing the government. The finding suggests that political fear is a common problem for transitional societies. Though Taiwan had already begun its transition to democracy at the time of the survey, we can still find residuals of authoritarian rule – that is, the fear of criticizing one's government.

Appendix B

TABLE B.2. *Correlation between Political Fear and Political Trust*

Types of Trust	Fear of Criticizing Government	Fear of Criticizing National Leaders
Incumbent-Based Trust	−0.04 (2334)*	−.013 (2399)
System/Regime-Based Trust	−0.01 (2489)	−.013 (2215)

*** p < .01; ** p < .05; * p < .1
Source: 2002 China Survey, Asian Barometer Survey I (N = 3,183).

Political fear may exist in a society, but such fear may or may not prevent people from telling interviewers their true feelings toward public authority. Can the high level of political trust in China be attributed to political fear?

The following hypothesis can be developed to determine whether people's answers to questions about political trust were contaminated by political fear:

If people who were fearful of political persecution lie to interviewers by claiming to trust the government, political fear should be positively correlated with political trust. Alternatively, if political fear exists in China but does not contaminate people's answers to questions on political trust, we should find that those fearful of political persecution are also distrustful of authority.

To test the hypothesis, I performed a Pearson correlation analysis between political fear and the two dimensions of political trust. The results are presented in Table B.2.

The Pearson correlation analysis shows that political fear is either negatively correlated with political trust or has no statistically significant impact on political trust. This finding shows that the high level of political trust in mainland China cannot be attributed to political fear. The analysis also suggests that a special kind of governmental legitimacy may exist in East Asia in general, and in China in particular, as discussed in Chapter 7.

VALIDITY OF OUR MEASUREMENTS OF THE SUPPLY OF DEMOCRACY IN MAINLAND CHINA

Analyses of people's evaluation of democratic supply reveal that people in mainland China possess a high appraisal of democratic development in their country. Can we rule out the possibility that the high appraisal of democratic supply in mainland China is caused by political fear?

Appendix B 243

If political fear prevents respondents in China from giving candid answers to interviewers, respondents may use two strategies to hide their true opinions: they can either lie to interviewers or tell interviewers that they do not know the answer. To find out whether respondents lied to interviewers to conceal their true opinion, in our survey we also asked respondents to evaluate democratic achievements in China before 1979 and in the mid-1990s. If political fear prevented people from revealing their true feelings about democratic achievements in 2002, we can expect them also to give a high appraisal of democratic development at other times. In 1979, China was just emerging from totalitarianism. Respondents' evaluation of democratic supply at that time was 4.85 (on a scale of 1 for completely undemocratic to 10 for completely democratic), indicating that most people perceived the regime as undemocratic. By the mid-1990s, however, the regime had recovered from the Tiananmen Square incident in 1989 and reopened to the outside world. Reflecting such a change, the mean score was 6.08. These analyses show that there is significant variation in respondents' appraisal of democratic supply in China at different times.

If respondents lied to interviewers to conceal their true opinions, we should also find that our political fear index is negatively correlated with people's appraisal of democratic supply. A simple correlation analysis shows that there is no statistically significant relationship between these two variables. These findings suggest that although political fear still exists in mainland China, it does not make people lie to interviewers when asked to evaluate democratic supply in their society.

It is more difficult, but not impossible, to rule out the possibility that people in mainland China used "don't know" answers (DKs) to conceal their true opinions. Although approximately one-quarter of respondents did not answer the democratic supply and demand questions, only 2 percent of respondents provided a straight refusal to answer (see Table B.3). If refusals were used to hide true opinions, the percentage would be too small to explain the high appraisal of democratic achievement in China. If people used DKs to hide their true opinion, the level of DKs in authoritarian China should be higher than in other societies. Comparing the level of DKs from China with the level of DKs in other societies included in the Asian Barometer Survey shows that the level of DKs in mainland China is indeed about 10 percent higher than that in other societies.[1]

---

[1] Combined "Don't know" and refusal answers in people's evaluation of the current regime is 9.1 percent in Japan, 10.7 in Hong Kong, 2.6 in Mongolia, .2 in the Philippines, 12.9 in Thailand, and 4.9 in Taiwan. Source: Asian Barometer Survey I.

244

Appendix B

TABLE B.3. *Missing Values in Democratic Supply and Demand Questions*

	Not Applicable	Don't Know	Refusal
Democratic Demand	.3 (9)	23.0 (732)	1.8 (57)
Democratic Supply before 1978	2.4 (78)	27.3 (869)	1.9 (60)
Democratic Supply in Early 1990s	1.3 (41)	24.7 (787)	2.0 (62)
Democratic Supply at the Time of the Survey	.3 (10)	27.1 (862)	2.2 (70)

Source: 2002 China Survey, Asian Barometer Survey I (N = 3,183).

There are two possible explanations for DK answers. One is political fear. A second plausible explanation would attribute the DKs to ignorance: people might give a DK answer when the question is beyond their comprehension and they do not know how to answer it.

Two propositions may be deduced to test which explanation is correct. First, if respondents used DKs to hide their true opinions, we should find that educated people are more likely to give DKs than less educated people. This is because educated people are more likely to understand the political risks of revealing their aspirations toward democracy under an authoritarian regime. On the contrary, if the cognitive deficiency hypothesis better explains the situation in China, we should find that education is negatively correlated to DKs. As education increases, people's ability to deal with complexity and abstract ideas increases, making more educated people more likely to be able to answer these questions

Second, people who are more interested in politics should be more likely to understand the meaning of democracy and, at the same time, know the political risks they face in expressing unorthodox opinions. Thus, if the political fear hypothesis is correct, we should find that people who are interested in politics are more likely to give DK answers to these two questions. On the contrary, if the cognitive deficiency hypothesis explains DKs better, we should find the relationship between political interest and DK answers is reversed – those who are not interested in politics are more likely to give DK answers to these questions than others.

Table B.4 presents the nonparametric correlation between education, political interest, political fear, and DK answers to questions measuring democratic demand and supply in China. In the upper part of the table, I present the tau-*b* and in the lower part of the table, I present Spearman's rho. The analyses show that both education and political interest are

Appendix B

TABLE B.4. *Impacts of Education, Political Interest, and Fear on Item Nonresponses*

	Democratic Demand		Democratic Supply	
	Refusals	*Don't Knows*	*Refusals*	*Don't Knows*
	Kendall's tau-b			
Education	−.043***	−.327***	−.054***	−.326***
Political Interest	−.029*	−.247***	−.083***	−.243***
Political Fear	−.014	−.014	.001	−.013
	Spearman's rho			
Education	−.051***	−.384***	−.064***	−.383***
Interest in Politics	−.031*	−.265***	−.088***	−.261***
Political Fear	−.015	−.041	.001	−.014

Note: * significant at .05 level, ** significant at 0.01 level, *** significant at .001 level (two-tailed).
Sources: 2002 China Survey, Asian Barometer Survey I (N = 3,183).

negatively correlated to DKs in China and that political fear has no statistically significant impact on DKs. Together, the analyses suggest that the cognitive deficiency hypothesis explains DK answers better than the political fear hypothesis. There is no empirical evidence to support the political fear hypothesis.

Appendix C

Comparing Different Measurement Models: IRT versus CMT

Two major theories have been developed for testing the dimensionality of latent constructs and for guiding scale building – classical measurement theory (CMT) and item response theory (IRT).[1] These two theories are built on different assumptions and have different requirements for questionnaire design. The properties of the scales derived from them are also different.

In CMT, researchers are required to assume that the observed variables represent the true scores of the latent constructs they are measuring for each respondent, plus an error term. The error is not differentiated into subcategories, that is, across item, time, and settings. The score in the CMT scale is a linear transformation of raw scores, and the confidence intervals of the scale are represented by a straight line for all scores, that is, the same confidence interval is applied to each score (Embretson and Reise 2000, 16). An important implication of those assumptions for questionnaire design is that in order to achieve precision, researchers must design each item measuring latent constructs similarly. Each item is supposed to tap the latent construct in the same way so that the standard error applies to the whole population after the raw data scores are transferred into scales. Unfortunately, such requirements can rarely be met in social surveys, and the above assumptions are usually violated. Furthermore, the relationships between raw scores and latent constructs

---

[1] Because the measurement theories were developed by psychologists to evaluate standardized tests, some scholars used the term classical test theory (CTT) for CMT. They are equivalent. See DeVellis (2003) and Embretson and Reise (2000).

Appendix C 247

may also be nonlinear. If the raw data scores are binary variables, the confidence interval band will become increasingly wide for extreme scores, violating another important assumption of CMT and also causing errors in estimation.

To address these problems with CMT, psychologists developed a new technique, IRT, to examine the dimensionality of latent constructs and to scale their data. IRT models depend upon three parameters – the capacity to discriminate, the difficulty of the item, and its susceptibility to false positives. All parameters are crucial for our study of norms. In testing, the "difficulty" of each item refers to how hard it is to get a correct answer to the question. As adapted to the measurement of attitudes, "difficulty" (as described in Chapter 3) is a measure of how unlikely it is that respondents holding the attitude under measurement will give a response to the question that reveals that attitude (hereafter, a "positive" response). In IRT, a higher difficulty score means that the item is weighted more heavily in the combined scale.[2]

For some questions, even limited commitment to a norm will make people give positive answers; for others, a strong commitment is required for people to give positive answers. For example, OTA3 ("When a mother-in-law and a daughter-in-law come into conflict, even if the mother-in-law is in the wrong, the husband should still persuade his wife to obey his mother," see Chapter 3) may be easy for people with hierarchical OTA to accept. However, OTA1 ("If a conflict should occur, we should ask senior people to uphold justice," see Chapter 3) could be more difficult for them to accept. Rather than treating each item as a roughly equivalent indicator of the same underlying phenomenon, IRT assigns different weights to different items when evaluating their contribution to latent constructs. The ability of IRT to differentiate difficult items from easy ones is especially useful in measuring people's normative orientations; it allows researchers to examine not only the qualitative differences in people's commitment to norms but also the strength of their commitment. This property of IRT is especially important as it can help researchers avoid Type I errors (false positive findings) in measuring norms.

Scores in CMT gain strength through their aggregation as a scale. An important implication of this property is that scale reliability is increased by redundancy – the more similar measurements are, the better the scale

---

[2] Although the survey items are designed as ordinal variables, the most important difference in the responses is the direction of the answers, which tells us the respondent's orientation.

performs. This can create problems when measuring norms. As we have emphasized, norms are situation-specific, and variations in people's commitment to norms is represented by the "jurisdiction" of norms perceived by its holders. Lower levels of commitment to a norm mean that actors perceive a smaller scope of issues as governed by the norm. Conversely, higher levels of commitment mean that actors perceive a wider scope of issues to be governed by the norm. This property of norms constitutes a specific problem in using CMT. Each survey question measures commitment to norms in a particular issue area, under specific situations. Questions designed to measure the different subdimensions of a norm are likely to be aggregated and used in the same model.

In IRT, the relationships between each item and latent construct are independently assessed. Standard errors are smallest when the items are optimally appropriate for a particular level of commitment to latent constructs and when the discriminatory power of the item is high. Unlike CMT, in IRT more items do not necessarily increase the reliability of the scale. The precision of IRT is enhanced by having items with specific characteristics that can capture a particular aspect of the latent construct. This property of the IRT model is especially useful in measuring norms, as it allows researchers to assess the level of commitment respondents have to a particular norm.

In CMT, factor structure is derived from a correlation of observable variables. Because the same covariance structure in CMT can be produced by different causal structures, an infinite numbers of configurations can in theory lead to the same correlation matrix. As a result, determining the configuration of factor structure by factor loading in CMT models with two or more factors is nothing more than guesswork (Kim and Mueller 1978, 38–39). In guessing the structure of latent constructs, researchers conventionally use factor loading as an acceptable threshold for assigning an observable variable to a particular factor, but this criterion is just a convention, not based on any theory. An advantage of confirmatory factor analysis based on the IRT model is that researchers do not need to make judgment calls to assess the relationships between observed variables and latent constructs. To test the dimensionality of a factor structure that has been developed based on theory, IRT uses fit statistics rather than loadings. As long as a variable's coefficient is statistically significant, we know that it contributes something to the latent construct.

Finally, when using IRT, respondents' positive or negative answers to an item have constant meaning with respect to their level of commitment to a given norm, irrespective of who the person is or the average level

Appendix C

of a particular orientation in a sample. Respondents are characterized by metrics independent of any specific sample. This means researchers can compare IRT scores across samples and time periods. This property makes IRT extremely useful in comparative studies of political cultures across nations and time. For our purpose, IRT is a superior method for testing the dimensionality of cultural norms in mainland China and Taiwan and for scaling the data for further analyses.

Appendix D

The Mechanism of Cultural Shifts: The Cases of Yu Luojin and "Running Fan"

In this appendix, I compare two cases that occurred in China in different eras in order to demonstrate the mechanism of cultural shifts that has been ignored by most students of political culture. The first one is the story of Yu Luojin. She was the sister of Yu Luoke, the author of *On Family Background*, who was executed by the Chinese Communist Party (CCP) in the 1970s. As a writer and somewhat of a celebrity herself, Yu Luojin's experience provides a baseline for understanding cultural shifts.

As a family member of one of the most famous and condemned counter-revolutionaries of the Cultural Revolution, Yu faced an extremely hostile political environment. She was "sent down" to Xingtai, Hebei province, and struggled to survive in an area stricken with extreme poverty. Although many people were reluctant to associate with her, some ignored political pressure and offered her help. One sent-down youth from Mulidawa Qi, a wealthier area in Heilongjiang, married Yu despite the political pressure and took her to the place to which he had been sent down. The couple had a child but later divorced because Yu had an extramarital affair.[1] After her divorce, Yu returned to Beijing to work as a nanny. In the face of the hostile political environment surrounding Yu, Cai Zhongpei, an electrician in Beijing, married her in July 1977. The marriage provided Yu with shelter and also made it possible for her to transfer her household registration from Heilongjiang to Beijing.

In 1979, Yu Luoke was posthumously rehabilitated by reformers in the CCP and thereafter was openly praised as a hero in the Chinese media. Yu Luojin subsequently found fame by penning a memoir about

---

[1] See http://jhyb2007.blog.sohu.com/56757639.html (accessed December 17, 2013).

250

Appendix D

her brother and her life during the Cultural Revolution. The article, which thoroughly condemned the Cultural Revolution, was published in China's most important literary journal, *Dang Dai* (*Contemporary*). Soon after, Yu decided to divorce Cai, claiming that they had nothing in common. Cai disagreed with the divorce and challenged her claim in court. In response, rather than settling things quietly with Cai, Yu published a series of articles in the Chinese media explaining her decision to divorce him. In these articles, she claimed that she had never loved Cai and asserted that marriage without love was immoral. She also insisted that she *should* and *would* divorce her husband (Yu 2009).

Yu's article generated heated debate among the public, eventually drawing well-circulated magazines such as *Xin Guancha* (*New Observer*) into the conversation. At the time, most people saw Yu's decision to divorce her second husband as a violation of the dominant cultural norms in Chinese society on two grounds: (1) Yu used "the self" rather than the family as the unit of analysis in her interest calculation; (2) in two different situations, she had betrayed a different man, each of whom had married her when she had been in a difficult situation. With the exception of a few liberal intellectuals and college students, people widely condemned her decision to divorce Cai.

Observers from abroad tend to interpret the widespread media criticism of Yu as orchestrated by the regime. My interviews of editors and reporters who participated in the debate, however, suggest that the criticism and condemnation were spontaneous. The criticism and condemnations can be considered powerful external policing acts on the part of dominant norm holders. Rumor also played a critical role in mobilizing Yu's opponents. The gossip and the vocal criticism of Yu allowed traditional norm holders to both reaffirm their moral superiority and to demonstrate to others their firm commitment to a dominant norm. Those critiques successfully put Yu in social isolation, a change that made her life miserable. In a later article, she claimed that her enemies were all around, making it difficult for her even to breathe. Before long, she fled the country to escape the painful social isolation that had been created by the external policing mechanisms of dominant norm holders in Chinese society. In a recently published book, Yu claimed that she had been a prisoner of Chinese culture since the late 1970s (Yu 2009).

Analyzing these events in terms of the theory presented in this book, we find that: (1) the trauma of the Cultural Revolution caused some people, especially liberal intellectuals and young students, to abandon allocentric DSI and to convert to idiocentric DSI; (2) pattern-maintaining change in

252   *Appendix D*

allocentric DSI might have occurred for some people, but the change did not affect the ways people dealt with relationships within their families. In other words, familial relationships were still effectively governed by allocentric DSI; (3) cultural flexibility had yet to occur for allocentric DSI at the individual level – those who subscribed to allocentric DSI did not hesitate to impose sanctions against norm violators like Yu; and (4) although deviating norm holders had begun to emerge in Chinese society, most of them were young and had yet to occupy strategic social positions. Neither Yu nor her supporters were politically skillful norm entrepreneurs.[2] Thus, although Yu had many supporters, they failed to provide her with the critical support necessary for her to survive socially; dominant norm holders were still able to socially isolate her. As such, external policing acts on the part of dominant norm holders in Chinese society created enormous pain and distress for her.

The second case is the story of Fan Meizhong, a graduate of the history department of Peking University, who taught at a private high school in Sichuan province. When the enormous 2008 Wenchuan earthquake occurred, Fan rushed out of the classroom, thereby abandoning his students. He subsequently posted an article on *Tianya*, one of the most popular Internet forums in China, expressing no regret for leaving his students behind. He defended his actions: "In such a life-and-death moment, I would give up my life only for my daughter. I would not do it for other people, even my mother."[3] His choice to run out of the classroom, along with the subsequent publication of his justifications for the decision he made, earned him the nickname Fan Paopao ("Running Fan")." Like Yu, Fan's decision to circulate his articles in a public forum made him a norm

---

[2] The concept of norm entrepreneur has been borrowed by regime scholars in International Relations, and is now widely used (Finnemore 1993, 1996; Finnemore and Sikkink 1998). Norm entrepreneur refers to a person who seeks to influence a group to adopt or maintain a norm. The norm entrepreneur may press for the creation or enforcement of a norm for reasons that are either humanistic or selfish. Some examples of norm entrepreneurs are human rights advocates and environmentalists. Howard S. Becker uses the term "moral entrepreneur" for norm entrepreneur, and argues that they fall into roughly two categories: rule creators, and rule enforcers. Rule creators can be seen as moral crusaders, who are concerned chiefly with the successful persuasion of others, but are not concerned with the means by which this persuasion is achieved. Successful moral crusades are generally accomplished by those in the upper strata of society. Moral crusaders must generate power, public support, public awareness of the issue, and be able to propose a clear and acceptable solution to the problem (Becker 1963, 147–53).

[3] The details about Fan's blog posting on *Tianya* can be found at: http://tech.hexun.com/2008-06-17/106747959.html (accessed December 15, 2013).

Appendix D   253

entrepreneur. However, unlike Yu, Fan was not punished with social isolation for his infraction of dominant social norms.

A comparison of the two cases reveals several important differences in the cultural environments that faced these two political actors: in 2008 (1) more people in their 20s and 30s had abandoned allocentric DSI for idiocentric DSI; (2) pattern-maintaining change in allocentric DSI had occurred in China, and the change had begun to affect the ways in which people dealt with issues related to the family; (3) cultural flexibility had also occurred for some individuals – some of those who subscribed to allocentric DSI were no longer willing to impose sanctions against norm violators for fear of being blamed or labeled as outdated (i.e., *laowangu*, or "old fogey"); (4) deviating norm holders had begun to occupy strategic positions in society, taking up roles such as university professors and editors in mass media. Moreover, the spread of the Internet and the community forums it hosted provided young people in China with critical outlets for expressing their opinions; and (5) greater numbers of deviating norm holders were willing to stand up for Fan than was the case in Yu's situation. These deviating norm holders' acts greatly reduced the dominant norm holders' capacity to socially isolate Fan. Although these changes could not prevent all people from imposing sanctions upon Fan, the effects of such sanctions were greatly reduced. Because the cultural environment had changed, the dynamic of interactions among societal actors was quite different in 2008 as compared with 1979.

Although both Yu and Fan violated allocentric DSI, they used fundamentally different strategies to justify their behaviors. Yu justified her decision by arguing that she was so miserable that she had no choice and that marriage without love was immoral; "Running Fan" directly challenged dominant cultural norms by claiming he had a natural right to save his own life over the lives of his students. Yu neither challenged the dominant norms in the society nor the norms' jurisdiction in her case. Instead, she blamed the social environment for putting her in such an awkward situation. Effectively, Yu's real argument was that her case should be exempt from the governance of allocentric DSI due to *force majeure*. In effect, she acknowledged that most people would perceive her decision to divorce her husband as a violation of dominant norms, and she implicitly recognized the right of others to impose sanctions against her. The tone of her articles even suggests that she harbored guilt over her actions. From her behavior, we may infer that pattern-maintaining change, rather than cultural discontinuity, had occurred to Yu. She recognized the right for dominant norm holders to impose sanctions against the violation of

254   *Appendix D*

allocentric DSI under *normal* circumstances but was pleading a personal exemption due to her special situation.

By contrast, Fan took a completely different strategy for dealing with criticism. Fan openly announced that it was within his natural right to choose "self" over the collective as the unit of analysis in his interest calculation and accused his critics of infringing upon his rights. Rather than feeling any guilt over abandoning his students, Fan perceived himself as morally superior to dominant norm holders in the society.[4] Fan's behavior suggests that he had converted to idiocentric DSI and that the norm provided him with different behavioral guidance. He had undergone a process of cultural discontinuity.

The even more important difference in these two cases was in the response from society. While few people in the late 1970s openly supported Yu, Fan enjoyed open support from certain groups of people. This shows that pattern-maintaining change had occurred for some people in 2008. Many sympathizers of "Running Fan" told me in interviews that although teachers should protect their students, they did not think a teacher should be asked to give up his life for his students.[5] For those people, even if Fan's choice was morally wrong, it could be justified by the circumstances he faced.

As a consequence of these changes, the cost for allocentric DSI holders to impose sanctions on norm violators was higher in 2008 than in the past. Because many people had either converted to idiocentric DSI or experienced pattern-maintaining change, they were no longer willing to join others in imposing incremental sanctions against norm violators. At the same time, norm violators like Fan were willing to fight back against external attempts to impose sanctions on them. Some deviating norm holders occupied strategic positions in society and deliberately used their position to promote the new norms. In fact, some of the official media in China either openly supported Fan's right to protect his own life or argued the exceptionalism of the case.[6] A group of idiocentric DSI holders were willing to provide critical social support for "Running Fan." They not only publicly defended his choice but also provided him with social shelter.[7]

---

[4] I personally believed that Running Fan misread the norm. Even in an individualist culture, teachers are still required to save their students in such a situation.

[5] Interviews conducted in Beijing in May 2008.

[6] For example, *Southern Weekend*: http://www.infzm.com/content/13259 (accessed December 17, 2013).

[7] In December 2008, Kaihua Educational Institution hired Fan as a teacher. Kaihua's decision generated serious debates. The important thing to note is that many people openly supported Kaihua's decision to offer Fan a job.

Appendix D 255

As a result of all these changes, external policing acts not only became more costly but also unreliable in their effectiveness. Although the majority of people in society still carried allocentric DSI, the dominant norm holders were no longer able to impose on Fan the unbearable social isolation that they had imposed on Yu thirty years prior. Despite his "Running Fan" moniker, Fan was neither made socially repugnant nor quelled by mounting social pressure. After the Ministry of Education ordered the school to fine him, Fan even threatened to sue the Ministry's spokesman.[8]

The most important lesson from these two cases with regard to the theory of cultural shifts is that the mechanism of cultural shifts is much more complicated than previously realized. As discussed in Chapter 4, the traditional theory of cultural shifts relies exclusively on changes in the distribution of alternative norms as indicators of cultural shifts. Such a method implicitly assumes that the ability for the dominant norms to control social interaction is linearly associated with the percentage of dominant norm holders in a society. Our analyses have challenged this assumption and suggest that the distribution of alternative cultural orientations may not be the only indicator of cultural shifts. Even if the distribution of norms remains unchanged, the ability of dominant norms at the societal level to control the behavior of political actors may decline or even vanish for the following reasons.

First, despite the fact that cultural discontinuity has yet to occur, pattern-maintaining change in allocentric DSI can change the scope of issues governed by that norm. If allocentric DSI required one to sacrifice his or her life for the collective interests of the majority in the past, after pattern-maintaining change, the norm may cease to apply to certain situations. In that case, even if the distribution of alternative norms in a society remains stable, *the boundary of issues* governed by allocentric DSI has changed.

Second, the case studies show how a dominant norm's ability to control individual behavior through an external policing system may not be linearly associated with the percentage of dominant norm holders in a society. As shown in Fan's case, the emergence of a small group of strongly committed deviating norm holders who are able to provide critical social support to deviating norm holders can have devastating

---

[8] According to the Wall Street Journal, Fan has some supporters. "There were many people like him [Fan]. But only he stood up and bravely said, 'I didn't save any person,'" one online writer commented on Sohu.com: "He is sacrificing himself for people's reconsideration about some systems. We need this kind of difference in views" (Chao 2008).

impacts on the effectiveness of the external policing system of dominant norm holders in a society.

Finally, the social status of deviating norm holders can also have a significant impact on the effectiveness of a norm's external policing system. Let us assume that there are three societies in which 20 percent of each respective population holds deviating norms. In society A, deviating norm holders are randomly distributed among the population; in society B, they are primarily youth; in society C, deviating norm holders are primarily elites – people who occupy leadership positions, control the mass media, and are recognized as public intellectuals. Even if the distribution of alternative norms in these three societies is identical, the dominant norm's external policing system's effectiveness at controlling social interaction can be extremely different. In society A, the dominant norm may still be able to effectively control people's behavior. In society B, the dominant norm may no longer be able to control the behavior of young people, but it can still effectively control the behavior of others. In society C, the presence of even a limited number of prominent deviating norm holders can void the dominant norm's ability to control the behavior of individuals in the society.[9]

If the mere prevalence of an alternative culture in a community or society is an unreliable indicator of a cultural shift, how should we measure cultural change at the group level? Since cultural norms are enforced by internal and external policing systems, cultural shifts must result from changes in the ability of the internal and external policing system of cultural norms to control social interaction. As suggested in Chapter 4, researchers must separately estimate changes in the effectiveness of the two policing systems associated with norms as well as the interactions between the two channels that control the behavior of individuals and the political processes in a society respectively. Therefore, a study of cultural shifts at the group level requires researchers to go through several steps of analysis.

First, researchers need to look for changes in norm distributions over time, which is the most important indicator of changes in the internal policing system of norms. If researchers find that the distribution of norms has changed, they need to carefully identify the sources of the change, that is, if such change was brought about by generational replacement, cultural

---

[9] It should be pointed out that the political skills of deviating norm holders and/or norm entrepreneurs can also have a significant impact on the effectiveness of norm policing mechanisms at the group level.

Appendix D

discontinuity, or life-cycle effects. If cultural discontinuity is shaped by generational replacement, we know that the behavior of certain individuals will be guided by different norms.

Second, even if the distribution of norms remains unchanged, pattern-maintaining change may occur to a norm, altering its scope. To find out, researchers need to explore whether the internal policing system of the norm plays the same role at different times, especially whether previously proscribed acts have now become acceptable. Empirically, this can be done by comparing the relationship between latent constructs and the observable variables that researchers use to measure a particular norm as well as the effect of latent constructs on people's political behavior over time. If pattern-maintaining change has occurred for a cultural norm, these two relationships will have undergone change.

Finally, cultural shifts may start with the collapse of the external policing system of cultural norms, that is, with cultural flexibility at the social level. Even when a large number of people in a society have not converted to deviating cultural norms, dominant norm holders may no longer be willing to impose sanctions against violators, or incremental sanctions in the society may become impossible. Note that cultural flexibility at the social level may not necessarily influence the effectiveness of *internal* policing system of norms. Although norm holders now refrain from punishing norm violators, they themselves may still strictly follow guidance of the norms into which they were socialized. Researchers can empirically test changes in the external policing system associated with norms by comparing the impact of the normative environment on individual behavior at different times, such as in the cases of Yu and Fan.

Appendix E

Analyzing Cross-County Variation in Government Salience and Political Participation: A Prerequisite for Hierarchical Linear Modeling

As discussed in Chapter 6, in order to determine whether hierarchical linear modeling (HLM) could be used for my analysis of the impact of culture on government salience, I needed to gauge whether there was sufficient variation across counties in government salience. The results of the analysis are presented in Table E.1.

Given a Bernoulli sampling model and a logit link function, the level-1 model is

$$\eta_{ij} = \beta_{0j}$$

where the level-2 model is

$$\beta_{0j} = \gamma_{00} + \mu_{0j}, \mu_{0j} \sim N(0, \tau_{00})$$

Here γ_{00} is the average log-odds of government salience across the county, while τ_{00} is the variance between counties in county-average log-odds of government salience. The estimated results are

$$\gamma_{00} = 1.512 \ (se = .0160), \tau_{00} = 3.040 \ (se = .174)$$

Assuming the average log-odds of government salience within a county, β_{0j}, to be approximately distributed normally within a mean of 1.512 and variance $\tau_{00} = 3.040$, we would expect about 95 percent of the counties to have a value of β_{0j} between

$$1.512 \pm 1.96 * \sqrt{3.040} = (1.905, 4.929).$$

Appendix E

TABLE E.1. *Hierarchical Logit ANOVA Model for Government Salience*

		DF
Fixed effect		
Intercept	1.507 (0.160)***	141
Random variance		
Intercept	3.032 (.147)***	141
95% CI of the mean probability at the second level		
Upper bound	98.88%	
Lower bound	8.38%	

*** p < .01; ** p < .05; * p < .1

Note: Restricted PQL estimator in HLM 6.06. Robust standard errors are in parentheses.

Source: 1993 Survey of Political Culture and Political Participation in Mainland China, Taiwan, and Hong Kong (China N = 3,287).

TABLE E.2. *Hierarchical Logit ANOVA Model for Political Participation*

	1993		2002	
Fixed effect		DF		DF
Intercept	.74 (.091)***	141	−.26 (.079) ***	125
Random variance				
Intercept	.81 (.076)***	141	.58 (.761)***	125
95% CI of the mean probability at the second level				
Upper bound	92.45%		88.77%	
Lower bound	26.40%		28.65%	

*** p < .01; ** p < .05; * p < .1

Note: Restricted PQL estimator in HLM 6.06. Robust standard errors are in parentheses.

Source: 1993 Survey of Political Culture and Political Participation in Mainland China, Taiwan, and Hong Kong; 2002 China Survey, Asian Barometer Survey I (1993 N = 3,287; 2002 N = 3,183).

If we convert these log-odds to probabilities, we will find 95 percent of the counties lie between (.130, .992) with respect to the probability of government salience. As mentioned in Chapter 6, the results of the analysis show that the average level of government salience in some counties is near zero but in other counties, nearly everyone holds the government responsible for their problems. The finding reveals significant cross-county variation in government salience, which requires the use of a hierarchical model for the analysis. I chose an intercept model for the final analysis because none of the random components of independent variables were found to be statistically significant, which indicates that no cross-level interaction was found in the analysis.

Likewise, to confirm that HLM could be used to analyze the effects of culture on political participation, I applied the same thinking and methods as above to determine sufficient cross-county variation in levels of political participation. Respondents who claimed that they did not have any problem to bring to government were removed from the sample, and therefore the populations of the study are only people who perceived government to be salient. The results are presented in Table E.2.

As demonstrated in the table, 95 percent of the counties in 1993 lie between (.265, .925) with respect to the probability people will participate in politics. In 2002, the lower bound is .287 and the upper bound is .888. On average, around 25 percent of people in some counties participated in politics, but around 90 percent of people in other counties engaged in some political acts. The variance findings helped pave the way for the use of HLM for the analyses of political participation.

References

Abramson, Paul R. 1972. "Political Efficacy and Political Trust among Black Schoolchildren: Two Explanations." *The Journal of Politics* 34: 1243–69.
  1983. *Political Attitudes in America: Formation and Change.* San Francisco: W. H. Freeman.
Abramson, Paul R., and John H. Aldrich. 1982. "The Decline of Electoral Participation in America." *The American Political Science Review* 76, 3: 502–21.
Adler, Emanuel. 1997. "Seizing the Middle Ground: Constructivism in World Politics." *European Journal of International Relations* 3: 319–63.
Adorno, T. W., Else Frenkel-Brunswik, Daniel J. Levinson, and Nevitt R. Sanford. 1950. *The Authoritarian Personality.* New York: Harper & Row.
Aiken, Leona S., Stephen G. West, and Raymond R. Reno. 1991. *Multiple Regression: Testing and Interpreting Interactions.* Newbury Park, CA: Sage.
Almond, Gabriel A. 1983. "Communism and Political Culture Theory." *Comparative Politics* 13, 1: 127–38.
Almond, Gabriel A., and Sidney Verba. 1963. *The Civic Culture: Political Attitudes and Democracy in Five Nations.* Princeton, NJ: Princeton University Press.
Anderson, Christopher J., and Yuliya V. Tverdova. 2003. "Corruption, Political Allegiances, and Attitudes toward Government in Contemporary Democracies." *American Journal of Political Science* 47, 1: 91–109.
Aronoff, Myron Joel. 1988. *Israeli Visions and Divisions: Cultural Change and Political Conflict.* New Brunswick, NJ: Transaction.
Banfield, Edward C. 1958. *The Moral Basis of a Backward Society.* Glencoe, IL: Free Press.
Barnes, Samuel H., Max Kaase, Klaus R. Allerbeck, Barbara G. Farah, Felix Heunks, Ronald Inglehart, M. Kent Jennings, Hans D. Klingemann, Allan Marsh, and Leopold Rosenmayr. 1979. *Political Action: Mass Participation in Five Western Democracies.* Beverly Hills, CA: Sage.
Barry, Brian M. 1970. *Sociologists, Economists and Democracy (Themes and Issues in Modern Sociology).* London: Collier-Macmillan.

Becker, Howard Saul. 1963. *Outsiders: Studies in the Sociology of Deviance.* London: Free Press of Glencoe.

Bedford, Olwen, and Kwang-Kuo Hwang. 2003. "Guilt and Shame in Chinese Culture: A Cross-Cultural Framework from the Perspective of Morality and Identity." *Journal for the Theory of Social Behaviour* 33, 2: 127–44.

Bedford, W. A. 2004. "The Individual Experience of Guilt and Shame in Chinese Culture." *Culture & Psychology* 10, 1: 29–52.

Bell, Daniel. 1996. *The Cultural Contradictions of Capitalism.* 20th anniversary ed. New York: Basic Books.

Benedict, Ruth. 1989. *The Chrysanthemum and the Sword: Patterns of Japanese Culture.* Boston: Houghton Mifflin.

Berelson, Bernard R., Paul F. Lazarsfeld, and William N. McPhee. 1954. *Voting: A Study of Opinion Formation in a Presidential Campaign.* Chicago: University of Chicago Press.

Berlin, Isaiah. 2002 (1969). *Liberty: Incorporating Four Essays on Liberty,* ed. H. Hardy. Oxford: Oxford University Press.

Bianco, Lucien. 1967. *Origins of the Chinese Revolution, 1915–1949.* Stanford, CA: Stanford University Press.

Böckenholt, Ulf, and Peter van der Heijden. 2007. "Item Randomized-Response Models for Measuring Noncompliance: Risk-Return Perceptions, Social Influences, and Self-Protective Responses." *Psychometrika* 72, 2: 245–62.

Braithwaite, Valerie A., and Margaret Levi. 1998. *Trust and Governance.* New York: Russell Sage Foundation.

Brown, Archie. 1984. *Political Culture and Communist Studies.* Armonk, NY: M. E. Sharp.

Campbell, Angus, Philip E. Converse, Warren E. Miller, and Donald E. Stokes. 1960. *The American Voter.* New York: John Wiley.

Chang, Gordon G. 2001. *The Coming Collapse of China.* New York: Random House.

Chao, Loretta. 2008. "Earthquake Lays Bare Ethical Faultlines in China: Teacher Who Left Class Faces Scorn and Loses His Job." *Wall Street Journal,* June 23. Online version available at: http://online.wsj.com/news/articles/SB121417134731295015 (accessed December 30, 2013).

Chen, Jie. 2004. *Popular Political Support in Urban China.* Washington, DC, and Stanford, CA: Woodrow Wilson Center Press and Stanford University Press.

 2005. "Popular Support for Village Self-Government in China: Intensity and Sources." *Asian Survey* 45: 865–85.

Chen, Pengren. 1989. *Preliminary Discussions on Dr. Sun Yat-sen's Thoughts (Sun Zhongshan Xiansheng Sixiang Chutan).* Taipei, Taiwan: Modern China Press.

Chow Tse-tsung. 1967. *The May Fourth Movement: Intellectual Revolution in Modern China.* Stanford, CA: Stanford University Press.

Chu, Godwin C. 1976. *Communication and Development in China.* Honolulu: East–West Center.

Chu, Yun-han, Larry Diamond, Andrew J. Nathan, and Doh Chull Shin, eds. 2008. *How East Asians View Democracy.* New York: Columbia University Press.

References

Cialdini, Robert B., Richard E. Petty, and John T. Cacioppo. 1981. "Attitude and Attitude Change." *Annual Review of Psychology* 32: 357–404.

Citrin, Jack. 1974. "Comment: The Political Relevance of Trust in Government." *American Political Science Review* 68, September: 973–88.

Citrin, Jack, and Christopher Muste. 1999. "Trust in Government." In *Measures of Political Attitudes*. Measures of Social Psychological Attitudes, vol. 2, ed. J. P. Robinson, P. R. Shaver and L. S. Wrightsman, 465–532. San Diego, CA: Academic Press.

Coleman, James Samuel. 1990. *Foundations of Social Theory*. Cambridge, MA: Harvard University Press.

Confucius. 1971. *The Four Books*. Taipei, Taiwan: Chengwen.

1999. *The Analects*. M. Yang, ed. Library of Chinese Classics. Changsha, China: Hunan People's Publishing House.

Confucius and Mencius. 1992. *The Four Books*. H. P. H. Translation Division, ed. The Chinese-English Bilingual Series of Chinese Classics. Changsha, China: Hunan People's Publishing House.

Craig, Stephen C. 1979. "Efficacy, Trust, and Political Behavior: An Attempt to Resolve a Lingering Conceptual Dilemma." *American Politics Quarterly* 7, 2: 225–39.

Craig, Stephen C., and Michael A. Maggiotto. 1982. "Measuring Political Efficacy." *Political Methodology* 8, 2: 85–109.

Craig, Stephen C., Richard G. Niemi, and Glenn E. Silver. 1990. "Political Efficacy and Trust: A Report on the NES Pilot Study Items." *Political Behavior* 12, 3: 289–314.

Dahl, Robert A. 1989. *Democracy and Its Critics*. New Haven, CT: Yale University Press.

Dalton, Russell J. 1996. *Citizen Politics: Public Opinion and Political Parties in Advanced Industrial Democracies*, 2nd ed. Chatham, NJ: Chatham House.

de Bary, William Theodore. 1991. *The Trouble with Confucianism*. Cambridge, MA, and London: Harvard University Press.

2004. *Nobility and Civility: Asian Ideals of Leadership and the Common Good*. Cambridge, MA: Harvard University Press.

Delli Carpini, Michael X. 1986. *Stability and Change in American Politics: The Coming of Age of the Generation of the 1960s*. New York: New York University Press.

Dessler, David. 1989. "What's at Stake in the Agent-Structure Debate?" *International Organization* 43: 441–74.

Deutsch, Karl W. 1961. "Social Mobilization and Political Development." *American Political Science Review* 55, 3: 493–514.

DeVellis, Robert F. 2003. *Scale Development: Theory and Applications*, 2nd ed. Applied Social Research Methods Series, vol. 26. Thousand Oaks, CA: Sage.

Diamond, Larry. 1992. "Economic Development and Democracy Reconsidered." In *Reexamining Democracy: Essays in Honor of Seymour Martin Lipset*, ed. G. Marks and L. Diamond, 93–139. Newbury Park, CA: Sage.

Diamond, Larry, Marc Plattner, Yun-han Chu, and Hung-Mao Tien. 1997. *Consolidating the Third Wave Democracies*. Baltimore, MD: Johns Hopkins University Press.

Diani, Mario, and Doug McAdam, eds. 2003. *Social Movements and Networks: Relational Approaches to Collective Action*. Oxford, UK and New York: Oxford University Press.

Dickson, Bruce J. 1992. "What Explains Chinese Political Behavior? The Debate over Structure and Culture." *Comparative Politics* 25: 103–18.

DiMaggio, Paul, and Walter Powell. 1991. "Introduction." In *The New Institutionalism in Organizational Analysis*, ed. W. Powell and P. DiMaggio, 1–38. Chicago: University of Chicago Press.

Douglas, Mary, ed. 1973. *Rules and Meanings: The Anthropology of Everyday Knowledge*. Harmondsworth, UK: Penguin Education.

1982. *Essays in the Sociology of Perception*. London and Boston: Routledge and Kegan Paul.

Douglas, Mary, and Aaron B. Wildavsky. 1982. *Risk and Culture: An Essay on the Selection of Technical and Environmental Dangers*. Berkeley: University of California Press.

Downs, Anthony. 1957. *An Economic Theory of Democracy*. New York: Harper & Row.

Durkheim, Emile. 1952 (1897). *Suicide: A Study in Sociology*, trans. John Spaulding and George Simpson. London: Routledge and Kegan Paul.

1964 (1893). *The Division of Labor in Society*, trans. George Simpson. New York: Free Press of Glencoe.

Easton, David. 1965. *A Systems Analysis of Political Life*. New York: Wiley.

1975. "A Re-Assessment of the Concept of Political Support." *British Journal of Political Science* 5: 435–57.

Easton, David, and Jack Dennis. 1969. *Children in the Political System: Origins of Political Legitimacy*. New York: McGraw-Hill.

Eckstein, Alexander. 1970. "Economic Development and Political Change in Communist Systems." *World Politics* 22, 4: 475–95.

Eckstein, Harry. 1975. "Case Study and Theory in Political Science." In *The Handbook of Political Science*, ed. F. I. Greenstein and N. W. Polsby, 79–138. Reading, MA: Addison-Wesley.

1988. "A Culturalist Theory of Political Change." *American Political Science Review* 82, 3: 789–804.

1996. "Culture as a Foundational Concept for the Social Sciences." *Journal of Theoretical Politics* 8, 4: 471–97.

Ellis, Richard. 1993. *American Political Cultures*. Oxford, UK and New York: Oxford University Press.

Embretson, Susan E., and Steven Paul Reise. 2000. *Item Response Theory for Psychologists*. Mahwah, NJ: Lawrence Erlbaum.

Fairbank, John King. 1983. *The United States and China*. 4th ed. Cambridge, MA: Harvard University Press.

1986. *The Great Chinese Revolution 1800–1985*. New York: Harper & Row.

Fairbank, John King, and Merle Goldman. 1998. *China: A New History*. Cambridge, MA: Belknap Press of Harvard University Press.

Falkenheim, Victor C. 1978. "Political Participation in China." *Problems of Communism* 27, May–June: 18–32.

References

265

1981. "Democracy, Modernization and Participatory Values in Post-Mao China." In *Political Participation in Communist Systems*, ed. D. Schulz and J. S. Adams. New York: Pergamon Press.

1987. "Citizen and Group Politics in China: An Introduction." In *Citizens and Groups in Contemporary China*, ed. V. C. Falkenheim. Ann Arbor: University of Michigan Center for Chinese Studies.

Fan, X., B. Thompson, and L. Wang. 1999. "Effects of Sample Size, Estimation Method, and Model Specification on Structural Equation Modeling Fit Indexes." *Structural Equation Modeling* 6: 56–83.

Feldman, Stanley. 1988. "Structure and Consistency in Public Opinion: The Role of Core Beliefs and Values." *American Journal of Political Science* 32, 2: 416–40.

Fenno, Richard F., Jr. 1978. *Home Style: House Members in Their Districts.* Boston: Little, Brown.

Festinger, Leon. 1957. *A Theory of Cognitive Dissonance.* Evanston, IL: Row, Peterson.

Finnemore, Martha. 1996. *National Interests in International Society.* Ithaca, NY: Cornell University Press.

Finnemore, Martha, and Kathryn Sikkink. 1998. "International Norm Dynamics and Political Change." *International Organization* 52, 4 International Organization at Fifty: Exploration and Contestation in the Study of World Politics: 887–917.

Fiorina, Morris P. 1981. *Retrospective Voting in American National Elections.* New Haven, CT: Yale University Press.

Flanagan, Scott C., Shinsaku Kohei, Ichiro Miyake, Bradley M. Richardson, and Joji Watanuki. 1991. *The Japanese Voter.* New Haven, CT: Yale University Press.

Fukuyama, Francis. 1995. *Trust: The Social Virtues and the Creation of Prosperity.* New York: Free Press.

Fung, H. 1999. "Becoming a Moral Child: The Socialization of Shame among Young Chinese Children." *Ethos* 27, 2: 180–209.

Gambetta, Diego. 1993. *The Sicilian Mafia: The Business of Private Protection.* Cambridge, MA: Harvard University Press.

Gerbner, George, Larry Gross, Michael Morgan, and Nancy Signorielli. 1994. "Growing Up with Television. The Cultivation Perspective." In *Media Effects: Advances in Theory and Research*, ed. J. Bryant and D. Zillmann, 17–42. Hillsdale, NJ: Lawrence Erlbaum.

Gibbs, Jack P. 1965. "Norms: The Problem of Definition and Classification." *American Journal of Sociology* 70, 5: 586–94.

Gilley, Bruce. 2004. *China's Democratic Future: How It Will Happen and Where It Will Lead.* New York: Columbia University Press.

Goel, Madan Lal. 1975. *Political Participation in a Developing Nation: India.* New York: Asia Publishing House.

Goffman, Erving. 1986. *Frame Analysis: An Essay on the Organization of Experience.* Boston: Northeastern University Press.

Goldhagen, Daniel Jonah. 1996. *Hitler's Willing Executioners: Ordinary Germans and the Holocaust.* New York: Knopf.

Goldstein, Judith, and Robert O. Keohane. 1993. *Ideas and Foreign Policy: Beliefs, Institutions, and Political Change*. Ithaca, NY: Cornell University Press.

Guang, Lei. 1996. "Elusive Democracy: Conceptual Change and the Chinese Democracy Movement, 1978–79 to 1989." *Modern China* 22, 4: 417–47.

Hamilton, Alexander, James Madison, and John Jay. 2009 (1787–1788). The Federalist Papers. In *The Federalist Papers: Alexander Hamilton, James Madison, John Jay. Rethinking the Western Tradition*, ed. Ian Shapiro, 3–445. New Haven, CT: Yale University Press.

Hardin, Russell. 2000. "The Public Trust." In *Disaffected Democracies: What is Troubling the Trilateral Countries?*, ed. S. J. Pharr and R. D. Putnam, 31–51. Princeton, NJ: Princeton University Press.

Hayes, Bernadette C., and Clive S. Bean. 1993. "Political Efficacy: A Comparative Study of the United States, West Germany, Great Britain and Australia." *European Journal of Political Research* 23: 261–80.

He, Qinglian. 2004. "How Chinese Government Controls the Media." *Modern China Studies (Dangdai Zhongguo Yanjiu)* 86, available online at: http://www.modernchinastudies.org/us/issues/past-issues.html (accessed December 27, 2013).

Higgins, E. T. 1989. "Self-Discrepancy Theory: What Patterns of Self-Beliefs Cause People to Suffer?" In *Advances in Experimental Social Psychology*, vol. 22, ed. L. Berkowitz, 93–136. New York: Academic Press.

Hirschman, Albert O. 1970. *Exit, Voice, and Loyalty*. Cambridge, MA: Harvard University Press.

    1984. "A Dissenter's Confession: 'The Strategy of Economic Development' Revisited." In *Pioneers in Development*, ed. G. M. Meier and D. Seers, 87–111. Oxford, UK and New York: Oxford University Press.

    1996 (1977). *The Passions and the Interests: Political Arguments for Capitalism before its Triumph*, 20th anniversary ed. Princeton, NJ: Princeton University Press.

Hobbes, Thomas. 1996 (1651). *Leviathan*, ed. Richard Tuck. Cambridge, UK and New York: Cambridge University Press.

Hofstede, Geert H. 2001. *Culture's Consequences: Comparing Values, Behaviors, Institutions, and Organizations across Nations*, 2nd ed. Thousand Oaks, CA: Sage.

Hong, Y. Y., and C. Y. Chiu. 1992. "A Study of the Comparative Structure of Guilt and Shame in a Chinese Society." *Journal of Psychology* 126, 2: 171–79.

Huntington, Samuel P. 1968. *Political Order in Changing Societies*. New Haven, CT: Yale University Press.

    1993a. "American Democracy in Relation to Asia." In *Democracy and Capitalism: Asian and American Perspectives*, ed. R. L. Bartley, 27–44. Singapore: Institute of Southeast Asian Studies.

    1993b. "The Clash of Civilizations?" *Foreign Affairs* 72, 3: 22–49.

Huntington, Samuel P., and Joan M. Nelson. 1976. *No Easy Choice: Political Participation in Developing Countries*. Cambridge, MA: Harvard University Press.

Inglehart, Ronald. 1977. *The Silent Revolution: Changing Values and Political Styles among Western Publics*. Princeton, NJ: Princeton University Press.

References

1988. "The Renaissance of Political Culture." *American Political Science Review* 82, 4: 1203–30.

1990. *Culture Shift in Advanced Industrial Society*. Princeton, NJ: Princeton University Press.

1997. *Modernization and Postmodernization: Cultural, Economic, and Political Change in Forty-Three Societies*. Princeton, NJ: Princeton University Press.

Inglehart, Ronald, and Christian Welzel. 2005. *Modernization, Cultural Change, and Democracy: The Human Development Sequence*. Cambridge, UK and New York: Cambridge University Press.

Inkeles, Alex. 1983. *Exploring Individual Modernity*. New York: Columbia University Press.

1997. *National Character: A Psycho-Social Perspective*. New Brunswick, NJ: Transaction.

Inkeles, Alex, and David H. Smith. 1974. *Becoming Modern: Individual Change in Six Developing Countries*. Cambridge, MA: Harvard University Press.

Jackman, Robert W., and Ross A. Miller. 1996a. "The Poverty of Political Culture." *American Journal of Political Science* 40, 3: 697–716.

1996b. "A Renaissance of Political Culture." *American Journal of Political Science* 40, 3: 632–59.

2004. *Before Norms: Institutions and Civic Culture*. Ann Arbor: University of Michigan Press.

Jennings, M. Kent. 1998. "Political Trust and the Roots of Devolution." In *Trust and Governance*, ed. V. A. Braithwaite and M. Levi, 218–44. New York: Russell Sage Foundation.

Jennings, M. Kent and Jan W. van Deth, eds. 1990. *Continuities in Political Action: A Longitudinal Study of Political Orientations in Three Western Democracies*. Berlin: Walter de Gruyter.

Johnson, Chalmers A. 1982. *MITI and the Japanese Miracle: The Growth of Industrial Policy, 1925–1975*. Stanford, CA: Stanford University Press.

Kaase, Max, and Andrew Kohut. 1996. *Estranged Friends? The Transatlantic Consequences of Societal Change*. New York: Council on Foreign Relations Press.

Kahn, Joseph. 2006. "Pace and Scope of Protest in China Accelerated in '05." *New York Times*, January 20. A10.

Kang, Xiaoguang. 2008. "Study of Restoration of Traditional Culture (*Fuxing Chuantong Wenhua Yanjiu*)." *Leaders* (*Lingdaozhe*) 20: 63–81.

Katzenstein, Peter J. 1996. *The Culture of National Security: Norms and Identity in World Politics*. New York: Columbia University Press.

Keohane, Robert O., and Joseph S. Nye. 1977. *Power and Interdependence: World Politics in Transition*. Boston: Little, Brown.

Kertzer, David I. 1988. *Ritual, Politics, and Power*. New Haven: Yale University Press.

Key, V. O., Jr., and Milton C. Cummings. 1966. *The Responsible Electorate: Rationality in Presidential Voting, 1936–1960*. Cambridge, MA: Belknap Press of Harvard University Press.

Kim, Jae-on, and Charles W. Mueller. 1978. *Factor Analysis: Statistical Methods and Practical Issues*. Sage University Paper series on Quantitative Applications in the Social Sciences, no. 07-014. Beverly Hills, CA: Sage.

Kim, Uichol, and Hakhoe Han'guk Simni. 1994. *Individualism and Collectivism: Theory, Method, and Applications*. Thousand Oaks, CA: Sage.

King, Gary, Christopher J. L. Murray, Joshua A. Salomon, and Ajay Tandon. 2004. "Enhancing the Validity and Cross-Cultural Comparability of Measurement in Survey Research." *American Political Science Review* 98, 1: 191–207.

Kish, Leslie. 1965. *Survey Sampling*. New York: John Wiley.

Kish, Leslie, and M. Frankel. 1970. "Balanced Repeated Replications for Standard Errors." *Journal of the American Statistical Association* 65: 1071–91.

Klotz, Audie. 1995. *Norms in International Relations: The Struggle against Apartheid*. Ithaca, NY: Cornell University Press.

Kluckhohn, Clyde. 1951. "Values and Value-Orientations in the Theory of Action" in *Toward a General Theory of Action*, ed. Talcott Parsons and Edward A. Shils, 388–343. Cambridge, MA: Harvard University Press.

Knight, Jack. 1992. *Institutions and Social Conflict*. Cambridge and New York: Cambridge University Press.

Kolb, Bryan, and Ian Q. Whishaw. 2003. *Fundamentals of Human Neuropsychology*, 5th ed. New York: Worth.

Korn, Edward Lee, and Barry I. Graubard. 1999. *Analysis of Health Surveys*. New York: Wiley.

Krasner, Stephen D, ed. 1983. *International Regimes*. Ithaca, NY: Cornell University Press.

Kratochwil, Friedrich V. 1989. *Rules, Norms, and Decisions on the Conditions of Practical and Legal Reasoning in International Relations and Domestic Affairs*. Cambridge, UK and New York: Cambridge University Press.

Kratochwil, Friedrich, and John Gerard Ruggie. 1986. "International Organization: A State of the Art on an Art of the State." *International Organization* 40, 4: 753–75.

Kreft, Ita G. G. 1996. "Are Multilevel Techniques Necessary? An Overview, Including Simulation Studies." Unpublished paper, California State University, Los Angeles.

Kuhn, Thomas S. 1970. *The Structure of Scientific Revolutions*, 2nd ed. Chicago: University of Chicago Press.

Lapid, Yosef, and Friedrich Kratochwil, eds 1997. *The Return of Culture in IR Theory*. Boulder, CO: Lynne Rienner.

Lee, Eun Sul, and Ron N. Forthofer. 2006. *Analyzing Complex Survey Data*, 2nd ed. Sage University Paper series on Quantitative Applications in the Social Sciences, no. 07–71. Thousand Oaks, CA: Sage.

Lehtonen, Risto, and Erkki Pahkinen. 1995. *Practical Methods for Design and Analysis of Complex Surveys*. Chichester, UK and New York: Wiley.

Li, J., L. Q. Wang, and K. W. Fischer. 2004. "The Organisation of Chinese Shame Concepts?" *Cognition and Emotion* 18, 6: 767–97.

Li, Lianjiang. 2004. "Political Trust in Rural China." *Modern China* 30, 2: 228–58.

References

Li, Lianjiang, and Kevin J. O'Brien. 1996. "Villagers and Popular Resistance in Contemporary China." *Modern China* 22, 1: 28–61.

1999. "The Struggle over Village Elections." In *The Paradox of China's Post-Mao Reforms*, ed. R. MacFarquhar and M. Goldman, 129–44. Cambridge, MA: Harvard University Press.

Linz, Juan J. 2000. *Totalitarian and Authoritarian Regimes*. Boulder, CO: Lynne Rienner.

Lipset, Seymour Martin. 1981. *Political Man*. Baltimore, MD: Johns Hopkins University Press.

Locke, John. 2000 (1728). *Two Treatises on Government*. Birmingham, AL: Palladium Press.

Loeb, Paul Rogat. 1994. *Generation at the Crossroads: Apathy and Action on the American Campus*. New Brunswick, NJ: Rutgers University Press.

Lukes, Steven. 1974. *Power: A Radical View*. London: Macmillan.

Lynch, Daniel C. 1999. *After the Propaganda State: Media, Politics, and "Thought Work" in Reformed China*. Stanford, CA: Stanford University Press.

Maas, C. J. M., and J. J. Hox. 2005. "Sufficient Sample Sizes for Multilevel Modeling." *Methodology* 1, 3: 86–92.

Magalhães, Pedro C. 2007. "Voting and Intermediation: Information Biases and Electoral Choices in Comparative Perspective." In *Democracy, Intermediation, and Voting on Four Continents*, ed. R. Gunther, H. J. Puhle and J. R. Montero, 254–308. Oxford, UK: Oxford University Press.

Manion, Melanie. 1994. "Survey Research in the Study of Contemporary China: Learning from Local Samples." *The China Quarterly* 139: 741–65.

2006. "Democracy, Community, Trust: The Impact of Chinese Village Elections in Context." *Comparative Political Studies* 39, 3: 301–24.

Mann, Jim. 1999. *About Face: A History of America's Curious Relationship with China, from Nixon to Clinton*. New York: Knopf.

Mao, Tse-tung. 1964. *Selected Works of Mao Tse-tung, vol. 4*. Beijing: Foreign Language Press.

March, James G., and Johan P. Olsen. 1984. "The New Institutionalism: Organizational Factors in Political Life." *American Political Science Review* 78, 3: 734–49.

1998. "The Institutional Dynamics of International Political Orders." *International Organization* 52, 4 International Organization at Fifty: Exploration and Contestation in the Study of World Politics: 943–69.

Marx, Karl. 1967. *Economic and Philosophic Manuscripts of 1844*. Moscow: Progress.

McAdam, Doug, John D. McCarthy, and Mayer N. Zald, eds. 1996a. *Comparative Perspectives on Social Movements: Political Opportunities, Mobilizing Structures, and Cultural Framings*. Cambridge, UK and New York: Cambridge University Press.

1996b. "Introduction: Opportunities, Mobilizing Structures, and Framing Process – Toward a Synthetic, Comparative Perspective on Social Movements." In *Comparative Perspectives on Social Movements: Political Opportunities, Mobilizing Structures, and Cultural Framings*, ed. D. McAdam, J. D.

McCarthy and M. N. Zald, 1–20. Cambridge, UK and New York: Cambridge University Press.

McAdam, Doug, Sidney G. Tarrow, and Charles Tilly. 1997. "Toward an Integrated Perspective on Social Movements and Revolutions." In *Comparative Politics: Rationality, Culture, and Structure*, ed. M. I. Lichbach and A. S. Zuckerman, 142–73. Cambridge, UK and New York: Cambridge University Press.

2001. *Dynamics of Contention*. Cambridge, UK and New York: Cambridge University Press.

McClosky, Herbert, and John Zaller. 1984. *The American Ethos: Public Attitudes toward Capitalism and Democracy*. Cambridge, MA: Harvard University Press.

McKown, Roberta E., and Robert E. Kauffman. 1974. "The Use of Background Factors in the Prediction of Attitudes: Some Empirical Considerations," Occasional paper, Dept. of Political Science, University of Alberta.

Merry, S. E. 1984. "Rethinking Gossip and Scandal." In *Toward a General Theory of Social Control, vol. 1: Fundamentals*, ed. D. J. Black, 271–303. New York: Academic Press.

Metzger, Thomas A. 1977. *Escape from Predicament: Neo-Confucianism and China's Evolving Political Culture*. New York: Columbia University Press.

Milbrath, Lester W., and Madan Lal Goel. 1982. *Political Participation: How and Why do People Get Involved in Politics?* Lanham, MD and Washington, DC: University Press of America.

Mill, John Stuart. 1993 (1859, 1863). *On Liberty and Utilitarianism*. New York: Bantam.

Miller, Arthur H. 1974a. "Change in Political Trust: Discontent with Authorities and Economic Policies, 1972–1973." Conference Proceedings, Annual Meeting of the American Political Science Association, Chicago, IL.

1974b. "Political Issues and Trust in Government: 1964–1970." *American Political Science Review* 68: 951–72.

1974c. "Rejoinder to 'Comment' by Jack Citrin: Political Discontent or Ritualism?" *American Political Science Review* 68: 989–1001.

Ministry of Public Security. 1987. *Population Statistics by City and County of the People's Republic of China (Zhongguo Chengxian Renkou Tongji)*. Beijing: Map Publishing House of China.

Mishler, William, and Richard Rose. 1997. "Trust, Distrust and Skepticism: Popular Evaluations of Civil and Political Institutions in Post-Communist Societies." *The Journal of Politics* 59, 2: 418–51.

Misztal, Barbara A. 1996. *Trust in Modern Societies: The Search for the Bases of Social Order*. Cambridge, UK and Cambridge, MA: Polity Press and Blackwell Publishers.

Moore, Barrington, Jr. 1966. *Social Origins of Dictatorship and Democracy: Lord and Peasant in the Making of Modern World*. Boston: Beacon.

Mote, Frederick W. 1989. *The Intellectual Foundations of China*. New York: Knopf.

Nathan, Andrew J. 1998. "Even Our Caution Must Be Hedged," *Journal of Democracy* 9, 1: 60–64.

References

2003. "China's Changing of the Guard: Authoritarian Resilience," *Journal of Democracy* 14, 1: 6–17.

Newton, Kenneth, and Pippa Norris. 2000. "Confidence in Public Institutions: Faith, Culture, or Performance?" In *Disaffected Democracies: What's Troubling the Trilateral Countries?*, ed. S. J. Pharr and R. D. Putnam, 52–73. Princeton, NJ: Princeton University Press.

Nie, Norman H., Bingham G. Powell, Jr., and Kenneth Prewitt. 1969a. "Social Structure and Political Participation: Developmental Relationships, Part I." *American Political Science Review* 63, 2: 361–78.

1969b. "Social Structure and Political Participation: Developmental Relationships, Part II." *American Political Science Review* 63, 3: 808–32.

North, Douglass C. 1996. "Epilogue: Economic Performance through Time." In *Empirical Studies in Institutional Change*, ed. L. J. Alston, T. Eggertsson, and D. C. North, 342–55. Cambridge, UK and New York: Cambridge University Press.

Nye, Joseph S., Philip Zelikow, and David C. King. 1997. *Why People Don't Trust Government*. Cambridge, MA: Harvard University Press.

O'Brien, Kevin J. 1990a. "Is China's National People's Congress a Conservative Legislature?" *Asian Survey* 30: 782–94.

1990b. *Reform without Liberalization: China's National People's Congress and the Politics of Institutional Change*. Cambridge, UK and New York: Cambridge University Press.

1994a. "Agents and Remonstrators: Role Accumulation by Chinese People's Congress Deputies." *China Quarterly* 138: 359–79.

1994b. "Implementing Political Reform in China's Villages." *Australian Journal of Chinese Affairs* 32: 35–59.

1996. "Rightful Resistance." *World Politics* 49, 1: 31–55.

O'Brien, Kevin J., and Lianjiang Li. 2000. "Accommodating 'Democracy' in a One-Party State: Introducing Village Elections in China." *China Quarterly* 162: 465–89.

2006. *Rightful Resistance in Rural China*. Cambridge, UK and New York: Cambridge University Press.

Offe, Claus. 1999. "How Can We Trust Our Fellow Citizens?" In *Democracy and Trust*, ed. Mark E. Warren, 42–87. Cambridge, UK: Cambridge University Press.

Oksenberg, Michel. 1998. "Will China Democratize? Confronting a Classic Dilemma." *Journal of Democracy* 9, 1: 27–34.

Olsen, Mancur, Jr. 1965. *The Logic of Collective Action*. Cambridge, MA: Harvard University Press.

Parry, Geraint, and Michael Moran. 1994. *Democracy and Democratization*. London and New York: Routledge.

Parsons, Talcott. 1968 (1937). *The Structure of Social Action: A Study in Social Theory with Special Reference to a Group of Recent European Writers*. New York: Free Press.

Parsons, Talcott, and Edward A. Shils. 1951. *Toward a General Theory of Action: Theoretical Foundations for the Social Sciences*. Cambridge, MA: Harvard University Press.

Patterson, S. C., J. C. Wahlke, and G. R. Boynton. 1973. "Dimensions of Support in Legislative Systems." In *Legislatures in Comparative Perspective*, ed. A. Kornberg, 282–313. New York: McKay.

Pei, Minxin. 2006. *China's Trapped Transition: The Limits of Developmental Autocracy*. Cambridge, MA: Harvard University Press.

Pelham, B. 1991. "On Confidence and Consequence: The Certainty and Importance of Self Knowledge." *Journal of Personality and Social Psychology* 60, 4: 518–20.

Pharr, Susan J., and Robert D. Putnam. 2000. *Disaffected Democracies: What's Troubling the Trilateral Countries?* Princeton, NJ: Princeton University Press.

Putnam, Robert D. 1993. *Making Democracy Work: Civic Traditions in Modern Italy*. Princeton, NJ: Princeton University Press.

Pye, Lucian W. 1985. *Asian Power and Politics: The Cultural Dimensions of Authority*. Cambridge, MA: Harvard University Press.

1988. *The Mandarin and the Cadre: China's Political Cultures*. Ann Arbor, MI: Center for Chinese Studies.

1992. *The Spirit of Chinese Politics*, 2nd ed. Cambridge, MA: Harvard University Press.

Qian, M. Y., J. L. Qi, and B. Xie. 2000. "An Experimental Study on the Differences between Shame and Guilt among Chinese College Students." *International Journal of Psychology* 35, 3–4: 423.

Raudenbush, Stephen W., and Anthony S. Bryk. 2002. *Hierarchical Linear Models: Applications and Data Analysis Methods*, 2nd ed. Advanced Quantitative Techniques in the Social Sciences 1. Thousand Oaks, CA: Sage.

Riker, William H. 1990. "Political Science and Rational Choice." In *Perspectives on Positive Political Economy*, ed. J. E. Alt and K. A. Shepsle, 163–81. Cambridge, UK and New York: Cambridge University Press.

Rogowski, Ronald. 1974. *Rational Legitimacy*. Princeton, NJ: Princeton University Press.

Rosenstone, Steven J., and John Mark Hansen. 1993. *Mobilization, Participation, and Democracy in America*. New York: Macmillan.

Ruggie, John Gerard. 1998. "What Makes the World Hang Together? Neo-Utilitarianism and the Social Constructivist Challenge." *International Organization* 52, 4 International Organization at Fifty: Exploration and Contestation in the Study of World Politics: 855–85.

Sabato, Larry. 2000. *Feeding Frenzy: Attack Journalism and American Politics*. Baltimore, MD: Lanahan.

Schattschneider, E. E. 1960. *The Semi-Sovereign People*. New York: Holt, Rinehart & Winston.

Schram, Stuart R., ed. 1973. *Authority, Participation and Cultural Change in China: Essays by a European Study Group*. Cambridge, UK and New York: Cambridge University Press.

Seligman, Adam B. 1997. *The Problem of Trust*. Princeton, NJ: Princeton University Press.

Seligson, Mitchell A. 2002. "The Impact of Corruption on Regime Legitimacy: A Comparative Study of Four Latin American Countries." *The Journal of Politics* 64, 2: 408–33.

References

Shao, Jun, and Dongsheng Tu. 1995. *The Jackknife and Bootstrap*. New York: Springer Verlag.

Shi, Tianjian. 1997. *Political Participation in Beijing*. Cambridge, MA: Harvard University Press.

1999. "Village Committee Elections in China: Institutionalist Tactics for Democracy." *World Politics* 51, 3: 385–412.

2001. "Cultural Impacts on Political Trust: A Comparison of Mainland China and Taiwan." *Comparative Politics* 33, 4: 401–19.

Shi, Tianjian, and Diqing Lou. 2010. "The Shadow of Confucianism," *Journal of Democracy*, 21, 4: 123–30.

2010. "Subjective Evaluation of Changes in Civil Liberties and Political Rights in China." *Journal of Contemporary China* 19, 63: 175–99.

Shirk, Susan L. 1982. *Competitive Comrades: Career Incentives and Student Strategies in China*. Berkeley: University of California Press.

Showers, C. 1992. "Evaluative Integrative Thinking about Characteristics of the Self." *Personality and Social Psychology Bulletin* 18, 6: 719–29.

Shyu, Huoyan. 2009. "Psychological Resources of Political Participation: Comparing Hong Kong, Taiwan, and Mainland China," *Journal of International Cooperation Studies* 17, 2: 25–47.

Skinner, C. J., D. Holt, and T. M. F. Smith. 1989. *Analysis of Complex Surveys*. Chichester, UK and New York: Wiley.

Smith, Adam. 1982 (1759). *The Theory of Moral Sentiments. The Glasgow Edition of the Works and Correspondence of Adam Smith vol. 1*, ed. D. D. Raphael and A. L. Macfie. Indianapolis, IN: Liberty Fund.

Snow, David A., E. Burke Rochford, Jr., Steven K. Worden, and Robert D. Benford. 1986. "Frame Alignment Processes, Micromobilization, and Movement Participation." *American Sociological Review* 51, 4: 464–81.

Spence, Jonathan D. 1999. *The Search for Modern China*, 2nd ed. New York: W. W. Norton.

Stipek, D. 1998. "Differences between Americans and Chinese in the Circumstances Evoking Pride, Shame, and Guilt." *Journal of Cross-Cultural Psychology* 29, 5: 616–29.

Stokes, Donald E. 1962. "Popular Evaluations of Government: An Empirical Assessment." In *Ethics and Bigness*, ed. H. Cleveland and H. D. Lasswell, 61–72. New York: Harper & Row.

Sun, T., V. Yuan, J. G. Payne, and B. Zhong. 2005. "Leadership Attributes Salient to Chinese Local Voters – Correlates of Voting Intentions among Chinese Constituents." *American Behavioral Scientist* 49, 4: 616–28.

Tan, Sor-hoon. 2003. *Confucian Democracy: A Deweyan Reconstruction*. Albany: State University of New York Press.

Tang, Wenfang. 2005. *Public Opinion and Political Change in China*. Stanford, CA: Stanford University Press.

Tarrow, Sidney. 1994. *Power in Movement: Social Movements, Collective Action and Politics*. Cambridge, UK and New York: Cambridge University Press.

Tocqueville, Alexis de. 1945 (1835, 1840). *Democracy in America*, trans. Phillips Bradley. New York: Knopf.

Townsend, James R. 1969. *Political Participation in Communist China*. Berkeley: University of California Press.

Triandis, Harry Charalambos. 1995. *Individualism and Collectivism*. Boulder, CO: Westview.

Tsai, Kellee S. 2007. *Capitalism without Democracy: The Private Sector in Contemporary China*. Ithaca, NY: Cornell University Press.

Tyler, Tom R. 1998. "Trust and Democratic Governance." In *Trust and Governance*, ed. V. A. Braithwaite and M. Levi, 269–94. New York: Russell Sage Foundation.

Uslaner, Eric M. 2002. *The Moral Foundations of Trust*. Cambridge, UK and New York: Cambridge University Press.

Verba, Sidney, and Norman H. Nie. 1972. *Participation in America: Political Democracy and Social Equality*. New York: Harper & Row.

Verba, Sidney, Norman H. Nie, and Jae-on Kim. 1978. *Participation and Political Equality: A Seven-Nation Comparison*. Cambridge, UK and New York: Cambridge University Press.

Verba, Sidney, Kay Lehman Schlozman, and Henry E. Brady. 1995. *Voice and Equality: Civic Voluntarism in American Politics*. Cambridge, MA: Harvard University Press.

Verba, Sidney, Kay Lehman Schlozman, Henry Brady, and Norman H. Nie. 1993. Citizen Activity: Who Participates? What Do They Say? *American Political Science Review* 87, 2: 303–18.

Vinken, Henk, J. Soeters, and P. Ester. 2004. *Comparing Cultures: Dimensions of Culture in a Comparative Perspective*, International Studies in Sociology and Social Anthropology, vol. 93. Leiden, Netherlands and Boston: Brill.

Walder, Andrew G. 1986. *Communist Neo-Traditionalism: Work and Authority in Chinese Industry*. Berkeley: University of California Press.

Wang, Zhengxu. 2005. "Before the Emergence of Critical Citizens: Economic Development and Political Trust in China." *International Review of Sociology* 15, 1: 155–71.

Wang, Zhengxu, Russell J. Dalton, and Doh Chull Shin. 2006. "Political Trust, Political Performance, and Support for Democracy." In *Citizens, Democracy, and Markets around the Pacific Rim: Congruence Theory and Political Culture*, ed. R. J. Dalton, D. C. Shin, 135–58. Oxford, UK and New York: Oxford University Press.

Weber, Max. 1947. *The Theory of Social and Economic Organization*. New York: Free Press.

Weir, Margaret. 1992. "Ideas and the Politics of Bounded Innovation." In *Structuring Politics: Historical Institutionalism in Comparative Analysis*, ed. S. Steinmo, K. Thelen and F. Longstreth, 188–216. Cambridge, UK: Cambridge University Press.

Wendt, Alexander E. 1987. "The Agent-Structure Problem in International Relations Theory." *International Organization* 41, 3: 335–70.

  1999. *Social Theory of International Politics*. Cambridge Studies in International Relations 67. Cambridge, UK and New York: Cambridge University Press.

Werlin, Herbert H., and Harry Eckstein. 1990. "Political Culture and Political Change." *American Political Science Review* 84, 1: 249–59.

White, Gordon. 1993. *Riding the Tiger: The Politics of Economic Reform in Post-Mao China*. Stanford, CA: Stanford University Press.

References

White, Lynn T. 2005. *Legitimacy: Ambiguities of Political Success or Failure in East and Southeast Asia*. Series on Contemporary China 1. Singapore and Hackensack, NJ: World Scientific.

Wildavsky, Aaron. 1987. "Choosing Preferences by Constructing Institutions: Culture Theory of Preference Formation." *American Political Science Review* 81, March: 3–21.

Wilson, Richard W. 2000. "The Many Voices of Political Culture: Assessing Different Approaches." *World Politics* 52, 2: 246–73.

Wolfinger, Raymond E., and Steven J. Rosenstone. 1980. *Who Votes?* New Haven, CT: Yale University Press.

Woo-Cummings, Meredith. 1999. *The Developmental State*. Ithaca, NY: Cornell University Press.

Xiong, Yuezhi. 2001. "'Liberty', 'Democracy', 'President': The Translation and Usage of Some Political Terms in Late Qing China." In *New Terms for New Ideas: Western Knowledge and Lexical Change in Late Imperial China*, ed. M. Lackner, I. Amelung and J. Kurtz, 69–93. Leiden, Netherlands and Boston: Brill.

Yamigishi, Toshio, and Midori Yamigishi. 1994. "Trust and Commitment in the United States and Japan." *Motivation and Emotion* 18: 129–66.

Yu, Luojin. 2009. *A Big Fairytale: My Forty Years in China (Yige Da Tonghua: Wo Zai Zhongguo de Sishi Nian) (1946–1986)*, 1st ed. Hong Kong: Morning Bell Press.

Zablocki, Benjamin David. 1980. *The Joyful Community: An Account of the Bruderhof, a Communal Movement Now in Its Third Generation*. Chicago: University of Chicago Press.

Zakaria, Fareed. 2004. *The Future of Freedom: Illiberal Democracy at Home and Abroad*. New York: W. W. Norton.

Additional Works Consulted

Aldrich, John Herbert. 1995. *Why Parties? The Origin and Transformation of Political Parties in America.* Chicago: University of Chicago Press.

Bell, Daniel A. 2000. *East Meets West: Human Rights and Democracy in East Asia.* Princeton, NJ: Princeton University Press.

Bell, Daniel A., and Chae-bong Hahm, eds. 2003. *Confucianism for the Modern World.* Cambridge, UK and New York: Cambridge University Press.

Blumberg, Rae Lesser, and Robert F. Winch. 1972. "Societal Complexity and Familial Complexity: Evidence for the Curvilinear Hypothesis." *American Journal of Sociology* 77, 5: 898–920.

Bratton, Michael, Robert B. Mattes, and Emmanuel Gyimah-Boadi. 2004. *Public Opinion, Democracy, and Market Reform in Africa.* Cambridge, UK and New York: Cambridge University Press.

Burns, Nancy, Kay Lehman Schlozman, and Sidney Verba. 1997. "The Public Consequences of Private Inequality: Family Life and Citizen Participation." *American Political Science Review* 91, 2: 373–89.

Canache, Damarys, Jeffery J. Mondak, and Mitchell A. Seligson. 2001. "Meaning and Measurement in Cross-National Research on Satisfaction with Democracy." *The Public Opinion Quarterly* 65, 4: 506–28.

Carmines, Edward G., and John P. McIver. 1981. "Analyzing Models with Unobserved Variables: Analysis of Covariance Structures." In *Social Measurement: Current Issues*, ed. G. W. Bohrnstedt and E. F. Borgatta, 65–115. Beverly Hills, CA: Sage.

Carr, Edward Hallett. 1946. *The Twenty Years' Crisis, 1919–1939: An Introduction to the Study of International Relations.* London: Macmillan.

Chang, Yu-tzung, Yun-han Chu, and Chong-min Park. 2007. "Authoritarian Nostalgia in Asia." *Journal of Democracy* 18, 3: 66–80.

Dalton, Russell J., and T. Ong Nhu-Ngoc. 2006. "Authority Orientations and Democratic Attitudes in East Asia: A Test of the Asian Values Hypothesis." In *Citizens, Democracy, and Markets around the Pacific Rim: Congruence*

278 *Additional Works Consulted*

Theory and Political Culture, ed. R. J. Dalton and D. C. Shin, 97–112. Oxford, UK and New York: Oxford University Press.

Dalton, Russell J., and Doh Chull Shin. 2006. "Democratic Aspirations and Social Modernization." In *Citizens, Democracy, and Markets around the Pacific Rim: Congruence Theory and Political Culture*, ed. R. J. Dalton and D. C. Shin, 75–96. Oxford, UK and New York: Oxford University Press.

de Bary, William Theodore. 1998. *Asian Values and Human Rights: A Confucian Communitarian Perspective*. Cambridge, MA: Harvard University Press.

de Bary, William Theodore, Wing-Tsit Chan, and Burton Watson, eds. 1960. *Sources of Chinese Tradition*. New York: Columbia University Press.

de Bary, William Theodore, and Tu Weiming, eds. 1998. *Confucianism and Human Rights*. New York: Columbia University Press.

Dickson, Bruce J. 2003. *Red Capitalists in China: The Party, Private Entrepreneurs, and Prospects for Political Change*. Cambridge, UK and New York: Cambridge University Press.

Eckstein, Harry. 1973. "Authority Patterns: A Structural Basis for Political Inquiry." *The American Political Science Review* 67, 4: 1142–61.

Edwards, R. Randle, Louis Henkin, and Andrew J. Nathan. 1986. *Human Rights in Contemporary China*. New York: Columbia University Press.

Emmerson, Donald K. 1995. "Singapore and the 'Asian Values' Debate." *Journal of Democracy* 6: 95–105.

Festinger, Leon. 1954. "A Theory of Social Comparison Processes." *Human Relations* 7: 117–40.

Finifter, Ada W. 1996. "Attitudes toward Individual Responsibility and Political Reform in the Former Soviet Union." *American Political Science Review* 90, 1: 138–52.

Finifter, Ada W., and Ellen Mickiewicz. 1992. "Redefining the Political System of the USSR: Mass Support for Political Change." *American Political Science Review* 86, 4: 857–74.

Finnemore, Martha. 1993. "International Organizations as Teachers of Norms: The United Nations Educational, Scientific, and Cultural Organization and Science Policy." *International Organization* 47, 4: 565–97.

Flanagan, Scott C., and Aie-Rie Lee. 2000. "Value Change and Democratic Reform in Japan and Korea." *Comparative Political Studies* 33: 626–59.

Freedman, D. A. 2001. "Ecological Inference and the Ecological Fallacy." In *International Encyclopedia of the Social and Behavioral Sciences vol. 6*, ed. N. J. Smelser and P. B. Baltes, 4027–30. Oxford, UK: Elsevier.

Friedman, Edward. 1994. *The Politics of Democratization: Generalizing East Asian Experiences*. Boulder, CO: Westview.

Glendon, Mary Ann. 2001. *A World Made New: Eleanor Roosevelt and the Universal Declaration of Human Rights*. New York: Random House.

Gunther, Richard, Hans-Jürgen Puhle, and José Ramón Montero. 2007. *Democracy, Intermediation, and Voting on Four Continents*. Oxford, UK: Oxford University Press.

Hall, David L., and Roger T. Ames. 1999. *The Democracy of the Dead: Dewey, Confucius, and the Hope for Democracy in China*. Chicago: Open Court.

Additional Works Consulted

Hall, Peter A., and Rosemary C. R. Taylor. 1996. "Political Science and the Three New Institutionalisms." *Political Studies* 44, 5: 936–57.

Hardin, Russell. 1982. *Collective Action*. Baltimore, MD: Johns Hopkins University Press.

Higgins, E. T., James Shah, and Ronald Friedman. 1997. "Emotional Responses to Goal Attainment: Strengths of Regulatory Focus as a Moderator." *Journal of Personality and Social Psychology* 72: 515–25.

Higgins, E. T., and O. Tykocinsky. 1992. "Self-Discrepancies and Biographical Memory: Personality and Cognition at the Level of Psychological Situation." *Personality and Social Psychological Bulletin* 18, 5: 527–35.

Hox, Joop J. 2002. *Multilevel Analysis: Techniques and Applications*. Mahwah, NJ: Lawrence Erlbaum.

Hu, L., and P. M. Bentler. 1999. "Cutoff Criteria for Fit Indexes in Covariance Structure Analysis: Conventional Criteria Versus New Alternatives." *Structural Equation Modeling* 6, 1: 1–55.

Huntington, Samuel P. 1996. *The Clash of Civilizations and the Remaking of World Order*. New York: Simon & Schuster.

Inkeles, Alex, and Raymond A. Bauer. 1959. *The Soviet Citizen: Daily Life in a Totalitarian Society*. Cambridge, MA: Harvard University Press.

Inkeles, Alex, and Daniel J. Levinson. 1969. "National Character: The Study of Modal Personality and Sociocultural Systems." In *The Handbook of Social Psychology, vol. 4*, ed. G. Lindzey and E. Aronson. Reading, MA: Addison-Wesley.

Katz, Elihu, and Paul Felix Lazarsfeld. 1955. *Personal Influence: The Part Played by People in the Flow of Mass Communications*. Glencoe, IL: Free Press.

Kline, Rex B. 2005. *Principles and Practice of Structural Equation Modeling*. New York: Guilford Press.

Krueger, Joachim I., and Melissa Acevedo. 2005. "Social Projection and the Psychology of Choice." In *The Self in Social Judgment*, ed. M. D. Alicke, D. A. Dunning and J. I. Krueger, 17–42. New York: Psychology Press.

Lazarsfeld, Paul Felix, Bernard Berelson, and Hazel Gaudet. 1944. *The People's Choice: How the Voter Makes up His Mind in a Presidential Campaign*. New York: Duell, Sloan and Pearce.

Le Bon, Gustave. 1960 (1896). *The Crowd: A Study of the Popular Mind*. New York: Viking.

Lenin, Vladimir Ilich. 1929. *What Should Be Done: Burning Questions of Our Movement*. New York: International Publishers.

Lin, Min, and Maria Galikowski. 1999. *The Search for Modernity: Chinese Intellectuals and Cultural Discourse in the Post-Mao Era*. New York: St. Martin's Press.

Lipset, Seymour Martin. 1959. "Some Social Requisites of Democracy: Economic Development and Political Legitimacy." *American Political Science Review* 53, 1: 69–105.

Luke, Douglas A. 2004. *Multilevel Modeling*. Sage University Paper Series on Quantitative Applications in the Social Sciences, no. 143. Thousand Oaks, CA: Sage.

Mackay, Charles. 2001 (1841). *Extraordinary Popular Delusions and the Madness of Crowds*. Amherst, NY: Prometheus.

Mansbridge, Jane. 1999. "Altruistic Trust." In *Democracy and Trust*, ed. M. Warren, 290–310. Cambridge, UK and New York: Cambridge University Press.

Markus, H. R., and S. Kitayama. 1991. "Culture and the Self: Implications for Cognition, Emotion and Motivation." *Psychological Review* 98: 224–53.

Marx, Karl. 1969 (1875). "Critique of the Gotha Programme." In *Marx/Engels Selected Works, vol. 3*, ed. K. Marx and F. Engels, 13–30. Moscow: Progress.

Milgram, Stanley, Leonard Bickman, and Leonard Berkowitz. 1969. "Note on the Drawing Power of Crowds of Different Size." *Journal of Personality and Social Psychology* 13: 79–82.

Millar, James R., ed. 1987. *Politics, Work, and Daily Life in the USSR*. Cambridge, UK and New York: Cambridge University Press.

Miller, Arthur H., Vicki L. Hesli, and William M. Reisinger. 1994. "Reassessing Mass Support for Political and Economic Change in the Former USSR." *American Political Science Review* 88, 2: 399–411.

1997. "Conceptions of Democracy among Mass and Elite in Post-Soviet Societies." *British Journal of Political Science* 27, 2: 157–90.

Mishler, William, and Richard Rose. 1994. "Support for Parliaments and Regimes in the Transition toward Democracy in Eastern Europe." *Legislative Studies Quarterly* 19, 1: 5–32.

Nathan, Andrew J. 1985. *Chinese Democracy*. New York: Knopf.

Nathan, Andrew J., and Tianjian Shi. 1993. "Cultural Requisites for Democracy in China: Findings from a Survey." *Daedalus* 122, 2: 95–124.

1996. "Left and Right with Chinese Characteristics: Issues and Alignments in Deng Xiaoping's China." *World Politics* 48, 4: 522–50.

Nie, Norman H., and Sidney Verba. 1975. "Political Participation." In *Handbook of Political Science vol. 4: Nongovernmental Politics*, ed. F. I. Greenstein and N. W. Polsby, 27. Reading, MA: Addison-Wesley.

North, Douglass C. 1990. *Institutions, Institutional Change, and Economic Performance*. Cambridge, UK and New York: Cambridge University Press.

Pateman, Carole. 1980. "The Civic Culture: A Philosophic Critique." In *The Civic Culture Revisited*, ed. G. A. Almond and S. Verba, 57–102. Boston: Little, Brown.

Powell, John Duncan. 1971. *Political Mobilization of the Venezuelan Peasant*. Cambridge, MA: Harvard University Press.

Przeworski, Adam, Michael E. Alvarez, Jose Antonio Cheibub, and Fernando Limongi. 2000. *Democracy and Development: Political Institutions and Well-Being in the World, 1950–1990*. Cambridge, UK and New York: Cambridge University Press.

Pye, Lucian W. 1981. *The Dynamics of Chinese Politics*. Cambridge, MA: Oelgeschlager, Gunn and Hain.

1986. "Political Psychology in Asia." In *Political Psychology*, ed. M. Hermann, 467–86. San Francisco: Jossey-Bass.

Additional Works Consulted

Robinson, W. S. 1950. "Ecological Correlations and the Behavior of Individuals." *American Sociological Review* 15, 3: 351–57.

Rogers, T. B., N. A. Kuiper, and W. S. Kirker. 1977. "Self-Reference and the Encoding of Personal Information." *Journal of Personality and Social Psychology* 35, 9: 677–88.

Rokeach, Milton. 1973. *The Nature of Human Values*. New York: Free Press.

Rose, Richard, and William T. E. Mishler. 1994. "Mass Reaction to Regime Change in Eastern Europe: Polarization or Leaders and Laggards?" *British Journal of Political Science* 24, 2: 159–82.

Scalapino, Robert A. 1989. *The Politics of Development: Perspectives on Twentieth-Century Asia*. Cambridge, MA: Harvard University Press.

Schlozman, Kay Lehman, Nancy Burns, and Sidney Verba. 1994. "Gender and the Pathways to Participation: The Role of Resources." *The Journal of Politics* 56, 4: 963–90.

Schlozman, Kay Lehman, Nancy Burns, Sidney Verba, and Jesse Donahue. 1995. "Gender and Citizen Participation: Is There a Different Voice?" *American Journal of Political Science* 39, 2: 267–93.

Sen, Amartya. 1999. *Development as Freedom*. New York: Knopf.

Shi, Tianjian. 1999. "Voting and Nonvoting in China: Voting Behavior in Plebiscitary and Limited Choice Elections." *Journal of Politics* 61, 4: 1115–38.

2000. "Cultural Values and Democracy in the People's Republic of China." *China Quarterly* 162: 547–66.

2008. "China: Democratic Values Supporting an Authoritarian System." In *How East Asians View Democracy*, ed. Yun-han Chu, Larry Diamond, Andrew J. Nathan, and Doh Chull Shin, 209–37. New York: Columbia University Press.

Shirk, Susan L. 2007. *China: Fragile Superpower*. Oxford, UK and New York: Oxford University Press.

Silver, Allan. 1989. "Friendship and Trust as Moral Ideals: An Historical Approach." *European Journal of Sociology* 30, 2: 274–97.

Simon, Herbert. 1957. *Models of Man*. New York: Wiley.

Solomon, Richard H. 1971. *Mao's Revolution and the Chinese Political Culture*. Michigan Studies on China, vol 1. Berkeley: University of California Press.

1973. "From Commitment to Cant: the Evolving Functions of Ideology in the Revolutionary Process." In *Ideology and Politics in Contemporary China*, ed. C. Johnson, 47–77. Seattle: University of Washington Press.

Steenbergen, Marco R., and Bradford S. Jones. 2002. "Modeling Multilevel Data Structures." *American Journal of Political Science* 46, 1: 218–37.

Stephens, Thomas B. 1992. *Order and Discipline in China: The Shanghai Mixed Court, 1911–27*. Seattle: University of Washington Press.

Sun, Yan. 1995. *The Chinese Reassessment of Socialism 1976–1992*. Princeton, NJ: Princeton University Press.

Tang, Wenfang, and William L. Parish. 2000. *Chinese Urban Life under Reform: The Changing Social Contract*. Cambridge, UK and New York: Cambridge University Press.

Tannen, Deborah. 1993. *Framing in Discourse*. New York: Oxford University Press.

282   *Additional Works Consulted*

Tanner, Murray Scot. 1999. *The Politics of Lawmaking in Post-Mao China – Institutions, Processes, and Democratic Prospects.* Oxford, UK and New York: Clarendon and Oxford University Press.

Tu, Weiming. 1984. *Confucian Ethics Today: The Singapore Challenge.* Singapore: Federal Publications.

    1985. *Confucian Thought: Selfhood as Creative Transformation.* Albany: State University of New York Press.

    1996. *Confucian Traditions in East Asian Modernity: Moral Education and Economic Culture in Japan and the Four Mini-Dragons.* Cambridge, MA: Harvard University Press.

Tu, Weiming, and Mary Evelyn Tucker, eds. 2003. *Confucian Spirituality, vol. 1.* New York: Crossroad.

Verba, Sidney. 1978. "The Parochial and the Polity." In *The Citizen and Politics: A Comparative Perspective,* ed. S. Verba and L. W. Pye. 3–28. New York: Greylock.

Walder, Andrew G. 1987. "Communist Social Structure and Worker's Politics in China." In *Citizens and Groups in Contemporary China,* ed. V. C. Falkenheim, 45–89. Ann Arbor: University of Michigan Center for Chinese Studies.

    1989. "Factory and Manager in an Era of Reform." *China Quarterly* 118: 242–64.

    ed. 1995. *The Waning of the Communist State: Economic Origins of Political Decline in China and Hungary.* Berkeley: University of California Press.

Wang, Shaoguang. 1995. *Failure of Charisma: The Cultural Revolution in Wuhan.* Oxford, UK and Hong Kong: Oxford University Press.

Wang, Zhengxu, and Ern-Ser Tan. 2006. "Self-Expression, Asian Values, and Democracy: East Asia in Global Perspective." In *Citizens, Democracy, and Markets around the Pacific Rim: Congruence Theory and Political Culture,* ed. J. Dalton and D. C. Shin, 50–72. Oxford, UK and New York: Oxford University Press.

Zakaria, Fareed. 1994. "Culture is Destiny: A Conversation with Lee Kuan Yew." *Foreign Affairs* 73, March-April: 109–26.

Zhao, Dingxin. 2001. *The Power of Tiananmen: State-Society Relations and the 1989 Beijing Student Movement.* Chicago: University of Chicago Press.

Zhao, Suisheng, ed. 2000. *China and Democracy: Reconsidering the Prospects for a Democratic China.* New York and London: Routledge.

Zhou, Xueguang. 2004. *The State and Life Chances in Urban China: Redistribution and Stratification, 1949–1994.* Cambridge, UK and New York: Cambridge University Press.

Index

ABS I. *See* Asian Barometer Survey I
  (ABS I)
ABS II. *See* Asian Barometer Survey II
  (ABS II)
Accountability without Democracy
  (Tsai), 39
"Actual self," 36–37
Affective encoding, 18
Africa
  level of democracy in, 193–94
  political trust in, 111, 112, 114
Age
  choice of confrontational acts,
    correlation with, 181
  cognitive diffidence, correlation
    with, 206
  perceived government salience,
    correlation with, 157, 161
  political trust, correlation with, 129
  understanding of democracy, correlation
    with, 213
All China Women's Association
  (ACWA), 231
Allocentric DSI
  in China, 91–93, 99
  choice of confrontational acts and,
    178, 183
  cognitive diffidence and, 207,
    208–9, 210
  complexity of effects of, 227
  in Confucianism, 48
  cultural discontinuity and, 82
  democratization, ramifications for, 145

Fan Meizhong and, 252–55
focus on in cultural theory, 223
interpretation of social action, effect
  on, 50–52
IRT analysis, 89
likelihood of participation and, 165–66,
  170–74
overview, 7–8, 9
pattern-maintaining change
  and, 255
perceived government salience and, 155,
  156, 163, 164
political participation and, 149–50,
  189–90, 225
political trust and, 117–18, 126,
  129–30, 224
protest potential and, 186, 189
safety valve for authoritarianism,
  providing, 227–28
shame and, 58
sources of affect, providing, 55
standards for evaluation of behavior,
  providing, 54
survey questions regarding, 66
understanding of democracy and, 193,
  211, 213–16, 226
Yu Luojin and, 251–52
Almond, Gabriel A., 4, 20–21, 26, 62,
  121–22, 146, 148
Altruistic explanations of cultural norm
  adherence, 36–37
Analects (Confucius), 199
Anomie, 81

283

Index

ANOVA models
  likelihood of participation, 166–67
  perceived government salience, 159
  political trust, 126–27, 130
  protest potential, 187
Anti-Spiritual Pollution Campaign
    (1983–1984), 97
Aristotle, 187
Asian Barometer Survey I (ABS I)
  commitment to democracy and, 8, 17
  data from, 62
  interviewers, 231–32
  likelihood of participation and, 166
  overview, 3
  perceived government salience and, 156
  political trust and, 119
  PPS method, 231, 236–37
  primary sampling units, 230–31
  quality control, 232
  "raking," 231, 237
  sample design for China survey, 230–32
  sample design for Taiwan survey, 236–37
  sampling process, 234
  secondary sampling units, 231
  tables, 237–38
  tertiary sampling units, 231
  understanding of democracy and, 192,
    194–96, 202
Asian Barometer Survey II (ABS II)
  data from, 63
  interviewers, 233
  overview, 3
  PPS method, 232–33
  primary sampling units, 232–33
  sample design for China survey, 232–33
  secondary sampling units, 233
  tertiary sampling units, 233
Attitudes
  characteristics of, 26–27
  cultural norms distinguished, 25–29
Authoritarianism in China
  economic development and reform,
    effect of, 14, 16
  Freedom House on, 194
  information barriers, 15–16
  institutional changes, effect of, 16
  particular Asian legitimacy as reason
    for, 16
  repression, level of, 15
  safety valve for, 227–28
  survival of in post-Tiananmen
    period, 14–15

Authority, orientation toward.
    See Orientation toward authority
    (OTA)

Backlash. *See* Cultural backlash
Bai Hua, 177
Barnes, Samuel, 185
Becker, Howard S., 252
Beijing University, Research Center for
    Contemporary China, 232, 233
Benedict, Ruth, 56
Bentler Comparative Fit Index, 69
Berlin, Isaiah, 200
Bitter Love (Bai Hua), 177
Böckenholt, Ulf, 39

Cai Zhongpei, 250–51
Cathexis, 18
CCP. *See* Chinese Communist Party (CCP)
CFI (Confirmatory Fit Index), 69
Change. *See* Cultural change
Chen Pengren, 201
China. *See specific topic*
China Survey (2002), 3
China Survey (2008), 3–4
Chinese Academy of Social Sciences,
    Institute of Sociology, 230
Chinese Communist Party (CCP)
  on democracy, 197, 204
  economic development and reform
    and, 14
  membership, correlation with political
    trust, 125–26, 129
  political trust of, 119–20
  Tiananmen Incident and, 13
  Yu Luoke and, 250
Chi-square test, 69
Chiu, C.Y., 57–58
Choice of confrontational acts, impact of
    culture on
  age, correlation with, 181
  allocentric DSI and, 178, 183
  cost-benefit analysis of, 175
  cultural norms, correlation with,
    175–77, 179–82
  degree of confrontation, 178–81
  education, correlation with, 181
  factor analysis, 178–81
  "free rider" problem and, 176
  gender, correlation with, 181
  Hierarchical Linear Modeling (HLM)
    and, 178–81

Index

hierarchical OTA and, 177–78, 181
idiocentric DSI and, 178, 181, 183
income, correlation with, 181
independent variables, 178–81
overview, 174–75
political efficacy, correlation
with, 181
political fear, correlation with, 175–76
political interest, correlation
with, 181–83
psychological resources, correlation
with, 181
rational actor model and, 175
reciprocal OTA and, 177–78
remonstration, 177–78
sociological resources, correlation
with, 181
SOEs and, 164–65
survey questions, 175–77
urbanization, correlation with, 181
Chu Yun-han, 2, 234, 236
Cialdini, Robert, 39
Citrin, Jack, 108
The Civic Culture (Almond and Verba),
121–22
Civic culture approach to cultural
theory, 20–21
Civic orientation, 31
Civil liberties in China versus Taiwan, 61
Classical Measurement Theory (CMT)
IRT compared, 246–49
overview, 69, 71
Cognitive decoding
as component of decision making, 18
cultural backlash and, 96
social action, effect of cultural norms on,
34, 52–53
understanding of democracy and, 211
Cognitive diffidence, 205–10
age, correlation with, 206
allocentric DSI and, 207, 208–9, 210
in China, 208–9, 210
cultural norms, correlation with, 207
"don't know" answers, analysis of,
243–45
education, correlation with, 206
gender, correlation with, 206
hierarchical OTA and, 207, 208–9, 210
idiocentric DSI and, 207
income, correlation with, 206
meaning of democracy versus suitability
of democracy, 207

perceived government salience,
correlation with, 206–7
political efficacy, correlation with, 206
political interest, correlation with, 206
probit models, 208
psychological resources, correlation
with, 206
reciprocal OTA and, 207
sociological resources, correlation
with, 206
study results, 208
in Taiwan, 209–10
urbanization, correlation with, 206
Cognitive dissonance, 19–20, 52, 97
Cognitive engagement, 205–6
Cohort analysis of cultural change, 86–96
allocentric DSI in China, 91–93, 99
generational effects, 87–88
idiocentric DSI in China, 91–93, 99
idiocentric DSI in Taiwan, 93–96
institutional theory and, 87, 93, 96
IRT analysis, using, 89
life-cycle effects, 87, 91
modernization theory and, 87, 93, 96
reciprocal OTA in China, 90, 91
reciprocal OTA in Taiwan, 93, 94
social-structural theory and, 87, 93, 96
study results, 89
Coleman, James, 28–29, 36–37, 38
Collective action problem, 42, 45–46
Collective consciousness, 33
"Collective mass incidents," 15
Collectivist nature of culture, 31
Communist Revolution (1949), 84–85
Confidentiality of interviewees, 239–40
Confirmatory Fit Index (CFI), 69–70
Conflict acceptance, 44
Conflict avoidance, 49
Confrontational acts, choice of. *See* Choice
of confrontational acts, impact of
culture on
Confucianism, 40
allocentric DSI in, 48
collective action problem and, 45–46
Communist efforts to eliminate, 62
conflict avoidance in, 49
courteousness in, 48
education in, 46–47
external policing system for enforcing
cultural norms in, 58
guardianship democracy and, 198–99
hierarchical OTA in, 49

Index

Confucianism (*cont.*)
  ren in, 46–47
  shame in, 58
  social contract theory contrasted,
    47–48, 50
  substantive justice in, 50
Confucius. *See also* Confucianism
  collective action problem and, 42
  criticism of, 62
  cultural backlash and, 97
  on human nature, 47
  minben and, 45, 46, 197, 199
  on political institutions, 41
Constraining power of government in
    democracy, 196–97, 202
Convergence theory, 68
Corruption Perception Index, 112
Cost-benefit analysis
  of choice of confrontational acts, 175
  of political participation, 147, 148–49
Cultural backlash, 96–102
  in China, 99, 100, 102
  in Chinese history, 97
  cognitive decoding and, 96
  Confucius and, 97
  cultural theory and, 96–97
  in Eastern Europe, 97
  education and, 98–99
  institutional theory and, 96–97
  in Iran, 97
  in Middle East, 97
  in other countries, 97–98
  overview, 96, 97
  study results, 99–102
  in Taiwan, 99–102
Cultural change
  allocentric DSI in China, 91–93, 99
  cohort analysis of, 86–96
    (*See also* Cohort analysis of cultural
    change)
  critique of theories regarding, 78, 79–81
  cultural backlash, 96–102
    (*See also* Cultural backlash)
  cultural discontinuity (*See* Cultural
    discontinuity)
  cultural flexibility (*See* Cultural
    flexibility)
  different types of change in normative
    orientations, 80–81
  external policing system for enforcing
    cultural norms and, 79–80, 257

generational effects, 87–88
geography, analysis of distribution of
    cultural norms across, 86
at group level, 83–86, 256
idiocentric DSI in China, 91–93, 99
idiocentric DSI in Taiwan, 93–96
at individual level, 81–83
internal policing system for enforcing
    cultural norms and, 79–80
jurisdiction of cultural norms, analysis of
    change in, 85–86
life-cycle effects, 87, 91
overview, 76–77, 103
pattern-maintaining change (*See* Pattern-
    maintaining change)
problems in defining, 79–80
reciprocal OTA in China, 90, 91
reciprocal OTA in Taiwan, 93, 94
regulation of social behavior by cultural
    norms, effect on, 85, 86
time, analysis of distribution of cultural
    norms across, 86, 256–57
Cultural discontinuity
  allocentric DSI and, 82
  cultural consequences of social
    discontinuity, 78
  defined, 80–81
  at group level, 84–85
  hierarchical OTA and, 82
  at individual level, 81–82
Cultural environment, correlation with
    political trust, 131, 132, 134–35
Cultural flexibility
  defined, 80
  at group level, 84
  at individual level, 83
  internal policing system for enforcing
    cultural norms and, 257
  pattern-maintaining change, relationship
    to, 83
  structural or institutional change, effect
    of, 85–86
  Yu Luojin and, 251–52
Cultural norms
  additional information, as guide
    for, 52–53
  allocentric DSI (*See* Allocentric DSI)
  altruistic explanations of
    adherence, 36–37
  attitudes distinguished, 25–29
  behavior and, 28

choice of confrontational acts, correlation with, 175–77, 179–82

cognitive diffidence, correlation with, 207

culture as norms, 221

defined, 27–28

DSI (*See* Definition of self-interest (DSI))

focus on in cultural theory, 223

geography, analysis of distribution across, 86

guardianship democracy, effect on, 204–5

hierarchical OTA (*See* Hierarchical OTA)

idiocentric DSI (*See* Idiocentric DSI)

as intermediate level of psychological orientation, 25

interpretation of social action, effect on, 34, 50–52

jurisdiction, analysis of change in, 85–86

legitimate goals, defining, 35, 55, 150

legitimate means, constraining, 35, 56, 150

likelihood of participation, correlation with, 165–66, 168–72

in literature, 40

measurement of, 222 (*See also* Measurement of cultural norms)

OTA (*See* Orientation toward authority (OTA))

perceived government salience, correlation with, 154–55, 159, 160–62

political participation, correlation with, 190–91

as preferred focal point for cultural study, 28–29

protest potential, correlation with, 185–86, 188

reciprocal OTA (*See* Reciprocal OTA)

regulation of social behavior, effect of cultural change on, 85, 86

sanctions for enforcing (*See* Sanctions for enforcing cultural norms)

social action, effect on, 34–35, 52–53, 222–23

as social phenomena, 28–29

sources of affect, providing, 35, 54–55

standards for evaluation of behavior, providing, 34–35, 54, 96, 149–50

time, analysis of distribution across, 86

understanding of democracy, correlation with, 211, 213–17, 218

values distinguished, 25–29

Cultural Revolution (1966–1976), 62, 84–85, 196, 250–52

Cultural theory

affective encoding, 18

attitudes, cultural norms distinguished, 25–29

change, problems in defining, 79–80

civic culture approach, 20–21

cognitive decoding, 18, 34

collectivist nature of culture, 31

complexity of effects of culture, 227

conventional theory distinguished, 221–22

critique of, 79–81

cultural backlash and, 96–97

cultural norms (*See* Cultural norms)

culture as norms, 221

different types of change in normative orientations, failure to account for, 80–81

evaluative encoding, 18–19

immediate social environment as unit of analysis, 33–34

individualist nature of culture, 30–31

intellectual origins of, 18–19

level-of-analysis problem in, 30–32

measurement of cultural norms in, 222 (*See also* Measurement of cultural norms)

mechanisms of cultural influence, 221–22, 227

normative orientations and, 18–19

normative rationality and, 24–25, 29–30, 226–27

orientations, failure to make distinctions between, 79

overview, 4–5, 78

political participation and, 149–52

social action, effect of cultural norms on, 222–23

social bias approach, 22–23

social character approach, 20

social constructivism approach, 23–24

symbols, rituals and myths approach, 21–22

unit-of-analysis problem in, 32–34

values, cultural norms distinguished, 25–29

Index

Dahl, Robert, 197–98
Dang Dai (journal), 251
Data
  from ABS I, 62
  from ABS II, 63
  reliability, indicators of, 64–65
  reliability, methods to ensure, 63–64
  from 1993 Survey, 62
Definition of self-interest (DSI)
  allocentric (*See* Allocentric DSI)
  idiocentric (*See* Idiocentric DSI)
  influence on behavior, 58–59
  orientation toward authority (OTA)
    distinguished, 223–24
  overview, 5
  survey questions regarding, 66
Democracy and Its Critics (Dahl), 197–98
Democracy Wall movement (1979), 78
"Democratic dictatorship," 196
Democratic Progressive Party (Taiwan),
  140–41, 204, 209, 234–35
Democratization
  allocentric DSI, ramifications of, 145
  hierarchical OTA, ramifications of,
    145–46
  political trust and, 145–46
  "Third Wave" of, 8, 13, 192
  United States, role of, 17
Dennis, Jack, 108–10
Design effects, 88–89
de Tocqueville, Alexis, 187
Deviating norm holders
  external policing system for enforcing
    cultural norms, effect on, 118, 255–56
  idiocentric DSI and, 132
  perceived government salience and, 159
  political trust and, 132
  reciprocal OTA and, 132
Discontinuity. *See* Cultural discontinuity
Dominant norm holders, effect on external
  policing system for enforcing cultural
  norms, 251–52, 255–56
Dong Zhongshu, 97
Douglas, Mary, 22
Downs, Anthony, 147, 148
Durkheim, Emile, 30–31, 81

East Asian Barometer (EAB), 3
Eastern Europe
  cultural backlash in, 97
  political trust in, 111, 112, 114

Eastern versus Western cultural norms,
  5, 41–42
Easton, David, 108–10, 116–17
Eckstein, Harry, 26, 31, 78, 80–82,
  151, 174
Economic development and reform
  authoritarianism in China, effect on,
    14, 16
  CCP and, 14
  China versus Taiwan, 61
  perceived government salience, effect
    on, 156
  political participation, effect on, 190
  political trust, effect on, 119–20, 130,
    132–33
  protest potential, effect on, 183–85
Education
  in China versus Taiwan, 61
  choice of confrontational acts,
    correlation with, 181
  cognitive diffidence, correlation
    with, 206
  in Confucianism, 46–47
  cultural backlash and, 98–99
  "don't know" answers, analysis
    of, 245
  likelihood of participation, correlation
    with, 167
  perceived government salience,
    correlation with, 157, 161, 162, 163
  political trust, correlation with, 123,
    129, 130–31, 132–33
  understanding of democracy, correlation
    with, 213
Efficacy. *See* Political efficacy
Elections in democracy, 196–97, 202
Elements of International Law
  (Wheaton), 201
Empirical data on culture, 5
Endogeneity, culture and, 2, 6, 77–78, 79.
  See also Independence of culture
English and Chinese Dictionary
  (Lobscheid), 200
Eurasia, level of democracy in, 193–94
Evaluative encoding, 18–19
External policing system for enforcing
  cultural norms
  in Confucianism, 58
  cultural change and, 79–80, 257
  deviating norm holders, effect of, 118,
    255–56

Index

dominant norm holders, effect of, 251–52, 255–56
"free rider" problem and, 38
heroic sanctions, 38–39
interaction with internal policing system, 39
overview, 36
External political efficacy
choice of confrontational acts, correlation with, 181
cognitive diffidence, correlation with, 206
likelihood of participation, correlation with, 167–70
perceived government salience, correlation with, 158

Factor analysis
choice of confrontational acts, 178–81
factor structure validity, 71, 73
independence of culture, 223–24
jurisdiction of cultural norms, analysis of change in, 85–86
measurement of cultural norms by, 68–72
OTA and DSI as separate dimensions, 69–71
overview, 68–69
performance of variables, 70, 72, 73, 74
political trust in China, 119–20
political trust in Taiwan, 140
protest potential, 186–87
statistically significant correlation, 70, 71
Fan Meizhong, 252–55
Fear. See Political fear
The Federalist Papers (Madison), 195
Festinger, Leon, 19–20, 52
Flexibility. See Cultural flexibility
"Four Olds," 62
Framing, 52–53
Freedom
in guardianship democracy, 199–201
in liberal democracy, 199–201
negative freedom, 200–1
positive freedom, 200–1
understanding of democracy and, 202
ziyou and, 200–1
Freedom House, 112, 193–96
"Free rider" problem
choice of confrontational acts and, 176
external policing system for enforcing cultural norms and, 38

protest potential and, 187–89
rationality of free riding, 38
French Revolution (1789), 187

Game theory, political trust and, 115
GDP in China versus Taiwan, 61
Gender
choice of confrontational acts, correlation with, 181
cognitive diffidence, correlation with, 206
likelihood of participation, correlation with, 167
perceived government salience, correlation with, 157, 161
political trust, correlation with, 129
Generational effects, 87–88
Gibbs, Jack, 28
Gilley, Bruce, 14
Global Barometer Surveys (GBS), 110–11
Goldstein, Judith, 25
Gossip, role in enforcing cultural norms, 39
Government responsiveness, correlation with political trust, 121–22, 127, 130, 132–33
Government salience. See Perceived government salience, impact of culture on
Grapevine rumors. See Xiaodao xiaoxi (grapevine rumors)
Great Leap Forward, 62
Guardianship democracy, 197–201
Confucianism and, 198–99
cultural norms, effect of, 204–5
freedom in, 199–201
ideal government, methods of building, 197–98
legitimacy, evaluation of, 198
liberal democracy contrasted, 197–201, 225–26
overview, 48, 192
political participation in, 198–99
public welfare as purpose of, 197
in Taiwan, 204–5
understanding of democracy and, 202–4
Guilt
idiocentric DSI and, 57
religion and, 57
shame contrasted, 56–58
Guo Haifeng, 15

Han Dynasty, 48, 97, 201
Hardin, Russell, 115
Henry Luce Foundation, 2–3
He Qinglian, 15–16
"Heroic sanctions," 38–39
Hierarchical Linear Modeling (HLM)
of China data, 119, 126–27, 133–36, 141–44
choice of confrontational acts and, 178–81
likelihood of participation and, 166–67
perceived government salience and, 159, 258–60
political participation and, 258–60
political trust and, 107–8, 119, 126–27, 133–36, 141–44, 224
protest potential and, 187
of Taiwan data, 141–44
understanding of democracy and, 213
Hierarchical OTA
additional information, as guide for, 52–53
choice of confrontational acts and, 177–78, 181
cognitive diffidence and, 207, 208–9, 210
complexity of effects of, 227
in Confucianism, 49
cultural discontinuity and, 82
democratization, ramifications for, 145
focus on in cultural theory, 223
interpretation of social action, effect on, 50–52
IRT analysis, 89
legitimate goals, defining, 55
legitimate means, constraining, 56
likelihood of participation and, 165, 170, 173–74
overview, 7–8, 9
pattern-maintaining change and, 82
perceived government salience and, 154–55, 156, 163, 164
political participation and, 189, 190, 191, 225
political trust and, 117, 118, 144, 224
protest potential and, 186, 189
safety valve for authoritarianism, providing, 227–28
sources of affect, providing, 54–55
standards for evaluation of behavior, providing, 54
in Taiwan, 144

understanding of democracy and, 193, 211, 213–16, 226
Higgins, E. Tory, 36
HLM. See Hierarchical Linear Modeling (HLM)
Hobbes, Thomas, 41, 42–43
Hofstede, Geert H., 30
Hong, Y.Y., 57–58
Hu Fu, 2, 234, 236
Huntington, Samuel P., 77, 78, 97–98, 156, 196, 199–200

"Ideal self," 36–37
Idiocentric DSI
change over time in China, 99, 100, 102
change over time in Taiwan, 99–102
in China, 91–93, 99
choice of confrontational acts and, 178, 181, 183
cognitive diffidence and, 207
cultural discontinuity and, 82
deviating norm holders and, 132
factor analysis (See Factor analysis)
Fan Meizhong and, 252–55
focus on in cultural theory, 223
guilt and, 57
interpretation of social action, effect on, 50–52
IRT analysis, 89
likelihood of participation and, 165–66, 170–73
perceived government salience and, 155, 161–63
political participation and, 149–50, 190–91
political trust and, 117–18, 136–38, 224
protest potential and, 186, 189
religion and, 57
sanctions for enforcing cultural norms and, 57
in social contract theory, 44
standards for evaluation of behavior, providing, 54
study results, 66–68
survey questions regarding, 66
in Taiwan, 93–96
understanding of democracy and, 193, 211, 213–16, 226
Yu Luojin and, 251–52
Income
choice of confrontational acts, correlation with, 181

Index

cognitive diffidence, correlation with, 206
likelihood of participation, correlation with, 167
perceived government salience, correlation with, 157, 161
Incremental sanctions, 39–40
Incumbent-based trust
in China, 119, 130, 134–35, 137–38
overview, 108, 109–10
Independence of culture, 1–2, 5–6, 150–52, 223–24. *See also* Endogeneity, culture and
Individualist nature of culture, 30–31
Inglehart, Ronald, 31, 78, 126, 129, 174
Institutional theory
cohort analysis of cultural change and, 87, 93, 96
cultural backlash and, 96–97
overview, 76, 77–78
political trust and, 138–39
on Taiwan, 138–39
Institutions. *See* Political institutions
Interest. *See* Political interest
Internal policing system for enforcing cultural norms
cultural change and, 79–80
cultural flexibility and, 257
interaction with external policing system, 39
overview, 36, 37
pattern-maintaining change and, 257
Internal political efficacy
cognitive diffidence, correlation with, 206
likelihood of participation, correlation with, 167–70
perceived government salience, correlation with, 157–58
Intra-Class Correlation Coefficient (ICCC), 126–27
Iran, cultural backlash in, 97
Item Response Theory (IRT)
CMT compared, 246–49
cohort analysis of cultural change using, 89
factor analysis (*See* Factor analysis)

Japan
authoritarianism in, 16
democracy, attitudes toward, 17
political participation in, 148
shame in, 56
understanding of democracy in, 194
Johnson, Chalmers, 16
Journal of Democracy, 13

Kaase, Max, 185
Kaihua Educational Institution, 254
Keji fuli (overcome selfish desires and restore traditional virtues), 97
Keohane, Robert O., 25
Kim, Jae-on, 147–48
King, Gary, 122, 236
Knight, Jack, 77
Kratochwil, Friedrich V., 23
Kuan, Hsin-chi, 2–3
Kuhn, Thomas, 80–82
Kulian (Bai Hua), 177
Kuomintang (Taiwan), 140–41, 234–35

Latent trait theory. *See* Item Response Theory (IRT)
Latin America, political trust in, 111, 112, 114–15
Lau, S.K., 2–3
Lazarsfeld, Paul Felix, 52–53
Legitimacy
authoritarianism in China, particular Asian legitimacy as reason for, 16
evaluation of in democracy, 198
political trust and, 110
Leninism, 197
Level-of-analysis problem in cultural theory, 30–32
Li, Lianjiang, 15, 167, 240
Liberal democracy
freedom in, 199–201
guardianship democracy contrasted, 197–201, 225–26
ideal government, methods of building, 197–98
legitimacy, evaluation of, 198
obstacles to in Asia, 228
overview, 196–97
political participation in, 198–99
public welfare as purpose of, 197
reciprocal OTA and, 196–97, 198
Life-cycle effects, 87, 91
Life satisfaction, correlation with political trust, 126, 129

Likelihood of participation, impact of culture on
  allocentric DSI and, 165–66, 170–74
  ANOVA models, 166–67
  conventional theories, 164
  county-level variables, 167, 173
  cross-county variation, analysis of, 166–67
  cultural norms, correlation with, 165–66, 168–72
  dependent variables, 166
  education, correlation with, 167
  gender, correlation with, 167
  Hierarchical Linear Modeling (HLM) and, 166–67
  hierarchical OTA and, 165, 170, 173–74
  idiocentric DSI and, 165–66, 170–73
  income, correlation with, 167
  individual-level variables, 167–73
  pattern-maintaining changes, 173
  political efficacy, correlation with, 167–70
  political interest, correlation with, 167, 170–73
  psychological resources, correlation with, 167–70, 171–72
  reciprocal OTA and, 165, 170, 173
  sociological resources, correlation with, 167
  study results, 173–74
  survey questions regarding, 166
  urbanization, correlation with, 167
Lin Biao, 62
Li Shimin, 198
Literature, cultural norms in, 40
Liu Binyan, 13
Lobscheid, William, 200
Locke, John, 41, 42, 43
Lu Xun, 40

Madison, James, 199
Mao Zedong, 62, 200
Martin, W.A.P., 201
Marx, Karl, 187
May Fourth Movement (1919), 84–85
Measurement of cultural norms
  Bentler Comparative Fit Index, 69
  chi-square test, 69
  choice between cultural norms required, 66
  Classical Measurement Theory (CMT), 69, 71, 246–49

Confirmatory Fit Index (CFI), 69–70
  conventional theory distinguished, 222
  DSI, survey questions regarding, 66
  factor analysis, 68–72 (See also Factor analysis)
  factor structure validity, 71, 73
  motives versus cultural norms, 65–66
  observable variables, 65
  OTA and DSI as separate dimensions, 69–71
  overview, 6, 60, 75
  performance of variables, 70, 72, 73, 74
  political referents avoided, 65
  reliability of data, indicators of, 64–65
  reliability of data, methods to ensure, 63–64
  Root Mean Square Error of Approximation (RMSEA), 70–71, 72
  statistically significant correlation, 70, 71
  Tucker-Lewis Index (TLI), 69–70
  validity of (See Validity of measurements)
Media access, correlation with political trust, 124–25, 129, 136–38
"Media malaise," 124
Mencius, 41, 42, 45, 47, 199
Middle East
  cultural backlash in, 97
  level of democracy in, 193–94
Mill, John Stuart, 200
Miller, Arthur H., 108
Minben (people-as-the-basis), 8. See also Guardianship democracy
Ming restoration movement, 97
Ministry of Education, 255
Minzhu (democracy), 201
Modernization theory
  cohort analysis of cultural change and, 87, 93, 96
  overview, 76, 77
Mongolia, understanding of democracy in, 194
Moral crusaders, 252
Moral entrepreneurs, 252

National General Team for Rural Surveys, 230
National People's Congress, 119–20, 155
National Population Databook (1987), 230
National Statistical Yearbook (1999), 231
National Taiwan University, 234, 236

Index

Nazism, 78
Negative freedom, 200–1
Negative liberty, 200
Nelson, Joan M., 77
Neo-Confucianism, 97, 102
New Left, 102
Nie, Norman H., 147–48
1993 Survey. *See* Survey of Political Culture and Political Participation in Mainland China, Taiwan, and Hong Kong (1993)
Nongovernmental organizations (NGOs), attitudes toward in China, 54
Normative orientations, cultural theory and, 18–19
Normative rationality, cultural theory and, 24–25, 29–30, 226–27
Norm entrepreneurs, 251–53
Norms. *See* Cultural norms

O'Brien, Kevin, 15, 167
Offe, Claus, 115
On Family Background (Yu Luoke), 250
Opium War (1840), 84–85
Orientation toward authority (OTA)
  definition of self-interest (DSI) distinguished, 223–24
  hierarchical (*See* Hierarchical OTA)
  influence on behavior, 58–59
  overview, 5
  reciprocal (*See* Reciprocal OTA)
"Ought self," 36–37

Pan Blue (Taiwan), 140–41
Pan Green (Taiwan), 140–41
"Paradox of voting," 148
Parsons, Talcott, 18–19, 20, 25, 28, 34
Participation. *See* Political participation, impact of culture on
Pattern-maintaining change
  allocentric DSI and, 255
  cultural flexibility, relationship to, 33
  defined, 80
  at group level, 84
  hierarchical OTA and, 82
  at individual level, 82
  internal policing system for enforcing cultural norms and, 257
  likelihood of participation and, 173
  Yu Luojin and, 251–52
Pearson analysis
  political fear, 242

understanding of democracy, 194–96
People's Communes (China), 62
People's Republic of China. *See specific topic regarding China*
People's University of China, Center for Social Survey, 229
Perceived government salience, impact of culture on
  age, correlation with, 157, 161
  allocentric DSI and, 155, 156, 163, 164
  ANOVA models, 159
  cognitive diffidence, correlation with, 206–7
  control variables, 157
  conventional theories, 154
  county-level variables, 159
  cross-county variation, analysis of, 258–60
  cultural norms, correlation with, 154–55, 159, 160–62
  defined, 152–54
  deviating norm holders and, 159
  economic development and reform, effect of, 156
  education, correlation with, 157, 161, 162, 163
  gender, correlation with, 157, 161
  Hierarchical Linear Modeling (HLM) and, 159, 258–60
  hierarchical OTA and, 154–55, 156, 163, 164
  idiocentric DSI and, 155, 161–63
  income, correlation with, 157, 161
  individual-level variables, 157–59
  political efficacy, correlation with, 157, 161
  political institutions, role of, 158–59
  political interest, correlation with, 157, 161
  PPS method, 159
  psychological resources, correlation with, 157–58, 161
  reciprocal OTA and, 154–55, 161–62, 163
  sociological resources, correlation with, 157, 161
  study results, 161–64
  survey questions regarding, 156
  understanding of democracy, correlation with, 213
  urbanization, correlation with, 157

Philippines, understanding of democracy in, 194

Plato, 197–98

Poland, Solidarity movement in, 15

Political efficacy
- choice of confrontational acts, correlation with, 181
- cognitive diffidence, correlation with, 206
- likelihood of participation, correlation with, 167–70
- perceived government salience, correlation with, 157–58, 161

Political fear
- in China, 240, 241, 242–43
- choice of confrontational acts, correlation with, 175–76
- "don't know" answers, analysis of, 245
- hypothesis regarding, 242
- Pearson analysis, 242
- political trust, correlation with, 123
- political trust, effect on validity of measurement of, 112, 240–42
- supply of democracy, effect on validity of measurement of, 242–43
- in Taiwan, 240–41

Political institutions
- China versus Taiwan, 61
- perceived government salience, role in, 158–59
- political participation, role in, 147–48, 151

Political interest
- choice of confrontational acts, correlation with, 181–83
- cognitive diffidence, correlation with, 206
- likelihood of participation, correlation with, 167, 170–73
- perceived government salience, correlation with, 157, 161

Political Order in Changing Societies (Huntington), 199–200

Political participation, impact of culture on
- allocentric DSI and, 149–50, 189–90, 225
- in China, 150–52, 153
- choice of confrontational acts (See Choice of confrontational acts, impact of culture on)
- cost-benefit analysis of, 147, 148–49
- cross-county variation, analysis of, 258–60
- cultural norms, correlation with, 190–91

cultural theory and, 149–52

economic development and reform, effect of, 190

in guardianship democracy, 198–99

Hierarchical Linear Modeling (HLM) and, 258–60

hierarchical OTA and, 189, 190, 191, 225

idiocentric DSI and, 149–50, 190–91

independence of culture, 150–52

in Japan, 148

in liberal democracy, 198–99

likelihood of participation (See Likelihood of participation, impact of culture on)

overview, 7–8, 147–49, 189–91, 224–25

perceived government salience (See Perceived government salience, impact of culture on)

political institutions, role of, 147–48, 151

protest potential (See Protest potential, impact of culture on)

reciprocal OTA and, 190–91

SOEs and, 149

in Taiwan, 148, 151

Political trust, impact of culture on
- in Africa, 111, 112, 114
- allocentric DSI and, 117–18, 224
- in authoritarian regimes, 109–10, 144–45
- in China (See Political trust, impact of culture on – China)
- conceptualizing, 108–10
- correlation of structural and institutional variables, 113
- defined, 108
- democratization, ramifications for, 145–46
- diffuse support, 109, 110, 116–17
- in Eastern Europe, 111, 112, 114
- education, correlation with, 123
- game theory and, 115
- Hierarchical Linear Modeling (HLM) and, 107–8, 224
- hierarchical OTA and, 117, 118, 224
- hypotheses regarding, 117–18
- idiocentric DSI and, 117–18, 224
- incumbent-based trust, 108, 109–10
- in Latin America, 111, 112, 114–15
- legitimacy and, 110
- multidimensional approach to, 108–9

Index

overview, 6–7, 107, 224
political fear, correlation with, 123
political fear, effect of on validity of
 measurement, 112, 240–42
reciprocal OTA and, 117, 118, 224
regional variants in determinants,
 110–15
SOEs and, 121
specific support, 109, 110
study results, 112–15
in Taiwan (*See* Political trust, impact of
 culture on – Taiwan)
in United States, 123
validity of measurements, 240–42
values and, 115–17
Political trust, impact of culture on – China
age, correlation with, 129
allocentric DSI and, 126, 129–30
ANOVA models, 126–27, 130
CCP membership, correlation with,
 125–26, 129
control variables, 123
corruption, correlation with, 123
county-level variables, 130–33
cross-level interaction between
 individual-level and county-level
 variables, 133–36, 137–38
cultural environment, correlation with,
 131, 132, 134–35
dependent variables, 119
deviating norm holders and, 132
economic development and reform,
 effect of, 121, 130, 132–33
education, correlation with, 123, 129,
 130–31, 132–33
factor analysis, 119–20
gender, correlation with, 129
government responsiveness, correlation
 with, 121–22, 127, 130, 132–33,
 136–38
Hierarchical Linear Modeling (HLM)
 and, 119, 126–27, 133–36
idiocentric DSI and, 136–38
incumbent-based trust, 119, 130,
 134–35, 137–38
independent variables, 120–26
individual-level variables, 127–30, 133
life satisfaction, correlation with,
 126, 129
media access, correlation with, 124–25,
 129, 136–38
overview, 107–8, 138, 224

political fear, correlation with, 124
random components of study, 130, 133
reciprocal OTA and, 126, 129–30, 138
regime-based trust, 119, 127, 138
variance in dependent variables, 126–27
Political trust, impact of culture
 on – Taiwan
county-level variables, 141
dependent variable, 139
differences between political institutions,
 effect of, 139–40
factor analysis, 140
Hierarchical Linear Modeling (HLM) in,
 141–44
hierarchical OTA and, 144
independent variables, 140–41
individual-level variables, 141, 142
institutional theory on, 138–39
measurement of trust, 139
overview, 108, 144, 224
Positive freedom, 200–1
Positive liberty, 200
"Priming," 52
Probability Proportional to Size (PPS)
 method
in 1993 Survey, 230, 234
perceived government salience
 and, 159
in 2002 Survey, 231, 236–37
in 2008 Survey, 232–33
Probit models
cognitive diffidence, 208
understanding of democracy, 213
Procedural justice, 44–45
Protest potential, impact of culture on
allocentric DSI and, 186, 189
ANOVA models, 187
in China, 185
collective effort, need for, 187–89
control variables, 187
cultural norms, correlation with,
 185–86, 188
dependent variables, 186–87
economic development and reform,
 effect of, 183–85
factor analysis, 186–87
"free rider" problem and, 187–89
Hierarchical Linear Modeling (HLM)
 and, 187
hierarchical OTA and, 186, 189
idiocentric DSI and, 186, 189
independent variables, 187

Protest potential, impact of culture on (*cont.*)
objective versus subjective opportunities, 185–86
overview, 183
psychological resources, correlation with, 189
reciprocal OTA and, 186
relative deprivation, correlation with, 187
social trust, correlation with, 187
sociological resources, correlation with, 189
SOEs and, 184–85
study results, 186
survey questions, 185–86, 187
Psychological resources
choice of confrontational acts, correlation with, 181
cognitive diffidence, correlation with, 206
likelihood of participation, correlation with, 167–70, 171–72
perceived government salience, correlation with, 157–58, 161
protest potential, correlation with, 189
understanding of democracy, correlation with, 213
Public welfare as purpose of democracy, 197
Putnam, Robert D., 36–37
Pye, Lucian, 110

Rational actor model, choice of confrontational acts and, 175
Rebellion in Chinese tradition, 49
Reciprocal OTA
additional information, as guide for, 52–53
in China, 90, 91
choice of confrontational acts and, 177–78
cognitive diffidence and, 207
cultural discontinuity and, 82
deviating norm holders and, 132
factor analysis (*See* Factor analysis)
focus on in cultural theory, 223
interpretation of social action, effect on, 50–52
IRT analysis, 89
legitimate goals, defining, 55
legitimate means, constraining, 56

liberal democracy and, 196–97, 198
likelihood of participation and, 165, 170, 173
perceived government salience and, 154–55, 161–62, 163
political participation and, 190–91
political trust and, 117, 118, 126, 129–30, 138, 224
protest potential and, 186
in social contract theory, 44
sources of affect, providing, 55
standards for evaluation of behavior, providing, 54
study results, 66–68
in Taiwan, 93, 94
understanding of democracy and, 211, 213–16, 226
Red Guards, 62
Regime-based trust
in China, 119, 127, 138
overview, 108, 109–10
Relative deprivation, correlation with protest potential, 187
Religion
guilt and, 57
idiocentric DSI and, 57
Remonstration, 177–78
Ren (Benevolence), 46–47
Renxin bugu (decline in public morality), 97
"Repeated games," 46
The Republic (Plato), 197–98
Republic of China. *See specific topic regarding Taiwan*
Risk and Culture (Douglas and Wildavsky), 22
Root Mean Square Error of Approximation (RMSEA), 70–71, 72
Rousseau, Jean-Jacques, 42, 43
Ruggie, John Gerard, 23
Rule creators, 252
Rule enforcers, 252
"Running Fan" (Fan Meizhong), 252–55

Salience. *See* Perceived government salience, impact of culture on
Sanctions for enforcing cultural norms
effectiveness of, 36
external policing system (*See* External policing system for enforcing cultural norms)
gossip, role of, 39

Index

297

"heroic sanctions," 38–39
idiocentric DSI and, 57
incremental sanctions, 39–40
internal policing system (*See* Internal
    policing system for enforcing cultural
    norms)
overview, 35–36, 40
"three selves" theory, 36–37
Self-interest, definition of. *See* Definition of
    self-interest (DSI)
Severe Acute Respiratory Syndrome
    (SARS), 155–56
Sex. *See* Gender
Shame
    allocentric DSI and, 58
    in China, 56
    in Confucianism, 58
    guilt contrasted, 56–58
    in Japan, 56
    socialization and, 58
Shang shu (Book of Documents), 201
Shils, Edward, 18–19, 20, 34
Showers, C., 37
Singapore, authoritarianism in, 16
"Small-street news.". *See Xiaodao xiaoxi*
    (grapevine rumors)
Social action, effect of cultural norms on,
    34–35, 52–53, 222–23
Social bias approach to cultural
    theory, 22–23
Social character approach to cultural
    theory, 20
Social constructivism approach to cultural
    theory, 23–24
Social contract theory, 42–45
    common characteristics, 43–44
    conditional exchange and, 43
    conflict acceptance of conflict
        in, 44
    Confucianism contrasted, 47–48, 50
    idiocentric DSI in, 44
    order and, 42–43
    popular sovereignty and, 43
    procedural justice in, 44–45
    reciprocal OTA in, 44
Socialization, 47, 58
Social-structural theory
    cohort analysis of cultural change and,
        87, 93, 96
    overview, 76, 77–78
Social trust, correlation with protest
    potential, 187

Socioeconomic development. *See* Economic
    development and reform
Sociological resources
    choice of confrontational acts,
        correlation with, 181
    cognitive diffidence, correlation
        with, 206
    likelihood of participation, correlation
        with, 167
    perceived government salience,
        correlation with, 157, 161
    protest potential, correlation with, 189
    understanding of democracy, correlation
        with, 213
SOEs. *See* State-owned enterprises (SOEs)
Sohu.com, 255
Southern Europe, attitudes toward
    democracy in, 17
South Korea
    authoritarianism in, 16
    democracy, attitudes toward, 17
    understanding of democracy in, 194
Soviet Union, collapse of, 13
State-owned enterprises (SOEs)
    choice of confrontational acts and, 164–65
    overview, 14–15, 16
    political participation and, 149
    political trust and, 121
    protest potential and, 184–85
State Security Bureau (China), 15–16
Subcultures, 33–34
Substantive justice, 50
The Sun and the People (film), 177
Supply of democracy, validity of
    measurements, 242–45
Survey of Political Culture and Political
    Participation in Mainland China,
    Taiwan, and Hong Kong (1993)
    data from, 62
    interviewers, 230
    likelihood of participation and, 166
    overview, 2–3
    perceived government salience and, 156
    PPS method, 230, 234
    primary sampling units, 229, 230
    reliability of interviews, 235
    sample design for China survey, 229–30
    sample design for Taiwan survey, 234–35
    sampling process, 234–35
    secondary sampling units, 229
    tables, 236
    tertiary sampling units, 229

Survey questions
  allocentric DSI, 66
  choice of confrontational acts, 175–77
  definition of self-interest (DSI), 66
  idiocentric DSI, 66
  likelihood of participation, 166
  perceived government salience, 156
  protest potential, 185–86, 187
  understanding of democracy, 212
Symbols, rituals and myths approach to
    cultural theory, 21–22

Taiwan. *See specific topic*
Taiwan Survey (2002), 3
Taiyang yu ren (film), 177
Tang, Wenfang, 15, 16, 52, 149, 240
Tang Dynasty, 198
Texas A&M University China
    Archive, 62
Thailand, understanding of democracy
    in, 194
"Third Wave" of democratization, 8,
    13, 192
Thought Reform Campaign, 62
"Three selves" theory, 36–37
Tiananmen Incident (1989), 13, 51
Tianya (Internet forum), 252–53
Tibet, protests in, 50–51
Triandis, Harry Charalambos, 48
Trust. *See* Political trust, impact of
    culture on
Tsai, Lily, 39
Tucker-Lewis Index (TLI), 69–70
2002 Survey. *See* Asian Barometer Survey
    I (ABS I)
2008 Survey. *See* Asian Barometer Survey
    II (ABS II)

Unconventional political participation.
    See Protest potential, impact of
    culture on
Understanding of democracy, impact of
    culture on
  age, correlation with, 213
  allocentric DSI and, 193, 211,
    213–16, 226
  Asia, diversity of views in, 193–96
  in China, 194, 213–16, 218–20, 225
  cognitive decoding and, 211
  cognitive diffidence, 205–10
    (*See also* Cognitive diffidence)

constraining power of government
    and, 202
cultural norms, correlation with, 211,
    213–17, 218
different understandings, 203, 218
"don't know" answers, analysis of,
    243–45 (*See also* Cognitive
    diffidence)
education, correlation with, 213
elections and, 202
freedom and, 202
guardianship democracy
    (*See* Guardianship democracy)
Hierarchical Linear Modeling (HLM)
    and, 213
hierarchical OTA and, 193, 211,
    213–16, 226
idiocentric DSI and, 193, 211,
    213–16, 226
independent variables, 213
liberal democracy (*See* Liberal
    democracy)
meaning of democracy versus suitability
    of democracy, 207
minben (*See* Guardianship democracy)
multinomial regression analysis,
    218, 219
other factors, 204
overview, 8, 192–93, 218–20, 225–26
Pearson analysis, 194–96
perceived government salience,
    correlation with, 213
political fear, effect of on validity of
    measurement, 242–43
probit models, 213
psychological resources, correlation
    with, 213
reciprocal OTA and, 211, 213–16, 226
sociological resources, correlation
    with, 213
in South Korea, 194
study results, 216–18
survey questions, 212
in Taiwan, 194, 216, 217, 218–20, 225
urbanization, correlation with, 213
validity of measurements, 242–45
United States
  democratization, role in, 17
  political trust in, 123
Unit-of-analysis problem in cultural
    theory, 32–34

Index

University of Michigan, Survey Research
  Center, 121–22, 123
Urbanization
  choice of confrontational acts,
    correlation with, 181
  cognitive diffidence, correlation
    with, 206
  likelihood of participation, correlation
    with, 167
  perceived government salience
    correlation with, 157
  understanding of democracy, correlation
    with, 213
Uslaner, Eric M., 115–17

Validity of measurements
  confidentiality of interviewees, 239–40
  overview, 239–40
  political trust, 240–42
  supply of democracy, 242–45
Values
  beliefs versus, 25
  characteristics of, 25–26
  cultural norms distinguished, 25–29
  defined, 25
  political trust and, 115–17
van der Heijden, Peter, 39
Verba, Sidney, 4, 20–21, 26, 121–22, 146,
    147–48, 175

Walder, Andrew G., 157
Wall Street Journal, 255

Watergate, 123
Weber, Max, 18, 21, 24–25, 30–31, 110
Weimin zuozhu (rule for the people), 201
Wenchuan earthquake (2008), 82, 252–53
Wendt, Alexander E., 23, 56–57
Wen Jiabao, 82
Western versus Eastern cultural norms,
    5, 41–42
White, Gordon, 14
Wildavsky, Aaron, 22
Woo-Cummings, Meredith, 16–17
World Values Survey, 240

Xiaodao xiaoxi (grapevine rumors)
  political participation and, 158–59,
    167–70, 181
  political trust and, 125, 129
  understanding of democracy and,
    206, 208
Xin Guancha (journal), 251
Xiong Yuzhi, 201
Xunzi, 47

Yamigishi, Midori, 115
Yamigishi, Toshio, 115
Yu Luojin, 250–52, 253–54, 255
Yu Luoke, 250

Zakaria, Fareed, 193
Zhang Dongsun, 200
Zhou Dynasty, 41, 45, 46
Ziyou (freedom), 200–1, 202